T0335233

A CENTURY OF
POPULIST DEMAGOGUES

A CENTURY OF
POPULIST DEMAGOGUES

EIGHTEEN EUROPEAN PORTRAITS

1918–2018

Ivan T. Berend

CENTRAL EUROPEAN UNIVERSITY PRESS

Budapest–New York

Published in 2020 by
Central European University Press

CEU Press is imprint of the
Central European University Limited Liability Company
Nádor utca 11, H-1051 Budapest, Hungary
Tel: +36 1-327-3138 or 327-3000
E-mail: ceupress@press.ceu.edu
Website: www.ceupress.com
224 West 57th Street, New York NY 10019, USA

ISBN 978-963-386-333-6 (paperback)
ISBN 978-963-386-334-3 (ebook)

Library of Congress Control Number: 2020938490

Table of Contents

Preface and acknowledgement

Demagogues and demagoguery are every day phenomena in many spheres of public life. They are, of course, very much present in politics. I am writing this introduction in the early summer of 2018, after the first one-and-half years of Donald J. Trump presidency in the United States. From this vantage point it looks like politics has once again become a perch for populist demagogues. In a way, this is quite simply a general lesson from the history of twentieth and early twenty-first century Europe. Though currently there is a resurgence of populism in Europe, populists have also suffered defeats in recent national elections in the Netherlands, France, and Germany. They are still present, quite a few of them are in power in Southern and Central Europe, others have emerged victorious in Austria and some, in spite of their electoral defeats, have only grown stronger, as in Germany.

The topic of this book is a very personal one for me. I was born and lived in Europe when dangerous demagogues ruled the continent, and I barely survived their rule. I experienced the impact of demagoguery, the relatively frequent regime changes, and the introduction of different types of authoritarian rules. I enthusiastically welcomed the foundation and development of the European Union and consider it a personal insult that various populist demagogues are seeking to destroy it.

This book tells the story of eighteen fascist, communist, left-wing, right-wing, and liberal-conservative populist demagogues from eleven European countries: Britain, France, the Netherlands, Italy, Austria, Hungary, Poland, Serbia, Croatia, Bosnia, and Romania. There were many more all over the continent during the last century. In a book twice as large as this, one could discuss the story of twice as many populist demagogues. Nevertheless, the selected ones are very representative of the phenomenon of populist demagoguery. Some of these demagogues caused the death of hundreds of thousands or even millions of people; others committed no major crimes against humanity. All were harmful to their countries and to Europe.

I wanted to write a popular book for the wider public in order to characterize populist demagogues, what they have preached, whom they called their "enemies," and the lies and false promises they offered. I broadly quote their speeches and writings to introduce them and their demagoguery as it was. That is the main goal of the book. I also try to explain the situation in which they were able to act and even gain power, and to confront what they said with what, in reality, they did. The case studies on populist demagogues discuss this phenomenon and the way it has flooded Europe. In a relatively lengthy introduction I will analyze this phenomenon with the help of a great deal of scholarly works on the topic.

I am very grateful for Kati, my wife, with whom I've talked endlessly about the new age of demagogues, and who played a key role in writing about this topic. She, as always, has helped me immensely with her library expertise, and critical and editorial skills. Without her, this book would not have been written. I am also thankful for Dr. Robert Levy, my former student and old friend, who, as quite a few times before, masterfully edited and polished my manuscript. Last but not least, I am also thankful to József Litkei and the Central European University Press for copy editing and publishing this work.

Ivan T. Berend
June 15, 2018.

Who are the populist demagogues, and how can they attain political power?

What is demagoguery and who is a demagogue?

What are the main characteristics of demagoguery and demagogues? Everyone has, at least, some notion and sometimes even some personal experience to answer these questions. However, to give an exact definition is not very easy. To start the most simplistic way one can turn to dictionaries and encyclopedias to look for a concise definition. What can we find? They tell us that the origin of the term "demagogue" comes from the Greek *demos agein* (leader of people), but in modern times it has a much darker meaning, "leader of the mob." The definitions contain that a demagogue is a political agitator who appeals to the passions and prejudices of the mob in order to obtain power. They normally stress the connection between populism and demagoguery, because both seek power from the people and not from the establishment. Some even quote H. L. Mencken, who once said pointedly that a demagogue "preaches doctrines he knows to be untrue to men he knows to be idiots and. . . he may use methods that violate logic, fairness, and sound judgment."[1]

This quotation is pointing to the fact that demagogues are—either by oversimplifications or deliberately—always lying. Of course, their lies have different origins. Often they are cynical calculations to gain support, but sometimes they are true believers and blindly believe their own ideology to such an extent that they see the whole world through it and are unable to see reality as it is. Difficult to say which populist demagogues are more dangerous. The quotation from Mencken also points to the best base of populist demagogues: the less informed people in the countryside and rust-belt industrial areas, under-educated or uneducated, many of them older and many of them desperate.

Still, it would behoove us to have a comprehensive explanation so that we can grasp the main characteristics of political demagoguery. This does not mean that all demagogues are similar. Not at all, rather different types will appear in this book: fascist-racist demagogues such as the Hungarian Gyula Gömbös or the Romanian Corneliu Zelea Codreanu; right-wing conservatives such as the Dutch Geert Wilders or the French Marine Le Pen; communist revolutionaries such as the Hungarian Béla Kun or the Romanian Nicolae Ceaușescu; and even liberal-conservatives such as the British Boris Johnson and the Italian Silvio Berlusconi. In many cases, their political messages are a mixture of right and left agendas.

Demagogues might be excellent orators such as the Austrian Jörg Haider or the Croat Franjo Tuđman, bad speakers like the Serb Slobodan Milošević, or even the less educated who could not speak without a written text such as Romanian Ceaușecu. Most of them lacked humor, but some were witty with a talent for comedy, occasionally acting like buffoons, like the Italian Silvio Berlusconi or the British Boris Johnson. They may be charismatic and driven by ideology, with a sense of mission, as was the case for the Hungarian Béla Kun, the Romanian Zelea Codreanu, the Austrian Ernst Rüdiger Starhemberg, and the Bosnian Alija Izetbegović. Others are calculating opportunists who, if needed, can change their political credo and possess a "manufactured" charisma such as the Serb Slobodan Milošević or the Hungarian Viktor Orbán. Or they might lack charisma altogether, have no genuine belief in any ideological mission, and serve instead their own petty ambition as is certainly the case with Berlusconi or Johnson.

Nevertheless, in analyzing the phenomenon of populist political demagoguery one may discern certain common features. Let me list some of the more important ones. One of the main characteristics of demagoguery is *over-simplification*. Ignoring the complexity of problems and the validity of competing arguments, they invariably approach serious issues in a one-dimensional manner, and seek to address those issues with instant solutions. The serious problem of unemployment is a good example. It might be caused by various factors, international recession or depression, foreign competition, technological development that makes certain branches of the economy obsolete and declining, etc. Demagogues exploit people's natural dissatisfaction with unemployment, give a one-dimensional explanation, for example arguing that it was caused by bad policy which did not defend the national market against competitors. This sounds realistic for many although it is probably far from the whole truth. The demagogues' easy solution to introduce high tariffs does not solve the problem, which is caused by several other factors besides foreign competition. The belief that a single cause is responsible for innumerable problems is often much more appealing to people than the complicated truth that each problem has countless causes. An oversimplified answer is, of course, a kind of half-truth or a lie. Demagogues are inveterate liars—some doing so without knowing it, most deceiving quite deliberately.

Over-simplification is closely connected to (and even overlaps) *half-truths*. Demagogues much prefer to build their arguments on half-truths. That makes their arguments more realistic and more rooted in real facts, letting people more easily self-identify with certain claims of demagogues. Most demagogue attacks against the European Union are based on half-truths. The sixty-year-old European Community is a *sui generis* institution, partly supranational, partly intergovernmental organization. Its parliament is not a real legislative body; these and other shortcomings are often summed up by the term of "democratic deficit." Anti-EU demagogues are always using these facts. They, however, neglect the EU's efforts and the gradual progress it has made to strengthen its democratic features. The parliament is now directly elected, the qualified majority vote is better than the veto right has been. The member countries' governments together with the parliament are parts of a decision making process that is not made by a non-elected bureaucracy. The EU's rich members are profiting from integration but the poorer countries do as well, and the EU supports, in a democratic process, member countries of less developed areas with generous aid. Presenting it in a distorted way as a bureaucratic, dictatorial, and even colonizing monster that endangers national sovereignty is a blatant lie.

One must also not forget: even two-hundred-year-old democracies have democratic deficits. That was quite obvious in the nineteenth and early twentieth centuries when even in the so-called traditional democracies half of the population, women, were excluded as well as certain less educated and low-income layers of the societies who did not have voting rights. In the United States even in the twenty-first century, one presidential candidate may get the majority of the votes but still lose the elections—as happened to Al Gore and Hillary Clinton—because of the Electoral College. Money plays a major role in informing or misleading voters that may deform the democratic procedure. One can speak nowadays about democratic deficit in quite a broad and general way. To get rid of shortcomings by further reforms and emerge on the road of further gradual democratization is the real solution. Demagogues, however, argued to leave the EU or stop its supranational activities. Their critique of the EU is based on a half-truth that is evidently also a half-lie, but it enables demagogues to appear more credible to the public nonetheless.

In connection with this over-simplification tactic it is important to note that demagogues often use the method of *framing* when articulating their message. The American linguist George Lakoff and the Dutch professor of management Hans de Bruijn call attention to this phenomenon, maintaining that reframing societal/political problems is a major weapon for demagogues. "A frame is a particular way of looking at the world: a 'mindset' or 'world view' people can easily identify with. Talented populist demagogues often attack the establishment by inventing their own frames and challenge established conventions. They use the most unusual and violent language to strengthen their frame and to make it known and easily accepted by many." People who believe in these frames do not trust in any information and argument that are incompatible with them. Language is what populists use to activate a particular frame. "Once a frame has become widely embedded, it can have a significant impact on public debate. . . . The power of a good frame is that it places your opponent at an enormous disadvantage. . . . Denying the frame often serves to confirm it."[2] It is a similarly weak position to argue that populist exaggerate isolated incidents and present them as general phenomena. This does not work because people who believe in the demagogue's frame are convinced that pointing to the problem is the most important thing regardless whether it is exaggerated or not. A good frame creates a base to identify with and voters identify with values that fit into their identity. George Lakoff said: "people do not necessarily vote in their self-interests. They vote their identity. . . . They vote for who they identify with." The solution is as Lakoff warns, not to step to someone else's frame but instead to reframe the debate by introducing an alternative frame. That is what demagogues often do and their opponents often walk into their trap.[3]

One of the frames today is about immigration: based on the idea that European society is founded on Judeo-Christian, humanist, and enlightened values, which Islam, in contrast, does not share. Consequently, an influx of Muslims into Europe will destroy European values. Thus, in this frame, multiculturalism is totally mistaken. Another favorite frame to discuss the problems of the European Union is to describe it as a bureaucratic, dictatorial system, harmful to individual national interests—thus "We have to stop Brussels."

One of the most important characteristics of demagogues is that they are exclusionists. They always *point to an enemy*, hidden or open, inside and/or outside the country, and to scapegoat them as the cause of their nation's problems. The demagogue's enemies can be a whole variety of "others": a foreign power, a segment of society, the very rich, an ethnic or religious minority, the Jews, the immigrants, the Muslims, or representatives of a political ideology as the American McCarthyism embodied it in the 1950s. Demagogues routinely cast their adversaries and rivals as "enemies of the nation," serving alien interests with no moral or legal basis to be engaged politically. In other words, demagogues always depict situations in black-and-white terms; they always reduce sides to two irreconcilable camps—"us" versus "them," the good guys and the bad guys. As we've seen, they adhere to a strict "Manichean vision of society (pitting the good people against the corrupted political elite), a conception of the people as a homogenous entity, and a defense of popular sovereignty."[4] The enemies that demagogues denounce always include the establishment, controlled by established parties and politicians. They are portrayed as corrupt, self-serving quislings in cahoots with special interests. Demagogues occasionally advocate for direct democracy, but are more likely than not to call for the strong, authoritarian rule of the charismatic leader who is "of the people and for the people."[5]

Successful demagogues are often strong charismatic personalities. Max Weber addressed the question of the legitimation of power. He differentiated among three types of legitimized authority. Besides the traditional (inherited) and the modern rational-legal (elected) authority, Weber maintained that charisma can be a legitimizing source of power for a leader, especially in crisis situations. This idea is very useful in helping us understand the success of populist demagogues. Charismatic people have "the authority of the extraordinary and personal gift of grace (charisma), the absolutely personal devotion and personal confidence in revelation, heroism, or other qualities of individual leadership." They have inner determination and restraint; they lead and the people follow. In earlier times they had been prophets and warlords; today they are populist demagogues, endowed with charismatic legitimacy. Nevertheless, charisma is sometime "manufactured" through propaganda about the extraordinary qualities of the "leaders," such as their instinct and determination to lead in a good direction. Weber also observed, however, that such legitimacy evaporates if a leader can no longer deliver success or fails to carry out the promises he made upon gaining power.[6] Charismatic demagogues always pose as "men of the people," as authentic representatives of the "little, forgotten man" or the "silent majority," and as the "embodiment of the national interest." They instinctively understand people's problems since they are "one of them." They are fundamentally anti-elite and intensely anti-intellectual. Occasionally they even believe in what they're doing. But they are always—and sometimes only—power-seeking personalities who are intoxicated by power and captivated by the limelight.

Demagogues have a distinct capacity to mobilize a crowd by appealing to hatred, popular prejudices, anxieties, fear, and a lust for vengeance. The fervent and rousing oratory of charismatic demagogues incorporates angry, bombastic rhetoric and deliberately employed violent language. In contemporary Europe, this would include rejecting so-called politically correct language and preferring provocative prose instead. In countries where open hate speech is banned, or where it is deemed to be counterproductive, demagogues revert to using coded language. Instead of Jews, demagogues cunningly refer to "cosmopolitan" elements, or blame one Jew in particular, as is the case for Hungarian, Polish, Slovak, and other populist demagogues who currently target George Soros, the Hungarian-born American multi-billionaire and philanthropic liberal. They do not have to say the word "Jew" for their audience to get the message.

Similarly, demagogues enjoy using calculated ambiguity "that serves to address multiple and contradictory audiences simultaneously," and provocative statements "that colonize the agenda" of news programs. "All these linguistic strategies in text and talk keep right-wing populism alive and kicking."[7] Hot-headed hyperbole and frenzied charges are par for the course in stirring a crowd. If nothing else, demagogues are masters at "inflating others' passion in order to obtain power for its own sake."[8] Keith Spencer Felton points to "an elevated use of language [that] can magnify meaning, and motivate beyond the facile measure. . . . The influence of language upon history is ineluctable. . . . [E]xemplary oratory buoys civilization over its perennial perils."[9]

In order to demonstrate successful oratory, Felton quotes William Shirer, the renowned writer on Nazi Germany, who skillfully described Hitler's command of oratory: Hitler "would begin invariably in a low, resonant voice, beautifully modulated, speaking slowly. . . . As he worked toward the inevitable climax of his discourse, the natural voice would reassert itself, the tone rising in scale, and, as the words came tumbling out in a torrent, it would become shrill and he would begin to shriek hysterically and reach . . . an orgasm of sound and fury, followed by an ecstasy . . . and which the awed listeners seemed to fully share. . . . At such time the born actor in him would emerge. . . ."[10] The less known Romanian fascist, Corneliu Zelea Codreanu, also used vehement language, colored with strong religious content. Posing as the messenger of Archangel Michael, a kind of patron-saint of Romania—created by nineteenth century romantic-nationalism[11]—who leads God's armies against Satan's forces on earth, Codreanu was able to hood-wink hordes of highly superstitious and religious peasants. Today, this kind of frenetic oratory might still appeal to fanatics.

"Elevated language" comes in various forms. Boris Johnson uses a witty, funny language. In Stephen Castle's characterization: "Shaggy-headed, bombastic and full of bravado and sunny optimism as he brushed aside the clouds hanging over Britain's fraught withdrawal from the European Union."[12] Silvio Berlusconi was enormously successful using simple, witty or vulgar language peppered with jokes like people often use around the kitchen table. Cas Mudde speaks about the "*Stammtisch* discourse," the language people speak in pubs or—in the infamous case of Donald Trump, the vulgar "locker-room talk." Berlusconi's dumbing down of political discourse with simple soccer terms worked wonderfully in soccer-loving Italy. Nigel Farage, the primary advocate of Britain's exiting the European Union, also employed simple language, mimicking his followers' crude depictions of the EU and of the state of affairs inside Britain as one of total chaos and decline. This helped convince a bare majority to vote to leave the EU.

To instigate angry reactions, demagogues over-dramatize existing circumstances and describe them as constituting a serious crisis that requires a strong and immediate response. The calculated method of constant repetition of the same idea, the same proclamations, and the same posters plastered everywhere over a long period of time creates a conditioned, reflexive response in people to embrace ideas that lack any logical foundation. Demagogic oratory evokes in the public the belief that these views are true and self-evident; it persuades the crowd that the speaker knows precisely what to do and is ready to act.

When demagogues are not excellent orators, political programs and promises may serve as effective substitutes to good oratory, as is the case with several demagogues like the Bosnian Alija Izetbegović or the Romanian Ceauşescu. Steadfastness and resistance against a superior power can have the same effect, as the Serb Milošević, the Romanian Ceauşescu, and the Dutch Geert Wilders all exemplify. A calculated behavioral pattern can at times take the place of zealous oratory. Occasionally a "gladiator" posture and exceptional athleticism can also create the necessary charisma, as was true with Jörg Haider and is true with Vladimir Putin. In other cases "pedestrian" behavior works just as well. Sometimes being a soccer fan and mingling with soccer aficionados can do the trick, as Silvio Berlusconi and Viktor Orbán demonstrated. Other times sitting in pubs and drinking with "ordinary people," or riding a bicycle to work in high office can prove quite effective, as shown by the examples of Nigel Farage and Boris Johnson, respectively. All these behaviors create a veneer of authenticity and help build a personal bond between leaders and followers.

Over-simplification, which uses half-truth and political framing, is itself a lie. But demagogues are often direct, deliberate liars. Adolf Hitler mused in *Mein Kampf* that people are more prone to accept big lies than small ones because the former have a veneer of credibility. Ordinary people routinely tell small lies, but they cannot fathom telling the colossal lies made by demagogues and thus more easily fall victim to them. This was also seen in the effective propaganda of the pro-Brexit demagogues in Britain. The "leave" campaign promised that the UK would save £350 million a week in membership fees to the European Union and would invest that entire amount into the ailing health service. This claim, which swayed a large number of voters, was simply a lie because Brexit demagogues "forgot" to deduct from the British payments the massive amounts the EU paid back as rebates, the extensive support given to British farmers as part of the EU's common agricultural policy, and the huge sums the EU delivered to Britain's less developed or rust-belt regions as part of its so-called cohesion policy. They also "forgot" to mention the gigantic EU grants for British education and research. These subsidies had to be replaced with funds from the British government after Brexit. Investment in healthcare, so appealing to many, was simply out of the question. The entire demagoguery surrounding payments to the EU was fiction pure and simple.[13]

As *The Economist* observed, while "politicians have always lied" over the years, in our politics of the 2010s the truth is often entirely left behind. The post-truth age indeed holds true for more than a few contemporary demagogues: the Berlusconis, the Le Pens, the Orbáns, the Kaczyńskis, the Johnsons, and the Farages. It is partly the consequence of the advent of more reckless, power-hungry demagogues who believe that their time has arrived. But *The Economist* is right to note that "post-truth" politics is in part the consequence of the growth of a new media, including social media, "in which lies, rumour and gossips spread with alarming speed. Lies that are widely shared online within a network, whose members trust each other more than they trust any mainstream-media source, can quickly take on the appearance of truth. . . . Well-intentioned journalistic practices bear blame too. The pursuit of 'fairness' in reporting often creates phoney balance at the expense of truth."[14] Lies and baseless accusations in politics unfortunately have no legal consequences. Political speeches and advertisements, *The New Statesman* bitterly noted after Britain's Brexit referendum, are "exempt from the regulation that would otherwise bar false claims and outrageous promises."[15] Lies have always been an organic part of demagoguery. In response to the Brexit vote, the *Guardian* angrily quoted Rudyard Kipling's short poem, *A Dead Statesman*, written about demagogues after World War I: "I could not dig: I dared not rob/ Therefore I lied to please the mob./ Now all my lies are proved untrue/ And I must face the men I slew./ What tale shall serve me here among/ Mine angry and defrauded young?"[16]

The above listed main characteristics of populist political demagoguery will be broadly presented in this book, which will quote various demagogues' speeches and writings throughout. I have chosen to allocate a great deal of space to the voices of demagogues themselves. This seems to be the best way to present demagoguery at work.

The psychology of demagogues

How do demagogues attract so many people? What is the psychological predisposition to becoming a demagogue? And how does it interrelate with that of their followers? How does the psychology of the crowd work in these historical situations? A number of psychological and psychoanalytical studies have addressed this topic. Some suggest that several of the demagogues are actually mentally disturbed.[17] Some psychologists emphasize their difficult childhoods and early adulthood experiences. It is enough to mention Adolf Hitler's humiliating failure as a painter as a young adult in *fin-de-siècle* Vienna (then a hotbed of anti-Semitism), which is often cited as an explanation for his later atavistic anti-Semitism.

Sometimes hysterical, even epileptic characteristics are also noted. Some demagogues are highly neurotic or suffer from delusions. Since delusion, if it is dominant, is tantamount to madness, demagogues often act in ways "normal" people do not. Their delusion might manifest itself as a strong belief or an obsession in a particular mission, which often makes a person especially fanatical, one who is easily agitated and who suffers from unusual internal conflicts. Some demagogues (like Corneliu Zelea Codreanu of Romania, Alija Izetbegović of Bosnia, or Jarosław Kaczyński of Poland) are deeply religious and embrace the banner of God and religion. Others, such as Austria's Jörg Haider and France's Marine Le Pen, or Holland's Geert Wilders are not religious at all.

Another kind of psychological "deformation" is unusually strong self-confidence: a pronounced self-adulation and inflated egotism that make demagogues believe that they can do no wrong and are destined for greatness. They are also brazen narcissists who crave the limelight and desire incessant acclaim. They begin to believe their own lies and are masters at imparting that conviction on to their electrified audience. At the same time, demagogues can be erratic and mercurial. Close friends one day become bitter enemies the next. Deep hatred seems to be second nature to them, which makes appealing to the crowd's animosities an easy task. Sometimes, however, they are just pampered personalities or self-interested performers, or calculating opportunists cynically seeking power. If it serves their political goals, some, like Viktor Orbán or Vladimir Putin, will even pretend to be religious. They may have certain ideas or principles, but quite often it is precisely their lack of principles or their ability to change their views on a dime that makes them appear intriguing and flexible. Who can forget how Silvio Berlusconi would say one thing in the morning and then deny he ever said it that evening?[18]

Demagogues may veer left or right, but occasionally they'll switch from one to the other. Some who started off as communists one day ended up as fascists the next. Many routinely combine both right-wing and left-wing ideologies. Mussolini already engineered this sort of hybrid ideology using elements of his early socialist views. Hitler even used the term "socialist" in the name of his "National Socialist" party. Populist demagogues naturally pose as defenders of the "forgotten" people, including workers. A number of modern demagogues—Brexit's Nigel Farage certainly come to mind—flatly deny the existence of the Right and Left at all. It would indeed seem that demagoguery and ideological inconsistency often go hand in hand.

The psychology of the crowd (the "base" of the demagogues)

Populist demagogues, as we will see below, are very successful in certain historical periods. But why and under what circumstances are people ready to follow them in such a fervent, almost religious, manner? Why do they accept their simplistic notions and outright lies? Why are they drawn even to the demagogues' repulsive personal traits? Why do they rejoice when demagogues bully their opponents and brutally threaten them?

Occasionally people accept a demagogue's positions because they simply ring true to them. In many cases they do so because the demagogue's program serves their real interests. Eliminating Jewish economic competition and providing vacated Jewish residences served certain people in the 1930s and 1940s quite well. Several people believed that the expropriation of the rich, the bourgeoisie will be good for them, or at least, eliminate those who they hated. Some envision a similar boon today by ridding their countries of immigrants, whose alien nature in any case cannot be trusted. When people fail to understand complicated problems, they tend to seek out simple explanations and superficial solutions. In other words, there are rational reasons for certain parts of the population to believe in and vote for a populist demagogue.

True as this may be, it still doesn't fully explain the resounding success demagogues enjoy in certain historical periods. Dozens of scholarly works have grappled with this enigma by studying the psychology of the masses. Mass psychology has a solid, scientifically established explanation.[19] Great minds have long recognized how the behavior of single individuals differs from that of individuals congregating in a crowd. In ancient Athens, Solon noted that a single Athenian is a wily fox, but that a group of Athenians are a flock of sheep. The ancient Roman proverb mused that "senators are good men, but the Roman senate is a noxious beast."[20] Friedrich Nietzsche assures us that "Madness is rare in individuals, but in groups, parties, nations, and ages, it is the rule."[21] In the mid-nineteenth century, Charles Mackay[22] warned that crowds are insane, unbridled, hysterical, and overly emotional, and that they at times partake in collective ecstasy, exhibiting signs of delirium and a total loss of self-control. In the twentieth century this statement sounds truer than ever before.

One finding of mass psychology is that, while the individual is conscious and reasonable, "the conscious activity of these individuals, when they are collected in crowds, vanishes and gives place to unconscious actions of a very powerful but elementary type."[23] The greater the crowd is, the lower its intellect. Hitler instinctively understood this when he declared in *Mein Kampf* that "The greater the mass of men whom it [the propaganda] is desired to reach, the lower must be the intellectual level of propaganda." In other words, the consciousness of individuals disintegrates in a crowd. The crowd is unconscious, so much so that an individual will forget his personal interests and easily succumb to blind delusions once part of a crowd. As one of the founders of mass psychology, Gustave Le Bon, once noted: "Profound altruism . . . is a collective virtue. All work of general import, demanding for its accomplishment a minimum of egoism and a maximum of blind devotion, self-abnegation, and sacrifice, can scarcely be accomplished but by crowd."[24] As Le Bon sees it, the crowd behaves like individuals under hypnosis.

The masses are de-rationalized by passion; their ideas and principles are recast as irrational impressions, rendering the crowd incapable of perceiving reality. Their actions are devoid of logic and moral standards. They become easy prey to blind impulses. As Serge Moscovici puts it, the crowd falls into a quasi-hallucinatory state: "When we observe a crowd we have the impression that we are in the presence of people in trance . . . who lost control of their physical reactions as well as their desires and thoughts."[25] The crowd unites people with very different occupations, lifestyles, educational achievements and backgrounds, and it bounds them together with intensified emotional displays of anger, fear, and pathos. They are, mass psychologists maintain, "insane, unbridled, hysterical; they are epitomized by the emotional outbursts with which a multitude of fans greets a star, in the tumultuous activity in the wake of some prophet, in the collective ecstasy of the faithful."[26] The intensified emotions of the crowd are "contagious," and the herd instinct takes over.

The grouping of individuals into a crowd that shares common ideas and emotions can also lead to positive outcomes. The unique behavioral patterns of the crowd could enable people to be less reticent in expressing joy and gratitude. At a theater, concert hall, or sports event, the quiet contentment of individuals is often replaced by loud and animated expressions of delight and happiness. The cautious behavior of an individual is often replaced by heroism in a crowd if someone leads them through example and begins rescuing people from burning houses or the ruins of a collapsed building. When bolstered by the crowd, some lose their fear of death and selflessly fight an armed police force or a foreign army in war. "It is crowds rather than isolated individuals," Le Bon observes, "that may be induced to run the risk of death to secure the triumph of a creed or an idea. . . . Such heroism is without doubt somewhat unconscious, but it is of such heroism that history is made."[27] The opposite, however, is also maybe true. World War I, as Alfred Adler described it, was the "most terrible of collective neuroses into which our neuropathic civilization has been thrown by its will to power . . . stifling the immortal sentiment of human solidarity or turning it to perverted uses."[28] Another mass psychologist expressed this ambiguity thus: "A crowd can be roused to fury and to readiness for violence, and also to delirious enthusiasm; it is true that it is capable of incredible cowardice or sublime heroism. But it is characteristic of it that it acts only under leadership, only when there are protagonists who manipulate it, soul engineers."[29] This draws attention to two important elements of crowd psychology: it can be altruistic but also criminal, destructive, and violent. The combative instincts of humans, even those who are considered highly civilized, become an elemental collective neurosis in crowds.

Psychologists have found several reasons why people in crowds cling to false beliefs. Some are simply engaged in wishful thinking, adhering to notions that make them feel good about themselves and that boost their self-esteem. At times, ascribing to certain simplified explanations of complex issues lets people deny their own lack of understanding of those issues. Other times people simply need something to believe in. "Evidence abounds to show that normal people cling to cherished but false beliefs and are extremely resistant to giving them up. . . . Self-delusion [is] commonplace. We all find it difficult to accept certain truths, and delude ourselves into believing in a glaring falsehood in spite of evidence to the contrary. . . . First and foremost, people cling to beliefs because they do not understand the concept of evidence. This failure to understand the nature of evidence allows people to point to just about anything they want and cite it as evidence for their beliefs."[30] This is even more the case when individuals are grouped together in crowds and are influenced, indeed "hypnotized," by a strong leader. This means that people can virtually become insane in crowds. The crowd is always delusional, and it easily embraces false beliefs contrary to reality. In several extreme cases in recent times, a number of religious sects were mesmerized by a crazed leader to such an extent that they were prepared to commit mass suicide.[31] This clearly proves the existence of shared delusions, a kind of common "madness." Mass behavior provides adequate backing and support for demagogues.

The other element that is extremely important is the crowd's connection with a Leader. An amorphous mass without a leader, crowds always need to be led; they are always looking for a savior. Crowds yearn for someone to lead and dominate them—a powerful leader, a strong man, demanding their obedience. The crowd seeks only to emulate the leader's ideas and actions. Under strong leadership, a spontaneous, nondescript crowd can be transformed into a cohesive, organized group with common beliefs and common capabilities far superior to the individuals who make up the crowd. This "artificial (organized) crowd" readily subordinates itself to the systematic guidance of the leader. If this self-appointed leader is an intolerant demagogue, his threats, his hatred, and his violent propaganda assure his ascendancy over a blindly submissive crowd. Psychologists call this group manipulation, this creation of pre-determined responses, as "psychical rape of the masses." The charismatic leader essentially quasi-hypnotizes the crowd. Only one in ten is able to resist.

Historical situations accommodating demagoguery: national humiliation

To understand the story and success of demagogues in modern politics one has to understand the historical environment in which they have been successful. Populist demagogues rarely surface or thrive in times of peaceful prosperity and social harmony. They usually succeed in times of major transformations, conflicts, social turmoil, economic crises, national defeat and humiliation, uncertainty, disappointment, and popular apprehension. In such a political environment people generally lose confidence in the existing leadership. They reject the established parties and politicians and embrace strong personalities outside of the establishment who, they believe, can lead them and help them realize their hopes and dreams. This is the environment in which—as Max Weber suggested—charismatic leadership emerges and becomes legitimized.[32]

In modern times, the hotbeds of demagoguery are profound national crises, affronts to national pride and endangered nationhood. This may be caused by military defeat, the failure of national dreams, the dissolution of a state formation, regime change, foreign occupation, or territorial losses. In these historical circumstances demagogues are able to exploit the uncertainty and fear of large numbers of people. These situations are especially advantageous for demagoguery in countries with a history of similar upheavals. At this point I must draw the reader's attention to the phenomenon of so-called *path dependence*, that mystical but very real and existing force of history. This is a kind of historical legacy that predominated in certain countries in the past, but seemed to later disappear. The people of countries which experienced upheavals in the past today live in an entirely different political environment. They appear to have forgotten the past of their parents' and grandparents' generations. Yet suddenly, the vanished and "forgotten" past has risen to the fore once again. Large numbers of people today are reacting to recent social or political challenges in ways reminiscent of their ancestors. The same coping mechanisms of previous generations are now plainly evident today. A demagoguery that preaches hatred, violence, and the mobilization against enemies has returned with a vengeance. The "forgotten," "dead" past is alive for all to see once again. For some contemporary observers, this renewed popularity of demagogues is shocking and incomprehensible. They clearly have a different and more sanguine impression of their societies. In reality, however, the old behavioral patterns and political culture that seemed to be buried in the past actually survived in an ever-changing political-cultural environment. It survived mostly in the private sphere, on the family level, in small communities and it simply tapped into sentiments that never really disappeared.

Before World War I, Germany was the most successful rising power in Europe. Because it was united only in 1871, and had thus begun competing for colonies far too late, it nurtured a persistent grievance and turned to traditional Prussian militarism to establish a colonial system and elevate Germany into the top tier of European power politics. Driven to wage war against its more fortunate neighbors, Germany was defeated, mutilated, and disgraced, its territory truncated and its imperial dreams smashed. After World War I it endured the most devastating inflation and economic decline in world history. This humiliated country produced the most infamous Nazi demagogue known to humanity, Adolf Hitler, who attained power after another socio-economic disaster, the Great Depression.

Unlike Germany, Italy belonged to the victors' camp after World War I. Still, it failed to realize its national dreams and did not receive the remuneration it sought for joining the Entente Powers. Like Germany, Italy had also dreamed of being a colonial power but was not too successful in achieving this goal. Victorious in the war, the Italian nation also felt deep humiliation and declined into chaotic postwar revolutionary turmoil: the *biennio rosso* (two red years) of 1919–1920. The country became the breeding ground of populist demagoguery and the bastion of leading demagogues who preached hatred against the organized working class and the socialists. The revolutionary chaos was followed by the preemptive fascist counter-revolution of Benito Mussolini.

Model demagogues: Mussolini, Hitler and fascism

Mussolini and Hitler are the most well-known and successful populist-fascist demagogues of modern Europe. They emerged in countries that offered the most fertile ground for demagogues after World War I. They embodied most of the core features of political demagogues: extreme self-confidence ("*Mussolini ha sempre ragione*"—Mussolini is always right—as he and his followers liked to say) and a certainty of their charisma as their nation's leaders. They offered simple solutions to difficult problems and focused on an enemy. Murderous Fascism and Nazism offered a new era. Both were adept at emulating others' ideas and synthesizing them into one consistent and easily understandable ideology. Hitler based his central ideology on recurrent Viennese anti-Semitism. Mussolini, an avid reader and autodidact, combined his former socialist ideas with the theories of Friedrich Nietzsche, George Sorel, and Enrico Corradini. Moreover, he repeatedly read the work of the French founder of mass psychology, Gustave Le Bon, and used it to maximize his impact on the crowd.[33]

Both Mussolini and Hitler were passionate and great orators with a flair for the theatrical. Their lives were in some ways similar. Both sought to avoid military service and did so by going abroad (Hitler to Germany, Mussolini to Switzerland), only to join their respective armies later during the war. Both rose no higher than the rank of corporal in the Great War. They shared a love of violence, uniforms, and regalia. They were able to mobilize and nearly mesmerize untold numbers at mass rallies. Their life ended in a quite similar way as well.

Hitler masterfully persuaded his followers that a single enemy was responsible for all of Germany's miseries: the Jews. Judaism, communism, and capitalism adhered together in a secret international Jewish conspiracy. Mussolini masterfully combined elements of anti-capitalism with his fascist ideology by creating the corporate state. Denying class struggle between the bourgeoisie and the proletariat (which he had subscribed to earlier), he now affirmed the idea of a struggle between the bourgeois and proletarian *nations*, originated by Corradini. Both Mussolini and Hitler were expansionist, and both were prepared to wage war for what Mussolini described as "spazio vitale" (vital space) and Hitler as "Lebensraum" (living space).

Psychological factors also played an important role. There was Hitler's poverty and failure as an artist in early twentieth-century Vienna, which was then the world's center of anti-Semitism; and there was Mussolini's socialist background during his childhood, his early commitment and advocacy of socialism, his subsequent expulsion from the socialist party, and his founding of fascism. Both were fanatics with an oversized ego, self-confidence, and narcissism who were most in their element when leading mass rallies and addressing hordes of enthusiastic, even hysterical followers.

Modern political demagogues often model themselves after Hitler and Mussolini, the quintessential Fascist-Nazi political demagogues. But neither Hitler nor Mussolini appear in this book, as there is a whole library of scholarly works about them, analyzing their personality and methods, their temporary success, their murderous deeds, and their ultimate failure.

Demagogues in time of major changes

Instead, I will discuss the stories of less consequential but still important, influential, and dangerous demagogues from several countries of modern Europe. My goal is to present several of them from the last century and this one to show how common the danger of demagoguery is to modern European civilization. There were and are many of them. This volume offers a relatively small selection of communist, fascist, nationalist, right-wing, and liberal demagogues from the interwar period to present day Europe that arose in times of crises promising for populist demagogues. These were demagogues from the successor states of Austria-Hungary after its dissolution in 1918, which led to national crises in several successor states. Austria, the former center of a huge empire, became a small country overnight. National sentiment became jumbled and confused. People lost hope and feared for the future of the new rump country, and they advocated unification with Germany, or, in the case of Vorarlberg (the western part of the country), with Switzerland. A number of right-wing demagogues, Ernst Rüdiger Starhemberg and Engelbert Dollfuss the most successful among them, predominated in politics and public life.

Hungary, a part of the former Habsburg Empire, won its independence after four centuries but lost two-thirds of the Hungarian Kingdom's original territory. Both left- and right-wing demagoguery prevailed in the political arena. Béla Kun's short-lived communist regime was followed by the right-wing nationalist authoritarian Horthy regime. Dangerous populist-fascist demagogues, such as Gyula Gömbös and Ferenc Szálasi, attained leading political positions. The irredentist slogan of the postwar Horthy-regime proclaimed: "Rump Hungary is not a country! Greater Hungary is the Kingdom of Heaven!" Demagogues called for taking back all lost territories with a majority of non-Hungarian inhabitants, or at the very least, the parts that were populated mostly by Hungarians. This slogan was repeated every day in schools for a quarter of a century. Every neighboring country was considered an enemy, as were those countries' Western allies and Hungary's internal adversary, the Jews.

Other parts of the former Austria-Hungary were incorporated in newly established smaller multi-national states, such as Czechoslovakia and Yugoslavia. Some Slovak (Vojtech Tuka) and Croat politicians (Stjepan Radić and Ante Pavelić), demanded independent statehood. National demagoguery flourished and culminated during World War II in a bloody civil war between Yugoslav communist partisans on the one side and Serb royalists and Croat fascist-Nazi collaborators on the other. This was repeated almost a half century later when communism collapsed together with the Yugoslav state. Three nationalist demagogues, the Serbian Slobodan Milosević, the Bosnian Alija Izetbegović, and the Croat Franjo Tuđman, mobilized three distinct ethnic (in reality ethnically mixed) parts of the country (Serbia, Bosnia, and Croatia), and fought a protracted civil war that horrified Europe during the first half of the 1990s.

After the collapse of the Soviet Union, somewhat similar phenomena were repeated in the successor states of Russia, Ukraine, and other newly independent countries. The Soviet Union's implosion in 1991 led to the formation of several independent states. The core country of the Soviet Union, Russia, though a significant military and nuclear power, degenerated from a super-power status to that of a mutilated and impoverished peripheral country. A decade of rapid decline, dramatically rising poverty, and even shortened life expectancies followed. In such a crisis-ridden socio-political and economic environment, national-populist demagogy naturally flourished. Appearing on the scene were political firebrands like Vladimir Zhirinovsky, who sought to reconstruct the old Russian Empire, incorporating Finland as well; Saparmurat Niyazov, the former communist boss of Turkmenistan, who reinvented himself into a nationalist leader and took the moniker *"Türkmenbashi"* ("Leader of all Türkmen"); and Alexander Lukashenko, who preserved a Soviet-type system in Belarus as president of what has been described as "Europe's last dictatorship."

Demagogues are sometimes possible even in times of positive changes that hasten development. In periods when societies undergo promising transformations, when established social relations and circumstances disappear and are replaced by new social-economic realities, people fear the uncertainty of an unknown future. When, for example, a traditional agrarian society loses ground and disappears in times of successful industrialization—even if industrial transformation is a positive change historically—it endangers the old order and leads to mounting apprehension. Every major historical change, regardless of whether it is a historical decline or an elevation, has its winners and losers. When modern big industry and retail chains began to predominate, this fundamental transformation of economic-social structures endangered large segments of society. Masses of workers in small-scale and handicraft industries, small farmers, and small shopkeepers and their employees lost their livelihood. These aggrieved groups were easy prey for populist demagogues.

The dramatic transformations of the British Industrial Revolution, which lifted Britain, Europe, and then the world to a higher stage of development, created the desperate Luddites movement of traditional handicraft workers, who destroyed the first machines that replaced their manual labor. On several occasions in peripheral Europe, such as in nineteenth-century Russia and post-World War I Romania, demagogues renounced industrialization and upheld a highly idealized peasant society. Capitalism and its concomitant individualism were anathema to them; the medieval egalitarian peasant village community was lionized. These demagogues saw urbanization as the source of all social and moral decline and they reviled progressive reforms that altered the cultural environment as threats to the old social order.

A recent example of this historical phenomenon is what happened in Eastern Europe after the collapse of communism. During the promising transformation towards a democratic market system around the turn of the twenty-first century, the people of these countries longed to return "Back to Europe!" (the ubiquitous slogan of 1990). Eleven countries of the region had gradually won acceptance into the European Union and thus became members of the same "Club" as the most advanced countries of Western Europe. Their dreams had come true! Massive capital inflow and EU assistance fostered the region's economic and social modernization. Nevertheless, this arduous transformation caused a huge social shock. Income distribution and differentials radically changed, and large layers of the societies could not adjust easily. The region became the hunting ground for populist, nationalist demagogues. Nationalism and xenophobia abounded. Viktor Orbán's Fidesz party in Hungary, now enjoying its fourth term in government, is an anti-European party with a program of "illiberal democracy." Its main opposition, the Jobbik Party, is more right-wing and even neo-fascist. This political trend strengthened considerably in Central Europe in late 2015, with the electoral victory of the demagogue populist-nationalist Jarosław Kaczyński and his *Prawo i Sprawiedliwość* (Law and Justice) Party in Poland. Kaczyński immediately proceeded on an illiberal course, purged public officials and journalists, and embraced an Orbánist political agenda combined with an anti-immigration and anti-EU policy.

Thus, as Karl Polanyi reminds us, major changes always have the potential to cause a *social shock*, even if they improve the situation in the long run. "Social calamity is primarily a cultural not an economic phenomenon that can be measured by income figures. . . . Not economic exploitation, as often assumed, but the disintegration of the cultural environment of the victim is then the cause of the degradation. . . . [I]t lies in the lethal injury to the institutions in which his social existence is embodied. . . . [I]t happen[s] to a people in the midst of violent externally introduced, or at least externally produced change . . . though their standard of life . . . may have been improved. . . . [People's lives were] disrupted by the very fact that a market economy [was] foisted upon an entirely differently organized community."[34]

Fertile soil for populist demagoguery: backwardness and economic crisis

Political demagoguery tends to flourish and populist demagogues tend to advance in backward, relatively poor peripheral countries that lag behind wealthy core neighboring countries. The state of economic backwardness and marginalization are themselves more than enough to create a sense of hopelessness and a predisposition for demagoguery. Throughout modern history, the peripheral countries in Europe's Mediterranean and East European regions could never attain more than half the economic levels and living standards of the affluent Western European countries. Since the turn of the century, the Central European and Baltic region has reached only 32 percent of the richer North-West European income level. The Russian and Balkan region declined to 40 percent of the Central European and only 13 percent of the North-Western level.[35]

The backwardness of these regions and their people's resultant frustrations were always easily exploited by demagogues. In the interwar decades Corneliu Zelea Codreanu in Romania, Ionnis Metaxas in Greece, and several Baltic leaders led vicious political revolts. These demagogues "discovered" the true culprit responsible for all the backwardness: landlessness and poverty in their countries. In some cases the enemies were an ethnic minority, the Jews, or a foreign country. Nowadays nationalist demagogues such the Hungarian Orbán and the Polish Kaczyński launch demagogic attacks against the "dictate" of the European Union and against the Jewish George Soros, who they claim wants to destroy Christian values and open the door to Muslim immigrants.

Major economic crises, even in the wealthy core countries of Western Europe, led to similar outcomes. Jacques Doriot, who started out as a leading communist in France, and Oswald Mosley, a Labor activist, Fabian socialist, and one of finest orators in Britain, both became fascists, founded their own fascist parties, and collaborated with Mussolini and Hitler. They targeted scapegoats whom they held "responsible" for their nations' problems along the lines of the Nazis, and they offered instant solutions à la Hitler. The Great Depression of the 1930s provided ample opportunity for populist political demagogues to flourish throughout the continent. Populist demagogues abound in affluent countries in periods when the country's normal standing is threatened, and when decline becomes a real possibility.

Why did populist demagoguery thrive in Europe at the turn of the millennium?

The turn of the millennium became a special historical period again when populist demagogues prevailed to a pathological degree in the political arenas of several countries in Southern, Eastern, and Western Europe alike. Why did this happen when there was no war, no economic decline, and no major catastrophe in Europe? This was a period of a revolution in technology and communications, comparable only to the British Industrial Revolution. Technological development and government policy established an era in which the economies of various countries and continents bound closely together. Free trade predominated and business was internationalized. The large banks of advanced countries began operating on a global scale and a massive network of subsidiaries and value chains connected the industries of advanced and less developed countries. Societies were subordinated to the vicissitudes of the market. The decades from the 1970s on became the age of neo-liberal *globalization*.

As is usual in times of big changes, there were winners and losers of globalization. The globalized economic system served the more advanced countries and their multinational corporations that were the nucleus of technological innovation. The latter created enormous new markets for their products. Multinational corporations proliferated between 1970 and the 2010s, increasing more than tenfold to eighty-thousand. They stripped national governments and institutions of control of their economies, and several of them became more prosperous than well-established but relatively smaller European states. They made use of the cheap labor force of the peripheral countries of Europe and the Third World—the latter becoming (to use Joseph Stiglitz's term) the "discontents" of globalization, with Russia at the top of the list.[36] Massive, sometimes violent demonstrations angrily protested this new kind of "colonization" throughout the world.

After nearly half a century, however, the advantages and disadvantages of globalization have begun to change. A number of developing countries, particularly the Asian Small Tigers and then China and India, have rapidly industrialized and have shot straight to the top of the list of global exporters. They successfully competed with the affluent core countries, even within their domestic markets. Poverty markedly decreased and living standard increased in China and several other Asian countries. Income inequality started decreasing *between* countries. Meanwhile, the opposite trend characterized the situation *within* countries. A shocking increase of inequality in advanced Europe radically changed the trend of the postwar decades between 1950 and the early 1980s. Indeed, after World War II major political considerations, the lessons of the war, rising feeling of solidarity, and the Cold War competition with the Soviet Union caused an "egalitarian revolution" in the West.

The inequality of early capitalism was replaced by growing equality. The Gini coefficient, a measure of income distribution, signaled a significant improvement. This index, if nearer to zero, reflects more egalitarian distribution. If it nears to one, it shows high inequality. In 1820, the global Gini index was 0.49 but by the early 1980s in Europe, it declined to 0.23–0.26. Apologetic interpretations, among them the American Simon Kuznets, maintained that advanced capitalism decreases inequality. However, as the French economist Thomas Piketty convincingly proved it, this was not the case. Political motivations led to reduction of inequality. From the 1970s on, in the time of globalization and the rule of neo-liberal practice, and then especially after the end of the Cold War, the postwar trend changed dramatically. "Income inequality has increased significantly in the rich countries" and returned to the level of early capitalism. The global Gini index in 2000 was already 0.66, much higher than in 1820.[37] Already during the first one-and-half decades between 1985 and 2000, the West European Gini index increased from 0.27 to 0.35. Some of the transforming Central and Eastern European former communist countries reflected the same trend. In the three Baltic countries—Estonia, Latvia, and Lithuania—that had been part of the Soviet Union but then became independent in 1991, the combined Gini index was 0.23 in 1985, but rose to 0.35 by 2000.[38] Wages mostly stagnated while profits and the income of the top one percent sharply increased. The world index of that shows the increase of income of the top one percent by 6.8 percent per annum while the average income of adults increased only by 2.1 percent. Since the 1960s, managers' income jumped to 10–17 times that of a factory worker by 1992, and to 13–25 times by 2000. In Britain, managers' income during the same period jumped to 25 times higher than average workers' income. In advanced countries that kept their social policy orientation such as Germany and Sweden, this discrepancy was smaller, 11 and 13 times respectively.[39]

Growing inequality became one of the main sources of dissatisfaction for the population and for the working masses' revolt against the elite. Additionally, most wealthy countries began restructuring their economies. Agriculture, which employed about 70 percent of the active workforce until the early nineteenth century and still about 30–35 percent until the mid-twentieth century, decreased to 2–4 percent in advanced countries. This long-term trend was also accompanied by de-industrialization. The manufacturing labor force declined from 40–45 percent in the early twentieth century to 15–25 percent by the early twenty-first century. Manufacturing employment was increasingly replaced with employment in financial and other service sectors branches. Blue collar workers in traditional sectors fell victim to growing joblessness and stagnating wages. True, millions of new jobs were also created but this work required new knowledge and much higher qualifications. This fundamental restructuring of the socio-economic system greatly devalued unskilled labor. Most coal mines were shut down even in Belgium, where the coal industry was a leading sector and an export industry. Education became emphatically emphasized. Already in the 1980s, 75 percent of the unemployed in Italy had no longer than eight years of elementary education, and 45 percent of them had even less. In Germany at that time unemployment among unskilled workers was twice as high as that of skilled workers.[40]

The traditional groups of workers, who lacked the requisite skills for the new economy, were simply unable to adjust and faced mounting peril, insecurity, and despair. Disillusioned and desperate workers are easy fodder for populist demagogues. A great part of the working class, the much-touted "proletariat" as Karl Marx and other socialists labeled them, which had long been the base for leftist revolutionary movements, now flocked to right-wing demagogues. This was not an entirely new phenomenon, for it had already happened during the interwar period when hordes of desperate workers joined fascist movements. One third of the members of the Nazi party in Germany were workers. The Hungarian "Arrow-cross" Nazi party won 40 percent of the vote in working-class regions in 1939.

The French populist demagogue Marine Le Pen and the advocates for Brexit in the UK in 2016 have successfully recruited the "forgotten" workers of their countries. In a way, this jump from Left to Right is understandable because both share one thing in common: a revolt against the establishment. The establishment was deemed responsible for the negative changes and rebuked as the enemy of "pure, ordinary people." Left-wing and Right-wing demagogues, usually not part of the political elite, offered an alternative leadership that promised radical change. Still, is it not a historical absurdity that the self-promoting billionaire Silvio Berlusconi, presenting himself as an anti-establishment, self-sacrificing savior, attracted the poor and under-unemployed working class of southern Italy?[41]

Populism and demagoguery

Discussing the historical environment in which populist demagoguery has gained ground and demagogues have become politically successful, it is time to speak about populism as a political phenomenon. Populism has become one of the most oft-discussed topics in politics as well as political science and history scholarship in recent years. Descriptions and definitions of populism are partly connected with different regional peculiarities of the phenomenon. Latin American populism has a much longer and somewhat different history than does European or North American populism, or newly emerging African populism.

Still, this is hardly a new phenomenon in Europe. John Abromeit rightly points to progressive populism of the French Revolution and its transformation via progressive socialist populism in mid-nineteenth century (of Pierre-Joseph Proudhon) and later nineteenth-century Russian and Balkan "peasantism," as the beginning of populist trend in politics. He also describes how this progressive populism transformed in the twentieth century and how "fascism was able effectively to place itself within" a transformed populism, using a variant of the same distinction between "virtuous producers and immoral parasites," by "incorporating progressive populist ideas that had emerged in the long nineteenth century." The Nazis' radical critique of the existing system and offering an alternative to both capitalism and communism exploited basic populist ideas. Therefore, fascism, originally a middle-class movement, was able via its populist agenda to conquer a great part of the working class.[42]

After World War II, however, populism hardly existed in Europe. Nevertheless, the gradual collapse of colonialism and the foundation of dozens of new states revitalized this political trend. In the first sentence of their edited book, Ernst Gellner and Ghiţă Ionescu, rephrasing the famous first sentence of Marx and Engels's Communist Manifesto, noted in 1969: "A specter is haunting the world—populism." They observed that when leaders of the newly established countries "embrace an ideology it tends more often to have a populist character."[43] It also crops up, they suggest, when political persecution mania is more acute and when there is a growing belief that unidentifiable conspiracies are at work against the public at large. As they characterize it, populism is a peculiarly negative ideology. It is anti-capitalistic, anti-urban, and xenophobic. Populists worship the people, especially the meek and the miserable, precisely because they are persecuted or neglected by the elite. Populism, they maintain, "has been more fundamental to the shaping of the political mind than is generally acknowledged."[44] Such words sound nothing short of prophetic nearly half a century later.

According to the *Oxford Handbook on Populism and Political Leadership*, populism "is an essentially contested concept . . . and discussing all the definitions of populism that have been developed in the scholarly debate would be a titanic endeavour."[45] One of the best experts of this topic, Cas Mudde in his small book written together with Cristóbal Rovira Kaltwasser, also noted that populism is "an essentially contested concept . . . academics and journalists use the term to denote very diverse phenomena."[46] Indeed, there are schools of thought that see populism as a political style, a strategy, a movement, a popular agency, and a positive force for radical democracy that strives to strengthen government power by directly connecting to a mobilized populace.[47] Others consider populism a pathological disorder of democracy. Large numbers of people are not really represented in the political system and in certain political situations become easily disillusioned and rebel against the existing political establishment, embracing instead the notion of popular sovereignty as opposed to imperfect political representation.[48]

At the core of the interpretation of populism is the conflict between the elite and the people. Yves Mény and Yves Surel stress the centrality of the "people," who are betrayed by the elite and to whom the populists want to restore primacy.[49] The concept of "the people" however, is more than questionable. Paul Taggard speaks about the "imagined entity of the people" and its hostility against representative politics that means "stealing power" from the people.[50] "The People" that is central to populism is a constructed construction, and may mean the common people or the entire nation. Jacques Rancière flatly stated that "the people does not exist." Bruno Bosteels added: "The question 'what is a people?' invites us to abandon the . . . presuppositions behind 'the' people and . . . talking about 'peoples' in the plural."[51] The "Elite," in this concept, might be the political, cultural elite, and the media, and they work against the general will of the people. In more contemporary terms, the elite often incorporates the European Union's bureaucrats who are against the member countries' peoples.

The already quoted Dutch scholar, Cas Mudde, gives one of the most precise definitions by saying that populism is: "an ideology that considers society to be ultimately separated into two homogeneous and antagonistic groups, 'the pure people' versus 'the corrupt elite', and which argues that politics should be an expression of the *volonté générale* (general will) of the people."[52] In his edited 641 pages long collection of 32 studies, *The Populist Radical Right* (2017), Cas Mudde defines the populist ideological phenomenon as a combination of three features: 1. Nationalist xenophobia (ethnic, religious, and racial prejudices such as Islamophobia and those against minorities and immigrants, and sometimes anti-Semitic, anti-Roma, and anti-neighbor policies). 2. Authoritarianism (strict conservative law and order policy, especially against "immigrant crime"). 3. Populist concept of a unified people whose will has to be realized and the corrupt elite and political class, together with their "political correctness," pushed out from power and thus eliminated.[53] The elite is self-serving and anti-democratic, the people are the exploited and neglected whom populists seek to mobilize.[54] Such mobilization may come from either the Left or the Right. Populism is "unrelated to the left-right distinction," not a coherent, but rather fluid, a "thin-centered ideology . . . almost always appears attached to other ideological elements, which . . . are appealing to a broader public. . . . This means that populism can take very different shapes."[55]

Indeed, populism might merge with communist, anti-capitalist ideology as well as fascist, racist, right-wing, anti-Semitic concepts (ethno-populism), it may appear as anti-European nationalism and may even be combined with neo-liberalism (as was the case with the Forza Italia, or the UK Independence Party). As some scholars point out, populism is always a kind of primitivism. Indeed, the notion of fraternity and cohesion of a pure people, the belief of the homogeneity of an entire population, and the assumption of some kind of common will of the public at large are nothing but a fantasy. The failure to recognize the existence of diverse and even conflicting interests of various segments of society is indeed the product of a primitive imagination.[56]

These over-simplified untruths are connected to "the belief in the value of belonging to a group or culture. . . . From this fraternity and this primitivism it is an easy step to intolerance, suspicion, fear of betrayal, and xenophobia."[57] One should add: the belief of belonging to a community often leads to exclusive nationalism. Populism has a "Manichean world view." This is an interpretation of the world as an ominous duality, as a struggle between good and evil, light and dark, love and hate. Its origins date back to a prevailing Iranian-born religion between the third and seventeenth centuries.[58]

From the political debates about populism it pays to quote the well-established view of Tony Blair, the former British Prime Minister:

> Rightist populism . . . [is] a new coalition, comprising formerly left-
> leaning supporters in working-class communities who feel left behind
> by globalization and traditionally right-leaning supporters who hate lib-
> eralism. Both constituencies believe that traditional culture is at risk
> from immigration and "political correctness". . . . Both feel let down by
> the so-called elites and think that the solution is an authoritarian fig-
> ure who dismisses what a biased establishment thinks. . . . The modus
> operandi of this populism is not to reason but to roar. . . . Its support-
> ers welcome the outrage their leaders provoke, so that even when they
> are in government, they act as if they were excluded from it. . . .[59]

Populist demagogues always present themselves as the people's true
representatives, as "their voice," merely one among the many, as the
"man on the street" who speaks the people's language and understands
their problems. On that basis, some scholars maintain that "populism
is regularly applied as [a] synonym for demagoguery."[60] This idea is
strengthened by the fact that as populism may merge with various ideologies, right or left alike, demagogues may also be communist, fascist,
or liberal. The very close connection between populism and demagoguery is evident, but they are not synonyms. Sometimes they are spontaneous mass movements without any definable leadership. That was the
case with the Russian left-wing Narodnik (populist) movement in the
second half of the nineteenth century, as well as the various Balkan populist peasant movements during the interwar period. That was also the
case with right-wing fascist groupings in Hungary before a strong demagogue, Ferenc Szálasi, consolidated them into a united Hungarian Nazi
party in 1935. Communist populist groups were found inside the established Social Democratic party in pre-World War I Russia, as they were
in post-World War I Austria, Hungary, Bulgaria, and elsewhere, often
without an unquestioned demagogue leader. (In the United States the
right-wing "Tea Party" movement established itself within one of the
oldest American political organizations, the Republican Party, without
a single leader. At the same time, the left-wing "Occupy Wall Street"
movement also had no single charismatic demagogic leader at all.) Populist movements thus do exist without demagogues leading them. Populism is not always the creation of political manipulators and ambitious
leaders, although it often ends up in such leaders' hands. Time and again
populist movements have sought out charismatic leaders, who are some-

times political outsiders, but are always strong and flamboyant personalities who promise instant solutions for people's pressing problems.

Populist demagogues in certain historical periods have been hugely
successful in attacking the political elite and their established parties.
They are dangerous. Populist demagogues, right-wing and left-wing
alike, tend to consider their electoral victories and their rise to power as
not merely a change of government, but as regime change. They see
themselves as opening a new chapter in the nation's history—a chapter
seemingly considered "permanent." Hitler spoke of a "Thousand-Year
Reich." Viktor Orbán, at his inauguration speech in 2018 when he started his fourth term in power, described the period between 2010 and
2030 as a single period when he rules the country.[61] They are fully prepared to eliminate or at least limit all opposition and undermine democratic institutions, subordinate the media and weaken the rule of law
that may endanger their rule. They are mostly advocates for strong government and the subordination of the various government branches—
including legislative and judiciary—to the executive branch. In the economic arena they are for state interventionism. Once in power, populist
demagogues try to concentrate as much power in their hands as possible to make their regimes permanent.

In the interwar decades, newly established left-populist communist
and right-populist fascist parties gained huge ground. As populism has
spread, support of traditional parties around the turn of the millennium's Europe diminished considerably, and at times completely evaporated, while new, mostly populist parties came to the fore. Soon after
the collapse of communism, the European communist parties, including the most powerful Italian one, virtually disappeared. In Italy, actually *all* the traditional parties disappeared, including the dominant postwar Christian Democratic Party. The social democratic parties lost a
huge part of their members and voters. The political vacuum was exploited handily by populist demagogues and newly founded populist
parties. "During the last twenty years," Gianfranco Bettin Lattes and
Ettore Recchi noted in 2005, one can see "the electoral growth of new
political formations, the Greens and the populist parties of the extreme
right."[62] The most important new development was definitely the spectacular rise of right-wing populism. The losers of modern transformation: de-industrialization and globalization flocked to politicians who

offered quick and easy solutions. This was first seen in Italy in the 1990s. Umberto Bossi's separatist *Lega Nord*, Gianfranco Fini's neo-fascist *Alleanza Nazionale*, and most of all Silvio Berlusconi's right-wing populist *Forza Italia* emerged triumphant. During the early 2010s the *Movimento Cinque Stelle*, the Five Star Movement, joined and became the strongest.

Populist political demagogues gained prominence throughout Europe. The list is a quite long one. A slew of new far-right populist opposition parties, led by influential demagogues, appeared on the scene in several countries, some openly espousing neo-fascist rhetoric and ideology. Among them are Greece's *Laïkós Sýndesmos – Chrysí Avgí* (Golden Dawn), Hungary's *Jobbik*, which came in second in the 2014 elections, and Germany's *Nationaldemokratische Partei Deutschland* (German National Democratic Party) and then, at the 2018 elections, the *Alternative für Deutschland*. Most of these parties are made up of extreme nationalists and minority and foreigner-hating xenophobes. Many have gradually turned against the "Brussels dictate" and European integration in general. They began to flourish as a reaction to the EU's enlargement in the decades between the 1980s and 2010s, and they strengthened with the migration crisis of the mid-2010s.

One of the oldest and strongest parties of this stripe, led by popular demagogues, is the French *Front National* of Marine Le Pen, which won a quarter of the votes at the last European Parliamentary elections in 2014. Marine Le Pen triumphantly declared that her party was "regaining" lost territory, among them the suburbs of big cities. Nevertheless, Le Pen lost the 2017 presidential and parliamentary elections. Geert Wilders's Dutch *Partij voor de Vrijheid* (Party of Freedom), which was founded only in 2005, came in third in the 2014 EU parliamentary elections and promptly proceeded to forge an alliance with the French National Front. At the 2017 national elections, however, the French National Front gained only 13 percent of the votes. Populist parties are present and even dominate several countries in turn of the millennium Europe. In Italy, one of the most extreme examples, populist parties dominate the entire political structure. The Five Star Movement, which won 25 percent of the vote in the 2013 national elections gained about one-third in 2018. Spain's *Podemos* (We Can) party emerged as the second largest in the country. Britain's conservative-nationalist Independence Party

(UKIP), captured 27 percent of the vote in 2014. Austria's far-right *Freiheitliche Partei Österreichs* (Freedom Party), a party that, despite having a longer pedigree, managed to win only 11 percent of the vote in national elections in 2006—yet at the October 2017 parliamentary elections it won more than 27 percent. The Greek left-wing *Syriza* party—in coalition with a far-right anti-establishment party—easily gained power in 2015 with 36 percent of the vote. In the Greek case, some of Syriza's leaders renounced populist demagoguery to retain power (having capitulated to the EU on the Greek debt crisis), while others disappeared from politics. Germany's anti-immigrations nationalist *Alternative für Deutschland* (Alternative for Germany), a party that was unimportant for long, increased their votes from 4.5 to nearly 13 percent in 2017.

Less influential examples of this political genre include Finland's *Perussuomalaiset* (True Finns Party), Belgium's *Vlaams Belang* (Flemish Interest Party), and small opposition groupings in Denmark, Croatia, and elsewhere. This is, however, not a stable situation. Some of these parties have begun to grow. The Neo-Nazi *Sverigedemokraterna* (Swedish Democrats Party) suddenly catapulted to the top of the polls in traditionally tolerant Sweden. Founded in 1988, it won 5.7 percent of the vote in 2010 (reaching the 4 percent parliamentary threshold), and then captured 13 percent in 2014. These parties, led by populist xenophobic demagogues, are adept at mobilizing mass resistance especially against immigration, but also against the "dictate of Brussels." They exploit anti-integrationist sentiments: in 2012, only 30 percent of Europeans told Eurobarometer pollsters that they believe the EU benefits them.[63] "Trust in the European Union," as the *Telegraph* noted a year later, was "at its lowest level since records began in 1997, with less than one in three EU citizens expressing trust in the EU in 2013."[64] Nevertheless, by 2017–18, popular feeling somewhat improved and more people trusted the EU than national governments.

The "Trump effect"

This book is about Europe. At this point, nevertheless, the connection with the similar populist trend in the United States has to be mentioned. The most dangerous momentum of the frightening deluge of populist demagoguery, a breakthrough worldwide was the election of Donald J. Trump as president of the United States, the dominant world power, in November 2016. The narcissistic, ego-maniac billionaire with a showman's mastery of the media and using a primitive, vulgar language was able to attract the angry, less educated, underemployed or unemployed workers, and the rural population whose income stagnated for decades. These layers formed his base. About a quarter of the eligible voters believed his promise that he would bring back lost jobs, would improve their situation, "protect" the country from Chinese imports and illegal Mexican immigrants, competitors for jobs, by closing the borders and building a huge wall along the Mexican border, and ban all Muslim immigrants from the country. His speeches and advertisements, presenting Mexican immigrants as criminals and rapists, Muslims as terrorists, his slogans of "America First!" and "Make America great again" successfully spread hatred and nationalism, strengthened and revitalized racism and white supremacists, and encouraged anti-Semitism. Trump attracted the support of the KuKluxKlan. His triumph story is an American tragedy but also closely connected to Europe. European populist demagogues celebrated his victory as the prefiguration of their own better future. Nigel Farage, Geert Wilders, Marine Le Pen, and Viktor Orbán openly endorsed and welcomed him. They welcomed the event as a watershed in Western politics, the opening of a new age. Trump's presidency, they thought, heralded a victorious future for them too. They did not foresee the endless series of lies—as fact checks proved—already two-thousands misleading, false statements in his first year in office. Innumerable scandals have been caused by his unpreparedness, total lack of understanding of the role of president, and total lack of concentration in performing it. One could not count the number of improvised, failed decisions, the lack of civility, his open lies, and attacks against both democratic institutions and the freedom of the press that have characterized Trump's presidency from the very first day. His demagoguery worked well during the election campaign and also to keep his base intact. The Republican Party gathered behind him and realized some of their old dreams such as a major tax cut and new Supreme Court judges, strengthening their domination of the judicial branch.

Europeans watched and some of them understood well: Donald Trump's electoral victory was both a danger and a warning, and caused the vast majority of Europeans to turn against his counterparts in Europe during the 2017 elections in the Netherlands, France, and Germany. His impact on worldwide populist demagoguery, however, remains ambivalent. On the one hand, he has encouraged similar European political trends, on the other, frightened a part of the electorate to be skeptical about populist promises.

The severe economic and social problems, however, that marginalized and left behind large blue-collar worker layers and the agricultural population in the countryside are still present. Increasing inequality returned to the advanced world. The consequences of the 2008 financial-economic crisis, followed by the 2015–16 migration crisis, and the way it was handled by the European Union, mobilized large segments of societies and fueled right-wing nationalism and anti-EU sentiments. The Trump factor is thus ambiguous and may be dangerous in Europe. Populism is rising in Europe and even losers of elections such as Geert Wilders and the Alternative for Germany, became stronger than before. The October 2017 Austrian parliamentary elections significantly strengthened the populist right-wing, including Jörg Haider's party (FPÖ) that finished second. The right-conservative, anti-immigration Austrian People's Party (ÖVP) and the Freedom Party of Austria together gained 57 percent of the votes and formed a coalition government. The Social Democratic Party (with 27 percent of the votes) came close—for the first time during the one-hundred year-long history of independent Austria—of not being among the first two parties at a national election. In the early summer of 2018, Italy was taken over by two populist parties in coalition and altogether about three quarters of the electorate voted for populists.

Populist parties dominate only Italy and Austria in the West, but virtually conquered Central and Eastern Europe. The region that was far behind the West, but started rising through market democracy after the collapse of communism in the 1990s, suffered a lot during the 2008 economic crisis and the austerity measures that were forced by the European Union to put the financial households in order, lost their ways, and turned to anti-EU populism. Populists are in power in Hungary, Poland, and in the four so-called Visegrád countries, they have won the election in Slovenia and are also in power in Greece. They are actually forming a rebellious group against the European Union. Populism flooded Southern and Central Europe and the European Union in general.

The story has not yet ended. The door is still wide open for populist demagogues to rape the masses and rape history. It is crucially important for Europe to learn the reality behind the demagogues' promises and their persuasive language in order to block their road into twenty-first century politics.

Endnotes

1 Kenneth F. Warren, ed., *The Encyclopedia of U.S. Campaigns, Elections, and Electoral Behavior* (Thousand Oaks, California: SAGE Publications, Inc., 2008), accessed April 25, 2008, http://dx.doi.org/10.4135/9781412963886.

2 Hans de Bruijn, *Geert Wilders Speaks Out: The Rhetorical Frames of a European Populist* (The Hague: Eleven International Publishing, 2011), 9–15.

3 George Lakoff, *Don't Think of an Elephant!: Know Your Values and Frame the Debate* (White River: Chelsea Green Publishing, 2004), 3–4, 19.

4 Stijn van Kessel, *Populist Parties in Europe: Agents of Discontent?* (Houndsmill: Palgrave Macmillan, 2015), 2. See in more detail: Paul Taggart, *Populism* (Buckingham, PA: Open University Press, 2000); Cas Mudde, "The Populist Zeitgeist," *Government and Opposition* 39, no. 4 (2004): 542–63. doi:10.1111/j.1477-7053.2004.00135.x.

5 Ghita Ionescu and Ernest Gellner, eds., *Populism: Its Meaning and National Characteristics* (London: Weidenfeld and Nicolson, 1969).

6 Max Weber, *Politik als Beruf* (Stuttgart: Reclam Verlag, [1919] 1992), 5.

7 Ruth Wodak, *The Politics of Fear: What Right-wing Populist Discourses Mean* (London: Sage Publications, 2015), 47.

8 Warren, *Encyclopedia of U.S. Campaigns*.

9 Keith Spencer Felton, *Warriors' Words: A Consideration of Language and Leadership* (Westport, CT: Praeger, 1995), xv.

10 Ibid., 65. Shirer quoted by Keith Spencer Felton.

11 See Constantin Iordachi, "God's Chosen Warriors: Romantic Palingenesis, Militarism and Fascism in Modern Romania," in *Comparative Fascist Studies: New Perspectives*, ed. Iordachi (London: Routledge: 2009), 316–57.

12 "British Foreign Minister is Center of Attention at a Party Conference," *New York Times*, October 4, 2017.

13 Donald Trump's 2016 presidential campaign in the US provides a good example. Trump disingenuously accused Hillary Clinton of questioning Barack Obama's American birth during the 2008 election campaign. He of course knew that this was a lie since he was the one, together with some extreme racist Republican politicians, who began the "birther" campaign in order to delegitimize Obama's presidency. He actually repeated this accusation several times for years, including at an early stage of the 2016 campaign.

14 "Art of the Lie," *Economist*, September 10, 2016, https://www.economist.com/leaders/2016/09/10/art-of-the-lie

15 "The Brexit lies," *New Statesman*, June 30, 2016.

16 Nick Cohen, "There are liars and then there's Boris Johnson and Michael Gove," *Guardian*, June 25, 2016, https://www.theguardian.com/commentisfree/2016/jun/25/boris-johnson-michael-gove-eu-liars?CMP=fb_gu.

17 I am not going to review the vast psychological and psychoanalytical literature, but, as a curiosum, permit me to mention a study on the Croat politician in the 1920s: Michael Bankovitch, *Stjepan Radić, eine psychoanalytische Studie* (Vienna: Adolf Lhotzky, 1928).

18 See Giovanni Orsina, *Berlusconism and Italy: A Historical Interpretation* (New York: Palgrave Macmillan, 2014).

19 Scholars from the turn of the twentieth century such as Gabriel Tarde, Gustave Le Bon, and Sigmund Freud were the first to systematically study mass psychology. They were followed by Alfred Adler, Serge Moscovici, Carl F. Graumann, and several others. They analyzed crowd behavior and distinguished it from individual behavior. In the following paragraphs I summarize some of the most important elements of their discoveries.

20 Carl F. Graumann and Serge Moscovici, eds., *Changing Conceptions of Crowd Mind and Behavior* (New York: Springer Verlag, 1986), 11. I used this book, especially the chapter "The Discovery of the Masses," written by Serge Moscovici, in the following analysis.

21 Quoted by Lawrie Reznek, *Delusions and the Madness of the Masses* (Lanham, MD: Rowman & Littlefield, 2010), 69. I used this book in the following analysis.

22 Charles Mackay, *Memoires of Extraordinary Popular Delusions and the Madness of Crowds* (Wells, VT: Page, [1841] 1932).

23 Serge Chakotin, *The Rape of the Masses: The Psychology of Totalitarian Political Propaganda* (New York: Alliance Book, 1940). I used this book in the following analysis as well.

24 Gustave Le Bon, *The Psychology of Socialism* ([New York: Macmillan, 1899] New Jersey: Transaction Publishers, 1982), 102.

25 Serge Moscovici, "The Discovery of the Masses," in Graumann and Moscovici, *Changing Conceptions of Crowd Mind*, 13.

26 Ibid, 7.

27 Gustave Le Bon, *The Crowd* (Harmondsworth: Penguin, [1895] 1977), 33–34.

28 Alfred Adler, *Le tempérament nerveux: Éléments d'une psychologie individuelle et applications à la psychothérapie* (Paris: Payot, [1929] 1948), quoted by Chakotin, *The Rape of the Masses*, 63–64.

29 Ibid., 47.

30 Reznek, *Delusions and the Madness of the Masses*, 48–49, 63.

31 The shocking stories of the American "Peoples temple" sect in 1978 in Jonestown and the "Heaven Gate" sect in 1997 in Rancho Santa Fe may serve as examples.

32 See Max Weber, *Economy and Society: An Outline of Interpretive Sociology* (Berkley, CA: University of California Press, [1922] 1978).

33 Mussolini said: "I have read all the work of Gustave Le Bon and I don't know how many times I have reread his *Psychologie des Foules*. It is a capital work to which I return frequently to day." Quoted by R. de Felice, *Mussolini il rivoluzionario* (Torino: Einaudi, 1965), 467.

34 Karl Polanyi, *The Great Transformation: The Political and Economic Origins of Our Time* (Beacon Hills: Beacon Press, [1944] 1957), 157–59.

35 Here and throughout this book, comparative GDP statistics are quoted from: "List of Countries by Projected GDP per capita 2017," *Statistical Times*, http://statisticstimes.com/economy/countries-by-projected-gdp-capita.php.

36 Joseph Stiglitz, *Globalization and its Discontents* (London: W. W. Norton &. Co., 2002).

37 Thomas Piketty, *Capital in the Twenty-First Century* (Cambridge, MA: Harvard University Press, 2014), 13–15. Piketty successfully rejected the postwar theory of Simon Kuznets that maintained the early capitalism is characterized by high inequality that decreases in mature capitalism.

38 Stephen Broadberry and Kevin H. O'Rourke, eds., *The Cambridge Economic History of Modern Europe, 1870 to the Present*, vol. 2 (Cambridge: Cambridge University Press, 2010), 398.

39 Ivan T. Berend, *An Economic History of Twentieth-Century Europe: Economic Regimes from Laissez-Faire to Globalization* (Cambridge: Cambridge University Press, [2006] 2016), 270.

40 Hans-Georg Betz, *Radical Right-Wing Populism in Western Europe* (New York: St. Martin's Press, 1994), 31; "Black and Jobless in America," *Economist*, May 2, 2011.

41 Similarly, unemployed former coal miners and steel workers in the US have placed all their hopes on the billionaire Donald Trump.

42 John Abromeit, "Transformation of Producerist Populism in Western Europe," in *Transformation of Populism in Europe and the Americas: History of Recent Tendencies*, ed. John Abromeit, Bridget Maria Chesterton, Gary Marotta, and York Norman (London: Bloomsbury, 2016), 236, 239, 254. See also the three studies in this volume about Russian and Balkan peasant populism from page 51 to 104.

43 Ionescu and Gellner, *Populism*, x.

44 Ibid, 3–5.

45 Cas Mudde and Rovira Kaltwasser, "Populism and Political Leadership," in *Oxford Handbooks Online*, ed. R.A.W. Rhodes and Paul 't Hart, doi:10.1093/oxfordhb/9780199653881.013.016.

46 Cas Mudde and Cristóbal Rovira Kaltwasser, *Populism: A Very Short Introduction* (Oxford: Oxford University Press, 2017), 2.

47 Kurt Weyland, "Clarifying a Contested Concept: Populism in the Study of Latin American Politics," *Comparative Politics* 34, no. 1 (2001): 1–22.

48 See Pierre Rosanvallon, *Counter-Democracy: Politics in an Age of Distrust* (New York: Columbia University Press, 2008), 265.

49 Yves Mény and Yves Surel, *Par le Peuple, Pour le Peuple: Le Populisme et les Démocraties* (Paris: Fayard, 2000); Yves Mény and Yves Surel, eds., *Democracies and the Populist Challenge* (New York: Palgrave Macmillan, 2002).

50 Paul Taggart, *Populism* (Buckingham, PA: Open University Press, 2000).

51 The concept of "People" is broadly discussed by Alain Badiou, Pierre Bordieu, Judith Butler, Georges Didi-Huberman, Sadri Khiari, and Jacques Rancière in *What is a People?* The Introduction is written by Bruno Bosteels. See Badiou et al., *What is a People?* (New York: Columbia University Press, 2016), 2, 102.

52 Mudde, "The Populist Zeitgeist," 543.

53 Cas Mudde, ed., *The Populist Radical Right: A Reader* (London: Routledge, 2017), 4–5.

54 Michael Kazin, *The Populist Persuasion: An American History* (Ithaca, NY: Cornell University Press, 1995), 1.

55 Mudde and Kaltwasser, *Populism: A Very Short Introduction*, 6, 8.

56 Donald MacRae, "Populism as an Ideology," in *Populism: Its Meaning and National Characteristics*, ed. Ghita Ionescu and Ernst Gellner (London: Weidenfeld and Nicolson, 1969), 154–65.

57 Ibid., 156.

58 Manicheanism was a major religious movement that was founded by the Iranian prophet Mani and prevailed between the third and seventh centuries. In its heyday, it was one of the most popular religions in the world.

59 Tony Blair, "How to Stop Populism's Carnage," *New York Times*, March 4, 2017.

60 van Kessel, *Populist Parties in Europe*, 9.

61 "Hungary's new parliament re-elected Viktor Orbán as prime minister," *Hungarian Daily News*, May 10, 2018, https://dailynewshungary.com/hungarys-new-parliament-re-elected-viktor-orban-as-prime-minister/.

62 Gianfranco Bettin Lattes and Ettore Recchi, eds., *Comparing European Societies: Towards a Sociology of the EU* (Bologna: Monduzzi Editore, 2005), 205.

63 *Standard Eurobarometer* 78, 2012, https://ec.europa.eu/commfrontoffice/publicopinion/archives/eb/eb78/eb78_en.htm.

64 Nassos Stylianou, "Trust in EU at an all time low latest figures show," *Telegraph*, January 22, 2014, https://www.telegraph.co.uk/news/worldnews/europe/eu/10586961/Trust-in-EU-at-an-all-time-low-latest-figures-show.html.

PART
1

Interwar populist
–communist and fascist–
demagogues

CHAPTER 1

A Hungarian communist demagogue: Béla Kun

Hungary's special postwar crisis and territorial shrinkage

The profound crisis and sense of desperation that characterized post-World War I Hungary were not normal occurrences in history. With its defeat along with Germany in 1918, Hungary fell into dramatic decline. A medieval great power, a part of the Habsburg Empire since 1526, a major component of the Austro–Hungarian Monarchy since 1867, Hungary found itself suddenly independent but bled white, humiliated, and mutilated.

The long war had depleted the economy and exhausted the society. More than 43 percent of the country's national wealth, the equivalent of two and a half years of prewar national income was squandered on war expenditures. Wheat production dropped to half, and agricultural and industrial output (in 1919 and 1920) fell to about 40 percent of prewar levels. Inflation had begun during the war and soared in the summer of 1919, when the value of the currency (the crown) stood at 15 percent the prewar level. After a failed attempt at stabilization in 1921, the inflationary spiral hit a ceiling in the spring of 1924, when the value of 100 gold crowns, which had been virtually equal to 100 Swiss francs a decade before, was worth only 0.0065 Swiss francs. Hyper-inflation eradicated the wages and savings of much of the middle class. Impoverishment, rationing of basic food items, and actual starvation afflicted the vast majority of the population.[1]

Hungarians were deeply demoralized throughout this period. The Hungarian media routinely reported on the suffering, chaos, and hopelessness throughout the country. *Az Est* (The Evening), one of the most popular Hungarian dailies, bemoaned that "what remains of Hungary's land is not cultivated . . . we do not have coal . . . home heating and lighting is frighteningly jeopardized. . . . The most tragic loss that is frightening this helpless nation . . . is the loss of people! We have no idea what will happen to us. Every single existing thing, every single life is mortally endangered!"[2] A month earlier the same paper reported: "The anarchy of hoodlums and looters prevails in the country. . . . Do we have any notion what will happen here this winter without coal and with paralyzed transportation? . . . Everyone has become our enemy because of our past sins . . . and we are unable to communicate to them how much we've developed. . . . We have to build a new life out of this misery and catastrophe."[3]

A little over than a year later the paper described the calamitous lack of consumer goods and the galloping high prices, exploited by "massive armies of black-marketers, smugglers and usurers. . . . During the French Revolution the death penalty could not stop these types of thieves and blood sucking leeches."[4]

Losing the war also led to a unique national crisis in Hungary. As was the Austro-Hungarian Monarchy as a whole, the Hungarian Kingdom was also broken up into disparate pieces, and from its various nationalities, comprising 20 million people in 1913, 54 percent of the country's population became citizens of neighboring states. The Croat National Assembly (the Sabor) declared independence from Hungary on October 29, 1918, and signaled its readiness to join the newly established Kingdom of Serbs, Croats, and Slovenes—later called Yugoslavia. On the next day the Slovak National Council ratified the Czechoslovak National Council's declaration joining the two nations to create Czechoslovakia. On November 9, the National Assembly of Romanians living in Hungary declared independence and formed a government of Romanian nationals; three weeks later, it formally announced its incorporation into Romania.

All these moves were spurred on by France. General Franchet d'Esperey, Commander of the French Balkan Army, handed a memorandum to the Hungarian government on the new "demarcation lines" (virtually the new borders of the country) and demanded that Hungary's army and state apparatus withdraw behind those lines. Even liberal newspapers decried the loss and humiliation imposed on the nation. "The big Entente's small friends have still not sobered up from such bloody intoxication. . . . They ship off our food to their countries, they remove entire industrial factories . . . they have emptied offices and institutions and send the furniture to their countries. . . . [The victors have to be made aware who it is] who tramples the Wilsonian stone tablet under their feet."[5]

In an editorial entitled "Martyrdom," *Az Est* bitterly complained: "Nothing similar could have been done for defeated and conquered countries. . . . One cannot tear out of Hungary's motherly heart Pozsony or Kassa or Kolozsvár. . . . There is no Hungarian who believes that it can remain this way."[6] Nevertheless, Pozsony became Bratislava, Kassa became Košice, and Kolozsvár became Cluj; the Versailles Peace Treaty in 1920 redrew Hungary's new borders accordingly. Hungary lost 60 percent of its prewar territory and nearly 40 percent of its population. It was due first of all to the ethnic minorities who left Hungary based on their right of self-determination after a long history of subordination and government attempts of "Magyarization." With them, however, some 3 million Hungarians—31 percent of Hungary's total Hungarian populace—also became citizens of neighboring countries. Hungarians internalized that as an unjust national humiliation that only compounded Hungary's postwar crisis.

In such desperate conditions, Hungary became the hunting ground of both Left-wing and Right-wing demagogues. There were countless numbers of them. One of them was Béla Kun, head of the just established communist party.

Béla Kun, his road to communism

Béla Kun was born in Transylvania in 1886 to a secular Jewish family. His father was the notary of the village of Lele. The talented young Kun studied at a German-type gymnasium and at the Law School of the University of Kolozsvár (today Cluj). In addition to his Hungarian mother tongue, he learned German, English, and later Russian. Socially sensitive, he joined the Hungarian Social Democratic Party and left the university prior to graduating to become a journalist. When war broke out in 1914, he was mobilized and sent to the eastern front, where he, along with hundreds of thousands of other Hungarians, was captured and held in a Russian prisoner-of-war camp in the Ural Mountains. In the spring of 1917, he welcomed the Kerensky Revolution and supported the Provisional Government in an article of the *Népszava* (the newspaper of the Hungarian Social Democratic Party). Together with some 100,000 Hungarian prisoners of war, however, the young officer would soon join the Bolshevik Party. He did so in January 1918 in Petrograd, where he began working at the Bureau of Prisoners of War and met Lenin. In March of that year, he founded the Hungarian Branch of the Russian Communist (Bolshevik) Party. He was sent back to Hungary in the fall of 1918 to spread the communist revolution there and establish the Communist Party of Hungary.

Two postwar revolutions, 1918, 1919

At the end of the war the country declined in the midst of a profound crisis and fell into economic and political chaos. A democratic revolution took place on October 31, 1918, with the promise of impending land reform and elections. Soon to follow was the dethronement of the Habsburgs and the establishment of an independent Hungarian Republic. The democratic regime, however, proved to be short-lived. President Mihály Károlyi resigned on March 20, 1919—a consequence of the French ultimatum demanding Hungary's withdrawal behind the Entente's newly created demarcation lines, which left Hungary with only a third of its prewar territory. Conditions were indeed ripe for demagogues.

In those tumultuous months Béla Kun worked hard to stage a communist uprising, even though there were only 10,000 members in Hungary's newly created Communist Party. The democratic government arrested him in February for organizing street fights and violent demonstrations. In prison, he signed a pact with the left-wing faction of the Social Democratic Party, splitting it in two. The seceding Social Democrats joined the Communists to form the Socialist Party of Hungary.

After President Károlyi's resignation, the newly formed Socialist Party took power without bloodshed and declared the establishment of a Hungarian Council (or Soviet) Republic on March 21, 1919.[7] This coup was the first step in an adventurous revolutionary experiment. Béla Kun emerged as the virtual leader of the revolution (although his official position was Peoples' Commissar for Foreign Affairs and later also Defense).

Kun: leader of the communist revolution

Kun took little heed of the actual conditions of the country and based his actions on the blind belief of his ideology, an inevitable international communist revolution. When he was still in Russia on February 1, 1918, he penned an article in *Pravda* declaring:

> The revolution is spreading from the East to the West. It started in Russia, and from there will go via Austria-Hungary to Italy, and will then emerge triumphant . . . in Germany and ultimately in the parasitic, rotten bourgeois regimes of the old imperialists states of England and France.[8]

Two weeks after the establishment of the Hungarian Soviet Republic, he repeated:

> I assume that the transformation to communism will happen all over Europe. . . . The victory of communism will not stop at Hungary's borders—that is already clear. Capitalism is dying and will be replaced by communism.[9]

His demagoguery was a utopian rejection of reality and a projection of sheer fantasy. Kun delivered agitated speeches at numerous mass rallies and published countless articles in his *Vörös Ujság* (Red Journal). His fervent demagoguery targeted all those despondent over the long war and its consequences. As a prisoner of war in Russia, and a recruiter of Hungarian solders into the Red Army, Kun appealed to thousands of soldiers, poor Hungarian peasants, and workers. He spoke to their hopelessness and longing for a better life. He understood just how much they despaired of the old regime, which had kept them landless and exploited and had sent them to the trenches for years. He instinctively inferred just how much ordinary Hungarians would be open to communist ideas, and was convinced that calls for a communist revolution would reverberate among them. His success in recruiting some 100,000 Hungarian soldiers into the Red Army assured him of the feasibility of mobilizing the mass of the Hungarian populace in destroying capitalism and establishing a communist regime.

In typical demagogic fashion, he divided Hungary and the entire world into two camps, good and bad, the world of the proletariat and the world of the bourgeoisie. Eliminating the latter, he affirmed, would solve everything. Appealing to anger and acrimony and offering easy solutions, he was able to mobilize large numbers of Budapest industrial workers, especially in the spring of 1919. Even in June 1919, a few weeks before the collapse of the Hungarian Soviet Republic, he still argued that the "objective economic prerequisites of the proletarian dictatorship" exist in Hungary and throughout the western world:

> The total bankruptcy of capitalism, its total collapse . . . and the collapse of the organization of the bourgeois state characterize the entire world. . . . The prerequisites of the proletarian revolution that existed in Hungary, exist in the other countries as well; both in the victors and defeated countries. . . . The economic situation, the bankruptcy of capitalism, is the absolute guarantee that the proletariat of the other countries will follow us. . . . When we see more and more signs every day that the international proletarian revolution, the base we have built upon of our fate and future, was not . . . humbug, but an objective reality. Thus we have to struggle until the international proletarian revolution will come to save us.[10]

Neglecting realities

The grim reality was rather different. Revolutionary ideas did indeed spread among industrial workers and left-oriented intellectuals in Budapest, but they frightened the rural middle class and most of the peasantry. Hungary was surrounded by the *Little Entente* countries, whose attacking armies had the upper hand. France had decided to create a strong ring of allied countries, a *cordon sanitaire*, behind Germany, and to prevent a restoration of the Habsburg Empire, Germany's assumed "natural" ally. At the same time, the French-led Little Entente sought to isolate Soviet Russia and block the spread of Bolshevik revolution to the West.

The Little Entente of Czechoslovakia, Yugoslavia, and Greater Romania was actually formed only in 1921–22, but *de facto* it had already existed in 1918. France had exploited its position as the strongest country on the continent in order to *create* this alliance in Central Europe, and it abused the Wilsonian principle of the right of self-determination at Versailles to do so. It backed the decision of the former national minorities in Hungary, comprising nearly 54 percent of Hungary's population in 1913, to join newly formed neighboring countries. But it flagrantly violated the very same principle when it denied the right of self-determination to the more than 3 million Hungarians who—living in the new border areas—now became citizens of Czechoslovakia, Romania, and Yugoslavia.

Hungary's new (officially temporary) borders were actually dictated by the Commander of the French Balkan Army, General Franchet d'Esperey, and signed by the democratic Hungarian government in November 13, 1918. (The Trianon Peace Treaty with Hungary set the permanent borders accordingly in 1920.) Hungary lost 60 percent of its prewar territory and nearly 40 percent of its previous population.

Béla Kun shared Hungarians' outrage over this unjust treatment and saw it as a unique mobilizing opportunity. He sought to convince the former ethnic minorities that their emancipation would come not in their new nation states but only with a communist revolution. During his brief spell in power, when the west Hungarian German minority in the so-called Burgenland region expressed the desire to join Austria, he convened a Council meeting in the region and declared:

> In Soviet-Hungary the national question does not exist. . . . Earlier all the nationalities were oppressed without distinction. In this region, national liberation has been achieved together with the social-liberation of the proletariat. This is proof that the path toward national liberation is possible only through the social liberation of the proletariat. National differences can be eliminated only by eliminating class differences. . . . We cannot believe that German proletarians would want to join to a capitalist state. . . . If the proletariat of German-Austria took power . . . we would be ready at any minute to form a federative country with the German-Austrian proletariat.[11]

He was oblivious to the fact that the population had been more affected by the country's territorial losses and was thus more amenable to nationalist appeals. In an era of virulent resurgent nationalism in Europe, Kun blindly believed that nationalism was evaporating and being rapidly replaced by proletarian internationalism. On June 10, 1919, when the Red Army of the Hungarian Soviet Republic had "liberated" Kassa (the former Hungarian city that became the Czechoslovak town of Košice) during its temporarily successful counter-offensive, Kun travelled to the city and repeated his black and white views at a rally:

> We have liberated you, inhabitants of Kassa, the proletarian Red Army has liberated you, demonstrating proletarian solidarity. The Red Army did not come here to oppress, as the Czech imperialist army did, but to liberate the workers regardless of what language they speak. . . . We know only two types of people, proletarian and bourgeois, oppressor and oppressed, those who exploit and those who are exploited. We are the liberators of the now liberated Slovak proletarians. . . . In this territory of the Soviet Republic, we are going to make our slogan "Proletarians of the World Unite!" a reality.[12]

Falsely anticipating an international proletarian revolution, or better said hoping for one, Béla Kun refused to accept the French demand on the demarcation lines. Two weeks into the Hungarian Soviet Republic, the Versailles Peace Conference sent General Jan Smuts to Hungary to verify whether the new government would accept the French Memorandum delivered to the previous government on the demarcation lines. Meeting with Kun and his deputy on April 4–5, Smuts left Hungary empty-handed.

Offering suffering and fight

This was a foolhardy rejection of reality. France's response was to launch a military attack from all sides. A few days later, on April 19, Kun addressed the Revolutionary Workers and Soldiers Council of Budapest:

> Comrades, you know about our [meeting] . . . with the Entente representative General Smuts. . . . We rejected the withdrawal of the demarcation line. . . . The two world orders, imperialist capitalism and Bolshevik socialism, are confronting each other over the Council Republic of Hungary. . . . We will not allow our liberated proletarian brothers

living in the neutralized zone to fall under the yoke of capitalism once again. . . . Now the Romanian Boyar regime has begun its offensive. This is part of the international class struggle. . . . The proletariat of Budapest must go to the front! . . . In any case we only have to wait for the international proletarian revolution. . . . Until the proletariat of the neighboring countries offers us their active assistance, we will have to settle for . . . the strength of the Hungarian proletarian revolution.[13]

Rejecting reality, and appealing to the anti-capitalist sentiment of a relatively small segment of Hungarian society, proved to be a futile exercise. Hungary's military strength had naturally been exhausted during the long war. The Austro-Hungarian Monarchy had mobilized 9 million people, 3.4 million of whom from its Hungarian regions. By the end of the war, three-quarters of Hungary's military-aged men had been mobilized. No fewer than 2.75 million men—81 percent of the Hungary's mobilized population—were killed, wounded, or captured during the war. The Hungarian Soviet Republic inherited a small army of some 30,000–40,000 badly equipped soldiers. However, when the Little-Entente offensive began with overwhelming superiority in troops and armament, Kun's fervent, actually nationalist rhetoric proved effective: the Soviet Republic had been able to successfully mobilize 200,000 people, including several former officers. Paradoxically, an attack by foreign armies and the national sentiment that it engendered—a sentiment disdainfully dismissed by Kun—helped the Soviet Republic fight back, for a time even successfully. In the long run, of course, the military situation was totally hopeless and the Commune's social base very limited.

Failure of utopian demagoguery: the collapse

Hungary's military standing was further weakened by the catastrophic economic situation of that surrounded and exhausted country. Hungary had not been an economically developed country prior to the war. Industrialization had begun during the last third of the nineteenth century, but Hungary remained a mostly agricultural country. Before the war, almost 60 percent of its exports were partly processed food products. Hungary continued to be a country of large estates comprising a third of its land mass, while more than half of the peasantry was either landless or in possession of 5 acres or less; 56 percent of postwar Hungary's gainfully employed population worked in agriculture, and 21 percent in industry. Still, some 40 percent of its industrial output came from the food processing industry. Its genuinely under-developed economy virtually collapsed at the end of the war. Impoverishment, the rationing of basic food items, and starvation characterized the situation of the vast majority of the population.

Béla Kun's demagoguery, however, offered a "solution." The day after the declaration of the Hungarian Soviet Republic, he stated:

> We do not make false promises about future progress. We have to suffer and starve. However, if we do suffer and starve, we do it for our own well-being and for the unification of the world proletariat.[14]

Another of his major themes was the solidarity between the urban proletariat and the poor peasantry:

> Go out to the villages! We have to awaken the brotherly feelings of the urban proletariat and the poor peasants. . . . Through propaganda, we have to break the resistance of those parts of the peasantry which, based on their social position, ought to be in solidarity with us.[15]

Again, he replaced reality with utopia and assumed an imaginary solidarity of workers and poor peasants. When he appealed to the entire populace, the bulk of the peasantry rejected him. Nevertheless, he denounced "anti-Marxist" attitudes claiming that the peasants would resist the collective cultivation of the land. In a country of pronounced landlessness, the Hungarian Soviet Republic, and Béla Kun personally, made the serious mistake of alienating the peasantry when, for doctrinaire reasons, they opposed land reform and the breaking up of the large estates into small parcels for landless peasants comprising some 60 percent of rural population. As it would be described during the interwar period, Hungary was a country of "3 million beggars" who had been waiting for land for over a century. Rebuffing them, the communist regime began collectivizing the nationalized big estates. In his very first speech after taking power, Kun declared:

Power will be in the hands of the councils of the workers, soldiers and poor peasants. The land is common property; we do not parcel out land . . . but [will rather introduce] common cultivation through the councils of the poor peasants.[16]

Kun adamantly rejected all "rumors" to the effect that the peasants would resist collectivization—which was another indication of Kun's stark departure from reality. The regime also introduced forced food requisitions: red troops and the so-called Lenin-boys attacked, searched and emptied the barns of the peasants. "Class rationing" was introduced: "We have to organize collections of stocks [of food] and rationing in such a way that only the workers can eat; if someone works more, he gets to eat more."[17]

These actions further weakened the revolution's social base. Moreover, in this crisis situation, Béla Kun, after a brief period of successful demagoguery, utterly misread the state of mind in the country and continually fed the population a steady stream of bromides of impending international solidarity. On March 30, he gave an interview to the Viennese *Neue Freie Presse* (also published in *Vörös Ujság* in Hungary) and offered help to Austria:

The Hungarian proletariat has shown courage and discipline when faced with starvation and developments on the international stage and it will show that it could suffer and starve for the proletariat that speaks other languages.[18]

He also believed that the prospect of rapid development in the future might convince people to accept the suffering in the present. Eradicating the enemy, capitalism, and bourgeoisie, he argued, would lead to an economic miracle in a couple of years. The revolution, he insisted, will rapidly cope with economic backwardness and, with "brutal" state intervention if necessary, will promote rapid, even miraculous, economic development:

[The proletarian state's] drastic intervention into the sphere of production and its organization can supersede today's state of lesser development. Today, using the state's power, we can do in one-two years what capitalist development had been unable to achieve in twenty-five years. . . . We can concentrate production in a way that even capital consolidation in America had failed to achieve. . . . Using the proletarian state's power, we can produce during a short period of dictatorship what we've been unable to achieve over fifty years of capitalist development.[19]

Throughout, Kun blithely dismissed reality and based everything on his doctrinaire daydreams, and he demagogically promoted policies and dictated actions solely on the basis of theories and utopias. He was forever confident that he could convince the entire nation, but his demagoguery quickly fell flat because he had little grasp of the true conditions in the countryside, the preponderance of the country. He never stopped believing that ordinary workers and poor peasants would follow him.

The Jewish question

Kun was also of the firm belief that religion was an outdated notion and that most people shared that view. On that basis, he maintained that the Jewish Question no longer existed in Hungary, a country that witnessed Europe's last Blood Libel hysteria in 1882–83, hardly a generation earlier. At that time, when a 14-year-old Christian girl disappeared in the Hungarian village of Tiszaeszlár, Jews were accused of killing her to use her blood for religious rituals. The trial triggered an explosion of anti-Semitism throughout the country, and the defendants' acquittal sparked renewed violence and pogroms nation-wide—fueled in part by a newly established Anti-Semitic Party.

In addition to, and as part of, the national question, the "Jewish Question" was an important component of the bloody reality of postwar Hungary. Budapest was the urban and industrial heartland of Hungary and the real base of the communist revolution. With its one million inhabitants, Hungary's capital was a Western island in a sea of peasants. Half of Budapest's inhabitants were industrial workers, living with the bulk of the Hungary's middle class, shopkeepers, handicraftsmen, clerks, medical doctors, lawyers, and others. The city enjoyed a cosmopolitan cultural and intellectual life and a pronounced coffee house culture on par with any Western capital. It was the center of all the country's main railroad lines and its banking industry. Beyond its borders, however, was countryside still dominated by the landed aristocracy and traditional gentry, ruling over an impoverished and uneducated backward peasantry that still constituted the vast majority of the country.

Connected with these socio-economic divisions was the simple fact that Budapest was an extensively Jewish city. Before the war, the notorious anti-Semitic mayor of Vienna, Karl Lueger, called it "Judapest." Indeed, while 5 percent of Hungary's population was Jewish, every fifth inhabitant of the capital was a Jew. They comprised more than half the medical doctors and shopkeepers, and they dominated the modern sectors of the economy: banking, industry, and trade.

Budapest's population was also highly educated, in stark contrast to the rest of the country. Hungary as a whole was preponderantly uneducated: nearly half of Hungarians above the age of 6 completed only 6 years of elementary education. Only four percent of the population completed eight years of primary and secondary education, and only one percent completed university. In other words, the Hungarian Soviet Republic, based in Budapest, had to confront an uneducated peasant countryside with deeply rooted superstitions and entrenched anti-urban sentiments—all under the strong influence of the Catholic Church.

Nevertheless, in Kun's mind, religious background had no importance whatsoever. He recklessly agreed to form a revolutionary government with nearly three-quarters of its "Peoples-Commissars" (cabinet ministers) and their deputies having Jewish origins. Other estimates maintain that some 60 percent of the regime's key positions, including the leaders of the political police and the Revolutionary Tribunal, were filled by Jews.

At the State-wide Council (Soviet) Meeting on June 21, 1919, it became clear that the revolution's desperate situation sparked anti-Semitic rancor even among the Council communist representatives. A number of anti-Semitic declarations, and even calls for pogroms, were heard during the session. One of the Peoples' Commissars, Béla Vágó, alerted the Council: "Anti-Semitic feelings are being expressed at our meeting by some of the delegates. Dissatisfaction and rebellion is being directed against the Jews." Kun shouted angrily: "How can our Red Army fight when anti-Semitic provocations and even calls for pogroms are taking place at our Council Congress?" But he showed his clear lack of understanding when he added: "My father was Jewish, but I did not remain a Jew because I became a socialist and a communist."[20] Kun also insisted that communism made absolutely no distinction on the basis of religion:

> We in the workers' movement never ask anyone about his religion or nationality. Clergymen, magnates, and Jewish capitalists are instigating pogroms against the "Jewish government," though no anti-Semite could have broken the Jewish capitalists as this so-called Jewish government has.[21]

Kun's point on this specific matter was actually true. Jenő László, the Jewish head of the Revolutionary Tribunal, had indeed "ordered the execution of several Jews for anti-revolutionary activities. Among the 387 representatives of the capitalist order held hostage by the regime in Budapest, 78 were Jewish, among them top bankers."[22] Nevertheless, in the end none of this made any difference. The counter-revolutionary forces were able to present the communist revolution as a Jewish plot against the nation. This became the principal and most effective demagogic point of the so-called "white terror" that took revenge after the defeat of the Red revolution. As Gyula Gömbös, one of the leading counterrevolutionary demagogues, suggested when introducing Hungary's (and Europe's) first anti-Jewish legislation in 1920: "The only practical and useful outcome of communism and revolution was that it made clear the great danger that we face. . . . The Jewish race has gained the upper hand in Hungary. If we do not defend ourselves against it . . . the Hungarian race will decline to servant status."[23]

It is worth noting that even twenty years later, with the commencement of the Holocaust in Nazi-occupied Hungary in 1944, huge placards appeared on the walls in Budapest with photos of the leaders of the communist revolution and their names, including the original (characteristically Jewish) and magyarized versions: Béla Kun-Kohn and, Otto Corvin-Klein. After nearly two decades, the regime sought to legitimize the Holocaust by emphasizing the "Jewish" communist revolution in 1919.

Béla Kun's demagogue rhetoric based on his blind, lunatic utopian dreams and his actions based on these ideas as the leader of the communist revolution, at the end did not lead to a harmless failed experiment. It generated a vicious right-wing reaction, a deadly counter-revolution led by Admiral Miklós Horthy and the foundation of a deeply anti-Semitic right-wing regime that later made an alliance with Hitler and contributed to the killing of half of the country's Jewish population.

Kun himself became the victim of his blind conviction. After the defeat of his revolution, he escaped to Vienna and then to the Soviet Union where he was received as a hero. Lenin appointed Kun Governor of Crimea. About twenty years later, however, he had to face the reality of Stalin's communism, the ideas and policy he shared, and ended his life in one of Stalin's Gulags.

Endnotes

1 Ivan T. Berend and György Ránki, *The Hungarian Economy in the Twentieth Century* (Beckenham, Kent: Croom Helm, 1985), 25–37.

2 "Hadonásznak," *Az Est*, December 4, 1918.

3 "Van lelkük," *Az Est*, November 10, 1918.

4 "Megtanultuk," *Az Est*, January 10, 1920.

5 "Felemelte szavát," *Az Est*, March 12, 1918.

6 "A mártír sors," *Az Est*, February 5, 1919.

7 See the definitive book on his life: György Borsányi, *The life of a communist revolutionary, Béla Kun* (Boulder, CO: Social Science Monographs, 1993).

8 Béla Kun, *Válogatott írások és beszédek* (Budapest: Kossuth Kiadó, 1966), 66. Originally published in *Pravda*, February 1, 1918.

9 Interview with the reporter of *Vaterland*, April 2, 1919, in ibid., 216.

10 Speech at the session of the Workers Council of Budapest, June 7, 1919, in ibid., 337, 343.

11 Speech in Sopron at the Council Meeting of West-Hungarian Germans, May 20, 1919, in ibid., 314–15.

12 Speech at the celebration of the liberation of Kassa, June 10, 1919, in ibid., 344.

13 Speech at the meeting of the Central Council of the Workers and Soldiers Councils of Budapest, April 19, 1919, in ibid., 242–45.

14 Speech at the Communist Party meeting on March 22, 1919, in ibid., 202.

15 Speech at the meeting of the Central Council of the Workers and Soldiers Councils of Budapest, May 24, 1919, in ibid., 1966, 323.

16 Speech at the Communist Party meeting on March 22, 1919, in ibid., 202.

17 Ibid., 322.

18 Kun's answers to the questions of the reporter of the Viennese *Neue Freie Presse*, March 30, 1919; *Vörös Ujság*, March 30, 1919.

19 Speech at the debate on the party program at the National Party Meeting, June 12–13, 1919, in Kun, *Válogatott írások és beszédek*, 350.

20 János Gyurgyák, *A zsidókérdés Magyarországon: Politikai eszmetörténet* (Budapest: Osiris Kiadó, 2001), 103.

21 Speech given at the "Engels" Military Barack with the title "Revolution and Counter-revolution," July 6, 1919, in Kun, *Válogatott írások és beszédek*, 414.

22 Gyurgyák, *A zsidókérdés Magyarországon*, 104.

23 Gyula Gömbös's speech in the Parliament on the anti-Jewish "Numerus Clausus" law on February 16, 1920, in Gyula Gömbös, *Válogatott politikai beszédek és írások*, ed. József Vonyó (Budapest: Osiris Kiadó, 2004), 68.

CHAPTER 2

A Hungarian fascist demagogue: Gyula Gömbös

Right-wing counter-revolution in Hungary, 1919

The "Christian Hungarian" counterrevolution began as an Anti-Bolshevik Committee in Vienna, a government in Arad, and a White Army under the leadership of Admiral Miklós Horthy in the southern Hungarian city of Szeged already during the 133 days of communist rule in Hungary. Various counterrevolutionary organizations were also formed, among them the Awakening Hungarians Association (*Ébredő Magyarok Egyesülete*) and the Hungarian Association of National Defense (*Magyar Országos Véderő Egylet*, MOVE). The latter was led by a staff officer with the rank of captain, Gyula Gömbös.

The Hungarian counterrevolutionary forces, including the White Army, waited until the French-organized offensive of the Romanian and Czechoslovak armies had defeated the Hungarian Red Army. The collapse of the Hungarian Soviet Republic was unavoidable in such a war-weary country: its economy ruined, its people starving, and its borders overrun by enemies on all sides. The Hungarian Soviet Republic collapsed and the Revolutionary Governing Soviet disbanded itself on August 1, 1919. The Romanian army then occupied Budapest. Béla Kun and several other Commune leaders who could escape fled to Austria and from there to Soviet Russia. Their genuinely hopeless revolutionary adventure played into the hands of a violent counterrevolution endeavoring to establish an authoritarian regime.

In August 1919, Hungary's new counter-revolutionary government took shape with a program of extreme nationalism, rabid anti-Semitism and territorial revisionism. The regime launched a cruel and brutal "white terror" along with a new type of demagoguery that was central to its establishment. One of its principal players was the fervent demagogue Gyula Gömbös.

Gyula Gömbös, a leading rightwing demagogue

Gyula Gömbös was born to a mixed Hungarian-German family in 1886 (in the same year as Béla Kun, the leader of the Hungarian communist regime in 1919) in the southern Hungarian village of Murga. His father was a Protestant teacher, the son of an ethnic German woman from the western Hungarian city of Sopron. Gyula's mother had also come from an affluent German family in Murga. His family moved to Sopron, where Gyula began training as a military officer in the Austro-Hungarian army in 1901 and graduated at the top of his class in 1905. In 1912, he was sent to an elite military school for staff officers in Vienna. Gömbös was sent to the front in 1914 but was wounded and placed in the Ministry of Defense two years later.

Gömbös began organizing a counterrevolutionary group of officers already in the fall of 1918, when the democratic revolution of Mihály Károlyi was taking place in defeated Hungary. In January 1919, he became the leader of the demobilized solders' organization, MOVE. When Admiral Miklós Horthy began recruiting his counterrevolutionary army, Gömbös assisted him and served as state secretary of the counterrevolutionary government. In the spring of 1920, after the collapse of the Commune and the establishment of a new regime, he became a member of the newly organized Parliament. In the early years of counterrevolution, Gömbös belonged to the extreme right wing of political-military groupings. As the renowned British historian Hugh Seton-Watson characterized him, "his most outstanding quality was his ambition. . . . Vaguely convinced that the future lay with 'totalitarianism,' he filled his speeches . . . with Fascist bombast unintelligible to all but the keenest brains."[1] In 1922, he was one of the leaders of the newly established government party, the Alliance of Christian Unity (*Keresztény Egység Tábora*).

Leader of the fascist opposition of the rightwing regime

A year later, however, in the summer of 1923, Gömbös broke away from the ruling party, which he deemed to be insufficiently radical. He established the even more extreme Racial Defense Party (*Fajvédő Párt*), which tried to push the government even further to the right.

Gyula Gömbös was central to assuring that extreme nationalism and racist anti-Semitism would prevail in interwar Hungary. His successful demagoguery was based on his long-held view that every Hungarian is instinctively anti-Semitic. In addition, he appealed to the nationalist fervor growing exponentially in the country as a result of Hungary's humiliating postwar losses. In other words, Gömbös offered Hungarians a national revival by purifying the nation and scapegoating the Jews for all its ills. In his mind, Jewish "bankocracy" was exploiting the country, Jewish landlords were occupying much of Hungary's land, and Jewish capitalism was ruining the nation. The salvation of Hungary's economic travails, he insisted, lay in solving the Jewish question. The Hungarians' economic misery was solely due to the Jews' overwhelming over-representation in the Hungarian economy. "Our economy would be healthy if it were a national economy, permeated . . . with religious morality."[2] The Jews had undermined the nation during the war, they did not do their fair share of the fighting at the front, and they had caused prices to skyrocket. The depiction of the Jew as archenemy and the exploitation of instinctive anti-Semitism stood at the heart of Gömbös's demagoguery. He has built connections with Hitler already in the 1920s. He was able to tap into long festering resentments and had a strong impact on the population. His influence remained strong even after his early death in October 1936. Several of his close associates were important players in Hungary's Fascist-Nazi movement and in the Hungarian Holocaust. A central theme in Gömbös's demagoguery was racism:

> A nation state can prosper and stabilize its existence only if the supremacy of a race is guaranteed. . . . The Hungarians have the right to supremacy in this country . . . [but] the Jews oppressed this [Hungarian] race and reduced it to slavery.[3]

Also key to his polemics was the Jewish role in Béla Kun's Soviet Republic. "[The Jews] had been preparing that great day of reckoning for centuries."[4] The leitmotiv of his demagoguery was the "unsolved Jewish Question." As early as April 1919, he argued that "socialism was subordinated to serve the interests of the Jewish race,"[5] and he predicted the people's ultimate revenge:

> Resurrection will come. We will break the shackles of bolshevism and the Entente. . . . The hour of revenge will come when the people indict those who have destroyed the country and robbed us from our national identity. The people demand to know the brutal truth.[6] [He then coined the term that the Nazis would soon put to use:] We are also socialists, Hungarian national socialists. [7]

Gömbös often used highly inflammatory demagogic language, with a clear goal of incitement:

> There is only a single Jewish objective that will not let up until historical Hungary is eradicated. . . . Jews are fighting against us. . . . We Christian Hungarians have to learn the lesson . . . that there is no middle way, there is no compromise.[8]
>
> We will exterminate the trouble-makers in Budapest.[9]
>
> The Jews must disappear from Hungary.[10]
>
> We demand that these useless aliens, especially those who perniciously speculate, be driven out of the country.[11]
>
> Our race cannot live side by side with other races. We need a Hungarian life. . . . Our slogan is "Racial separation!"[12]
>
> [Moreover,] Jewish big capital that represents the Jewish international . . . we must exterminate them as well to assure the future of the Hungarian race.[13]
>
> My principal stance regarding socialism . . . is that we have to liquidate international social democracy.[14]
>
> [The] terror of the trade unions . . . that takes the bread of Christian workers. . . . Against their terror, I recommend a national terror in the interest of the nation.[15]

The "theoretical" basis of his anti-Semitic rabble rousing was borrowed from Houston Stewart Chamberlain, the racist English writer and son-in-law of Richard Wagner, who had moved to Germany and published *Die Grundlagen des neunzehnten Jahrhunderts* (The Foundations of the

Nineteenth Century) in 1899. Gömbös often quoted the "unquestionable truth" of this "bible" that Jews should never exceed quarter of one percent (0.25 percent) of any country's population. In 1920, Gömbös reminded Hungarians of Chamberlain's claim "that every country where the percentage of Jews is larger than that will decline under the yoke of Jewish rule. In our country the percentage of Jews is five percent. . . ." In a powerful speech at the Hungarian Parliament on February 16, 1920, he successfully called for the introduction of Europe's first anti-Jewish legislation, the so-called *Numerus Clausus* law limiting the number of Jews at universities based on their proportion of the population in the country.

> Jews have been able to rise to dominance because . . . our Western orientation has caused us to gradually lose our genuine racial traits. . . . We adjusted to Europe . . . but distanced ourselves from our authentic racial selves. . . . Liberalism anesthetized our nation and placed power entirely into the hands of the Jews. . . . I realized already in 1917 . . . that the Entente powers would win the war because the ratio of Jews and Christians in England and the Entente countries was 1:227, while it was 1:56 in the Central Powers. . . . It was inevitable that the greatest collapse would take place in Hungary. . . . Freemasonry was already entirely Jewish, and the social democrats put innocent workers under the Jewish yoke. . . . What we need is radical surgery, a deep cut to solve this question once and for all.[16]

A few weeks later he spoke of the "diligent, hard-working and talented Hungarian people that was put on liberalism's sacrificial altar thanks to racially short-sighted politics."[17] Utilizing the racist theories of his friend Lajos Méhely, Gömbös asserted that "Jewish blood-cells are stronger than Hungarian blood-cells and assimilate the latter."[18] Ignoring the fact that his own body was composed of 75 percent "German blood-cells" (from three ethnic German grandparents), he added that Hungarian blood-cells are stronger than German ones and assimilated the latter.

Populist agenda—economic nationalism and agrarism

Though centered on anti-Jewish instigation, Gyula Gömbös's demagoguery focused on other elements as well. He described his program as the unity of three main ideas:

The Christian, national, and agrarian ideals in one political world-view. . . . The realization of the . . . pure and fertile Christian religious morality. . . . The national ideal requires the merciless extermination of all anti-national aspirations, organizations, and gatherings. . . . The agrarian ideal means . . . an explicit pro-agrarian policy . . . , in contrast with past . . . mercantilist policies that are actually based on the big banks.[19]

Our entire life has to be based on Hungarian agriculture.[20]

Capital and industry must be Hungarian and serve agriculture.[21]

He also pushed for economic self-sufficiency and the defense of the domestic market with high tariffs. He insisted on restricting imports only for "raw materials, semi-products, and goods for mass consumption . . . [and for imposing] state monopoly of exports-imports."[22]

At the Parliamentary debate on new protectionist tariffs, he called for a "tariff policy that is life-affirming. . . . If we speak of an independent Hungary, we are talking about independence in every respect."[23] Gömbös stressed several times that he wished to maintain the agrarian economy of a not yet industrialized Hungary. Moreover, he wanted to preserve the big estates (accompanied by a limited settlement policy for small-holders). In 1921, he proudly declared that

We did not redistribute land with cheap demagoguery because . . . only very cautious progress leads to permanent results in the economic sphere.[24]

A year later he honestly added:

I, a defender of the Hungarian race, must say that, for me, based on national interest, it is more important to defend the big estate with four-five thousand *hold*[25] [5–7000 acres] if the owner has Hungarian blood.[26]

The racial idea is based on Hungarian brotherhood, rejects the existence of social classes, and unites all of Hungarian society.[27]

There are no differences among social classes, since all of us have Hungarian blood-cells; consequently social class differences do not exist. . . . The Hungarian magnate also comes from the Hungarian race; they also have Hungarian blood in their veins.[28]

Authoritarian regime

In Gömbös's mind, the defense of the Hungarian race required the rejection of democracy.

> I accuse those who, though being conservative, are still playing with democratic slogans.[29]

> It was a mistake to smuggle in various Western ideas such as democracy.[30] "Western" democracy . . . has already led to the near collapse of the nation. . . . [Democracy] is declining throughout the world. . . . We are replacing it with self-sacrificing Hungarian life and brotherly love.[31]

> It is not the law that is really important. What we need to defend is the interest of the eternal nation. . . . Accepting general voting rights with a secret ballot today would lead to the collapse of Hungary. . . . We want strong government . . . the supremacy of order.[32]

> Every nation in Europe that wants to keep on living cries out for strong government.[33]

> If the prosperity and the strengthening of the Hungarian people is possible through dictatorship, then I am all for it.[34]

Gömbös's fervent demagoguery was virtually the same as Nazi and Fascist demagoguery. But it's important to note that he did not copy Mussolini and Hitler, for he had started using this rhetoric earlier than they did. His flirtation with dictatorship and fascism was already complete by 1919–1922. Throughout the 1920s he was in the extreme-right opposition faction within Governor Miklós Horthy and Prime Minister Count István Bethlen's right-wing regime, in which he resisted their policy of realpolitik that tried to maintain Hungary within the existing European order. Gömbös angrily accused Bethlen of betraying the national cause.

The Prime Minister: new rhetoric and waiting for Hitler

Gömbös was powerless to carry out his radical program in the opposition. In 1928, he quite suddenly renounced his place in the right-wing opposition, halted all criticism of the government, and rejoined the government party. He was welcomed with open arms and appointed deputy minister and then minister of defense. When the Great Depression hit Hungary hard, and with the regime's leaders terrified of a resurgence of the labor movement, Gömbös was appointed prime minister in October 1932. At last he had attained the power he needed to make all his ideas and dreams a reality. To the great surprise of his contemporaries, however, Gömbös did not carry out his programs and pet projects. In fact, he renounced most of his previously held ideas and gave up his extreme right-wing positions. He continued on with his demagoguery, but he now utilized it for completely different ideas.

In several speeches, he almost apologized for not imposing a dictatorship, which everyone expected him to do when he became prime minister. Instead, he denounced the very concept of dictatorship. In a radio speech to the nation immediately after his appointment, he revealingly and suspiciously repeated his new outlook again and again:

> I tell all those who equated my appointment to the premiership with the imposition of dictatorship that I have no intention of being a dictator and will not be.[35]

> Many times, it was said that I dream about dictatorship. I do not want dictatorship. . . . A strong spiritual dictatorship will emerge, a concentration of spirit . . . that will exclude those who do not want to wear the national cloth.[36]

> Many demanded brutal measures when I became the head of the government . . . [but] our spiritual and economic life cannot be brutalized.[37]

After a visit with Hitler in 1933, he returned to the issue again:

> I was accused of having dictatorial goals and people are now especially worried that I sought inspiration in Berlin. . . . Just as we can't plant an Italian orange tree here . . . , we can't import the German system.[38]

Probably the most surprising statement he made in his first speech to Parliament as prime minister was the following: "I openly and honestly tell Jews that I have revised my views. I consider those parts of Jewry that identifies with the nation as my brothers, in the same way as I view my Hungarian brothers. I knew Jewish heroes in the war . . . and I know that they fought heroically and courageously."[39]

From that time on, over the next four years until his death, Gömbös completely avoided committing any kind of anti-Jewish outrage and even refrained from mentioning the "Jewish Question." He rescinded most of his other previous positions as well. Surprisingly enough, he expressed loyalty to István Bethlen, the country's former prime minister between 1921 and 1931, whom he had bitterly opposed beginning in 1923 and had accused of betraying Christian national interests. Now as prime minister, Gömbös quite suddenly praised Bethlen and seemed to apologize for his earlier attacks:

> My blood, especially in my earlier years, was boiling . . . because I had seen the many obstacles that were preventing me from attaining my goals. The staff officer in me was awakened and knew that I had to destroy and not ignore those obstacles. István Bethlen . . . valued me as a young man who was surging ahead in all circumstances, because he certainly knew that I would change and . . . choose the road of reality.[40]

> I want to go down the road that he [Bethlen] treaded.[41]

Gömbös now all of the sudden rejected the economics of self-sufficiency and protectionism, which he had so ardently promoted:

> Everyone is isolated from other countries. . . . We need an economic policy that ends protectionism. . . . Today . . . everybody is building Chinese walls instead of working on assuring a healthy economic blood flow in Europe.[42]

Gömbös also took back his attacks on the Little Entente: "I do not propose a fight against our neighbors but peace and understanding." He also changed his views on promoting an anti-democratic open ballot system: "Regarding voting rights, I am for a secret ballot." Instead of bitterly attacking the Jewish "bankocracy," as he had regularly done for a decade, he flatly stated:

> No one should count on radical steps from me. . . . [I]f the representatives of the capitalist economy follow a temperate and realistic policy, we will be able to solve the workers' problems as well.[43]

> We have to launch a conscious populist policy . . . and all the social classes will unite. . . . We understand the worker who only wants to earn a living, and the worker understands the capitalists who only want to produce. . . . Only harmony among all social classes can save Hungary.[44]

Gyula Gömbös announced a new reform policy embodied in a highly propagated 95 point governmental plan—a self-proclaimed "wise moderate policy" intended to meet the "demands of the age."[45] All in all, he became a completely different Gömbös from the one of the 1920s. Did he really change? Did he truly give up all his previously held political goals? Did he sincerely turn against the demagoguery of his earlier years? Analyzing his speeches and writings after 1932, and particularly his deeds during his four years of premiership (1932–1936), I would have to answer with a definite "no." What instead happened was an accommodation to new circumstances, and a use of modified demagoguery that hid his real intentions and camouflaged his actions.

He had been forced to do so in part because he did not have an entirely free hand in office, for Governor Miklós Horthy had demanded that he shelve his extremist programs already in 1928 when he appointed him to the defense ministry.[46] A historian of the Horthy regime described the compromises he had to make to be appointed prime minister. "Gömbös later explained to his colleagues, he had to make concessions to Bethlen, the Party and the Regent [Horthy]. Gömbös reluctantly agreed to the ground rules finally stipulated by Horthy."[47] His position as prime minister was strongly dependent on István Bethlen, who remained extremely influential in part through his close connection to Governor Horthy, and in part because his men predominated in party and government posts. "Those factors that would be responsible for supporting and realizing the prime minister's plans [the government party and the entire state and county administration], became the most important obstacle for them."[48] The historian of Horthy's regime concluded: "The formal appointment of Gyula Gömbös . . . on October 1, 1932, caused a considerable stir both in Hungary and abroad, but of course, few observers were aware of the severe restrictions that had been placed on his freedom of maneuver."[49]

Probably the most important reason for Gömbös's radically transformed rhetoric was Hungary's altered international position during his years as prime minister. He repeated several times in his speeches that Hungary was no longer alone. He hoped for strong and enduring support from Fascist Italy and Hitler's new Germany, and began working on drafting an alliance with those countries. At the center of Gömbös's policy from the time of his appointment was the building of the closest possible alliance with Mussolini's Italy. After 1933, when Hitler attained power, Gömbös endeavored to seize the opportunity and build a strong alliance with Nazi Germany. This became the primary means to achieve his goals. Hungary's new situation led him to change his demagoguery and use different rhetoric.

Earlier, Gömbös had always emphasized that a consistent racial policy would "regenerate Hungary . . . and restore Hungary's world political position, due to her historical role in Central Europe."[50] He repeatedly asserted that Hungary was "destined to leadership in Central Europe."[51] In Gömbös's view, Hungary's leadership in the region would only happen by redrawing the country's borders and recreating a Greater Hungary. In early 1921, he condemned the lack of determination in the country "to direct our entire policy . . . toward recapturing historical Hungary."[52] But he clearly realized that a revision of the Trianon Treaty was impossible with the existing European order of the 1920s, and repeatedly urged patience.

At the same time, Gömbös recognized long before it actually happened that Europe's politics was destined to change. Beginning in the early 1920s, he pinned his hopes on two major countries, Italy and Germany, which were just as dissatisfied with the Versailles Treaty system and France's continental leadership. He anticipated reconciliation between Germany and Italy and hoped to build a strong alliance with both countries. Long before this actually occurred, as early as 1922, he saw that a German-Italian axis was inevitable:

> The countries of the Little Entente follow a common program and want to destroy Hungary. . . . They reject any kind of reconciliation. . . . Nevertheless, I assume that European politics will soon revolve around the axis of Rome and Berlin. The differences between Germany and Italy will be overcome and countries will flock to this axis.[53]

The government of István Bethlen had already established an alliance with fascist Italy in April 1927 when it signed a Treaty of Friendship and Cooperation between the two countries. Mussolini's Italy was Horthy's Hungary first ally. The two countries signed an economic treaty in 1928 as well. Moreover, the Brocchi Plan called for the creation of a customs union between Mussolini's Italy, Horthy's Hungary, and Dollfuss's Austria. Although they signed the Semmering Accord in

1932, the plan that it envisioned was not realized. Still, the three countries signed the Rome Protocol in 1934 and formed strong trade ties. This step of strengthening Hungary's fascist orientation was made by the Gömbös government. A close alliance with fascist Italy had always been a dream of Gömbös. He has never hid his admiration for Mussolini and fascism. In October 1923, he declared:

> We have to act. We have to go ahead and take the road of the iron discipline of fascism. We cannot copy fascism. . . . A defeated country is incapable of doing what a great power easily does. . . . But I salute the formation of a united Hungarian fascism out of our movement and from the ideals we are propagating.[54]

> The Duce, the towering leader of Italy, [who] plays a historical world role. . . . We are no longer alone but will get enormous help.[55]

> Mussolini is an instinctive state-creating genius . . . he embodies the truth of Hungary and understands its historical mission.[56]

After signing the Rome Accord he stressed that

> The Rome Accord is not yet accomplished, it is just the beginning of something much greater.[57]

> We are extremely grateful to the brilliant leader of Italy, the Duce who established unbreakable historical and real political ties between Italy and Hungary. The . . . very first serious and honest step for a peaceful solution to the question of Central Europe.[58]

> We have unchanging strong sympathies for Germany, the Third Reich, after its first natural difficulties of establishing power, will assume the place she deserves in the community of European states.[59]

Between 1932 and 1936, Gömbös often returned to the great importance of an alliance between Italy, Germany, and Hungary. After visiting Hitler, he stressed:

> From a real political consideration, we must and we will strengthen our friendship with the great and powerful German Empire.[60]

> Germany asked for equality. Since she did not receive it, she gave it to herself. . . . We are unable to follow Germany down that road . . . but we hope that with the help of our Italian friends and all our other friends, we will achieve our goals.[61]

Gömbös began intense negotiations with the Nazis behind the scenes. Some aspects of his talks with Hitler were never made public. Only with the opening of the Hungarian and German archives do we have a clear picture of what transpired.[62]

Within 24 hours of Hitler's attaining power, Gömbös rushed to contact him. He dispatched a message to Hungary's ambassador in Germany, Kálmán Kánya, and ordered:

> As soon as possible pay an introductory visit to Chancellor Hitler. Give Chancellor Hitler my best regards and good wishes. Remind him that ten years ago we already had contact . . . on the basis of our common principles and worldview. . . . My firm belief is that our countries must cooperate on foreign and economic policy. Call his attention to the fact . . . that unfortunately commercial relations between Germany and Hungary are pretty week. . . . Germany is not providing Hungarian agriculture as much as our common destiny requires.[63]

Hitler received Ambassador Kánya on February 7 and sent the following message to Gömbös:

> One of [Hitler's] main goals in foreign policy is strengthening the foundation of Italian-German friendship. . . . He also believes that Hungarian-German relations will become more and friendlier and intimate . . . he believes that in economic questions it is not just economic but also political matters that have to be considered. From this respect, adopting a similar policy towards all the agricultural countries is a mistake. He will use his influence to modify German policy accordingly. He, Hitler, has the Chancellery not for four years but for a long, long time.[64]

During the first few months of Hitler's tenure, Gömbös waged intensive diplomatic activity. In March 1933, István Bethlen, in Germany on a lecture tour, met with Hitler with the expressed purpose of conveying the solidarity of Horthy's regime with Nazi Germany. In April, Gömbös invited the German Ambassador Schön and assured him "that his policies will be friendly toward Germany, but that doing so required German economic [market] concessions. . . . Gömbös mentioned that he should visit Hitler as soon as possible to discuss all these issues."[65]

The next day, Gömbös sent a letter to Hitler containing strong anti-Semitic language that he no longer expressed publicly:

Hungary, governed by a strong hand, has always looked to Berlin with
hope and sympathy. . . . Your Excellency certainly was informed that I
censored that racist Jewish journal that attacked your Excellency and
the German government. This also proves that I remain on your side
not only on principle and [our common] worldview but also from real
political considerations. . . . I know that your principles are the same as
mine. . . . We old comrades-in-arms for racial defense, who share the
same worldview, should understand and assist each other.[66]

In his answer on April 28, 1933, Hitler assured Gömbös: "The leaders
of the national government want nothing more than to deepen our mu-
tual spiritual understanding and turn it into a political agreement. . . .
Our strongest goal is to examine and consider the economic question as
a political one."[67] Quite unusually, in the spring of 1933, Werner Daitz,
the head of the foreign trade department of the Nazi Party, and not a
German government representative, arrived in Hungary and began extensive negotiations on trade relations. At the same time, Daitz issued
an invitation of the National Socialist Party (and not the government)
for Gömbös to visit Hitler. On June 16, 1933, hardly more than four
months after Hitler rose to power, the Hungarian prime minister traveled to Berlin and met with Hitler. This made news around the world as
Gömbös was the first foreign leader to visit Hitler. Curiously, he came
to Berlin as a private person without informing the Hungarian embassy
there or the press. He discussed with Hitler foreign policy issues, particularly the question of Hungary's territorial revision and Germany's *Anschluss* with Austria. Hitler also assured Gömbös that he agreed with his
main political line. However, the content of the meeting remained secret
and was not even disclosed to the Hungarian cabinet. Within a short
time, Gömbös's endeavors began to bear fruit: in February 1934, Nazi
Germany and Gömbös's Hungary signed a new trade agreement, the first
in the framework of the Nazi *Neuer Plan* for war preparations, followed
by pacts with other East and South-East European countries. The German goal was rather complicated. It wanted to build up an economic alliance system of *Grossraumwirtschaft*, a controlled economic area near its
borders that will assure regional self-sufficiency in the case of war. In addition, "Germany's goal with this agreement is to bind the Hungarian
economy by the increase of trade closely and unbreakable to the German
one."[68] Hitler began to build a larger *Lebensraum*.

Plan to copy Hitler

Gömbös's actions behind the scenes went beyond establishing close ties with Nazi Germany. In 1935, Herman Göring, Hitler's second in command, visited Hungary. In September of that year, Gömbös made a second trip to Berlin and met with both Hitler and Göring. During his talks with Göring, Gömbös reached a secret agreement with Nazi Germany. The only source of its content is Gömbös's friend from the Szeged counterrevolutionary camp, Miklós Kozma, a leading member of Horthy's inner circle, who noted in his diary that became public only long after his death as a file in the Hungarian National Archive:

> I realized without doubt that Gömbös and Göring had reached a German-Hungarian agreement that was much more far-reaching than anyone imagined, including [foreign minister] Kánya. This agreement concerned the political system, the question of totalitarianism and the Jewish question.[69]

According to Kozma's undocumented information, Gömbös had promised that he would set up a Nazi-type totalitarian regime in Hungary within two years. In his public statements, however, he never mentioned it. His demagoguery, however, changed accordingly. He began all his public speeches with the words: "My Hungarian Brothers." In a radio interview on February 15, 1935, the interviewer openly asked Gömbös: "According to some, your Excellency wants to disband the government party and govern with the support of new political forces. . . . People are also talking about your involvement in the so-called 'reform-generation' movement of university students and their evolving activities."[70] Although Gömbös never admitted this, he in fact ordered his right-hand man, Béla Marton, secretary general of the National Unity Party, to reorganize the traditional Party of National Unity as a modern mass party in the summer and fall of 1935. "The Gömbös faction considered the reorganization of the government party into a fascist-type mass party as one of the most important steps toward attaining its goals."[71] He suggested as much when he declared:

> In my program, when I say the party, I mean an organization with a goal. . . . I want to organize a large Hungarian family. . . . Many peo-

ple are suspicious of this and see this attempt as a kind of imitation. But I built this organization together with my friends on Hungarian soil, with Hungarian ideas. . . . My brothers, let's unite in this camp because it has a great mission. . . . We will recognize that there is no need for various parties. . . . I call the entire Hungarian nation to form one camp. One camp . . . led by me. . . . Come to this camp where brotherly understanding rules . . . and where the feeling of a shared destiny creates great unity. It will make the Hungarians great, strong and unbeatable.[72]

We are building our new home. It requires that Hungarian society becomes organized on the basis of a common world-view and common political ideas. . . . We know that we have to eradicate the past . . . and to create a new Hungary.[73]

Behind this oblique wording was the determined organizing of a mass movement. Béla Marton's regular circular letters to the local party units were written with clear fascist terminology:

The Leader [*Vezér* in Hungarian, the translation of the Italian *Duce* and the German *Führer*], Gyula Gömbös, created the National Unity Movement to establish the unity of the nation. . . . By destroying artificially built separation-walls and balancing various political beliefs, he has established the organization and its units in the firm conviction that the noble idea of national solidarity is burning in every honest Hungarian soul.[74]

The Leader's strong Hungarian will . . . has awakened the belief that the nation can fulfill its historical mission only by . . . one will under one leader. . . . Our Leader and his political past, the guarantee that the future of the nation is in preordained hands.[75]

The instructions called for organizing a youth movement and creating female sections of each unit, together with regular programs, question and answer debates, etc. The organization of the Gömbös-led national movement and the cult of the strong Leader were preparatory steps for regime change. The demagoguery of his deputies and the language they employed were already imbued with fascist-Nazi rhetoric.

Gyula Gömbös's demagoguery and actions, however, did not lead to what he had planned. He became ill in 1934, grew increasingly worse during the last two years of his premiership, and died in 1936 in a hospital in Munich. Nevertheless, he greatly contributed to building a massive social and political base for extreme right-wing politics and a fascist-Nazi orientation in Hungary. He was, of course, not alone in doing so, but was *primus inter pares* in a group of Hungarian politicians. His demagoguery significantly contributed to the tragedy that followed: first, a series of draconian anti-Jewish laws that began to be introduced two years after his death. With his personal ties and institutionalized agreements, he associated himself with those politicians who moved Hungary closer and closer to Hitler—all leading to the fatal step, five years after his death, of joining Hitler's war, which culminated in the death of nearly one million citizens, one of every ten Hungarians. Included among the dead were roughly 400,000 Jews, half of Hungary's Jewish population, who perished during the final episode of the European Holocaust in 1944–45.

Notes

1 Hugh Seton-Watson, *Eastern Europe Between the Wars, 1918–1941* (New York: Harper Torchbooks, 1967), 193.

2 Speech in the Parliament about the defense of the race and the Jewish question, June 16, 1922, quoted in Gömbös, *Válogatott politikai beszédek*, 161.

3 Speech in the Parliament on defense of the race, on social democrats and voting rights, June 16, 1922, quoted in Gömbös, *Válogatott politikai beszédek*, 124

4 "Az Ellenforradalom" [The Counterrevolution], published by *Budapesti Hírlap*, 1920, quoted in ibid., 40.

5 Article in the *Bécsi Magyar Futár*, April 8, 1919, "Marx-Kautsky és a magyar forradalmi szocialisták," in ibid., 28.

6 Article in *Bécsi Magyar Futár*, March 26, 1919, "Magyarország bolsevista kormánya Leninnel szövetkezett," in ibid., 24.

7 Article on Marx-Kautsky and the Hungarian revolutionary socialists, in the *Bécsi Magyar Futár*, April 8, 1919, in ibid., 27–28.

8 Speech in the Parliament about the voting rights and the Jews' political role, June 16, 1922, in ibid., 293.

9 Speech at Derecske for the delegation of the voters, May 3, 1922, in ibid., 113.

10 Speech at the dinner party of the Racial Defense Party, February 27, 1925, in ibid., 289.

11 The recommendations of the Racial Defense Group at the meeting of the government Party of National Unity, *Szózat*, August 3, 1923, in ibid.,177.

12 Speech at a mass rally, October 5, 1926, in ibid., 308.

13 Speech in the Parliament on the electoral law and the political role of the Jews, May 25, 1925, in ibid., 293.

14 Speech in the Parliament, January 25, 1927, in ibid., 330.

15 Ibid., 331.

16 Gömbös speech in the Parliament on the [anti-Jewish] "Numerus Clauses" on February 16, 1920, in ibid., 68–76.

17 Article in *Szózat*, August 10, 1920, in ibid., 66.

18 Speech in the Parliament on internal questions regarding a foreign loan, December 17, 1923, in ibid., 217.

19 Declaration of the Defenders of the Race, August 3, 1923, in ibid., 169–70.

20 Speech in the Parliament about the defense of the race and the Jewish question, June 16, 1922, in ibid., 165.

21 "The policy of 1921," *Szózat*, January 29, 1921, in ibid., 89.

22 Speech in the Parliament about the tariffs, May 31, 1924, in ibid., for the entire speech, see 268–77.

23 Speech in the Parliament about tariffs, June 16, 1922, in ibid., 270, 273–74.

24 Speech about the land reform law in the Parliament, June 16, 1922, in ibid., 83.

25 1 hold = 0.57 hectares

26 Speech about the land reform law in the Parliament, June 16, 1922, in ibid., 206.

27 Speech at the rally in Abádszalók on the defense of the race, April 19, 1922, in ibid., 107.

28 Appeal to Hungarian society to support racial defense, August 22, 1923, in ibid., 182–83.

29 Speech in the Parliament about the electoral law and the role of Jewry, June 16, 1922, in ibid., 291.

30 Speech in the Parliament at the debate about changing the Numerus Clausus law, January 25, 1927, in ibid., 354.

31 Speech at the National Unity Party's rally in Budapest, November 14, 1933, in ibid., 554.

32 Speech in the Parliament on social democracy, racial defense and electoral rights, June 16, 1922, in ibid., 121, 133–34.

33 Speech in the parliament on racial defense and the Jewish question, December 16, 1922, in ibid., 148.

34 Speech in the Parliament about the modification of the Numerus Clausus Law, February 23, 1928, in ibid., 355.

35 Announcement on the radio after his appointment as prime minister in October 1932, in ibid., 385.

36 Article in the *Budapesti Hírlap*, December 6, 1932, in ibid., 484.

37 Speech at the meeting of the National Association of Industrialists, *Nemzeti Figyelő*, May 15, 1933, in ibid., 516.

38 Speech at the Chamber of Agriculture, *Függetlenség*, June 21, 1933, in ibid., 525.

39 Speech at a mass rally in Berettyóújfalu on September 12, 1933, in ibid., 547.

40 Introductory speech at the Parliament as prime minister, 1932, in ibid., 414.

41 Answer to a toast at the dinner party of the National Unity Party on October 5, 1932, in ibid., 402.

42 The first speech as prime minister at the meeting of the National Unity Party in 1932, in ibid., 390.

43 Speech at the Upper House, answer to the debate, October 23, 1932, in ibid., 461–62.

44 Ibid., 409, 413, 416, 419.

45 Introductory speech in the Upper House, in ibid., 440.

46 In his "Conclusion" of the selected speeches and articles of Gyula Gömbös, the editor of the book, József Vonyó, stated: "This was not the first time that Gömbös had promised the representatives of Hungarian Jewry [in 1932] that he had given up his racist policy. That was the prerequisite for his reentry in the government party and his appointment as deputy minister of defense." Ibid., 719.

47 Thomas Sakmyster, *Hungary's Admiral on Horseback: Miklós Horthy, 1918–1944* (Boulder: East European Monographs, 1994), 170–71. Sakmyster described the events as such: Horthy received Bethlen on September 23, 1932, and asked him what he thought of Gömbös's appointment as prime minister. Bethlen agreed to "the experiment," but also insisted on placing certain constraints on him so "that the more radical parts of the Szeged program could not be implemented." Horthy shared this view. Horthy, Bethlen and Gömbös met the following week, and Gömbös made the required concessions.

48 See József Vonyó's conclusion in Gömbös, *Válogatott politikai beszédek*, 727.

49 Sakmyster, *Hungary's Admiral on Horseback*, 171. "Gömbös discovered that he was not able even to select his own cabinet, for Horthy had apparently granted Bethlen the right to veto appointments he opposed."

50 Gömbös, *Válogatott politikai beszédek*, 122.

51 The Big Party, *Szózat*, June 29, 1920, in ibid., 64.

52 The policy of 1921, January 1, 1921, in ibid., 77.

53 Speech at the Parliament on the defense of the race and the Jewish question, July 24, 1922, in ibid., 123.

54 Speech at the dinner party of the Christian opposition about a strong government and fascism, *Szózat*, October 5, in ibid., 191.

55 Speech broadcast on the radio about the first ten months of the government and its plans, *Függetlenség*, August 2, 1933, in ibid., 539.

56 Speech at the "Mussolini-Dinner" of the Council of Social Associations, November 19, 1933, in ibid., 567.

57 Speech at the meeting of the financial Committee of the Parliament, April 20, 1934, in ibid., 603.

58 Address in the radio on the occasion of the second anniversary of his appointment as prime minister, October 2, 1934, in ibid., 631–32.

59 Ibid., 632.

60 Speech at the national meeting of the Grand Council of the Party of National Unity, *Uj Magyarország*, October 11, 1935, in ibid., 690–91.

61 Speech at the Budapest rally of the Party of National Unity, *Függetlenség*, March 27, 1935, in ibid., 673.

62 My late friend and co-author György Ránki and I conducted this archival research, using documents from the archives of the Hungarian and German Foreign Ministries. Our findings were published in our book, which is the source of the archival quotation below: Ivan T. Berend and György Ránki, *Magyarország a fasiszta Németország "életterében," 1933–1939* (Budapest: Közgazdasági és Jogi Kiadó, 1960).

63 *Hungarian National Archive*, Ministry of Foreign Affairs, Küm. Political Department, 158, 21/7, February 1, 306/1933.

64 Ibid.

65 *Deutsches Zentral Archive* (DZA), Potsdam, AA. Abt.II, 41283, Ambassador Schön's telephone report.

66 Gömbös's letter and its copy are in the archives of both the German and Hungarian ministries of foreign affairs: *Hungarian National Archive*, Küm. Political Department, 158, 21/7 206/1933; *Deutsches Zentral Archive*, Potsdam, AA. Abt. II, 41283.

67 Hitler's answer is also available in both archives: *Hungarian National Archive*, Küm. Political Department, 158, 21/7, 306/1933; *Deutsches Zentral Archive*, Potsdam, AA. Abt. II, 41283.

68 *Deutsches Zentral Archive*, Potsdam, AA. Abt.II, 41288.

69 *Hungarian National Archive*, Kozma Iratok (Kozma Files), 7. The trip to Berlin.

70 Radio interview about the political situation, *Függetlenség*, February 15, 1935, in Gömbös, *Válogatott politikai beszédek*, 648, 651.

71 József Vonyó, *Gömbös Gyula és a jobboldali radikalizmus: Tanulmányok* (Pécs: Pannonia Könyvek, 2001), 68.

72 Speech at the electoral rally in South Budapest, *Uj Magyarság*, October 18, 1935, in Gömbös, *Válogatott politikai beszédek*, 694.

73 Detailed organizational instruction to the Budapest unit, February 1935, in József Vonyó, ed., *Gömbös pártja: A Nemzeti Egység Pártja dokumentumai* (Budapest: Dialóg Campus Kiadó, 1998), 214.

74 19/1934, Circular letter to all units, June 1934, in ibid., 151, 152.

75 28/1934, Circular letter to all units, September 1934, in ibid., 165.

CHAPTER 3

A Romanian fascist demagogue: Corneliu Zelea Codreanu

Romania after World War I

Romania joined the Triple Alliance on the side of Germany in 1883, but it declared neutrality in 1914 and did not enter World War I when the hostilities began. It was only in 1916 that it entered the war, when it foresaw an impending Entente victory. Joining the Entente against Austria-Hungary, Romania was promptly defeated and lost a significant part of the country, including Bucharest, to German military occupation. Despite its dreadful war performance, Romania belonged to the winners and was lavishly rewarded by the Entente with sizeable territories. As the renowned British historian Hugh Seton-Watson observed, "of all the Eastern European states Roumania was the most fortunate at the Peace Settlement . . . Roumania's success at the Peace is almost solely due to the panic about Bolshevism."[1]

Indeed, France proceeded to create a chain of allied countries, a *cordon sanitaire*, not only to shield itself from its arch enemies, Germany and Austria-Hungary, but also to isolate Bolshevik Russia. France contributed toward the establishment of bigger and stronger countries in its allied chain, the so-called Little Entente. This comprised the newly formed Czechoslovakia and Yugoslavia, as well as *România Mare* (Greater Romania). The latter acquired a huge territory and population: from the prewar 137,000 square kilometers and 7.5 million inhabitants, postwar Romania could now claim 304,000 square kilometers and 18 million inhabitants. Greater Romania obtained Bukovina, Dobrudja, and part of the Banat. It also incorporated Bessarabia, with a large Ukrainian and Russian minority, from Russia, and Transylvania, with altogether two million Hungarians, from Hungary.[2]

Romanian nationalism emerged triumphant and became even more virulent. The country had a vast minority population, comprising nearly a third of its citizenry. In addition, 5 percent of the population was Jews, who were considered aliens and denied citizenship before the war. A significant part of Romanian Jewry was not assimilated, did not speak Romanian well, dressed in traditional Jewish garb, and maintained separate Yiddish-Hebrew schools. Large Jewish minorities could be found in several regions and in many cities, and they made up a third of Bucharest's population. They were heavily involved in all the modern capitalist sectors of the country, in what was still an overwhelmingly peasant society. More than half, in some areas, three-quarters of Romania's shopkeepers, industrialists, and bankers were Jews. They constituted huge majorities in the intellectual and cultural fields as well. In this fundamentally uneducated agrarian country, ethnic minorities, and Jews foremost among them, disproportionately helped develop capitalism.

Romania was one of Europe's least developed countries. Its people endured unbearable economic hardships after the war, including galloping inflation, and they continually clamored for change. Production of the country's most important export items plummeted. Crude oil output dropped from 1.9 million tons to 0.9 million, wheat exports from 3 million tons to 1 million. A great part of the Romanian economy was in foreign hands: 91 percent of the crucial petroleum industry, 74 percent of metallurgy, 72 percent of the chemical industry, and 95 percent of electric and gas production. The financial sector was very much the same: 70 percent of insurance firms and roughly a third of bank assets were owned by foreigners. All of Romanian society cried out for change.

Corneliu Zelea Codreanu and his background

These postwar dilemmas were tailor-made for populist demagogues who dominated Romania's political scene after the war and rode an ever-growing wave of Romanian nationalism. They readily identified a domestic enemy responsible for all the miseries of the country, and they offered an immediate and simple solution. Among these demagogues was a handsome, charismatic, fervently religious and infuriated young man, a disciple of some of the country's most influential intellectuals, who was viewed by an army of fanatical followers as the reincarnation of Jesus Christ. He never attained power but influenced Romanian politics during the interwar period more than practically anyone else.

His name was Corneliu Zelea Codreanu, the prophet of Romania's rebirth with religious peasant-fascism. His personal history and family background were, psychologically speaking, rather textbook. This exalted Romanian nationalist was a neophyte, born into an immigrant family. His father moved to Romania from Bukovina (a part of Austria-Hungary) at the end of the nineteenth century; his original name, Ion Zieliński, suggests Polish or Ukrainian origins. (Others maintain that the family's name was Polonized in Bukovina from its original Romanian.) His mother, Elizabeth Brunner, was born to a German-Bukovinian family originally from Bavaria. Employed as a school teacher, Zieliński joined the extreme nationalist and anti-Semitic movement of Professor Alexandru C. Cuza. He Romanized his name to Zelea, and added Codreanu on to it because his father and grandfather had been foresters (forest in Romanian is *codru*). He gave his children extremely nationalist, partly invented names. He named his first born son in 1899 Corneliu after the Roman centurion Cornelius who had converted to Christianity. His daughter was named "Irredenta"; two others were named after Dacian (Decebal) and Romanian (Horia) heroes. This tells us a little bit about the home life of this immigrant "new Romanian" family.

In the populist, anti-Semitic movement

Besides his family, the young Codreanu, who turned eighteen at the end of the war, fell under the strong influence of several older ideologues. At the age of 19, he joined Constantin Pancu's *Garda Conştiinţei Naţionale* (Guard of National Consciousness), an embodiment of left-wing Romanian populism (*poporanismul*). Pancu denounced Westernization and capitalism, the "Golgotha of capitalist development," as well as the Jews, the "representatives of vagabond capital."[3] The Guard recruited an amalgam of extreme nationalists, left-wing egalitarians, anti-capitalists and statist-corporatists, and was a violent working-class movement known for waging fierce street fights. It attacked Yiddish theaters in several Romanian cities in the summer of 1922.

Romania's postwar generations grew up under the political influence of a renowned Romanized historian of Greek origin, Nicolae Iorga, who promoted an extreme nationalist program: "Romania of the Romanians, only of the Romanians and of all Romanians. . . . The solution of the Jewish problem must be accomplished through the elimination of Jews, the development of the productive powers of Romanians, and the protection of their enterprises."[4]

Alexandru Cuza, a professor of economics at the University of Iaşi and an ardent nationalist and anti-Semite, mentored Codreanu at the university. In March 1923, Cuza established the *Liga Apărării Naţional Creştine* (Christian National Defense League), which appropriated the Romanian National Fascio and the Romanian Action movements two years later. Codreanu became the leader of the League's youth section and committed multiple violent attacks in the city of Iaşi. When the city's prefect tried to restore order, Codreanu shot him and several policemen dead in a court room. He was later acquitted because, the judge scandalously suggested, he had not killed for personal gain. He returned to Iaşi as a hero, blessed by priests and greeted by cheering, flower-throwing crowds. Fascism was born in Romania with a confused mix of social, national, anti-democratic, and anti-capitalist forces.

Founding the fascist Legion of Michael the Archangel

Codreanu came of age during a period when anti-capitalism in Romania was thoroughly transformed into fervent anti-Semitism. In the summer of 1927, Codreanu founded his own movement and issued a military-style Order No. 1:

> Today, Friday, June 24, 1927 (The feast of St. John the Baptist), 10 o'clock in the evening is founded under my leadership, the Legion of Michael the Archangel. . . . This first meeting lasted only one minute, only long enough for me to read the above order. After this, those present left in

order to ponder whether they felt sufficiently determined and courageous to join an organization like this, without a program other than
the example of my life.[5]

Zelea Codreanu fanatically believed in his mission to create a new
type of Romanian man—a typically demagogic idea. He noted:

> We had no program at all. . . . This country is dying of a lack of men,
> not of lack of programs. . . . It is not programs that we must have, but
> men, new men. . . . The greatest national peril is the fact that [our peo-
> ple] have deformed, disfigured our Daco-Romanic racial structure, giv-
> ing birth to this type of man, creating this . . . moral failure. . . . As a
> consequence . . . the Legion stands [to reform] man. . . . The Legion . . .
> will be more a school and an army than a political party. . . . A new man
> [*Omul Nou*] will have to emerge, a man with heroic qualities.[6]

His words regarding a "Daco-Romanic racial structure" clearly re-
flect the fact that he, of all the Romanian nationalists up till then, had
embraced the Daco-Roman romantic myth on the origins of the national identity and culture of modern Romania. According to this concept, the Romanian people were the descendants of Trajan's Roman
colonizers of Transylvania, the ancient Dacia (as the last province of
the Roman Empire had been named for some 170 years); there, the conquering Roman troops intermixed with the local Dacians. As Petru
Maior, one of the founders of nineteenth-century Romanian nationalism, suggested in 1812,[7] this myth of Romanians' being the "grandsons
of the ancient Romans" served to solidify Romanian national consciousness.

Codreanu also firmly believed that he had been chosen by God to
lead the Romanian people, and was fully prepared to sacrifice his life
for this mission. He turned the League of Michael the Archangel (also
known as the Legionnaires) into nothing less than a death cult. As his
movement's mouthpiece proclaimed:

> The most beautiful aspect of Legionary life is death. The Legionary
> death has nothing in common with ordinary death. Through his death
> the Legionary becomes one with Eternity; through his death the Le-
> gionary becomes the earthly incarnation of history. He becomes a leg-
> end. . . . The death of the Legionary is a symbol and cult.[8]

Codreanu issued "Eight Commandments." The first demanded "moral purity," the second a total submission to the community and a rejection of personal gain.[9]

> [The legionnaire has] to fight, in order to learn how to be brave and strong; to work, in order to learn the habit of working; . . . to suffer, in order to steel himself; to sacrifice, in order to get used to transcending his own person in the service of the people.[10]

Führer principle

Ion Moța, Codreanu's closest lieutenant, affirmed: "An organization cannot be built and developed without order and hierarchy, but most of all without a Leader. Our organization has a Leader . . . the great leading personality . . . who with his secret strength established the first disciplined net of our organization. . . . Our Leader is Corneliu Zelea Codreanu."[11] In other words, the Legion was based on the Führer-Principle, common in all fascist movements. The charismatic Leader, *Căpitanul* (Capitan) as he was called, was the ultimate authority. The movement's members had to follow the Leader's orders without questions and with iron discipline. Codreanu himself explained the principle this way:

> From an organizational point of view we have settled on the idea of leader and discipline. Democracy was excluded. . . . We have lived anti-democracy from the very start. I always led. . . . It was not the fighters electing me leader, but I choosing them to follow. I never . . . put propositions to vote.[12]

Anti-democratic, authoritarian ideology

Codreanu denounced democracy as a contemptuous Western-Jewish conspiracy against Romania and sought to establish fascism with authoritarian powers. "Romania needs broad reforms that are fascist in character," he adamantly asserted.[13]

[Democracy] is a worn-out framework . . . [that] breaks the unity of the Romanian people . . . stirring it up, and exposing it, disunited, to face the united forces of Judaism. . . . Democracy forms millions of Jews into Romanian citizens, by making them their equal. . . . Democracy is incapable of authority. It lacks sanctions . . . [and] it is at the service of great finance. . . . The people are unsuited to govern themselves . . . just as the bees elect their queen [the people must elect their own elite].[14]

He further argued that:

Europe's national movements such as the legionary movement, fascism, National-Socialism are neither dictatorship nor democracies . . . they represent a new form of government. . . . The leader is no longer "master," a "dictator". . . . He is the incarnation of this unseen state of spirit, the symbol of this state of consciousness. . . . He is guided . . . by the interest of the immortal nation.[15]

The hierarchy of interests and religious mystique

Codreanu's fanatic nationalism and unwavering belief in the charisma of the self-selected Leader, himself, led him to define the national interest as the supreme value over individual interests and human rights:

Human rights are not limited only by the rights of other humans but also by other rights. There are three distinct entities: 1. The individual. 2. The present national collectivity that is the totality of all the individuals of the same nation, living in a state at a given moment. 3. The nation, that historical entity whose life extends over centuries . . . and with an infinite future. A new great error of democracy based on "human rights" is that of recognizing and showing an interest in only one of these three entities, the individual; it neglects the second or ridicules it, and denies the third. . . . The individual must be subordinated to the superior entity, the national collectivity, which in turn must be subordinated to the nation.[16]

Codreanu never actually asked who would determine the interests of the present "national collectivity" of the nation. From everything he said, however, it was clear that it was not going to be any kind of election or referendum, which he denounced as destructive to the nation. Even more important, he never asked who was equipped to determine the "infinite future" interests of the eternal nation. Again, it was clear from all he said that the self-chosen Leader, sent by God, was the sole person who comprehends and can tell the people, or more accurately, order the people what to do to protect the eternal national interest.

To achieve his goals, Codreanu organized the Legion in a rather unique way—not as a party, but in small "nests" of 5 to 13 people. He instructed his followers that the nests had to help local people and solve local problems, be it repairing a small bridge or digging a small village well. He also distributed "The Nest Leaders Manual" and ordered mandatory religious practice: "The legionary believes in God and prays for the victory of the Legion. It should not be forgotten that we are here on this earth by God's will and the blessing of the Christian Church. . . . We the Romanian people . . . kneel to receive God's blessing."[17] Deep religious devotion was imperative for all in the movement. He introduced the cult of the icon Michael the Archangel, and founded the League with a prayer: "At ten o'clock, we all set off for the Church of St. Spiridon, dressed in national costume with *căciulă* [a cap made of lamb skin] and the swastika over the our hearts, marching in columns." From that point on, every meeting of the Legionaries began with a religious service.

Pathological anti-Semitism

The organization grew quickly. The number of "nests" multiplied from 4,000 to 34,000 in just a few years. The *Echipa Morţii*, a suicide commando squad, was also established to punish all the nation's enemies: rival politicians, ethnic-Romanian "traitors," and most of all the main enemy, the Jews. Codreanu's unsparing social critique, his irate denunciation of moral degradation and corruption, and his unrestrained anti-capitalist demagogy were all transformed into passionate, even pathological, anti-Semitism. Very much on the list of enemies were the country's bourgeoisie: "The Legion," he thundered, "cannot tolerate the existence of the bourgeoisie . . . because there is no need to continue the old bourgeois form of life."[18] All the problems that Romania faced, and all the hardships that Romanians endured, were caused by the Jews. If one can speak of any precise platform of his movement, it was the elimination of Jews and their influence. Solving the Jewish Question was the sum and substance of all of his speeches and writings, and was reflected in his journal *Ancestral Land*:

> In Romania, Fascism could only mean the elimination of the dangers threatening the Romanian people, namely the removal of the Jewish threat. . . . The Romanian people finds itself [in the difficult situation] menaced in its very existence by an alien people that grabbed our land and tends to grab the leadership of the country. . . . We determinedly rise around a new and sacred ideal, that of defending our fatherland against Jewish invasion. . . . We do not face some isolated Jews but a constituted power, [the conspiracy of] the Jewish community . . . an army that comes into our land to conquer us . . . according to a well-established plan. The great Judaic council probably seeks to establish a new Palestine on a section of land . . . covering half of Romania to the Black Sea. . . . The Jews are our enemies and . . . Romanian leaders who cross into their camp are worse than enemies: they are traitors. The first and fiercest punishment ought to fall first on the traitors, second on the enemy.[19]

The Jewish minority in Romania comprised 5 percent of the country's population, the same as in Hungary at that time. Poland and Lithuania, countries Codreanu mentioned as parts of the "planned" Jewish state, had the relatively largest Jewish population, 10 and 7 percent respectively. Codreanu passionately spoke of a Jewish danger and the absolute need to persecute Jews, who were behind corrupt politics, promote democracy, capitalism and communism, and exploited the Romanian people.

> The Judeo-Liberal power . . . is always for "democracy". . . . For democracy will break up the unity and the spirit of a people. . . . Communism's triumph coincides with Judaism's dream of ruling and exploiting the Christian nations. . . . By the triumph of communism . . . [Romania would place] under the heel of complete Jewish domination. . . . Every Jew, merchant, intellectual or banker-capitalist . . . was an agent of these anti-Romanian revolutionary ideas.[20]

Codreanu's movement preached anti-Semitism as the key for Romania's revival and committed anti-Jewish atrocities. When in March 1923 the country's parliament decided to grant citizenship to Jews (the last in Europe to do so), he organized a massive and violent protest demonstration in Iaşi. "We fulfilled our duty and beat everything to the ground which blocked our way. We were determined to show the Jews that Iaşi, the old capital of Moldavia, was still Romanian." On another occasion, "Codreanu and Moţa went from café to café and hit every Jew they met in the face."[21]

Violence became an everyday phenomenon. The Legionnaires not only advocated the punishment of ethnic-Romanian "traitors," those politicians who, in their eyes, served Jewish interests, but they killed them outright: three members of a Legionnaire commando unit, the *Nikadori* (using their initials) assassinated Prime Minister Ion Duca, who dared to attack the Legionnaires in 1933 and arrest 18,000 of their members. Ten activists from a Legionnaire death squad (the *Decemviri*) killed and dismembered Mihai Stelescu, who had left the Legionnaires and attempted to establish his own movement.

Anti-modernization Christian peasant orthodoxy

In 1936, the movement was reorganized as a political party named *Totul pentru Ţară* (All for the Fatherland), but was mostly known as *Garda de Fier*, the Iron Guard. In 1928, Codreanu described his political strategy concisely: the country is to be rebuilt on Romanian-peasant-Orthodox values; and the nation is to be liberated from "Jewish influences," from corruption, modernization, capitalism and democracy, and from Marxist communism. Christian Orthodoxy formed the nucleus of the movement embodying a triumvirate of nation, church, and state. Historian Nicolas Nagy-Talavera went so far as to state: "Not only did Romanian peasant Orthodoxy strongly influence the ideology of the Legion, but it became synonymous with it . . . a nationalist revival had to bring into motion a religious revival."[22]

The Iron Guard was a populist movement that strongly opposed modernization, industrialization, and education. Codreanu's right-hand man and deputy, Ion Moţa, who translated the infamous Protocols of the Elders of Zion and later joined Franco's troops in Spain, proclaimed:

From its very beginning, the industrial age destroyed our spiritual culture but it did not (offer) anything better in its place. It rather established a false culture, which corrupts us. . . . Under the existing conditions our ideal has to be an illiterate country.[23]

The Iron Guard recruited 270,000 members and won half a million votes in 1937, thus becoming a fascist, Nazi-type mass party that was unique in East-Central Europe and the largest outside Italy and Germany. Their paramilitary uniforms were not the fascist black shirts or the Nazi brown shirts, but green shirts. Echoing the Nazis and the Italian fascists, they saluted their leader with *Sănătate, Trăiască Legiunea şi Căpitanul!* (Heil! Long Live the Legion and its *Căpitan*).[24] The Iron Guard won an increasing share of voters in elections during the first half of the 1930s—gradually rising from 2 to 16 percent of the vote. Codreanu boldly declared prior to one election: "I am against the great Western democracies. I am against Little Entente. . . . I have no use for the League of Nations. In forty-eight hours after the Legionary victory, Romania will have a close alliance with Rome and Berlin."[25]

The peasant base of the fascist Iron Gard

Like its German and Italian counterparts, the Iron Guard sought to incorporate a small part of the country's industrial workers and established a special Workers Corps in 1936, as well as a Student Corps in 1937. Copying Mussolini's health care program, the Guard founded the Predeal Hospital that cared for the poor free of cost and asked others to pay what they could afford. However, unlike the Italian fascist and German Nazi parties, the Iron Guard was basically a peasant party. This was unique but to be expected given that Romania was a preponderantly peasant country. Before World War I, there were as many industrial workers in the entire country as there were in a single large factory in Germany or England. Yet, 50 percent of the land of this peasant nation belonged to the boyar landed aristocracy, and most of the peasants—until the postwar land reform—were landless or owned small, dwarf-sized parcels that could not sustain a family. The long-neglected Romanian peasantry—uneducated, religious, highly oppressed and mercilessly exploited—became Codreanu's natural acolytes. It pays to quote an account of one eyewitness to an appearance he made in a Romanian village, delivering a speech that the police had barred him from making:

> There was suddenly a hush in the crowd. A tall, darkly handsome man dressed in the white costume of a Romanian peasant rode into the yard on a white horse. . . . His childlike, sincere smile radiated over the miserable crowd. . . . Charisma is an inadequate word to define the strange force that emanated from this man. He was more aptly simply part of the forest, of the mountains, of the storms. . . . He had no need to speak. . . . An old, white-haired peasant woman . . . whispered to us, the emissary of the Archangel Michael![26]

Codreanu described his regular visits to the country's villages:

> As we rode from village to village . . . we entered villages singing. . . . Villagers were expecting us everywhere. . . . I felt how I was penetrating into those undefined depths of soul. . . . Romanians came out of Christian homes pouring pailfuls of water across our path—an old custom wishing us . . . the fulfillment of our hopes.[27]

Describing another visit, Codreanu recalled:

> The Christians came out from their homes and followed us. They did not know us, but saw the white crosses on our coats and the feathers in our hats. We rode along the streets singing: "Awake, awake, ye Romanian!" Over 7,000 peasants gathered around us in no time at all . . . a sea of uncovered heads welcomed us, with . . . an impressive church like silence. . . . Some of them were crying.[28]

The Iron Guard recruited a massive number of Romanian peasants. One of those peasants, a certain V.I. Onofrei from the village of Tungujei, wrote to Codreanu: "I am a poor peasant ploughman. . . . I shall help you with my money, my pen, by deed and word, asking you to give me a little corner in 'The Ancestral Land'." Codreanu boasted.[29] His appeal among peasants was predictable given the dismal state of Romania's agrarian system. The bulk of the peasantry worked for *arendași*, rural intermediaries who represented the worse aspects of feudal and capitalist agriculture. The landowning boyar aristocracy basically lived in Western Europe. Some of them, like Dimitrie Sturza, the grandson of a former *hospodar*, never once had stepped foot on his large estate. The boyars rented out their land—75 percent of the estates over 3,000 hectares—to merchants. The renters were often Romanian Jews or foreigners (such as the Austrian Fischer Brothers Company). These renters did not cultivate the land, as their counterparts had in many European countries from England to Hungary. Rather, they sub-leased the land to peasants who had to pay with half of their harvested crops. This extremely exploitative arrangement enabled both owners and renters to amass huge profits, while leaving the peasants with little income after paying their fees. When struck by bad harvests or price fluctuations, peasant families often starved. Writes Robert Seton Watson: in "the Golden Age of irresponsible landlordism . . . the peasant found himself as much exploited, as fatally tied to the soil, as in the vanished days of serfdom."[30]

This uniquely backward system led to several revolts in the countryside beginning in the late nineteenth century. An initial uprising in 1888 ushered in a long period of continuing tension and recurrent riots. When the government imposed an additional tax on the peasants in November 1906, the countryside erupted. At the Sturza estate, managed by the Fischer Brothers in Botoşani in northern Moldavia, peasants nearly lynched the estate administrator who offered them a new and even more exploitative contract for the following year. Peasant rebellions in Europe had been regular occurrences in the fifteenth and sixteenth centuries, but Europe's last *jacquerie* took place in Romania in early 1907. The "Great Peasant Revolt" saw peasants' rising up in various parts of the country—attacking cities, looting and burning shops and houses of local *arendaşi*, killing several Jewish merchants and shopkeepers, and occupying all of Moldavia. A gigantic peasant army marched on Bucharest, demanding land, justice, and fair contracts.

In the end, 120,000 Romanian troops slaughtered 10,000 peasants in an unprecedented bloodbath. As Radu Rosetti then observed, the Great Peasant Revolt had sought to quash the ubiquitous latifundia and the neo-feudal contract system in the Romanian countryside. But since the boyar landowners were nowhere to be found, the rebelling peasants turned on the local renters, merchants and innkeepers—the exploiters whom they knew. As half the country's renters, shopkeepers and innkeepers were Jews, the uprising turned into a bloody pogrom. Only a few days before the uprising, the newspaper *Moldova de Sus* published an editorial on December 30, 1906, stating that the "Yids" are the enemies of the Romanian people, and that Romanians "will rise up and start a new hetairia against the Yids. . . . All true Romanians will give it assistance and will struggle until they have achieved such a crucial victory, so as to save our ancestral land and our race."[31] In other words, Romania's exploitative agrarian system was blamed on the Jews.

Land reform was enacted in Romania after World War I: all estates over 500 hectares, and, in some areas (such as the newly incorporated Bessarabia and Transylvania, where the landowners were not Romanians), all estates over 100 hectares were broken up. A third of all arable land was redistributed among 1.4 million peasants, who received small parcels for which they had to make payments over a 25-year period. The reform was politically motivated and failed to modernize Romanian agriculture. The peasants tended their tiny parcels without modern machinery and technology. Hence, most of the peasantry remained steeped in poverty.[32] Codreanu seemed to be a godsend for these impoverished peasants, who responded to his calls for an egalitarian peasant society, to his diatribes against merchants and bankers, and to his promises for a greater redistribution of the land. His social program was encapsulated by the slogan: *Omul şi Pogonul* (one man one hectare of land). Tens and even hundreds of thousands of peasants flocked to him.

The martyr and his legacy

Codreanu was able to mobilize the people, but could not attain power. He came close in 1934–1935. Both King Carol and Prime Minister Tătărescu maintained furtive contacts with the Legion, tolerated its activities, and were open to future collaboration.[33] However, rivalries among other authoritarian parties (the short-lived Goga-Cuza fascist government in 1937–1938 and King Carol's so-called Royal Dictatorship in 1938) led to Codreanu's arrest. He was sentenced to ten years in prison and, along with eighteen other Iron Guard leaders, was "shot while trying to escape" (on the king's orders) when he was being transported to another prison on November 30, 1938. Codreanu became a martyr of his movement, and his populist demagoguery had a profound impact on Romania. His work was continued by his successor, Horia Sima, at the helm of the Iron Guard, which won a large number of new members and ultimately formed a government, the National Legionary State, in September 1940. At that time the Iron Guard was declared the only political party of Romania, and was the only fascist party outside Italy and Germany to rise to power without direct foreign (Nazi) intervention.

Horia Sima became the vice-premier of the new government—"chosen by God . . . as resolute as a rock . . . [and] bigger than the mountains,"[34] as his party described him. He avenged Codreanu's killing by executing sixty-four former dignitaries and officers, and by launching a horrible pogrom in Bucharest in January 1941. But the National Legionary State would not last a year: on January 22, 1941, General Ion Antonescu, Romania's "law and order" soldier, who brought the Iron Guard to power in 1940, removed and destroyed the Iron Guard with Hitler's personal blessing in 1941. In many ways, however, Antonescu would follow in Codreanu's footsteps: joining Hitler's war, he introduced a fascist type of military dictatorship that led to the extermination of half of Romanian Jewry.[35]

Endnotes

1 Hugh Seton-Watson, *Eastern Europe between the Wars, 1918–1941* (New York: Harper Torchbooks, 1967), 198.

2 Ivan T. Berend, *Decades of Crisis: Central and Eastern Europe before World War II* (Berkeley: University of California Press, 1998), 176–77.

3 Nicholas M. Nagy-Talavera, *The Green Shirts and Others: A History of Fascism in Hungary and Romania* (Stanford: Hoover Institution Press, 1970), 348.

4 Corneliu Zelea Codreanu, *For My Legionaries: The Iron Guard* (Madrid: Editura Libertatea, 1976), 7, 83. Codreanu wrote this book in 1936 and included several documents about his movement. An émigré follower republished his book in English in Francisco Franco's Spain.

5 Codreanu, *For My Legionaries*, 210.

6 Ibid., 220–21.

7 Petru Maior, *Istoria pentru începuturi a românilor în Dachia* (Buda, 1812).

8 Quoted by Nagy-Talavera, *The Green Shirts and Others*, 372.

9 Codreanu, *For My Legionaries*, 231.

10 Ibid., 320.

11 Armin Heinen, *Die Legion "Erzengel Michael" in Rumänien: Soziale Bewegung und politische Organisation* (Munich: Oldenburg, 1986), 131, 135, 142.

12 Codreanu, *For My Legionaries*, 48.

13 Heinen, *Die Legion "Erzengel Michael,"* 146–47.

14 Codreanu, *For My Legionaries*, 304–9.
15 Ibid., 242–43.
16 Ibid., 312.
17 Ibid., 247.
18 Nagy-Talavera, *The Green Shirts and Others*, 373.
19 Codreanu, *For My Legionaries*, 34, 45, 52, 103, 106, 118.
20 Ibid., 106, 148, 271, 4.
21 Quoted by Nagy-Talavera, *The Green Shirts and Others*, 365, 369.
22 Ibid., 349, 350.
23 Ibid., 268.
24 Ibid., 382.
25 Ibid., 410–11.
26 Ibid., 345.
27 Codreanu, *For My Legionaries*, 268.
28 Ibid., 271, 274.
29 Ibid., 240.
30 Robert W. Seton Watson, *The History of the Romanians from Roman Times to the Completion of Union* (London: Archon, 1963), 369.
31 Ion Ilincioiu, *The Great Romanian Peasant Revolt of 1907* (Bucharest: Editura Academiei Române, 1991), 54, 138, 179, 275–76.
32 Wim van Meurs, "Land Reform in Romania—A Never Ending Story," *South-East Europe Review for Labour and Social Affairs* 2 (1999): 109–22.
33 Nagy-Talavera, *The Green Shirts and Others*, 403.
34 Vlad Georgescu, *The Romanians: A History* (Columbus: Ohio State University Press, 1991), 213.
35 See Stephen Fischer-Galati, *Twentieth-Century Romania* (New York: Columbia University Press, [1970] 1991).

CHAPTER 4

A fascistoid Austrian demagogue: Ernst Rüdiger Starhemberg

Rump Austria after World War I

After World War I, most of Europe fell into desperation, disintegration, and chaos. The populace had little hope for the future because of high inflation and rampant starvation. The entire region consequently became the playing field of the Mussolinis and the Hitlers. While a number of the defeated countries and some of the victorious ones went through similar difficulties, practically none of them plummeted to such a degree as the newly created Austrian Republic. Austria-Hungary, the former great power, had extended over all of Central Europe; its population spoke eleven languages. But, in early 1918, as it was nearing defeat in World War I, nearly a million of its citizens were in the streets demanding an alleviation of their plight. The Monarchy collapsed. The beloved emperor, Franz Joseph, had already died in 1916, and his successor, Charles I, was forced out of the country. Austria-Hungary disintegrated, and in its place arose several newly created independent countries. The Treaty of Saint Germain, part of the Versailles Treaty system, detached the German-Austrian part of the former Monarchy and established it as a small independent state. France had sought to destroy Austria-Hungary, the "natural ally" of its arch German enemy. In the place of the 676,443 square kilometers that comprised the Monarchy, the new Austria could claim only 85,533 square kilometers; the Monarchy's 51.4 million inhabitants were reduced to Austria's mere 6.5 million. All of this may be compared to the breaking up of a corporate empire into dozens of smaller units (including raw material extraction sites), with its administrative headquarters transformed into an independent entity. The Austrian provinces (along with Bohemia) comprised the industrial center of the Empire, dependent on the supply of food and raw materials from Hungary and other provinces. Suddenly the truncated new Austria found itself isolated and devoid of its old contacts. In addition, as occurred throughout postwar Europe, agricultural production in war-weary Austria dropped to half its pre-war levels. Food shortages multiplied: milk consumption in Vienna dropped to seven percent of what it was prior to the war; bread and flour was rationed to 10–15 grams a day. Industrial output declined to a third of prewar levels. Railroads ceased to function because of a lack of coal.[1]

In such dire circumstances, few believed in the viability of the newly independent Austria. Paradoxically, both the Right and the Left called for *Anschluss*, i.e. joining Germany. The extremist right-wing Austro-German *Volksbund* supported Anschluss under the slogan of "One People One State!" The social democratic leader, Otto Bauer, left the Renner government in 1920 because Anschluss was not on its agenda. Plebiscites in the early 1920s revealed that 93 percent of the residents of Tirol, and 98 percent of Salzburg's voted for Anschluss. The majority of the *Nationalrat* (National Council) also signed an Anschluss declaration. Voralberg, the western part of the country, supported joining Switzerland.

Desperation led to political chaos and the rise of populist demagogues. There were many to choose from at both sides of the political spectrum. Powerful Left-revolutionary and fascist-type mass movements emerged. In this upheaval, a young soldier from one of Austria's oldest aristocratic families, Ernst Rüdiger Starhemberg, stepped on the political stage.

Starhemberg's background

His family's renown dated back to medieval times. One of his most famous ancestors, the legendary Count Ernst Rüdiger Starhemberg, had heroically defended Vienna in 1683 against the Ottoman Turks and halted the Ottoman conquest of the continent. His ancestors rose to the rank of *Reichsgrafen* in the mid-17th century and *Reichsfürsten* in the mid-18th. Ernst Rüdiger, who was born in 1899, inherited 20,000 acres of forestry and 13 castles along with the exalted rank of prince. Towards the end of the World War I, he went to the Italian front.

The young prince was the son of a high-ranking officer and was raised in a family who believed in serving the Emperor and the Empire. As he described later in his memoirs, he was inculcated with the discipline of the cavalry and quite naturally became a soldier:

> My toys were tin soldiers, miniature horses and cannon. Before I could even scribble, I knew how to use my little sword. . . . For a Starhemberg, no any other calling seemed possible. In no other profession can the nobleman cultivate the virtues he has inherited.[2] [But along with the defeat of the war] came the first tragedy in my young life. My country, the Austro-Hungarian Monarchy, collapsed. The imperial Austrian army dissolved . . . the young soldier . . . deceived in all his hopes.[3]

Everything had collapsed. There was no emperor to serve, and nothing but revolution on the horizon. The young Starhemberg, however, gradually found his bearings and rose to defend his humiliated country from the impending danger of revolution.

Under the magic spell of Hitler

As early as 1919, Starhemberg had headed a paramilitary unit in his home district. The peasants of the politically conservative countryside had spontaneously organized their own paramilitary forces, *Feld- und Flurwache* (rural defense force). "My own group had the satisfaction of being invited by the municipality of Linz to restore order on the street . . . when Linz was attacked by anarchist elements early in 1919."[4] The young soldier went to Innsbruck in the fall of 1920, when a major confrontation was in the making with the Social Democrats: "Placing myself at the service of the Tyrolese Heimwehr [Home Guard], I took command of a group of young volunteers . . . to defend the inner quarters of the town . . . against the attack by armed Socialist formations."[5] But Starhemberg had more ambitious goals in mind. He looked to Germany as a possible savior. He described his thinking in his memoirs in

1942: "To put things right again, it doesn't matter where we start. . . . And if in that way Germany can be made strong again, our own Austria will rise with her. . . . A strong and powerful Germany means the renaissance of my own country."[6] Starhemberg would later make the same argument when explaining his decision to go to Germany to join the right-wing paramilitary *Freikorps* (Free Corps). He was at the site where Hitler's National Socialist movement was launched. In his early twenties, the young soldier became an ardent admirer of Hitler. As he later described it, he had seen Hitler as an "embodiment of higher powers." He was "captivated" by his speeches that portrayed social problems as national issues, and he became his "enthusiastic follower and fighter." The culmination of Starhemberg's years in Munich under Hitler's enthralling influence was his participation in Adolf Hitler's first attempt at gaining power with a failed *putsch* in 1923.

Confrontation between Left and Right

In the early 1940s, Starhemberg admittedly acknowledged that he had been a "putschist and adventurer" in those *Sturm und Drang* years, and had acted not as a politician, but as a soldier. Upon returning to Austria in 1923, however, he desisted from his earlier posture.[7] He found his desperate country in the midst of a heated conflict between the Left and the Right—both with their own paramilitary armies. As was often the case in Central Europe, the urban centers leaned sharply to the Left, while the countryside was deeply entrenched with Catholic conservatism. After the war, workers' and soldiers' councils were spontaneously created. A few days after the war's end, the provisional National Assembly accepted the social democratic leader Karl Renner's constitution for a democratic republic. The revolutionary socialists founded the Vienna *Volkswehr* (People's Guard), a 17,000-strong private army equipped with artillery. One of its units was called the Red Guard. For a short period, Austria was surrounded by revolutionary communist regimes in Bavaria and Hungary.

When the Hungarian Soviet Republic called on the Austrian socialists to follow in its footsteps in March 1919, the more reasonable Austrians declined. As the celebrated socialist Viktor Adler put it in his answer to the Hungarian communist leader Béla Kun in *Arbeiter Zeitung:* "We would joyfully . . . [follow you] but unfortunately cannot. . . . There is no food in our country. . . . Thus we are entirely the slaves of the Entente." Another leading social democrat, Otto Bauer, added: "The great difference between our situation and that of Russia is, above all, the Russian peasant . . . is quite different from our peasant here. While the Russian peasant . . . feels like a proletarian . . . , our peasants feel like a bourgeois and [are] determined enemies of the working class."[8]

The Communist Party barely existed in Austria. Its more sober socialists did not relish risking a reckless uprising in the country, and thus purged their paramilitary forces of communists and even arrested a number of them to avoid political disaster. Clashes, even armed clashes, were nonetheless regular occurrences between the opposing Right and Left paramilitary units. *Volkswehr* units occupied Vienna's city center and opened fire on Left-wing demonstrators. The Austrian Right detested "Red (and 'parasitic') Vienna" and forced the social democrats out of the government in the fall of 1920. The Right, including Nazi and fascist forces, gained ground in the country. The German Nazi party established an Austrian branch, which marched under red flags with swastikas on May Day of 1920. One of its leaders told a rally in September of that year that Vienna's housing problem could easily be solved by expelling 200,000 *Ostjuden* (Eastern Jews). The Austrian Nazis formed their own paramilitary army, the *Vaterländischer Schutzbund* (National Protection Alliance), in 1923.

In this chaotic political climate, Starhemberg gradually established himself as an authoritarian nationalist leader. He considered himself a soldier defending his homeland, and remained under Hitler's influence. As he later admitted, "Hitler made a big impact on me" when the two met again in the summer of 1930.[9] This meeting with Hitler, however, marked the beginning of Starhemberg's political transformation:

> Hitler asked me . . . in Munich, whether I had made contact with Mussolini and the Italian Fascist Movement. . . . I said no, because [of the South Tirol conflict between the two countries.] Hitler relied: You are wrong. . . . An alliance with fascist Italy and Mussolini's support may make all the difference in your chances. . . . Go and see Mussolini.[10]

Mussolini's traumatic influence

Starhemberg indeed visited Mussolini in July 1930. They discussed the Austrian political situation, the leftist radicalization of the young generation and the inaction of the nationalist forces. Mussolini suggested:

> You must attract the youth . . . with simple principles and simple slogans: God, people and country. . . . [Mussolini asked:] What is your attitude to an Anschluss with Germany? . . . I frankly replied that the idea was popular among the masses. . . . I personally reject the Anschluss. . . . Instead, I stand for a union. I believe that an essentially independent Austria . . . has strong common bonds with the German Reich. . . . This enraged Mussolini, who, gesticulating violently, said: An Anschluss with Germany must never be permitted, nor a union either. . . . Austria must survive as an Austrian, not a German, land. . . . Prussia means barbarism. That is why you must fight for an "Austrian" Austria. . . . You must become sole leader of the Austrian Heimatschutz. . . . You must defend Austria against the Communist danger, but also against any attempt of an Anschluss with Germany. . . . I shall always be at your disposal in the fight for Austria.[11]

Starhemberg described the traumatic impact of this conversation upon him. He changed his plans, stayed in Rome for two more days, and walked endlessly throughout the city reflecting on his talk with Mussolini:

> The words of Mussolini . . . seemed in an extraordinary way to clarify my feelings about my own country. . . . What is Prussia? The . . . modern equivalent of the barbaric hordes. . . . The last island of the German race in Europe is Austria. . . . Under the influence of the Duce's words, I was anxious to seize leadership of the Heimatschutz at the first opportunity.[12]

Leader of Heimwehr: Austrian fascism

At the age of 31, Starhemberg did indeed take over the "supreme and sole leader[ship] of the Austrian *Heimwehr* (Home Guard) movement." From that point on, he began to distance himself from Hitler and German Nazism. As Mussolini advised him, he began looking for a genuine Austrian, Catholic version of Italian fascism. The Heimwehr gradually grew into a national organization. "I wanted to select some 40,000 to 50,000 men out of the 200,000 in the Heimwehr to form storm battalions."[13] This was a larger number than the 30,000 soldiers in the Federal army. Mussolini was the model to emulate and, if need be, was a close ally. The young soldier rose to become a national leader. He was invited to join the Government as Minister of Interior, as well as head of the police and gendarmerie, but he had no intention of stopping there:

> I frankly admit that I entered the Cabinet with the goal of carrying out a coup d'état. . . . [I devoted] all [my] attention to maintaining the movement's military preparedness. The fate of Austria would not be decided in Parliament. The struggle would eventually take place on the streets.[14]

The new profile of independent Austria

Starhemberg, with Engelbert Dollfuss, head of the Austrian Christian Social party, became the leading figures of Austrian authoritarian-fascist nationalism in the making. This was the time, more than a decade after the end of the war, that the idea of an independent Austria finally coalesced. A sundry of intellectual and political forces embraced the idea of an independent Austria with its own national consciousness and Catholic identity. The influential historian Hugo Hantsch published a history of Austria from the 18th to the 20th century to build the historical foundation for this program. The Austrian Action, a radical legitimist Catholic youth organization, called for building Austrian national consciousness: "The Alpine Austria today is culturally and racially different. The Austrian is racially a synthesis of German and Slav, culturally a synthesis of Roman and Byzantine. . . . Austria cannot return to the Reich, since it had never belonged to the German Reich of today."[15] In the 1930s, the Austrian government established the *Staatspreisen für Literatur, Music, und bildende Kunst*, a state award for writers and artists who effectively propagated the *Österreichische Idee*, Austrian Christian nationalism. The writer Heinrich Waggerl's novel, *Jahr des Herrn*, won the award because it was a *Heimatroman* (patriotic—

literally: fatherland—novel), a "liturgy of the peasantry" and the sacred land.[16] Josef Wenter's *Im heiligen Land Tirol* (In the holy land of Tirol), another awardee, was even more pronounced. The last sentence of the novel read: "this holy land is a jewel in the holy empire . . . the thousand year old 'Ostmark,' Austria."[17] A number of didactic propaganda pieces promoted independent Austrian culture, peoplehood and governance, the Österreichische Idee. Starhemberg became one of the leading espousers of this concept. In a major speech in Vienna on September 22, 1934, he advocated the Austrian Idea:

> We are increasingly committed to Austrian patriotism and Austrian self-assertiveness. . . . Over the centuries, Austria was the stronghold of all of Europe and of German culture and peoplehood as a whole. . . . Austria was a living fortress for Christianity . . . against the attacking East. . . . The struggle of the past is strikingly similar to the struggle of the present. . . . [We are] fighters for an Idea . . . the Austrian Idea is strongly bound to the Catholic faith. . . . We Austrians with our national consciousness . . . are standing on our good national soil. . . . The Austrian Miracle is going to be carried out again![18]
>
> In the pre-Dollfuss times, there was no patriotic politics [*Vaterländische Politik*] in Austria; there was only party politics. The Österreichische Idee is expressed in a comprehensive unity with the *Patriotic Front*.[19]

Starhemberg insisted that the *Idea* is immortal, and one that Austrians were ready to die for and would never renounce. At the same time, he linked Austrian nationalism to the newly established Patriotic Front. In the early 1930s, Starhemberg rose to become the second most important leader of Austria. He was the *Führer* of the powerful Heimwehr, a cabinet minister, deputy head of the Christian Social Party since 1931, close ally of the party leader Chancellor Engelbert Dollfuss, *Führer* of the *Vaterländische* (Patriotic) Front, and finally Vice-Chancellor. He launched an aggressive demagogic nationalist campaign: "Austria First!" "Austria awake!" "Long live New Austria!" His political credo now became both anti-socialist and anti-Anschluss, thus anti-national socialist.

Austro-fascism against "Red and Brown Bolshevism"

His Heimwehr units occasionally clashed with social democratic demonstrators and paramilitary units. One of those altercations in Schattendorf in January 1927 sparked riots across the country. Starhemberg's Heimwehr sought to eliminate the socialist paramilitary armed forces. In early 1934, various Heimwehr units, led by the head of the Vienna branch, Major Emil Fey, started confiscating the weaponry of the socialist *Schutzbund* (Defense Alliance). The commander of the Linz Schutzbund resisted, and a general uprising began. The Heimwehr's provocations led to all-out civil war. Between February 12 and 16, fighting took place in several cities, including Vienna. Emil Fey massacred several hundred socialist workers and arrested some 1,500. The Social Democratic Party, which had traditionally resisted reckless violence after the war and was no match for the more confrontational communists, was brutally disbanded and banned. Starhemberg welcomed these developments in a demagogic radio message to the nation calling for national unity:

> Austria was safeguarded from a catastrophe. I should like to mention a man, my comrade for many long years in the Heimatschutz, . . . Major Fey, who, in February proved what kind of man he is . . . by rescuing Austria from monumental danger. . . . We are invincible if we stand united.[20]

In June 2, 1935, addressing the Vienna Heimwehr, he added:

> You were the first to fight. Special thanks to the excellent *Führer* of the Vienna Heimwehr, Comrade Fey . . . [who] led the Vienna Heimwehr as an efficient combat unit and strike force.[21]

A united and independent Austria led by an authoritarian government, with strong Austrian national consciousness and a sense of superiority, became especially important when the pro-Anschluss, pro-Hitler Austrian Nazis attempted a coup and murdered Chancellor Dollfuss in the summer of 1934. This took place six months after Dollfuss and Starhemberg had destroyed the Austrian Social Democratic Party, their potential ally against the Nazis. The clash between the Heimwehr and the Nazis was not a new phenomenon. As Starhemberg recalled: "There were clashes between National Socialists and the Heimwehr. . . . Nothing fortifies a political idea more firmly than the exchange of blows."[22] From 1934 on, rhetoric defending an independent Austria and demagogically equating Social Democracy with Nazism became the *leitmotif* of Starhemberg's propaganda. He praised the Austrian nation as the

> most exquisite form of Germaneness (*Deutschtum*), the only one that can play a role in the world. . . . Anschluss will not happen if we know that it would be nothing else than turning Austria into a colony of Prussian-Berlin. . . . Austria is crucially important for a peaceful rebuilding of Europe, or otherwise we will fall into a world war. . . . We are fighting for freedom, independence and Austria's influence on world history. . . . The Austrian mission is also a world-mission. . . . The coming year will again be a year of wonderful victories . . . an Austrian miracle.[23]

He used strong words when referring to Nazi Germany, speaking of Nazi *Banditentum, Gengstertum,* and *Nazi Barbarians.* In several speeches Starhemberg extolled Austria's "fight against Red and Brown Bolshevism." He flippantly equated communism with Nazism. Both are forms of "purloined radicalism" that arose out of economic despair. One is "called Bolshevism over there and [the other] National Socialism over here."[24] Austria is fighting against both forms of "twentieth-century barbarism."[25]

In the 1930s, his political agenda became clear. Chancellor Dollfuss commissioned him to form the *Patriotic Front* in 1933 out of the Heimwehr and various rightwing parties and groupings. All other parties were banned. As *Führer* of the Patriotic Front, he contributed mightily to the rise of a one-party, "Austro-fascist" state. Together with Dollfuss, he proclaimed a new constitution in May 1933, established the *Ständestaat* (a corporative state) similar to Mussolini's, disbanded Parliament, and cancelled all elections. Based on Italy's fascist corporatist model, four corporatist councils[26] appointed the supreme state body, the *Staatsrat* (State Council). Presidential decrees now took the place of democratic legislation, with close to 500 "emergency laws" enacted in this manner.

Starhemberg abhorred parliamentarianism, embraced authoritarian rule, and decried "corrupt" and unpatriotic democracy. He was fond of recollecting that as early as 1930 Heimwehr had devised the Korneuburger Program that called for an end to democracy and parliamentary rule, and promoted an Italian-type fascist regime in Austria. "This was the program that laid down the basis of our existing state system and represented a turning point in the history of Austria."²⁷ The main points of this program were laid out in various speeches:

> The Heimatschutz [another name for the Heimwehr] is the backbone, and is our destiny; it is the present and future of this state. The fact is that the Heimatschutz created the idea of the Ständestaat (corporate state) that is so popular among the people. The Heimatschutz destroyed the parliamentary corruption in Austria. . . . We want to create real [patriotic] Austrian workers from the Marxist, international-oriented Austrian proletariat. . . . The state has to rebuild the economy.²⁸

> The modern thinking of *Führerprinzip* is spreading throughout the world as the highest idea [of leadership]. It requires trust between leaders and followers with mutual good faith.²⁹

He developed his ideas under the influence of Hitler and Mussolini, history's greatest fascist demagogues, but, quite unlike them, he was enormously uneasy as a public speaker: "I always had stage-fright," he confessed. "However, contact with the audience made me a good speaker. . . . Every meeting, small or large, was successful."³⁰ An added benefit was certainly his family name, of which every Austrian school child was familiar. His speeches were animated by his fervent enthusiasm, his idealistic populist nationalism, and his genuinely friendly demeanor. He presented the authoritarian corporative one-party system as a higher stage of democracy and social planning that would create new cooperative relations between entrepreneurs and workers:

> In my view, although it seems paradoxical, this authoritarian Ständestaat is much more democratic than most of the democratic states, and is definitely more democratic than our state was in the past. . . . Unlimited exploitative capitalism (*Ausbautungskapitalismus*) . . . will end and will be replaced by service to the state and society. . . . The authoritarian state creates the possibility for the improvement of the lives of the economically weaker classes . . . economic egotism disappear from both the entrepreneurs and workers.³¹

> Austria is not a [traditional] capitalist state any longer . . . [power] is increasingly shifting from the entrepreneurs to the state. . . . The Christian principle of love will permeate the economic realm as well, The entrepreneurs have to learn . . . to defend their workers and their human rights.³²

Starhemberg and the Austro-fascist Patriotic Front began winning support not only among peasants, but also among certain segments of the working-class. He proudly reported:

> The trade unionists . . . of industrial centers have closed ranks behind, and voted solidly for, the Heimwehr. . . . [Peasants] have been ready to take up arms and risk their lives and in later years some have actually died with the words on their lips: Heil Heimatschutz! Heil Starhemberg![33]

The Anschluss: Nazi-Austria

However, neither the country's military success nor Starhemberg's rhetorical impact would prove to last. Austria could barely cope with the world economic crisis and even less with Hitler's growing power. Mussolini's assistance against the first Nazi Anschluss attempt—sending the Italian army to the Brenner Pass—also evaporated thanks to Italy's isolation after its Ethiopian adventure and its consequent embrace of Hitler. Kurt Schuschnigg, who had followed Dollfuss into the chancellor's office in Ballhausplatz, tried in vain to proffer a compromise, but Hitler's troops triumphantly marched on Vienna on March 4, 1938, enthusiastically welcomed by the majority of the Austrians and Austria became part of the Third Reich. Ernst Rüdiger Starhemberg left the country, first to France and then (in 1942) to Argentina. He was allowed to return to Austria in 1956, and died there that same year.

Endnotes

1   Ivan T. Berend and György Ránki, *Economic Development of East-Central Europe in the Nineteenth and Twentieth Centuries* (New York: Columbia University Press, 1974), 173–75.
2   Ernst Rüdiger Prince Starhemberg, *Between Hitler and Mussolini: Memoires* (New York: Harper and Brothers, 1942), 2–3.
3   Ibid., 4.
4   Ibid., 5.
5   Ibid., 6.
6   Ibid., 18. Much later, when Starhemberg was living as an émigré in Western Europe, he amended his description: "the exact opposite was the truth, that Germany's greatness spelt Austria's downfall, [this] was a bitter truth I learned fifteen years later . . . . The fact that . . . I found my way into a German volunteer movement and thence to Adolf Hitler, passing part of my youth in

the camp of militant radical nationalism and in the nursery of the young Nazi movement, has astonished some people by its apparent inconsistency with my family origins and my essentially Austrian and conservative upbringing. But it came about naturally enough." Ibid., 20.

7 Ernst Rüdiger Starhemberg, *Die Erinnerungen* (Vienna: Amalthea Verlag, 1991), 22, 59, 60.

8 Francis Carsten, *Revolution in Central Europe, 1918–1919* (Berkeley: University of California Press, 1972), 113, 31.

9 Starhemberg, *Die Erinnerungen*, 74.

10 Ibid.

11 Ibid., 22–27.

12 Ibid., 28, 29.

13 Ibid., 30–31.

14 Ibid., 34–35.

15 Stanley Suval, *The Anschluss Question in the Weimar Era: A Study of Nationalism in Germany and Austria* (Baltimore: John Hopkins University Press, 1974), 200.

16 Rudolf Bayr, *Karl Heinrich Waggerl: Der Dichter und sein Work* (Salzburg: Müller, 1948); Engelbert Gutwenger, "Liturgie des bäuerlichen Lebens," in *K.H. Waggerl genuer betrachtet*, ed. Lutz Besch (Salzburg: Residenz Verlag, 1967), 36–39.

17 Josef Wenter, *Im heiligen Land Tirol* (Graz: Verlag Styria, 1937), 80.

18 Speeches in Vienna on September 22, 1934, and in Klagenfurt, December 9, 1934, in Ernst Rüdiger Starhemberg, *Die Reden des Vizekanzlers E.R. Starhemberg* (Vienna: Oesterreichischen Bundespressedienst, 1935), 27–35.

19 Speech in Eisenstadt, June 16, 1935, in ibid., 99.

20 Radio speech in Wiener Rundfunk, July 27, 1934, in ibid., 15.

21 Speech at the Spring Parade of the Vienna Heimwehr in June 2, 1935, in ibid., 76.

22 Starhemberg, *Between Hitler and Mussolini*, 48–49.

23 Speech in Linz on January 5, 1935, in Starhemberg, *Die Reden des Vizekanzlers*, 74–75.

24 Speech at the Vienna Heimwehr's meeting on October 25, 1934, in ibid., 54, 56.

25 Speech in Bergenz, March 31, 1935, in ibid., 64.

26 Four corporatist councils were established: the Staatsrat (Federal State Council), the Bundeskulturrat (Federal Cultural Council), Bundeswirstschaftsrat (Federal Economic Council), and Länderrat (State Council). These councils appointed the National Council without an election.

27 Speech in Innsbruck, May 19, 1935, in Starhemberg, *Die Reden des Vizekanzlers*, 84.

28 Speech in Innsbruck, April 4, 1935, in ibid., 80–82.

29 Speech at the Fatherland Front's meeting, December 4, 1934, in ibid., 78–79.

30 Starhemberg, *Die Erinnerungen*, 19, 21.

31 Speeches in Mödling, April 28, 1935, and Vienna, November 19, 1934, in Starhemberg, *Die Reden des Vizekanzlers*, 94, 116, 117.

32 Speeches in Vienna, December 4, 1934, and November 19, 1934; and in Graz, February 15, 1935, in ibid., 18, 110–21.

33 Ibid., 49–50.

PART
2

Turn of the millennium populist demagogues

CHAPTER 5

An Austrian far-right demagogue, Jörg Haider

The Nazi past of Haider's family

The Austrian national-fascism of Starhemberg and Dollfuss failed miserably. Hitler's Nazi party had strong roots and a multitude of followers in German Austria. One of them, a shoemaker named Robert Haider, joined the *Deutsche Nationalsozialistische Arbeiterpartei*, the Austrian affiliate of Hitler's *Nationalsozialistische Deutsche Arbeiterpartei* (as the Nazi party was officially called) in 1929. In 1933, when Dollfuss and Starhemberg suppressed Austria's Nazi movement, Haider moved to Munich, Germany, and joined the Austrian Legion, a division of the Nazi *Sturmabteilung*. Returning to Austria in 1938 soon after the *Anschluss*, he served in the Wehrmacht as a lieutenant during the war. In 1945, he married Dorothea Rupp, the former leader of the *Bund Deutscher Mädel*, a Nazi women's organization.

After the war, the couple was investigated for Nazi activities, as were millions of Germans and Austrians. The denazification process, however, was mild and short-lived with the escalating Cold War confrontation. The denazification tribunal classified the Haider couple as *Minderbelastet* (compromised to a lesser degree), prohibited Dorothea from practicing her profession as a teacher, but allowed Robert to return to work at a shoe factory. The couple had a child, Jörg, born in 1950 in the Upper Austrian Bad Goisern.

Jörg Haider,[1] graduated at the Vienna Law School and, indoctrinated at home, followed in his parents' footsteps. He joined the right-wing dueling student organization, *Burschenschaft Albia*, and then the right-populist *Freiheitliche Partei Österreichs* (FPÖ, Freedom Party of Austria). The leader of the Party's youth organization in 1970, he served as its representative in Parliament in 1979 and became the head of the Party's section in *Kärnten* (Carinthia), Austria's southernmost Eastern-Alps *Land* (or Austrian state) in 1983. He was made leader of the Party three years later and *Landeshauptmann* (Governor) of Carinthia in 1989.

Head of the right-populist Freedom Party of Austria

Founded in 1956, the Freedom Party of Austria was a right-wing Nazi-sympathizing populist organization. This type of populist party was not common in Europe at that time, and became so only thirty to fifty years later. Its provenance in mid-1950s Austria is fairly mysterious. One of Europe's most firmly established Right-populist parties, Jean-Marie Le Pen's National Front, was founded over a decade and a half later in 1972. Why did such a party emerge in Austria, so soon after the signing of the Austrian State Treaty in May 1955, in which the occupying powers left the country and Austria became a neutral independent state? The question is an important one, even though the Freedom Party did not become a significant political force until the 1980s, and it never attracted more than 5–8 percent of the electorate.

Certainly one explanation for the early rise of the Austrian Freedom Party is the fact that its first leader, Anton Reinthaller, an SS officer and champion of pan-Germanism, was a former minister in Austria's Nazi cabinet after the Anschluss. In other words, the party's followers were recruited from Austria's pan-German Nazi nationalists and neo-Nazis, who were mostly from the countryside.

Stable and prosperous Austria

During the 1960s and 1970s, Austria was hardly a bastion of anti-establishment populism. The country was the model of stability and prosperity. It was the birthplace of the so-called *Sozialpartnerschaft* after the war, creating corporatist cooperation between entrepreneurs, workers and the state in a democratic framework. In August 1947, the first wage-price agreement was signed by the powerful trade unions, the entrepreneurs' organization, and the government, followed by four additional agreements over the next four years.[2] Like several other Western countries, Austria created a well-functioning welfare state. Public expenditures on social institutions rose from 19 percent of the gross social product in 1950 to almost 50 percent by 1980. The country had one of the most egalitarian divisions of income in Europe. A mixed economy, a combination of private- and state-owned sectors, was a common phenomenon in postwar Europe, but Austria's state-owned sector was the largest in the West. In 1946, Austria's Parliament ratified its first nationalization act, which appropriated the entire engineering and oil refinery industries and nationalized the three biggest banks as well as the German-owned branches of a number of industries. The proportion of industrial output by state-owned companies and those controlled by state-owned banks reached 70 percent.[3] State ownership of certain companies notwithstanding, Austria's entire economy operated in a free market system.

Between 1970 and 1983, the three successive governments of Chancellor Bruno Kreisky ("Kaiser Bruno") were enormously popular. His home telephone number was listed in the Vienna Telephone Directory, and his reelection victories speak for themselves. Since its economic collapse in 1945, the country had more than doubled its national income and had surpassed prewar economic levels as early as 1950. When Haider took over the Freedom Party in 1988, Austria could claim virtually full employment. The country's exports were two and a half times, and its GDP 4.23 times larger than they were in 1950 and on par with West European levels.

Defending the Nazi past

When Jörg Haider joined the Freedom Party in the 1970s, he was simply emulating his Nazi parents and pursuing views he had learned in his parents' home. Accordingly, he often defended the Nazi past. Although every time he did so he created huge political scandals both home and abroad, he found a captivated audience in the Austrian countryside. An outspoken defense of the past became extremely important and popular among a great many Austrians during the second half of the 1980s. Until 1986, Austria's conscience was clear and Austrians unquestionably ascribed to the postwar propaganda line that they had not been Nazis and were in fact Hitler's first victims! Facing the past was not part of the Austrian vocabulary, lying about it for long was.

After 1986, a dramatic change took place. When Kurt Waldheim was elected president of the country, when his wartime role in Hitler's army and his lies about it all became known, and when the country's former Western allies boycotted Austria, Austrians were forced for the first time to face their past. The *Vergangenheitsbewältigung* (to come to terms with the past) generated endless debates and compelled Austrians to accept the truth about the country's Nazi past. Discarding the "first victim" bravado, Austria finally accepted responsibility. It was widely discussed how Austrians had enthusiastically welcomed Hitler in March 1938, when he triumphantly toured the country by car. Old newsreels were rediscovered with hordes of adoring Austrians, their arms raised saluting Hitler. Hitler himself had boastfully declared that "when I crossed the former frontiers, there met me such a stream of love as I have never experienced." Austrians could no longer ignore the fact that Austria had a higher percentage of SS membership per capita than did Germany. Austria made up only 8 percent of the Reich's population but 13 percent of SS membership, and Austrians comprised 40 percent of the concentration camps' staff and 75 percent of its commanders.[4] In the days after the Anschluss, Jews were humiliated and forced to clean the streets with toothbrushes—all triumphantly photographed and now serving as inconvenient testaments. Some 130,000 Jews fled the country; of those who remained, 65,000 were killed. This painful reckoning with the past made large numbers of Austrians uncomfortable and was not to their liking.

A typical demagogue, Haider appealed to these discontented Austrians and became their voice. He rejected the new politically correct attitudes and never hesitated to openly defend the Nazis and Austria's Nazi past. Austria's old-style politicians had never dared to do that, and their previous silence on the wartime period was now replaced with Haider's vitriol. His fervent demagoguery echoed in Austria's extremely conservative countryside, among those who had enthusiastically welcomed Hitler, as well as their children. In January 1985, Austrian Defense Minister and Freedom Party member Friedhelm Frischenschlager publicly welcomed Walter Reder, a former SS officer and commander of the 16th Armored Infantry Division, who had been sentenced to life in prison in Italy in 1951 but was released and returned to Austria. In the fall of 1944, Reder had committed one of Austria's most brutal war crimes when his unit murdered some 1,800 civilians, 200 of them children, in the Italian township of Marzabetto and its neighboring villages. The Freedom Party minister's official welcome of Reder sparked immediate outrage across Austria, but Haider adamantly defended his party colleague:

> He did not receive a criminal but a soldier who did his duty for his fatherland during the war . . . . If you are going to speak about war crimes, you should admit such crimes were committed by all sides and not pick on a few German soldiers.[5]

On another occasion, in May 1995, the governor of the Carinthian region honored a gathering of Waffen SS veterans. Jörg Haider delivered a speech at the gathering and declared:

> Dear Friends, . . . there are still simple and decent men who have character and who, even with a strong countervailing wind, stand by their convictions and have remained true to their beliefs . . . [T]he Wehrmacht and members of the German Wehrmacht are portrayed as criminals. . . . I shall always with my friends speak up so that this older generation will be treated with respect . . . , respect for all that they have preserved for us. . . . And anyone who today . . . says that the members of the war generation, the Wehrmacht, were all criminals is in the end besmirching their own parents. . . . And a people that does not hold its forefathers in honour, is condemned to doom.[6]

The speech had serious negative repercussions throughout the country, and was denounced by Interior Minister Franz Loeschnak. Haider did not hesitate to criticize the minister for his

> primitive attacks on respectable war veterans. A people that does not honor earlier generations is a people condemned to ruin. We shall prove that we are not to be wiped out. . . . The Waffen SS was part of the Wehrmacht [the regular German army] and because of that it deserves every honor and recognition.[7]

Nevertheless, Haider was "flexible" enough to say the opposite at times as well. In an interview on December 14, 1995, for the German magazine *Bunte*, he insisted:

> I always describe the Third Reich as the most heinous criminal regime. The worst thing about it was anti-Semitism and racism which led to mass extermination. . . . National Socialism cannot be justified.[8]

But only months earlier, in the summer of 1995, he went so far as to claim that Hitler had actually helped establish postwar European democracy by invading Russia:

> I have said that the soldiers of the Wehrmacht have made democracy in its existing form in Europe possible. If they had not resisted, if they hadn't been in the East, if they had not conducted military campaigns, we would have [under communism].[9]

On several occasions, Haider also positively commented the Nazi regime. In 1991, he called for reducing unemployment compensation and proposed mandating forced labor for those who receive it. When he was accused of emulating Nazi policies, he immediately replied: "No, they did not have that in the Third Reich, because in the Third Reich they had a proper (*ordentliche*) employment policy." He was more careful when talking about the Holocaust, which he always denounced. But he regularly equated it with "crimes" (meaning retribution) against Germans. In an interview in September 1998, Haider suggested:

> Two different measurements are being applied here. If Jewish emigrants are making claims, then there will be endless reparations. If the Sudeten Germans ask the Austrian government to demand reparations in their name from the Czech authorities, it will be said that this part of history needs to be considered finished. . . . One cannot treat equal things unequally.[10]

A pronouncement of the coalition government of which Haider's party took part, and signed by Haider as well, also equated the crimes against the Jews with the postwar retribution against Austrian-German Nazis:

> Regarding the matter of Nazi slave labor, the Federal Government . . . with due regard of the primary responsibility of the companies con-

cerned, will work . . . for fair solutions to . . . all persons compelled to perform forced labor during the Second World War, [including] Austrian prisoners of war and the German-speaking population expelled to Austria as a result of the Beneš decrees.[11]

Haider often made guarded anti-Semitic remarks as well: "The Holocaust serves as a 'cash cow,' a method of manipulating interests with high moral standards."[12] When a historians' commission was established to examine anti-Jewish reprisals in Austria, his Party complained that there were too many Jews in it:

> This is where I question the credibility of this "independent" commission, because, as a matter of fact, Austria's Jewish population is exceptionally well represented in high governmental and private positions, and in banks. But as soon as one talks like that, one is considered a "racist" and intimidating.[13]

To please part of his rightwing constituency, he endorsed pan-Germanism. In a televised debate in August 1988, he quipped: "You know as well as I do that the Austrian nation was a miscarriage, an ideological miscarriage."[14]

Turn to modern anti-establishment, xenophobic populism

Pride in the Nazi past, however, could not give him the political breakthrough he sought. When he became the leader of the Freedom Party, he realized that he had to amplify and update its agenda and rhetoric. Giovanni Metteo Quer calls our attention to this change:

> While the constituency of former Nazis and nostalgia decreased, Haider refined its political language and adopted the old tenets of racial superiority . . . by gradually introducing the concept of cultural and national distinctiveness. While hate speech was criminalized, Haider redirected its racial focus toward cultural identity . . . in order to denounce cultural mixing. Consequently, the ancient ideology of *Volk* and *Rasse* are substituted by *Kultur* in opposition to multiculturalism and "racial mixture" instead of "culture mixture" (*Kulturmischung*).[15]

Haider, indeed, significantly changed the Freedom Party and established it as a mainstream modern right-wing populist, radical nationalist, anti-emigration, anti-establishment, and later anti-European Union organization. After 1986, when Haider took over the party leadership, these kinds of populist ideologies and movements began to be more evident in European politics. In October 1989, Austria's Freedom Party issued its official St. Lorenzen Declaration, its first unambiguously anti-foreign and anti-immigration declaration that spoke of the *Überfremdung* (foreign swamping) of Austria and called for the racist exclusion of foreigners and particularly black foreigners. In early 1993, the Party launched the "Austria First" referendum asking voters to decide on twelve matters. The first asked them to agree on a constitutional amendment stipulating that "Austria is not a country of immigration." It also asked whether they agree if it was necessary, "to deal with the problem of illegal foreigners and organized crime," a statement symptomatic of Haider's brand of demagogy that forever equated immigrants with crime. The referendum also proposed a discriminatory policy against immigrants by limiting the number of students "with foreign mother-tongues to a maximum of 30 percent." Haider and the Freedom Party were quite successful in their anti-foreigner, anti-immigration rhetoric: in 1990, only 11 percent of the population believed that the Freedom Party could solve the problem; four years later, 36 percent did.[16]

The new party platform in 1993 propagated the slogans "Austria First" and the "Right to a Homeland," reflecting the party's extreme anti-immigration stance. It also rejected the concept of multiculturalism, because it "leads to and results in social conflicts." Instead of upholding the equality of Austria's citizens, it separated the population into various autochthonous national groups (*Volksgruppe*) and declared that the "overwhelming majority of Austrians belongs to the German autochthonous group."[17]

Replicating the American demagogue Newt Gingrich, Haider announced his own "Contract with Austria." This contained twenty pledges to assure "thrift," "more democracy," "more freedom," "more justice," and "lean government," and promised to "slash privileges," "cut taxes," "safeguard the health service," and "limit immigration." At his rallies Haider attracted large numbers who responded to his calls to distinguish between "pure and respectable" Austrians and "undesirables" in the country, and to his demand to ban immigration. He often used particularly derogatory and sometimes racist terminology to make distinctions between people. Discussing new medical legislation in 1998, he asked: "Where will we be when any bushman (bushnigger) will have a chance to provide medical treatment to our fellow Austrians?"[18] One of his favorite arguments, echoing other European populist parties, was to blame immigrants for unemployment:

> Immigration policy affects the labor market. In Austria's eastern region, about 10,400 new jobs were created between 1984 and 1992. Out of those, all, that is, 100 percent of them, were filled by cheap foreign laborers. At the same time, Austrians lost 1,300 jobs.[19]

At an election rally in 1999, Haider mocked newspaper accounts of the "tragic death" of an illegal immigrant drug dealer and said:

> How poor are the victims . . . of these drug dealers, our children, our youth. We [have to] protect the victims and not the perpetrators . . . Someone who comes to us, who stays here illegally, who becomes a criminal here in Austria, has not even for a minute the right to be in Austria, and should be expelled.[20]

In typical populist fashion, Haider regularly denounced the Austrian political establishment. He accused them of inaction and of causing a steep moral decline in the country, "The ruling Austrian executive class grabs this land."[21] "People are fed up with the old parties that never live up to their promises. . . . They want action for everyday problems, whether it is job security, housing, or uncontrolled immigration."[22] Haider accused the pseudo-elite, as he called them, for all of these problems:

> This land, in various respects, is ruled by authoritarian, morally complacent pseudo-elite. . . . They are broken spiritually. . . . Egotism, a lack of social coherence and the fiction of a universal multicultural world-society, the spiritual outcome of the nightmarish 18th century Enlightenment. . . . What is the essence of liberalism in which we are living? Chasing personal success, egotism, lack of social coherence, accumulation of luxuries. . . . Should we passively observe this meaningless Western industrial society submerged in hedonism and spiritual bankruptcy? Society is in danger . . . its moral and ethical base is broken . . . and traditions are broken . . . All this has led to a society that is void of values.[23]

Against the European Union

In the 1990s, Austria, along with a number of other neutral countries, applied for membership in the European Union. Haider was an enthusiastic supporter. In 1992, in the party's Vienna Declaration, he proclaimed: "Whoever goes with me stands for FPÖ, which supports a United States of Europe as the lasting guarantee for peace." A year later, he realized that his supporters had little inclination to join the EU and changed his position. He praised the nation and the nation-state and disavowed "abstract" nationless Europe:

> Maastricht is the wrong signal for today's Europe. . . . [Loose form of intergovernmental cooperation] is a model which will bring more self-determination . . . rather than some arbitrary centralized supra-national body. Only the nation state can protect the heritage and culture of a people.[24]

He also insisted that

> Europe is not united culturally and linguistically as those Brussels bureaucratic blood wolves imagine. . . . An abstract European culture and an abstract European people do not exist. . . . If the role of people as the highest sovereign is questioned, then democracy is questioned. . . . The European Community is the creation of a postwar Europe . . . the Cold War and not the primacy of freedom, peace, and security for all of Europe. . . . A kind of global civil-war [began] between two international utopias: Marxism-Leninism on the one side, and the liberal-capitalist world system with its cultureless individualism on the other. Both sought the eradication of the nation . . . the nation-state today and tomorrow will survive.[25]

In a populist way, Haider suggested—as the Brexiters did several years later—that payment to the EU was an unacceptable burden to the Austrian taxpayer, who had to fork out 150 million schillings a day for the privilege of membership. Where is all this money going? Isn't much of it being squandered thanks to the EU's notorious fraud and anarchy? He conveniently "forgot" to take into account the massive amounts Austria receives from the Union. He never mentioned the huge sums that went to Austria as a result of the EU's eastward expansion incorporating ten former Soviet Bloc countries. Austria's banks, for example, predominate in the financial sectors of those countries. Haider pushed for a "no" vote on joining the Union. Nevertheless, two thirds of Austrians voted "yes" in 1994. Haider's followers comprised only 33.4 percent of those who voted "no." With classic populist demagoguery, Haider imagined himself as the voice of the forgotten people. He often spoke about physical laborers, the "little" people who are being left behind. He employed conservative family values when he argued: "Women should be able to choose between a family and a career, free from ideological trappings. . . . Kindergarten is no substitute for a mother . . . instead kids get fast food, stress, and pre-packaged education from television."[26] On the other hand, he spoke about leading a revolution: "What we have in mind is more than a change of government. We want to bring about a cultural revolution. . . . We want to overthrow the ruling political class and the intellectual caste [by means of direct democracy]."[27] He also declared:

> Our freedom rules out every sort of patronage which stops people from making their own decisions . . . [We want] less oppression by the party machines and more freedom for citizens. . . . A break from bureaucratic chains and more intellectual autonomy instead.[28]

In a typical populist way, he fashioned his rhetoric, right-wing or left-wing, according to his audience, and his demagoguery worked. His success was partly the result of his personality. He was handsome, tall, and always suntanned—an enthusiastic athlete who excelled at rock climbing, marathon running, and cross-country skiing. He liked wearing the popular national fashions like *Lederhosen* and spoke in popular slang. Haider loved to be on stage. His childhood dream was to be an actor, which came true in politics. He loved to play the "gladiator" in the political arena battling the lions in power, the overwhelming enemy. Some political analysts, however, "supposed that deep in Haider's psyche lay a tiny 'Adolf' trying like Houdini to break free."[29] Most of all, he was an excellent speaker, some would even say a master speaker, who always spoke his mind and made calculated gaffes to attract all types of potential followers. The Freedom Party was first and foremost Jörg Haider, and its propaganda always revolved around him, as one of their election slogans demonstrated: "Simply honest, simply Jörg! They are against him because he's for you!"

In 1999, his Freedom Party won 42 percent of the vote in Carinthia, and 42.5 percent five years later. While the Freedom Party won only 5 percent of the vote in national elections in 1983, it won 27.5 percent (more than one million votes) in 1996 under his leadership—close to the 29 percent of the two establishment Austrian Peoples Party and the Social Democratic Party. In 2000, in coalition with the Österreichische Volkspartei (ÖVP), Haider won the election. He should have been named chancellor but allowed ÖVP leader Wolfgang Schüssel to take the post because of the international outcry. From time to time, the always controversial Haider was severely criticized and had to step aside, but he remained popular among his followers.

However, his story remained an incomplete one: going to his mother's 90th birthday party, he, as usual, drove his car at twice the speed limit. The alcohol content in his blood was almost three times the legal limit. He lost control of the car, hit a concrete pole, rolled several times, and died. The obituary in *The Economist* correctly stated:

> All this hard-right politicking gave the jitters to some. But Mr. Haider, sly as a snake and sharp as a razor, was not so easily defined. When Austria's ruling parties opposed Turkish membership of the EU, he supported it. Austria's own accession he first endorsed, then passionately resisted (leading the "No" forces in the 1994 referendum), then accepted. When Saddam Hussein was a pariah, he went to Baghdad to shake his hand. His most admired politician was Archduke Johann, a modernizing 19th-century governor of Styria, closely followed by Newt Gingrich and Tony Blair. His ideology shifted, conservative one moment and leftish the next, as changing as the suits, jeans, Robin Hood outfits, puffer ski-jackets and medieval robes which he clad himself in. It was often said that the only "ism" he ever embraced was populism. Jörg Haider, an Austrian populist, died on October 11th [2008], aged 58.[30]

Eight–ten years later

In 2016, the presidential candidate of Haider's Freedom Party, Norbert Hofer, lost the national election by fewer than 31,000 votes or 0.6 percent, thanks to the combined efforts of all of the other parties. However, because of irregularities, the election was annulled by the Constitutional Court and had to be repeated. Nevertheless, Hofer lost the election by nearly seven percentage points. History, it seemed, would not grant Haider a post mortem success. Next year in October 2017, however, at the parliamentary elections, Haider's Freedom Party almost finished second behind the Austrian Peoples Party with 26 percent of the votes. The two rightwing parties together gained almost 58 percent of the votes. This, in the end, became a kind of post mortem success of Haider.

Endnotes

1 Jörg Haider has been the subject of a great deal of scholarly work. See: Klaus Ottomeyer, *Jörg Haider, Mythenbuilding und Erbschaft* (Klagenfurt: Drava Verlag, 2009); Knut Lehman-Horn, *Die Kärtner FPÖ 1955–1983: Vom Verband der Unabhängigen (VdU) bis zum Aufstieg von Jörg Haider zur Landesparteioberman* (Klagenfurt: Universitätsverlag Carinthia, 1992); Kurt Piringer, *Die Geschichte der Freiheitslichen: Beitrag der Dritten Kraft zur Österreichischen Politik* (Vienna: Orac Verlag, 1982).

2 Felix Butschek, *Die östereichische Wirtschaft im 20. Jahrhundert* (Stuttgart: Gustav Fischer Verlag, 1985), 101–109.

3 Donald Sassoon, *One Hundred Years of Socialism: The West European Left in the Twentieth Century* (New York: The New Press, 1996), 161.

4 See David Art, *The Politics of the Nazi Past in Germany and Austria* (Cambridge: Cambridge University Press, 2006).

5 "Haider in His Own Words," *Time*, February 7, 2000, content.time.com/time/world/article/0,8599,2056294,00.html.

6 Haider's sppech in Krumpendorf, quoted in Melanie A. Sully, *The Haider Phenomenon* (New York: East European Monographs, 1997), 139.

7 Ibid.

8 Ibid., 132.

9 Interview with Haider, *Profil*, August 21, 1995. Quoted by Ruth Wodak and Anton Pelinka, eds., *The Haider Phenomenon in Austria* (New Brunswick: Transaction Publisher, 2002), 37.

10 Ibid., 38 (ORF Interview, ZIB, September 2, 1998).

11 Ibid., 55.

12 *Neue Freie Zeitung*, September 2, 1998.

13 Wodak and Pelinka, *The Haider Phenomenon in Austria*, 39.

14 "Haider in His Own Words."

15 Giovanni Matteo Quer, "Israel-Washing: The Radical Right in Europe, Anti-Semitism, and Israel," in *Central Europe (Re-)visited: A Multi-Perspective Approach to a Region*, ed. Marija Wakounig and Ferdinand Kühnel (Vienna: LIT Verlag, 2015), 111–12.

16 Wodak and Pelinka, *The Haider Phenomenon in Austria*, 20–24.

17 Ibid., 25–26.

18 *Der Standard*, October 13, 1998. Quoted in ibid., 35.

19 Rolf-Josef Eibicht, ed., *Jörg Haider: Patriot im Zwielicht?* (Stuttgart: DS-Verlag, 1997), 66.

20 Speech launching the election campaign in Klagenfurt, September 11, 1999, quoted in Eibicht, *Jörg Haider*, 164.

21 Ibid., 64.

22 Quoted in Matt Schudel, "Jörg Haider; Politician Made Far-Right Party a Force in Austria," *Washington Post*, October 12, 2008.

23 Eibicht, *Jörg Haider*, 63–70.

24 Quoted in Sully, *The Haider Phenomenon*, 92–93.

25 Eibicht, *Jörg Haider*, 63–70.

26 Sully, *The Haider Phenomenon*, 59.
27 Excerpt from Haider's book, *The Freedom I Mean*, quoted in Sully, *The Haider Phenomenon*, 32.
28 Ibid., 33.
29 Sully, *The Haider Phenomenon*, 62, 69.
30 "Jörg Haider, an Austrian populist, died on October 11th, aged 58," *Economist*, October 16, 2008.

CHAPTER 6

A Romanian communist demagogue: Nicolae Ceauşescu

Nicolae Ceauşescu was born in a small township near Bucharest toward the end of World War I. He was the child of a very poor, alcoholic worker with a family of ten children. Ceauşescu was never educated—having worked in a factory from the age of 11 after only completing elementary school. He was just 14 years old when he joined the Communist Party in 1932 during the midst of the Great Depression. He was arrested the following year, and would be repeatedly later, spending many years in prison. In 1936, he found himself in Doftana prison, infamous for its abusive conditions. In 1940, Ceauşescu was sent to the Târgu Jiu internment camp where, until his release in 1944, he shared a cell with a communist seventeen years his senior, Gheorghe Gheorghiu, one of the heroes of a communist revolt in the Transylvanian town of Dej, a member of the Communist Party's Central Committee since 1936, and head of the party's prison faction. To distinguish him from another prisoner named Gheorghiu, the Romanian police added "Dej" to his name (from the name of the city where he had spent several years in the 1930s).

There was a lot in common between the two men. Gheorghiu-Dej was also an industrial worker who began working at the age of 11. Dej had found an admiring protégé in Ceauşescu, and he would serve as an important mentor to him. This accidental meeting led to Ceauşescu's sudden rise after World War II.

Rise to power and boring success propaganda

Romania was one of the first countries to be Sovietized in Central and Eastern Europe. The Romanian Communist Party took power soon after the war under Stalin's wing. Gheorghiu-Dej, named General Secretary of the Party in 1945, paved the way for Ceaușescu's rise. Under his protection, the 26-year-old Ceaușescu began a fast ascent in the communist hierarchy. In 1945, he was appointed Brigadier General of the army. Four years later, he became Deputy Minister of Agriculture. In 1952, he was elected member of the Party's governing body, the Central Committee.

The real power within the communist party in the immediate postwar years, however, was in the hands of the so-called Muscovites, those communist leaders who spent the war years in the Soviet Union. Several of them were Jewish. The leading figure in the Romanian Communist Party was the legendary Ana Pauker, who had been the actual leader of the party in the early postwar period and maintained close connections to Moscow. She was not only Jewish, a huge disadvantage in a strongly anti-Semitic Romania, but her father and brother also lived in Israel. Party infighting between the Muscovites, who were led by Pauker, and the home communists, led by Gheorghiu-Dej, was unavoidable, and it would not be resolved until 1952. At that time Dej was able to take advantage of the bloc-wide, Stalin-directed purges of the communist parties and to monopolize power. These purges began in 1948 with the Gomułka case in Poland and the Pătrășcanu case in Romania—both "home communist" leaders. Home communists were also targeted in the notorious Rajk-trial in Hungary and the Kostov trial in Bulgaria in 1949. It was only with the Slánský trial in Czechoslovakia in 1952, targeting "Zionist traitors," when the victims became Jewish Muscovite communist leaders. In that year Gheorghiu-Dej was finally able to purge Ana Pauker and take over the leadership of the Romanian communist party.[1]

From that time on there was nothing stopping Ceaușescu's climb to the top. He was made a member of the Politburo in 1954, and was aptly positioned when Gheorghiu-Dej died in 1965. As Dej's loyal protégé, the then 47-year-old Nicolae Ceaușescu was elected head of the communist party, president of the State Council, and later in 1974, when the office was created for him, he became president of the country. It was an unprecedented career for a simple man with only an elementary-school education.

His first act was to rename the party. On Stalin's instructions, the Central and Eastern European communist parties in the early postwar period absorbed the social democratic parties and rebranded themselves as Workers Parties. At the Ninth Party Congress in 1965, Ceauşescu took back the Communist Party name.[2] This denoted a sharp turn to the left. During Ceauşescu's first three years in power, his demagoguery was standard fare for East European communist leaders. In frequent speeches he routinely falsified history, praised the Soviet Union, and celebrated the unity of the international communist movement. He also never stopped flouting the triumphant progress the country was making in modernization and industrialization, and the rising living standards of the Romanian people. In typical Stalinist-Zhdanovist fashion, the uneducated leader often "educated" writers and artists on the content of their work and regularly instructed young Romanians on how to emulate past generations of revolutionaries.

In his first three years in power, Ceauşescu incessantly raved about the party's successes and the grandiose plans of its leadership. His bombastic speeches and articles from those years were published in two volumes of nearly 1,200 pages. Allow me to quote a few characteristic paragraphs:

> The fundamental tasks . . . regarding the development of the national economy . . . have been successfully carried out. . . . This year [1965], industrial output is 2.24 times bigger than in 1959. . . . The output of electric power is 2.6 times bigger than in 1959. . . . The generalization of eight-year schooling has been completed and this marked a new stage in the history of Romanian public education. . . . The real wages in 1970 shall be 20–25 percent higher than in 1965. . . . [In December 1966 he announced his plan for] consolidation of the family, growth of the birthrate, [and] reduction in the number of divorces . . .[3]

This was typical Stalinist rhetoric. Given that Romania had one of the least developed economies in Europe with one of the lowest standards of living, Ceauşescu's unceasing propaganda of ever-greater achievements was unlikely to sound credible, though his oft-repeated rosy claims of Romania's rapid development and prosperous future did have some impact on Romanians. His references to the "consolidation of the family" was a deceptively simple code for drastic state policies that restricted divorce and prohibited abortion and birth control.[4]

It would be reasonable to question the label demagogue in the case of Ceauşescu because he was in fact a horrendously bad speaker. He gave incessantly long speeches, penned by others, with only a rare glance away from the script to his audience. It was plain for everyone attending that his words had no relation to everyday reality. He had, however, some skill in organizing celebrations and reaching out to people. His success in foreign policy and opposition against the Soviet Union were highly popular. Ceauşescu's demagoguery was only partly successful.

Rewriting history

Nevertheless, Ceauşescu's perennial rewriting, or more accurately falsifying, of history in a demagogic way did lead to some success. The wartime and postwar generations were still alive and could compare his grandiose descriptions of recent Romanian history with their own experiences. Ceauşescu presented the previous two decades as a triumphant battle of the communist party to destroy Antonescu's fascist regime and establish a socialist Romania. He depicted King Michael's coup d'état in 1944, carried out by the Romanian army without Soviet participation, as a heroic communist action and a genuine anti-fascist revolution:

> Strikes and acts of sabotage against the war and German occupation organized by the workers . . . were intensified. . . . Resistance to the fascist dictatorship and Hitler's Germany included broad circles. . . . The Communist Party, in collaboration with the other anti-Hitler forces, intensified the fight for the overthrow of Antonescu's government, the turning of weapons against Germany. . . . The Party . . . elaborated the plan of action for the carrying out of the armed insurrection. . . . On August 23, Antonescu's government was arrested in the Royal Palace.[5]

In this same speech he also "reinterpreted" the communist takeover of the postwar government, based on an agreement between Churchill and Stalin in October 1944—nicknamed the "percentage agreement."

Churchill wanted a free hand in Greece to fight the communist partisan army that had virtually taken over the country, which would have endangered the British position in the Middle East. He offered Stalin a division of sphere of interests in the Balkans, giving Stalin a free hand in Romania and Bulgaria, two Black Sea countries that were crucially important to the Soviet Union, in exchange for Britain's free hand in Greece. Stalin immediately agreed.

Stalin, indeed, allowed the British army to disarm and defeat the Greek communist partisan army. Within a few months, he cashed the check received from Churchill and presented an ultimatum to Romania's King Michael to appoint a communist-led government and disarm the Romanian army. Ceaușescu described this event as a successful revolution:

> Under the leadership of the Communist Party, huge masses of the population engaged themselves in a sharp struggle against reaction. . . . It was . . . political, economic, and social battles waged by the mass of the people . . . the Government of broad democratic concentration . . . was set up in March 1945 . . . in which the working class had the leading role.[6]

Successful nationalist demagoguery in 1968

As a demagogue, Ceaușescu strove to completely rewrite history and indoctrinate his people, but he found little success prior to 1968. Then, three years after he attained ultimate power in Romania, he began to use a more compelling demagoguery. Ceaușescu combined the typical bombast of communist leaders with popular nationalist rhetoric, even though nationalism was strictly prohibited by communist leaders of the Soviet Bloc countries. Ceaușescu started to distance himself and his country from the Soviet Union and openly stressed the reestablishment of Romanian sovereignty and a nationalist agenda.

This was a reasonable calculation. The Soviet army had already crushed the riots in Berlin in 1953 and the uprising in Hungary in 1956. In August 1968, Warsaw Pact armies invaded Czechoslovakia to overthrow the reform-communist government of the country. Keenly sensing that attacking Romania militarily would be a bridge too far for Leonid Brezhnev, Ceaușescu openly opposed the Soviet action in Czechoslovakia. Romania was a member of the Warsaw Pact, but he, and he alone, refused to participate in the invasion. Instead, he traveled to Prague in solidarity with the besieged Czech reform communists and openly denounced the invasion as an illegitimate foreign intervention into the domestic affairs of a sovereign state.

On August 14, 1968, just prior to the invasion, Ceaușescu made a calculated risk and openly expressed his differences with the Soviet leadership:

> Observance of the independence of each Party [and] non-interference in domestic affairs are fundamental conditions for the establishment of relations of equality and mutual trust among the communist and workers' parties and among the socialist countries. . . . Differences of opinions and divergences emerging between various Parties can be solved not by invectives and labeling, but by direct negotiations. . . . Our Party has expressed from the onset its full sympathy for the activity carried on by the Communist Party of Czechoslovakia. . . . In the next few days, a Party and State delegation of our country will pay a friendship visit to the Czechoslovak Socialist Republic.[7]

Immediately after the Warsaw Pact military intervention in Czechoslovakia on August 21, 1968, Ceaușescu convened a special session of the Romanian Grand National Assembly and dramatically declared:

> The Grand National Assembly . . . is called upon to analyze . . . the situation created by the military intervention in Czechoslovakia. . . . Our whole Party . . . looks upon the military intervention . . . with profound anxiety. We consider this a flagrant transgression of the national independence and sovereignty of Czechoslovak Socialist Republic. . . . We refuse to accept such an interpretation [that it was a brotherly help to protect socialism against counter-revolutionary threat]. . . . Our assessment accords with . . . the broadest circles of world public opinion. . . . I am addressing . . . solidarity to the brother Czechoslovak people.[8]

That was a new voice—a courageous, highly unusual, and sympathetic stand for most of the Romanian people, and one that was surprising but gladly welcomed in the West. Ceaușescu became extremely popular at home and admired the world over. Although this was widely seen as a brave and dangerous act, Ceaușescu had not seen it as an overly risky one at all. For one, he maintained an iron grip inside his country and could not be accused of endangering communism. There were no Soviet troops in Romania, for they had pulled out after the 1956 Hungarian revolution. The Soviet Union could not risk a second military intervention within the Soviet Bloc. Moreover, Romania had the option of turning to China, a major communist country already in conflict with the Soviet Union.

Playing the China card

Indeed, Ceaușescu played the China card at virtually the same time as Nixon and Kissinger. After an initial visit in the mid-1960s, he visited Mao Zedong a second time in 1971, in the midst of Mao's Cultural Revolution. He sought to forge an alliance with China in order to strengthen his independent rule in Romania without Soviet control and direction. He also presented himself as a mediator between China and the Eurocommunist parties of Western Europe. The transcripts of Mao's and Ceaușescu's conversation reveal that it was mostly political small-talk expressing their full agreement in criticizing the Soviet Union. For Ceaușescu, the importance of his visit was its demonstrative effect. Let me quote a very shortened version of their talk:

> *Mao*: There are certain [communist] parties that insult other parties; they think that truth is on their side . . .
> *Ceaușescu:* Unfortunately, it is true, that there still exists this practice of name-calling, of insulting other parties.
> *Mao*: Certain parties insulted us for over ten years. They [were] forced to insult us. . . . The meeting that took place in Bucharest in 1960, was that not imposed on you?
> *Ceaușescu:* It is true that the meeting took place there, and in a way, we too are at fault, since we could have refused to hold that meeting. Today such a meeting could not, and does not, take place in Romania. . . .
> Of course, it would be good if we reached an end to the insults and labeling. I have to tell you that many parties . . . —even big parties—refused to ally with the condemnation of the Chinese Communist Party, and are trying to find ways to establish relations with the CCP . . . the

Italian, Spanish [communist parties] . . . asked us to transmit their desire to reestablish contacts . . . we talked to them. . . . Now we are
[called] nationalists.

Mao: You too are being labeled. . . . You have so been labeled because
you are resisting the pressure. . . . We speak of socialist-imperialism.

Ceaușescu: Many parties have condemned the invasion [of Czechoslova-
kia]. . . . We were in Czechoslovakia a few days before the invasion . . .
there was no danger to socialism.

Mao: At that time they had great plans, not only against Czechoslovakia, but also against you and Yugoslavia . . . you are prepared, especially in the military field. If they shall come, you will fight.

Ceaușescu: We are a small country, but we do not want to live under [for-
eign] domination.[9]

Ceaușescu's visit to China caused a global sensation. The West, including the United States, established special relations with Romania
and with Ceaușescu personally. A year after the Soviet invasion, President Richard Nixon paid an official visit to Romania in August 1969.
At the airport, Nixon stated, "This is an historic occasion . . . it is the
first visit of a President of the United States to Romania, the first state
visit by an American President to a socialist country or to this region
of the continent of Europe."[10] High-level contacts between the US and
Romania continued throughout the 1970s, culminating in Ceaușescu's
state visit to Washington. Romania joined the General Agreement on
Tariffs and Trade (GATT) in 1971 and the IMF and the World Bank the
following year. In 1975, President Ford granted most-favored-nation status to Romania. Ceaușescu and his wife visited France, Britain, Spain,
and Japan, and were received with great fanfare. Ceaușescu began me-
diating international conflicts and served as a key negotiator between
the Americans and the Chinese in 1969 and the Israelis and the Egyp-
tians in 1977. Romania was the only Soviet Bloc country to maintain
diplomatic relations with Israel and Pinochet's Chile. He garnered respect for Romania abroad and popularity at home. Romania remained
a member of the Soviet-led economic bloc, the Comecon, and the Warsaw Pact, but it was posed as a neutral country by participating in both
the Moscow Olympics in 1980 (boycotted by the West) and the Los An-
geles Olympics in in 1984 (boycotted by the East). Ceaușescu received
the Legion of Honor award in France and the Knight Grand Cross of

the Order of the Bath in Britain. His wife, Elena, was appointed member of several Western academies of sciences, including that of the United States, and both were awarded honorary doctorates at several Western universities.

Ceauşescu's elevation as a "world leader" filled Romanians with pride and enthusiasm. They rejoiced at the spectacle of their *Conducător* (Leader) winning Romania such international esteem. Paradoxically, the "internationalist" communist hard-liner was lauded inside Romania for pursuing nationalist policies. His national demagoguery worked remarkably well and he was well received both home and abroad after 1968. For many Romanians, Ceauşescu's international successes initially offset their dire domestic troubles and economic plight. Many at first believed his inflated claims of rapid development and trusted that Romania's modernization would improve their lives. Ceauşescu continually bet that his own international reputation during an escalating Cold War and his propagandistic promises of a better life inside Romania would protect him from a popular backlash against domestic Stalinism, harsh repression, lack of freedom, low living standards, and economic misery in Romania.

Failure of demagoguery, crisis, and collapse

Ceauşescu lost the bet. The first oil crisis of 1973, and another at the end of the decade, plunged Romania and all other Soviet Bloc countries into a deep crisis. Rapid industrialization and economic growth ground to a sudden halt. The economy fell into recession and never recovered. The skyrocketing prices of oil and raw materials, as well as a rapidly emerging revolution in technology and communications that bypassed the Soviet sphere, undermined all of the transitory advantages that the communist regimes enjoyed. Romania (and the others) had to turn to the West for imports, and now half of Romania's foreign trade was with Western free market economies. The country quickly found itself unable to pay for imports through its export of its obsolete and low quality products. Some Soviet Bloc countries accumulated vast amounts of foreign debt, could not repay, and fell into bankruptcy.

As an oil-producing country, Romania was in a somewhat different situation. Ceauşescu hoped to profit from the oil crisis by building a huge oil refining industry. As usual, he opted for grandiose plans to make Romania Europe's leading oil refining country. He borrowed $13 billion from the West for the investment. Slow and inefficient work led to disaster. Oil prices started dropping in the 1980s and Romania was unable to repay the loans. Unlike Poland and Bulgaria, which asked for a rescheduling of their loans, Ceaușescu decided to impose the world's harshest austerity measures to repay the debt. These measures were unprecedented: homes were unheated during cold winters and dark at night. Families were allotted one electric bulb for their homes and were given replacement for faulty bulbs only if they turned in the old ones. Cities and streets were dark. In 1985, Romania's electricity consumption dropped to 20 percent of its 1979 levels. Shops were emptied of their goods, and almost nothing was made available for consumers. Romania's per capita GDP, only 28 percent the West European average in 1973, declined to 23 percent by 1989—one of the lowest in East Central Europe. The region's average that year was 37 percent of Western Europe's.

Some communist regimes like Hungary and later Poland turned to market reforms. The new Soviet leadership under Mikhail Gorbachev also introduced reforms, *Glasnost* and *Perestroika*, in the second half of the 1980s, and tried to push recalcitrant Bloc countries to reform. Ceaușescu resisted all pressure to do so. He hoped that his demagogic rhetoric of national independence would work again. In early 1989, *România Liberă* published a semi-official article underscoring his firm resistance:

> It is the specific merit of the Romanian Communist Party . . . to have struggled decades ago against the dogmatic views of a "common pattern". . . for building socialism. As there are no patterns for building the new society, there can be no compulsory pattern or recipes for improving socialist construction . . . any tendencies to pose as "judges" or "teachers" that teach others . . . is absolutely inadmissible.[11]

Reforms either did not take place at all in certain Soviet Bloc countries, or, when they did, were too little and too late to do any good. The Soviet Bloc countries were unable to cope with the crisis and began collapsing in 1989. First to fall was Poland in the summer of that year, when the opposition Solidarity movement formed the region's first anti-communist government. Hungary's reform communist leadership had already resolved to hold free elections in early 1990.

Ceauşescu sought to stop the unstoppable. This time, quite desperately and contrary to his 1968 stance, he proposed a joint intervention in Poland to the Soviet leaders. On August 19, 1989, *Gazeta Wyborcza* reported that Ceauşescu suggested to Gorbachev a "united action of the members of the Warsaw Pact against Solidarity's moves to take over the government in Poland."[12] This time, however, intervention was rejected.

Intoxicated by the unique cult of personality he had cultivated and enjoyed for years, Ceauşescu was arrogantly convinced that he could cope with all of Romania's problems. By 1989 the ruthless austerity restrictions had indeed worked for Romania, as it was the only Soviet Bloc country that successfully repaid its debt. The restrictions could finally be lifted, but nevertheless neither Ceauşescu nor his regime would survive the year. A revolt broke out in Timişoara, a city near the Hungarian border with a mixed population. Large crowds protested the arrest of a highly critical Hungarian priest. To quell the revolt, the *Securitate* killed more than hundred people—shocking the country. In the midst of the unrest, an over-confident Ceauşescu flew to Iran for a state visit, but was forced to return home when the rebellion continued.

Still defiant and self-assured, Ceauşescu convened a mass rally in the center of Bucharest on December 21, 1989, and addressed the crowd from the balcony of the Central Committee building. He blamed a fascist-anti-Romanian (i.e. Hungarian) conspiracy for the riots. He reasoned that anti-Hungarian nationalist rhetoric would work, as it had so many times before. This time, however, the desperate masses were not appeased. As the entire country watched in astonishment on state television, a major riot erupted in the square, forcing a shocked Ceauşescu to stop his speech and flee the balcony. Armed battles engulfed Bucharest, with the army joining the uprising against the regime. The Ceauşescus tried to make a Hollywood-type escape from the capital by helicopter and then a car, but they were quickly captured. Tried by a hastily convened military tribunal and sentenced to death, both Nicolae and his wife Elena Ceauşescu were immediately executed on Christmas Day of 1989. The old believer communist demagogue died singing the Communist International. The least capable of demagogues had enjoyed fleeting success but came to an ugly end.

Endnotes

1 The purge of Ana Pauker is brilliantly analyzed by Robert Levy. See Robert Levy, *Ana Pauker: The Rise and Fall of a Jewish Communist* (Berkeley: University of California Press, 2001).

2 Nicolae Ceaușescu, "Report of the Central Committee of the Romanian Communist Party on the Activity of the Party in the period between the Eight Congress and the Ninth Congress of the Romanian Communist Party, July 19, 1965," in Nicolae Ceaușescu, *Romania on the Way of Completing Socialist Construction: Reports, Speeches, Articles July 1965–September 1966*, vol. 1 (Bucharest: Meridiane Publishing House, 1969), 67.

3 Ibid., vol. 1, 9–12; Ibid., vol. 2, 34, 149.

4 Ceaușescu's reproduction policy is dramatically presented by Gail Kligman, *The Politics of Duplicity: Controlling Reproduction in Ceausescu's Romania* (Berkeley: University of California Press, 1998).

5 Speech delivered at the festive meeting held on the occasion of the 45th anniversary of the foundation of the Romanian Communist Party, May 7, 1966, in Ceaușescu, *Romania on the Way of Completing Socialist Construction*, 355–57.

6 Ibid., 361.

7 Nicolae Ceaușescu, *Romania: Achievements and Prospects: Reports, Speeches, Articles, July 1965–February 1969* (Bucharest: Meridiane Publisher, 1969), 659–61.

8 Ibid., 663–66.

9 "Minutes of the conversation between Nicolae Ceaușescu and Mao Zedong in Beijing on June 3, 1971," Woodrow Wilson International Center for Scholars Digital Archive, https://digitalarchive.wilsoncenter.org/document/117763, accessed July 24, 2018.

10 Nixon's Remarks on Arrival at Bucharest, Romania, August 2, 1969, *The American Presidency Project*, https://www.presidency.ucsb.edu/documents/remarks-arrival-bucharest-romania-0, accessed March 19, 2019.

11 *România Liberă*, January 17, 1989.

12 *Gazeta Wyborcza*, September 29, 1989.

CHAPTER 7

Two contemporary French demagogues: *Le Diable* and *La Fille du Diable*,[1] Jean-Marie and Marine Le Pen

France's postwar success, prosperity, and stability

France experienced one of its most successful periods in the quarter-century after World War II. It was hardly a breeding ground for demagogues during that time. The country was one of the main recipients of American aid from the Marshall Plan—receiving roughly a fifth of the funds earmarked for 16 countries. Like several other West European countries, France reorganized and modernized its economy during the postwar period. It developed a well-functioning mixed economy, with private and state-owned sectors working together in a free market system. The preamble of the 1946 French Constitution declared: "All property and all enterprises . . . shall have the character of a national public service, or a monopoly in fact must become the property of the community."[2] The postwar nationalization of the Bank of France, insurance, electric, and gas industries, air travel, eighteen mining and several large industrial companies, including the Renault car company, made up a fifth of France's national income.

France was also the first to introduce a new form of non-mandatory planning, involving state financing in a free market system, and generated several Four-year Plans. The first Plan of 1946–1950 (later expanded to 1952) concentrated on eight sectors, including energy and steel production, and carried out significant modernization. Although planning was not compulsory, the state easily met its targets. The third plan, for example, called for an increase of construction by 60 percent, industrial output by 30 percent, and agriculture by 20 percent. The country not only met but exceeded most of its original targets.

France's economic plans were put together by the *Comités de Modernisation*, with the participation of thousands of industrial managers. The planners and functionaries of the country's *Commissariat du Plan*, headed by Jean Monnet, "come from the same social background; they attended the same schools. . . . Indeed, to an alarming extent, they were the same people [as ranking civil servants and managers of big business]."[3] Planning was the vehicle of reconstruction and modernization leading to "a twentieth century industrial revolution in France."[4] The country came out with four Four-year Plans by the late 1960s, with each plan targeting the modernization and competitiveness of certain sectors. The second plan launched an ambitious nuclear power program and built France's first nuclear power station in 1956. Ultimately, nuclear power would uniquely comprise 78 percent of the country's electrical energy production. Its energy consumption increased by 250 percent between 1950 and 1970, while the proportion of coal in energy production dropped from 74 to 17 percent. Annual labor productivity in agriculture and industry increased by 6 percent and over 5 percent respectively in those decades. France also jointly developed the highly successful Airbus program in the late 1960s.

Acceding to an American plan, France was also the initiator of European integration beginning in the early 1950s. Its economy greatly expanded on the common market—leading to almost full employment and significantly increased living standards. Consumerism proliferated, and a newly emergent welfare state provided social security, free education, and health services for every French citizen. A similarly impressive expansion could be seen in housing. Between 1950 and 1970, more than a quarter of all investments went to the housing sector. As a consequence, modern housing mushroomed markedly: in 1960, only a quarter of French residences had indoor bathrooms and lavatories; by the early 1970s, two-thirds of them did. In the early 1950s, only one in five French households was in possession of a car; by 1962, 60 percent of them did. In the mid-1950s, only 8 percent of French households owned refrigerators and washing machines; by 1972, 60–80 percent did.[5]

The great change after the late 1960s

The first quarter of a century after World War II, therefore, was a time of prosperity and stability. All of this, however, changed dramatically at the turn of the 1960s and 1970s. The student revolution in May 1968 coincided with the outbreak of staggering general strikes (with the participation of 11 million workers) and the occupation of universities and factories throughout the country—all of which paralyzed the entire economy. The country was on the threshold of revolution and civil war. The situation deteriorated to such an extent that President Charles de Gaulle secretly left the country for a short time. A few years later, the 1973 oil crisis ended the postwar prosperity in Europe. The turmoil of the late 1960s and early 1970s vividly transformed France's political scene. This was the time when a very provocative demagogue first appeared.

Jean-Marie Le Pen and his background

Born in 1928 to a family of fishermen in La Trinité-sur-Mer in Brittany, Jean-Marie Le Pen lost his father at the age of 14 and quickly turned to extremism. After the war, he studied law and wrote a dissertation on the French anarchist movement, but he never finished his studies. He was drawn to extreme right-wing ideologies and movements, and became the head of a right-wing student union in Toulouse that attacked communists. In 1951, however, he was expelled from the organization. He joined the Foreign Legion in 1954 and fought in the French colonial war in Indochina. He was then sent to Egypt in 1956, and served in Algeria in 1957.

One can discern Le Pen's early indoctrination in far-right ideologies from his own statements. As a young man, Le Pen openly expressed admiration for the leaders of the Vichy regime and for early fascist and anti-Semitic writers:

> Until 1945, I kept a photo of Marshal Pétain and retained my admiration for him. Nor did I renounce the authors of my youth just because they were in prison like Maurras, or among the executed, like Robert Brasillach.[6]

In his later years, he retained his admiration for dictators and for the "order" they kept. In addition to Hitler and Mussolini, he often praised Franco, Pinochet, Perón, Salazar, and Saddam Hussein. Moreover, he expressed understanding of young people's emulation of "martyred" Nazi SS soldiers:

> Young people need order and purity. At a time when atheism has made formidable progress, there is a resurgence of the need for a moral order. . . . From this perspective the SS with its uniform is like a kind of priest with his cassock. Although he disappeared in the apocalypse of fire, bombs, and blood, Hitler's soldier has become a martyr for these young people looking for purity, even if it is the purity of evil.[7]

Place in rightwing populism

Small wonder, then, that, at the age of 28, Le Pen joined Pierre Poujade's *Union de Défense des Commerçants et Artisans* (UDCA; Defense Union of Shopkeepers and Craftsmen). Poujadisme (Poujadism) was a right-wing populist movement in postwar France that displayed elements of neo-fascism and opposed industrialization, big business, urbanization, and American-style modernization, which it saw as a threat to France's identity as a rural country comprising small businesses. UDCA pushed for keeping France's colonies and was strongly anti-Semitic. Le Pen became the Parliament's youngest member on the Poujadist list in 1956, but broke with Poujade two years later. He then joined the *Centre National des Indépendants et Paysans*, a liberal organization headed by Antoine Pinay that opposed economic interventionism and *dirigisme*. Nevertheless, Le Pen held firm to all the ideas of Poujadism: he demanded the rehabilitation of Nazi collaborators and had nothing but disdain for de Gaulle ("It was much easier to resist in London than to resist in France"). He always relished his role in the opposition as an election spoiler and master provocateur. An unmitigated bully, he regularly got in fistfights during childhood and was convicted on several occasions for assault as an adult. Even when he was nearly seventy, he was prosecuted for physically assaulting Annette Peulvast-Bergeal, a socialist candidate for the European Parliament. He lauded the use of violence or any other method against his political enemies. In an interview on the Algerian war with the journal *Combat* in November 1962, he proudly declared:

> I have nothing to hide. I tortured because it was necessary to do it. [Against Algerian terrorism] there is no place for the rules of classic warfare, still less for those of civilian legality. If it is necessary to use violence . . . if it is necessary to torture one man to save a hundred, torture is thus inevitable . . . and just.[8]

Leader of nationalist far-right

In the late 1960s, Le Pen's primary ambition was to unify all extreme right-wing groups and movements. "Everything that is national," he quipped, "is ours." In addition to the small far-right organizations *Occident*, *Jeune Révolution*, *Group Union Droit*, and *Fédération d'Action Nationale et Européenne*, he set his sights on the neo-fascist *Ordre Nouveau* (New Order), established in 1969 and containing more than 3,000 mostly young members in 1972.

In October 1972, during France's turbulent crisis, Jean-Marie Le Pen established his own party, the *Front National*. At his side from the beginning were Pierre Bousquet, a former member of the Waffen SS, Jacques Bompard, a former member of the terrorist-colonialist OAS (*Organisation de l'armée secrète*), and Roland Gaucher, a Nazi collaborator and former member of the fascist RNP (*Rassemblement National Populaire*) during the years of the Vichy regime. For the 1973 national elections, the Front National nominated 104 candidates to the National Assembly, a third of them were leaders or members of the Ordre Nouveau. Although the neo-fascists were extremely influential and active in the Front, Le Pen skillfully rid the party of his political rivals and monopolized the leadership. He was able to accomplish this within a year, when he evicted Ordre Nouveau from the Front. His intention was to lead a right-wing but politically more acceptable party.

> For almost one hundred years in France, there was no political party which dared claim to be Right, until 1972, when the National Front decided to define itself as the national, popular and social, right . . . .[9]
>
> [This means] first and above all . . . a defensive reaction: refusing the

left, its system, its objectives and its program . . . [and attaching the party] to traditional values . . . and to our national culture . . . a taste for order, authority, hierarchy . . . admiration for glory.[10]

Authoritarian racist as defender of the nation?

Jean-Marie Le Pen was an extreme far-Right populist promoting a mixed ideological agenda that negated basic Enlightenment principles such as égalité and abrogated the French Revolution's "crusade against the cross." His program espoused both overt and implicit anti-Semitism and neo-fascism, and it always openly heralded racism, xenophobia, and extreme nationalism. As a former soldier who fought in defense of the French colonies, he linked France's surrender of "French Algeria" to the subsequent Arab "invasion" and "colonization" of the country. He liked to remind people that he had predicted that losing French Algeria would invariably lead to the rise of an "Algerian France."[11]

Le Pen was a charismatic orator who employed folksy language and humor, who was always on the attack, and who was rife with anti-establishment demagoguery. All this attracted a certain element of French society. He delighted in creating scandals, and his followers delighted in watching him doing it. Le Pen ran the Front National as an autocratic leader. As an insider described, "The Political Bureau [of the Front] was the court of King Jean-Marie I. Around him, courtiers, friends, and the faithful listened. No one confronted the King under penalty of triggering a frightful rage . . . that the target wanted to disappear under his chair, while all around was a deathly silence."[12] The Front indeed cultivated the *Führerprinzip*, equating party and program with the supreme leader, and requiring absolute obedience to the party leadership. The Front National carried out a forced unity of the myriad of heterogeneous far-right factions inside the party. Le Pen tolerated not even a modicum of competition within the party. When his second-in-command, Bruno Mégret, rose in prominence in the party ranks, Le Pen waged a "deMégretisation" campaign in the party and expelled Mégret and his closest associates. "This period of crisis is widely remembered by party workers . . . as one in which Le Pen's megalomania was unsurpassed."[13]

Nationalism was the core of Le Pen's program. In one of his first speeches in Parliament as a Front National representative, he declared:

> The common designation of our movement . . . [is] the idea of nation. . . . There are Communists, Socialists and liberals, but we are before all nationalists. . . . The interests of France and the French are of premier significance. French people first![14]

He often employed heated rhetoric to define the eternal nation:

> [France] is the land of our fathers, the soil cultivated and defended throughout the centuries; the country fashioned in the landscape, the cities, the language, the history . . . fertilized by their sweat and blood. . . . The people of France are the heirs to nearly two-thousand million human beings. . . . France is not only people of the moment, but also those of yesterday who are now dead, and those of tomorrow who are still to be born.[15]

He was always careful to use the most poignant theatrics at Front National meetings, including the "use of the most sophisticated media and lighting techniques . . . , [with] attention paid to creating a sense of privileged community . . . a sense of togetherness, of shared destiny . . . of like-minded people around an exceptional leader."[16]

Le Pen's central message, and the *leitmotif* of his program and rhetoric, was the *defense of an endangered nation*. He firmly insisted that this required the strengthening of French identity and national unity. One of the Front's publications was named *Identité*:

> In choosing the title *Identité* . . . [we] wanted to get to the heart of the problem of our future. What will be tomorrow if by reason of the demographic, social and political changes of our century, we are incapable of defining ourselves?[17]

> Today, the defense of sectoral interest fragments national solidarity and . . . the *unity* of our country.[18]

> Without national unity there no longer is a homeland![19]

Le Pen's often hysterical notions of an *endangered nation* focused on external threats from the Soviet Union and its communist agents in France. It also focused on the demographic explosion within the Third

World that led to mounting immigration to France, especially from its former colonies. This latter factor was exacerbated, he argued, by France's demographic decline. And these dangers were combined with a pronounced cultural threat as well. In Le Pen's thinking, Americanization undermined traditional French values.

He was never shy to specifically name the "enemies" who posed such frightening dangers to France. In a typical populist way, the main enemies were the treacherous establishment parties and secret Jewish influences that spread cosmopolitanism (or *mondialism*) throughout the country. Somewhat later, beginning in the early 1990s (after the Treaty of Maastricht), he would add a dire new enemy: the European Union. Jean-Marie Le Pen prided himself as a non-politician, as the representative of the *petit homme*, the little men of France. Running for president, he presented himself in the following way:

> As candidate to the post of President of the Republic, I am nothing more than a French citizen like any of you. War orphan, state-funded pupil, student activist, combat officer, businessman, family man . . . I know your fear, your problems, your worries, your distress and your hopes because I have felt, and continue to feel them.[20]

At the same time, he boldly described himself as the savior of the nation who must heroically act at this eleventh hour:

> [T]he fate of our country will be decided in the years between now and the Millennium. . . . This is why I am engaged in a battle for our future: the people of France must be able to express their will with all firmness and freedom.[21]

He would love to brag that he was the present-day embodiment of Joan of Arc, and the Front, in the early 1980s, propagated a cult of Joan of Arc as a nationalist heroine. Le Pen proclaimed in 1998 that *Joan and he* shared the same objectives: the strengthening of French identity and fighting against foreign enemies. He brashly affirmed that he was following in her footsteps in fighting for the liberty of France. In 1986, the Front's primary message was *Le Pen – Joan of Arc – The Same Battle.*

Open and coded anti-Semitism

For Le Pen, anti-Semitism was a fundamental part of defending the nation. He embraced anti-Semitism early in life, imbibing the Jews-hatred of old-time anti-Semites from the interwar period. However, any open anti-Semitic sentiment was considered taboo after Auschwitz, as it was closely connected to Europe's and France's shameful collaboration with Hitler in the Holocaust. Le Pen thus ardently denied being anti-Semitic:

> I have said it several times. . . . If anti-Semitism consists of persecution of Jews because of their religion or their race, I am certainly not an anti-Semite. But I don't believe I am obliged to like the Veil law [proposed by a Jewish member of the Parliament on abortion], to admire Chagall's paintings, or to approve Mendès-France politics.[22]

In a speech at a Front National festival in the fall of 1985, he singled out by name a number of journalists with clear Jewish names who had criticized him (J-F. Kahn, J. Daniel, I. Levai, J-P. Elkabbach), denouncing them as "lying anti-France snakes of calumny and hate" without explicitly noting that they were all Jewish. He coded his message by mentioning that some had the "excuse of only recently learning French."[23]

A member of the Political Bureau of the Front National precisely articulated Le Pen's core belief of the Jews' secret dominance of France and their "secret decision-making oligarchy" in French establishment politics:

> [They are working in] secret committees consisting of men who carefully avoid presenting themselves in elections. . . . The connection of these high civil servants with the Masons, or B'nai B'rith and CRIF[24] [the latter two are Jewish organizations] is crucial. . . . The façade of democracy hides the true power of secret committees . . . [and the] oligarchy.[25]

On one occasion, Le Pen openly accused President Chirac of being on the payroll of Jewish organizations. Le Pen's anti-Semitism, however, always created costly scandals and led him to prefer the use of coded language. His favorite code words were *cosmopolitanism*, or *cosmopol-*

itan oligarchy, or (even more to his liking) *mondialism*, as well as *Masonic* (Free Mason), behind the scenes *lobbies' rule*, and the *politico-media class*. When he denounced conspiracies behind the scenes of lobbies and oligarchs, when he attacked the political establishment of "obeying orders," and when he condemned the forces that are undermining national identity and advocating multiculturalism, he was using code words that were clearly understood by his audience.

To be sure, Le Pen at times explicitly linked these code words to Jews. In 1977 he openly affirmed:

> Everybody has a right to a country, and each people must have a nation, but that doesn't imply the takeover of French politics by lobbies. Israel must exist, not the Jewish lobby. The large number of Jews in the areas of information or politics implies a certain pressure of a cosmopolitan tendency. . . . These people always oppose nationalism and the idea of nation. Their large number and their common attitude explain many things. It's up to the law to reduce and eliminate these abnormal oligarchies.[26]

Similarly, in an August 1989 interview for *Présent*, he discarded his typical coded language when he said:

> Freemasons . . . and the . . . Jewish International play a not unimportant role in the creation of antinational spirit. I will say that it is almost natural that those forces . . . collide with national interests. But it is necessary to be careful when one says that the Freemasons and the Jewish International play a role.[27]

In the two-page preamble of the Front National's election platform in 1993, he pointedly proclaimed that the political establishment has, "in a servile fashion, aligned itself with external foreign powers and internal lobbies, and, with the complicity of media power under orders, systematically gagged those who tried to speak the truth."[28] Le Pen explicitly expressed similar views to his close friends. At a meeting of the Front National's Political Bureau in May 1988, he angrily noted:

> I have a copy of a letter that Théo Klein, the President of CRIF [*Conseil Représentatif des Institutions juives de France*], addressed to Jacques Toubon [Secretary General of the Gaullist *Rassemblement pour la Ré-*

publique or RPR]. And do you know what he asked him? . . . The Boss of the CRIF clearly stated that the RPR would not benefit from any support from the Jews if it did not erect a complete roadblock against the National Front.[29]

At a subsequent press conference, he openly declared:

In any case, the PRP and UDF [*Union pour la Démocratie Française*] are only obeying orders. [Who gives these orders? – a journalist asked] The lobbies. . . . If you had read the letter that Mr. Klein sent to . . . the RPR! Even I wouldn't have spoken to my servants that way.[30]

A favorite talking-point of Le Pen that he repeatedly pontificated on (in 1987, 1997, 2009, and on other occasions) was diminishing the Holocaust. The gas chambers may have existed, he conceded, but "I believe that it was just a detail of the history of World War II. If you take a 1,000 page book on World War II, the concentration camps take up 2 pages and the gas chambers 10 to 15 lines."[31] Le Pen was convicted six times for racism and Holocaust denial.[32] At one of his trials in 1992, the Court of Appeal in Chambéry concluded: "Mr. Le Pen does not hide his resentment towards Jews. . . . He never hesitates to speak of a Judeo-Masonic plot, inciting therefore anti-Semitism."[33]

One might wonder why he would risk falling into such serious political trouble, all of which earned him the designation of being the "devil of France," a hated man among the majority of French voters. Perhaps the best explanation may be found in his character. Although he ran for the presidency several times, Jean-Marie Le Pen was never much interested in attaining power. He much more preferred to be an aggressive opponent of power. Still, he was quick to announce his candidacy for president only two years after establishing the Front National, but was able to win only 0.74 percent of the votes in that election. In 1981, he could not even get the required 500 signatures from notabilities to enable him to run again. However, he would repeatedly run for the presidency in 1988, 1995, 2002, and 2007. He won nearly 17 percent of the votes in the first round of the 2002 elections, and ran against Chirac in the second round. At that time the entire Right and Left united against "the devil of the Republic" and gave Chirac 82 percent of the vote.

Against immigration—and for conservative values

Although anti-Semitism was always present in his demagoguery, it was more of an automatic reflex than the central issue for Le Pen. Even in Nazi terms, the so-called "Jewish question" did not exist in postwar France. Even considering the French North-African (Moroccan and Algerian) Jewish immigration to France in the 1950s and 1960s, the country could claim only 550,000 Jewish citizens out of total population of 64.5 million inhabitants—amounting to less than one percent.

In the early part of Le Pen's political career, anti-communism and hostility to the Soviet Union were at the forefront of his views. This was still the core issue of his 1974 election campaign, one in which he incessantly lamented the Soviet danger and the communist subversion in the country. Nevertheless, his demagoguery was always characterized by xenophobic, racist, and reactionary nationalism. This fact guaranteed that he would invariably focus on immigration. As early as the late 1970s, xenophobic anti-immigration policy would gradually form the nucleus of the Front's program and Le Pen's demagoguery.

In a March 1978 article, Le Pen asserted that "for months the National Front has mounted a very active campaign against immigration, and it has based its electoral campaign on this problem."[34] This campaign would in time develop into an elaborate program based on the basic tenet that immigrants are the source of every problem, let it be AIDS or unemployment, and aggravate insecurity in the country through their criminal activity that ranges from petty crimes to drug trade, and includes even "attacks on old women."[35] But the threat, in Le Pen's view, was ultimately existential. Proclaiming that France is on the verge a civil war, he warned that

> The influx of immigrant families means the demographic submersion of France and the substitution of a Third World population. . . . Let's not fool ourselves: the very existence of the French people is at stake.[36]

The Front's election posters frivolously equated the number of unemployed to the number of immigrants: "4 million immigrants = 4 million unemployed." They falsely claimed that state expenditures on immigrants were equal to the entire amount French citizens pay in payroll taxes. Le

Pen called for an end to immigration and for deporting millions of immigrants. His fiery rhetoric quite intentionally incited hatred of immigrants: "Tomorrow the immigrants will move in with you, eat your soup and sleep with your wife, with your daughter or your son."[37] Using folksy jokes, Le Pen compared immigration to a visit of the mother-in-law:

> When we invite our mother-in-law to stay, we are very happy the first week, a little less the second week, even less the third, and at the end of the fourth we say: It is her or me. It is a little similar with immigrants.[38]

Attacking a new law granting citizenship within six months, "The Front National says NO to immigration-colonization. . . . With Jean-Marie Le Pen and the Front National, defend French France!"[39] The Front also sought to change the immigration law by replacing the traditional *jus soli* (the territorial concept of citizenship) by *jus sanguinis* (the blood related right for citizenship). Le Pen called for changing the law retroactively and stripping French citizenship from all post-1974 immigrants. He professed to accept anyone who completely assimilated into French society, all immigrants, including French Jews, must renounce their origins:

> If you are loyal to France, if you love it, if you adopt its laws, morals, language, way of thinking . . . if you integrate yourself completely, we will not refuse you. . . . But if you are loyal to your roots . . . and you are just pretending to live under our laws, with your own morals and culture . . . it is better that you return home because otherwise it could all end very badly.[40]

This anti-immigration advocacy was organically combined with a cult of conservative French values. For Le Pen, "real France" was traditional France—the France of "peasants-fishermen: my absolute national priority." The party program, *Agriculteurs pour le Front National*, avowed:

> For the Front national and Jean-Marine Le Pen. . . . French agriculture and peasants have an important future. . . . The rural world defends our traditional values. The peasant world has an equal role to play at the heart of our society. . . . The Front National counts on the farming world to assure the serenity for values.[41]

In Le Pen's mind, genuine "French values" were fundamentally connected to the Catholic Church. Christianity was emphasized as the basis of French identity. The implication was that non-Christians—Jews and Muslims—were the cause of the oft-lamented "moral decline" of the country. For Le Pen, French values necessarily included family values and the cult of large families, the Front employed a slogan of the Vichy regime: "Work, Family, Country!"

Jean-Marie Le Pen called for a demographic resurgence and vehemently opposed abortion, which, the party platform insisted, kills a third of all "infants waiting to be born."[42] "One of the gravest menaces facing France . . . is *dénatalité*. . . . I want to say to the young girls and young women of France that they hold the destiny of the country in their hands."[43]

When abortion was legalized during the presidency of Valéry Giscard d'Estaing (initiated by the Jewish Health Minister Simone Veil), Le Pen angrily shouted that "Killing the child is killing France" and spoke of an "anti-French genocide."[44]

Hand in hand with his demographic policies, Le Pen held conservative views on the role of women in society and suggested that women's foremost patriotic task was to take care of their children at home:

> The egalitarian movement, which consists in leveling out ages, sexes and peoples . . . masks reality, which is fundamentally inegalitarian. . . . There are inequalities which are just and equalities which are unjust. We are for justice and not for equality.[45]
>
> Official speeches have . . . tried to devalue the role of the mother and to abolish all differences in the functions of men and women. This utopian attitude denies biological and cultural reality which gives women a special responsibility in procreation and in the education of children.[46]

Le Pen and the Front proposed a maternal salary, equivalent to the *Salaire minimum interprofessionel de croissance*, for mothers of large French families. The Front's Lyon section demanded a doubling of the maternity allowance for mothers with a second child. As with every aspect of his program, these genuine conservative pro-natal positions went hand in hand with xenophobic anti-immigration rhetoric. Le Pen spoke of the "hegemony deriving from the demographic explosion of the Third

World and in particular in the Arab-Islamic world, which currently is penetrating our country and progressively colonizing it."[47]

The Front's mouthpiece warned of "14 million Muslims occupy[ing] our country . . . it is as the same as an army of occupation."[48] Le Pen began to speak of the danger of an Islamic France:

> An Islamic France could exist instead of a French, Christian and Western France. . . . The peace of the world is menaced by the Third World and Islamic demographic explosion. . . . The pro-immigration lobbies collaborating with Islam . . . [are] destroying our identity. . . . Pacific coexistence between Europe and Islam is impossible.[49]

He also viciously attacked the establishment parties, maintaining that they are betraying France and the interests of the French people and are responsible for all that is increasingly threatening France: "There sometimes emerge in the history of societies decadent elites, oligarchies who are far removed from the people."[50] Le Pen's rebellion against the political establishment at times coincided with violent acts. In October 1987, Le Pen and several other Front representatives "heaped insult on the other deputies and deluged the president of the chamber. . . . For ten hours during that night and early morning, there was pandemonium in the National Assembly." Le Pen defended their actions by affirming: "In the face of the political class which betrays the will of the people, the National Front puts itself forward as the defender of the interests of the French people."[51]

Appealing to the xenophobic-nationalism of certain segments of French society, Jean-Marie Le Pen's populist demagoguery won him increasing support in various parts of France. The core of his support came from the southern and western agricultural and wine-growing regions of the country. A part of the workers and small-business owners also supported the Front. His base was once called the "static France," which proved to be the most fertile soil for Le Pen. He also attracted a relatively large number of former communist and socialist working-class voters. During the 1995 presidential elections, he won 27 percent of the workers' votes, more than any other candidate.

Against the European Union

With his anti-establishment and anti-global populist nationalism, Le Pen invariably turned against the European Union. Especially after the Maastricht Treaty (1992), he began to attack the EU as inimical to the interests of the French nation. First and foremost, it was *mondialiste* and endangered France's national borders. The European Community, he argued, is "one of the keys of a true *mondialiste* and internationalist plot. . . . The promoters of Maastricht make no mystery of the hatred toward the nation . . . [and] to national values."[52]

The party's newsletter fervently declared that, "Our frontiers have disappeared. . . . The Schengen convention deprives our country of one of the essential aspects of sovereignty: the control of frontiers. [Schengen opened the door to a] Europe of immigration, of drugs and of organized crime."[53]

Against the federalization or supranationalization trend of the European Union, Le Pen returned to de Gaulle's *Europe des États* (Europe of Nations), or the notion of a confederated Europe. From that time on, similarly to other populists in Europe, hostility to the European Union remained the primary feature of Le Pen's and the Front National's demagoguery.

End of his career

Jean-Marie Le Pen's skillful political maneuvering and demagoguery gradually distanced the Front National from neo-fascism and made the party into a more or less ordinary turn of the millennium populist party.[54] At the age of 83 in 2011, he decided to retire from the daily management of the Front National but vowed to remain its spiritual leader as Honorary President. He passed the baton over to his youngest daughter, Marine, who was already a member of the party leadership. At the helm, Marine Le Pen continued full speed ahead her father's nationalist, anti-immigration, anti-establishment, and anti-European Union ideology.

Marine Le Pen—daughter of her father

Marine Le Pen, born in the troubled year of 1968, grew up in a transformed country. She was Jean-Marie's third and youngest daughter, but really the daughter of the Front National. The Front became her everyday environment and her all-consuming interest; it became her life. Graduating Law School, she worked as a lawyer for six years and, strangely enough, at times defended illegal immigrants. But aside from that, she worked in and lived for the Front National. She was eight years old when a bomb exploded in Le Pens' house in a botched assassination attempt. This experience, she would later relate, influenced her entire life. "Our childhood was marked by a sense of injustice concerning our father. . . . That forged my character and it also strengthened me."[55]

In 1986, she joined the party at the age of eighteen. In 2000, she became a member of the party's Executive Committee and was elected its vice-president in 2003. She married in 1995, divorced in 2000, married again in 2002, and divorced a second time in 2006. Both of her former husbands were Front National functionaries. Since 2009 she has been involved with Secretary General of the Front National and her vice-president. The Front appears to be her entire family.

Marine Le Pen was devoted to her father and worked closely with him until his retirement in 2011. Her real story now began. In 2010–11, she launched an intense campaign to be elected her father's successor and won 68 percent of the members' votes. Marine continued where her father left off. In one of her striking speeches during the campaign, she compared Muslims taking over certain streets to pray outdoors in predominately Muslim neighborhoods to the Nazi occupation of France. She offered nothing but a repetition of her father's earlier comparisons of Muslim crowds in parts of certain cities with foreign occupation.

Emerging from her father's shadow

From her father, Marine Le Pen inherited the skill of delivering penetrating speeches and excelling as a "media phenomenon." She regularly drew millions of viewers when she appeared on television panels and debates. But she has turned out to be a much shrewder tactician than her father ever was. She shies from scandals and refrains from making provocative statements so as not to denigrate the Front National as a serious, established third party with a real potential of attaining power. Although she consistently shared her father's views during the quarter-century she worked at his side, she today skillfully distances herself from his notorious extremism and works as a moderating force within the party. She renounced the party's previous anti-Semitism, which had delegitimized it in post-Auschwitz Europe, and declared that the Holocaust was the "height of barbarism." While she retained the rudiments of the Front's ideology, and allowed certain extremists (like the *Bloc identitaire* of Philippe Vardon, a close follower of Jean-Marie Le Pen) to remain a force within the party, she banned skin-heads from the Front's meetings and purged those far-Right party leaders (such as the rabid anti-Semite Yvan Benedetti and the Nazi-admirer Alexandre Gabriac) who jeopardized her ambitious plans. When, in April 2011, her father repeated his favorite anti-Semitic remark that the gas chambers were an unimportant detail of the war, and when he called on France to get along with Russia in order to "save the white world," the hardnosed, steely-gazed Marine Le Pen did not hesitate to suspend his party membership and even to remove him as the party's Honorary Chairman, so as to "steer [the Front] away from the overt racism and anti-Semitism of its past."[56]

Marine Le Pen, the *Guardian* commented, "made an unprecedented televised appeal to her aging father, Jean-Marie, to quit politics and fall on his own sword following his inflammatory comments belittling the Holocaust and hailing France's Nazi-collaborationist Vichy regime." The news was shocking because "the close-knit yet rather dysfunctional blonde clan . . . runs the Front National as a family business and until recently all lived together in a grandiose, historic manor[57] perched on a hill."[58]

Marine Le Pen explained her harsh response by declaring: "Jean-Marie Le Pen has entered on a downward spiral heading to . . . political suicide."[59] Marion Maréchal-Le Pen, Jean-Marie's granddaughter and a rising new star in the Front (and a blond one at that), who was elected to Parliament at the young age of 22, also sided with her aunt in their family feud. The *Guardian* noted:

There is a crucial difference between the gruff former paratrooper Jean-Marie and his public relations-savvy daughter who took over the party in 2011. Le Pen senior . . . , nostalgic for colonial Algeria and Vichy, unapologetic in his belief in the "inequality of the races" and who would later be convicted more than 15 times for hate-speech and contesting crimes against humanity, has always been an outsider. Delighted to be detested, proud to be subject of a protest vote, he never wanted power. Marine Le Pen very much wants power, and her ambitions go right to the presidency.[60]

"Dédiabolisation" of the Front National

Once renown as *la peste blonde* (echoing the la *peste noire* or the Black Death and the *la peste brune* or the Nazi menace*)*, Marine Le Pen has begun a systematic "repackaging," or as *The Economist* put it, "a self-conscious process of *dédiabolisation* (decontamination or de-demonization)" of the Front National. Her father had emphasized that all collaborationist Pétainists, all defenders of French Algeria, and all diehard right-wingers had a place in the Front. He had also maintained that "the Jews conspired to rule the world." His daughter sought to free herself from such harmful opinions. Comparing father with daughter, the French political scientist Michel Winock observed: "whereas Jean-Marie was anti-abortion, socially conservative, and a staunch advocate of small government, Marine is pro-choice, gay-friendly, and economically interventionist, with a populist streak." For her, notes Winock, "Islam now represents the enemy, when it used to be the Jews for Daddy's radical right."[61]

As she acknowledged in an interview, "I have damage to repair, damage between the French people and the National Front." The *New York Times* in 2011 (before the expelling of her father from the party) explained this statement thus: "[she] works assiduously at the fine political balancing act of remaining loyal to her father—and maintaining the support of the party's base—while distancing herself from the elder Le Pen's outrageousness."[62] Others compared her maneuvering to walking a tightrope between redeeming the party's image and jettisoning or abandoning its fundamental core. The German magazine *Spiegel*, citing her father's angry retort after his expulsion that "I am the Front National, I am at home in Front National," frankly noted, "The 47 year old [Marine Le Pen] wants to make the foreign-hating party more respectable looking to gain new voters."[63]

Indeed, at the time of her father's expulsion, Marine Le Pen had quite rationally dropped the toxic elements in the Front's program that so alienated such a vast number of people and weakened the party's standing. At the same time, she retained the key elements of extreme nationalism and xenophobia, especially its anti-Muslim, anti-immigration, and anti-European Union agenda, which were well-received in France. The unchanging nature of her political views is closely connected to her father's notions of "France First!" and his ideas on national unity, along with his populist beliefs on people and nationhood. She presents these views, however, in more acceptable ways, placing them on the continuum of French history and also exploiting deeply rooted anti-capitalist sentiments:

> I am convinced that loving the French nation and the concept that the Nation is the natural framework of political action, neither implies nor supports any confrontation with any other love or national conviction. . . . One can recognize certain will in the French people . . . to reconstruct the unity of the Nation that follows the same pattern as the one realized from Joan of Arc to Henry IV, from Richelieu to de Gaulle. We feel the will to reestablish moral, political, and economic barriers against the expression of senseless egoism and unrestrained selfishness . . . persisting against the ideology of *mondialism* and global markets; against perverse liberalism in which everything is for sale.[64]

Modern populism: anti-establishment, anti-EU

She has also continued assailing the establishment parties and their politicians, and she has repeated her father's attack against a borderless Europe within the European Union—using, however, more acceptable language:

> My single unique criterion is: love France! . . . I could not lead those who turn their back on France; those who have a post-national vision, who do not believe in the people, in democracy, and who run for the protection of Europe, America, or Germany; candidates like Juppé, Macron,

Sarko[zy], Hollande, Bayrou. . . . On the other hand, I promise you, I will lead you . . . we will move mountains, reach the highest summits. . . . Yes! Europe of Schengen is equal to Europe of thieves and fences. . . . We must reestablish national borders. . . . Schengen's Europe is also the Europe of terrorism, terrorism that endangers France more than ever.[65]

At the same time, she has embraced a new populist agenda: "She has come out with a detailed critique of capitalism and a position promoting the state as the protector of ordinary people."[66] Unlike her father, she distinguishes between "mondialisation" and "mondialisme," and does so in a much more sophisticated way. The first roughly means globalization, i.e. the continuous integration of global markets that cross national borders. She recognized that, at this new stage of development, each and every country has to adjust to and learn how to live in this environment. "Mondialisme," on the other hand, is an ideology that fundamentally denies the role of nations and nation states. In her view, this ideology posits that people are mere consumers and citizens of the world. Needless to say, Marine Le Pen doesn't think much of it: "Mondialisme is above all an ideology that permits the unlimited domination of a sacrosanct, supposedly 'self-regulating' market, which has become deified throughout the world . . . not disputable—would not you call it of divine nature?"[67]

She has, however, moderated her critique, which is based on the formerly mainstream (and thus acceptable) Keynesian analysis. She has called for regulation and maintains in typical populist fashion that only the nation state can implement it. The nation state is the only counterforce that can mitigate the power of money. The national government alone can limit and discipline the market. This market, she contends, is embodied in a form of hyper-capitalism that is dominated by finance and is disseminated everywhere, thanks to the gradual elimination of national constraints and the imposition of totally free exchange.

> With its financial, but also ideological, strength . . . , this hyper-capitalism can easily attract the enthusiastic support of the elites that constitute part of it and are compensated by it.

In a classically populist way, she has linked her critique of self-regulating, over-financialized global capitalism to anti-Americanism. However, quite unlike her father, who had espoused both anti-modernization and anti-Americanism, Marine Le Pen does not reject modernization but—with reason—only extreme American deregulation. In the United States, she points out, the market has also taken over the health and education sectors, achieving not just, as the proponents of the almighty market want us to believe, increased efficiency and reduced costs, but also an erosion of quality and unequal access. At the same time, the market in the US plays a huge role, she critically notes, in important state sectors like domestic and national security (private prisons and even mercenary firms that began to operate in Iraq and Afghanistan)—a genuine "privatization" of warfare. She has underscored the "perverse effect" of over-privatization by publicizing the notorious "kids for cash" scandal, in which American judges were revealed in 2008 to have been paid by private prisons for sentencing minors to serve time in their jails.[68]

Critique of Anglo-Saxon capitalism

Her critique of today's globalized, Anglo-Saxon-type capitalism is meant to lay the groundwork for the solution she offers:

> I am deeply convinced that France and the French people, more than ever, need a strong State. State and nation are understood as inseparable entities in our country. In others, the State is considered more as an instrument of collective action. . . . This is the Anglo-Saxon conception—countries where nations are older than states. These countries accommodate very easily to a minimal State that is not expected to disturb the free play of markets. France, I believe, does not offer itself for this model. . . . [In France] it is the State that forged the nation.[69]

The conclusion of her rather sophisticated argument is ultimately no different from her father's idea of the strong "law and order" populist state, a state of the "little man":

> We are proposing a strong State, i.e. a sovereign State that also maintains order and has zero tolerance everywhere; an authentic State based on solidarity that would help the most ordinary French people, the elderly, and all those who have been forsaken by the high ranks. A protective State that would support our factories, our employment, our French workers who are vulnerable to unrestricted globalization . . . and a Europe that accelerates all of this.[70]

Against a "European Soviet Union"

One of Marine Le Pen's pet-projects, as part of her nationalist agenda that has gradually emerged at the forefront of the Front's program, is uncompromising opposition to the European Union. She regularly employs extreme demagogic rhetoric to depict the EU as an institution that strips countries of national sovereignty, serves only German interests, and is against the core interests of France.

> The EU doesn't live up to the utopia they have sold us. . . . I want to destroy the European Union, not Europe! I believe in a Europe of nation-states. I believe in Airbus and Ariane, in a European-based cooperation. But *I don't want this European Soviet Union*. . . . The EU is deeply harmful, it is an anti-democratic monster. . . . These treaties promote German interest. . . . I place the blame with our own leaders who are not defending our interests. . . . Be careful Ms. Merkel . . . [who] wants to impose her policies on others. . . . The French want to regain control of their own country.[71]

In Le Pen's estimation, the European Union is not a guarantor of European peace, but is rather a force that increases hostility among European countries. The Greeks are denounced as fraudsters, and the French ridiculed as lazy. It is just not true, she insists, that the EU has protected the peace, for Europe is engulfed in economic warfare.

Brexit and the "Spring of the European People"

In 2015 and 2016, a number of new developments significantly strengthened the position of the Front National. The results of the British referendum on leaving the European Union and a series of Islamist terrorist attacks in France have provided Marine Le Pen an opportunity to change her demagoguery in order to accommodate the feelings of a larger part of the French population. Prior to the British referendum, she had even planned to go to Britain to campaign for Brexit. In the spring of 2016, the *Guardian* reported: "Marine Le Pen, the leader of France's far-right Front National, is considering coming to the UK to campaign for the country to leave the EU. . . . She has seized on the UK's EU referendum to boost her own critical stance on Brussels. Her anti-immigration and anti-euro party has said it would seek to renegotiate the terms of France's EU membership if it took power, and hold a referendum on the EU. Le Pen has hailed the UK's referendum. . . . That will prove it's possible to live outside the European Union. . . . She said every European country should also be able to decide whether or not to stay in the EU." The *Guardian* also reported, however, that the political forces behind Brexit did not want "an alliance of Vladimir Putin, Marine Le Pen, and Donald Trump."[72]

Indeed, Marine Le Pen began to build an anti-EU block, an alliance of Eurosceptic parties and forces. Nigel Farage, the leading anti-EU Brexit demagogue, spoke of Le Pen's activities:

> Not long after the election result, Marine did a deal with the Northern League in Italy, also Eurosceptics, to join her European Freedom Alliance. The Dutch PVV party (led by Geert Wilders), the Austrian nationalist party (the Freedom Party of Austria) and the Belgian Vlaams Belang Party all joined as well. Marine was desperate for us to follow suit . . . she would welcome UKIP with open arms into her anti-European alliance. It drives me mad. . . . My problem was and is not with Marine . . . but the fact remains that anti-Semitism is in the party's DNA. . . . But she will never manage to truly reform the party and shed it of its anti-Semitic past.[73]

In June 2016, Marine Le Pen celebrated Brexit's electoral victory and called the European Union "an undemocratic authority" and the prison of nations. She proudly proclaimed: "I chose France, I chose the sovereign nation, I chose freedom." Her anti-EU demagoguery was animated by hate:

> Do we want an undemocratic authority ruling our lives, or would we rather regain control over our destiny? . . . A cage remains a cage. . . . The European Union has become a prison of peoples. Each of the 28 countries . . . has slowly lost its democratic prerogatives. . . . Different economies are forced to adopt the same currency. . . . [The EU Parliament is] based on a lie: the pretense that there are a homogenous European people. . . . Brexit . . . [is] the people's first victory. . . . The People's Spring is now inevitable![74]

Although the term "Spring of Europe" may have reminded many of the devastating disaster of the "Arab Spring" a few years before, Marine

Le Pen promised that, should she attain power, she would pull France out of the euro-zone and, during her first six months in office, hold a referendum on France's continued membership in the European Union.[75] She has also launched a broader campaign to recruit allies against the EU. On the latter occasion she declared:

> Look at how beautiful history is when liberty succeeds through the will of the people! . . . It's the cry of love, of a people, for their country. The British have chosen a route which it thought was closed for all time. . . . [and] that the European Union is irreversible. . . . [The EU is being] built on the backs of ordinary people. . . . The United Kingdom has committed the heresy of breaking the chains of the EU.[76]

Terrorism and gaining ground

At the same time, the Islamist terrorist attacks in France have offered Marine Le Pen a huge opportunity to promote her anti-Islamization and anti-immigration ideology. She condemned the Bastille Day attacks in Nice, blaming it on the rise of Islamic fundamentalism, on ISIL, and "their murderous ideology that we let develop in our country." Accusing French leaders of inaction and complacency in the face of terror, she claimed that the terror attacks were "the fault of a state, failing in its first priority, which is the protection of our citizens," concluding that "we can't watch these successive terrorist attacks and count the dead without acting."[77]

Marine Le Pen's first reaction suggested that the disaster she had long predicted had finally arrived. France and the French, she said, are no longer safe. She demanded a crackdown on Islamists, and urged to "expel foreigners who preach hatred on our soil" and to strip binational Islamists of French citizenship.[78]

After the terrorist attack on the satirical weekly *Charlie Hebdo* in January 2015, Le Pen refused to agree to national unity and continued to criticize the government from the outside. After the Paris and Niece attacks, she changed her rhetoric and embraced national unity in order to present herself as a responsible leader of a major party and one primed for the presidency. Because of her rhetoric, and partly because of the population's growing alarm about Islamic terrorism and immigration, all of the establishment parties have shifted their positions towards more restrictive, defense-oriented policies. These factors have combined to place Marine Le Pen's Front National well into the mainstream of French politics. Against, as her father phrased it, the traditional parties' "betrayal" of the country, or, as she describes it, their "post-national vision" and their "turning their backs on France," Marine Le Pen offers authentically French leadership and national revival. As she declared on May 1, 2016: "We must reestablish national borders; borders that protect, borders that separate. Schengen's Europe is also a Europe of terrorism; terrorism that endangers France more than ever."[79] Marine Le Pen's altered rhetoric is approximating the changing view of the French people on immigration, Muslims, and the EU. Consequently, she thought to have become more acceptable and potentially more successful. Indeed, a majority of French voters predicted that she will be a candidate in the second round of the presidential elections in 2017, and that she has a good chance of winning. Her most tactful and flexible demagoguery has seemingly worked.

After Donald Trump's victory in the United States, the Front National and Marine Le Pen have become more energized and more enthusiastic. According to reports, she has suggested that "It shows that when the people really want something, they can get it. . . . When the people want to retake their destiny in hand, they can do it, despite this ceaseless campaign of denigration and infantilization."[80] When she appeared in an old coal mining town where 20 percent of the miners are unemployed, one of the eleven cities that have given their vote to the Front National, Marine Le Pen received an effusive reception. The mayor of the city, Steeve Briois, a member of the Front, expressed the hope of his constituents: "France is no longer France. . . . There is the same desire to change politics in France" as in the United States, and "the only one who can do it is Marine Le Pen."[81]

Nevertheless, Le Pen's successful advance, as happened in other cases as well, stopped after the election of Donald J. Trump as president of the United States. At the 2017 French presidential and then parliamentary elections, she was unable to mobilize a larger electorate than the traditional base of the Front, and at the second round of the presidential election suffered a severe defeat from the centrist and strongly pro-European Union Emmanuel Macron.

Endnotes

1 The "Devil" and the "daughter of the Devil"—as Jean-Marie Le Pen and his daughter Marine were often called in France. Several hostile analyses were published about Jean-Marie Le Pen in France. It is worth mentioning: Raymond Castells, *Hitler, Le Pen, Megret: Leur Programme* (Paris: Raymond Castells, 1998); and Maurice Rajsfus, *En Gros et en Détail: Le Pen au quotidien, 1987–1997* (Paris: Mediterranée, 1998).

2 Donald Sassoon, *One Hundred Years of Socialism: The West European Left in the Twentieth Century* (New York: The New Press, 1996), 164.

3 Stephen S. Cohen, *Recent Development in French Planning* (Washington, D.C.: United States GPO, 1977), 65–66.

4 Sima Lieberman, *The Growth of European Mixed Economies, 1945–1970: A Concise Study of the Economic Evolution of Six Countries* (Cambridge, MA: Schenkman, 1977), 5.

5 François Caron, *An Economic History of Modern France* (New York: Columbia University Press, 1979), 211, 214–15.

6 Quoted by Harvey G. Simmons, *The French National Front: The Extremist Challenge to Democracy* (Boulder: Westview Press, 1996), 12. This book is the source of several quotations from French newspapers, among them *Le Monde* and *Présent*. The two men who influenced Le Pen's views, and are mentioned by him, are Charles-Marie-Photius Maurras, an extreme rightwing, anti-Semitic writer, a forerunner of fascist ideas, and founder of Action Française; and Robert Brasillach, a journalist who supported fascism and collaborated with the Nazi occupation of France.

7 Ibid., 64.

8 Ibid., 38.

9 Jean-Marie Le Pen, *Les Français d'abord* (Paris: Carrère-Michel Lafon, 1984), 67, quoted in English in Simmons, *The French National Front*, 63.

10 *Le Monde*, December 27, 1972, quoted in Simmons, *The French National Front*, 63.

11 Peter Davies, *The National Front in France: Ideology, Discourse and Power* (London: Routledge, 1999), 31. This book is also the source of several quotations from French newspapers (such as *Le Monde*) as well as Front National leaflets and other publications.

12 Quoted by Simmons, *The French National Front*, 190–91.

13 Catherine Fieschi, *Fascism, Populism and the French Fifth Republic* (Manchester: Manchester University Press, 2004), 176.

14 *National Hebdo*, no. 91, April 17–23, 1986. Quoted in Davies, *The National Front in France*, 67.

15 Jean-Marie Le Pen, *Pour la France* (Paris: Albatross, 1985), 29–30.

16 Fieschi, *Fascism, Populism*, 157.

17 From a promotional leaflet of *Identité*, quoted in Davies, *The National Front in France*, 67.

18 Le Pen, *Les Français d'abord*, 302. Quoted in English in Fieschi, *Fascism, Populism*, 156.

19 Fieschi, *Fascism, Populism*, 156.

20 *Appel aux Français*, presidential campaign flyer, "Le Pen président," 1995, quoted in Fieschi, *Fascism, Populism*, 166.

21 Quoted from a Front National brochure by Davies, *The National Front in France*, 69.

22 Le Pen, *Les Français d'abord*, 221. Quoted in English in Simmons, *The French National Front*, 79.

23 *Le Monde*, October 22, 1985. Quoted in Simmons, *The French National Front*, 103.

24 The B'nai B'rith is a worldwide Jewish community service organization that is also fighting against anti-Semitism and anti-Israel bias; CRIF is a French Jewish organization (Conseil Représentatif des Institutions Juives de France).

25 Quoted by Simmons, *The French National Front*, 129–30.

26 Quoted by ibid., 127.

27 *Présent*, August 12, 1989, quoted by Simmons, *The French National Front*, 222.

28 Front National, *300 mesures pour la renaissance de la France* (Paris: Edition Nationales, 1993), 392, quoted by Simmons, *The French National Front*, 128.

29 Ibid., 133.

30 *Le Monde*, May 19, 1988, quoted in Simmons, *The French National Front*, 133–32.

31 See several of Le Pen's anti-Semitic statements in Rajsfus, *En Gros et en Détail*, 197–99.

32 "Le Pen wegen Holocaust-Verharmlosung verurteilt," *Spiegel Online*, April 6, 2016.

33 *Le Monde*, November 29–30, 1992, quoted in Simmons, *The French National Front*, 140.

34 *Le Monde*, March 12, 1978, quoted in Simmons, *The French National Front*, 79.

35 Le Pen, *Les Français d'abord*, 121–23.

36 Ibid., 175–76, 103–5, 121, quoted in Simmons, *The French National Front*, 160.

37 *Le Monde*, April 4, 1987; Le Pen, *Les Français d'abord*, 227. Quoted in Simmons, *The French National Front*, 240.

38 *Le Quotidian de Paris*, January 13, 1986, quoted by Davies, *The National Front in France*, 139.

39 Quoted by Davies, *The National Front in France*, 76–77.

40 *Le Monde*, April 4, 1987, quoted in Davies, *The National Front in France*, 78.

41 APFN policy leaflet, 1990–91, quoted in Davies, *The National Front in France*, 111.

42 Front National, *300 mesures pour la renaissance de la France*, 54.

43 *La National*, no. 8, May–June 1979, quoted by Davies, *The National Front in France*, 120.

44 Jean-Marie Le Pen (avec J.P. Gabriel et Pascal Gannat), *L'Espoir* (Paris: Albatros, 1989), 15, quoted in Davies, *The National Front in France*, 130.

45 Quoted by Simmons, *The French National Front*, 244.

46 Le Pen, *Pour la France*, 134, quoted in Simmons, *The French National Front*, 248.

47 *Le Monde*, February 15, 1984, quoted in Simmons, *The French National Front*, 78–79.

48 *National Hebdo*, no. 241, March 2–8, 1989, quoted in Davies, *The National Front in France*, 157.

49 *Identité*, no. 6, March–April 1990, quoted in Davies, *The National Front in France*, 124.

50 Jean-Marie Le Pen, "Déstabiliser l'établissement," *Identité*, January 1990, quoted by Fieschi, *Fascism, Populism*, 156.

51 *Le Monde*, October 14, 1987, quoted in Simmons, *The French National Front*, 85.

52 *Le Monde*, August 25, 1992, quoted in Simmons, *The French National Front*, 129.

53 Davies, *The National Front in France*, 101–2.

54 "Le Pen's success should be seen as the result of an evolution of the candidate from proto-fascist political agitator to populist, quasi-respectable—although arguably no less political menacing—populist figure." Fieschi, *Fascism, Populism*, 154.

55 Russell Shorto, "Marine Le Pen, France's (kinder, gentler) extremist," *New York Times Magazine*, April 29, 2011.

56 "France's National Front party expels founder Jean-Marie Le Pen," *Guardian*, August 20, 2015.

57 Jean-Marie Le Pen became a millionaire by inheriting the wealth (and an opulent mansion) of one of his multi-millionaire friends.

58 Angelique Chrisafis, "Le Pen family feud is a battle for the soul of the Front National—and France," *Guardian*, April 10, 2015.

59 Paul Ames, "France's Far-Right Leading Family is in a Family Feud," *USA Today*, April 13, 2015.

60 Chrisafis, "Le Pen family feud is a battle for the soul of the Front National."

61 Quoted in Cécile Alduy, "The Devil's Daughter," *The Atlantic*, October 2013, https://www.theatlantic.com/magazine/archive/2013/10/the-devils-daughter/309467/.

62 Shorto, "Marine Le Pen, France's (kinder, gentler) extremist."

63 "Jean-Marie Le Pen nach Ausschluss: Der Front National bin ich," *Spiegel Online*, August 8, 2015.

64 Marine Le Pen, *Pour que vive la France* (Paris: Grancher, 2012), 106–7.

65 Marine Le Pen, speech at May 1, 2016, accessible at http://www.frontnational.com/2016/05/1er-mai-2016-discours-de-marine-le-pen/.

66 Shorto, "Marine Le Pen, France's (kinder, gentler) extremist."

67 Le Pen, *Pour que vive la France*, 28.

68 Ibid., 28–29.

69 Ibid., 186.

70 Ibid., 190.

71 Mathieu von Rohr, "Interview with Marine Le Pen: 'I don't want this European Soviet Union'," *Spiegel Online*, June 3, 2014, https://www.spiegel.de/international/europe/interview-with-french-front-national-leader-marine-le-pen-a-972925.html, italics added.

72 Angelique Chrisafis, "Marine Le Pen could campaign for UK to leave EU," *Guardian*, April 20, 2016.

73 Nigel Farage, *The Purple Revolution: The Year that Changed Everything* (London: Biteback Publishing, 2015), 36–38.

74 Marine Le Pen, "After Brexit the People's Spring is inevitable," *New York Times*, June 28, 2016.

75 Elisabeth Zerofsky, "Marine Le Pen prepares for a Frexit," *New Yorker*, June 29, 2016.

76 Victoria Friedman, "Marine Le Pen in Euro Parliament: 'UK Sent A Signal Of Freedom Out To The Entire World'," *Breitbart*, June 28, 2016, https://www.breitbart.com/europe/2016/06/28/marine-le-pen-uk-liberty-glowing-future/. To hammer out a broader anti-EU alliance has a better chance after the Brexit. The Dutch Party for Freedom, Geert Wilders, and the Danish People's Party are also seeking a referendum on the Netherlands's and Denmark's membership.

77 Joanna Plucinska, "Marine Le Pen: Nice attacks proof of Islamic fundamentalism's rise," *Politico European Edition*, July 16, 2016, https://www.politico.eu/article/marine-le-pen-bastille-day-nice-attacks-proof-of-islamic-fundamentalisms-rise/.

78 "Marine Le Pen's Anti-Islam Message Gains Influence in France," *New York Times*, May 17, 2015.

79 Marine Le Pen's speech on May 1, 2016, accessible at: http://www.frontnational.com/ 2016/05/1er-mai-2016-discours-de-marine-le-pen/.

80 Adam Nossiter, "After Trump win, parallel path is seen for French Right," *New York Times*, November 11, 2016.

81 Ibid.

CHAPTER 8

An entertaining but harmful buffoon-type demagogue: Italy's Silvio Berlusconi

Italy in crisis: the 1980s-1990s and the rise of new parties

The quarter-century-long *miracolo economico* Italy experienced after World War II made it one of the most prosperous countries in Europe. Its economy grew by more than 5 percent a year, creating millions of jobs and attracting 9 million people from the poverty-ridden *Mezzogiorno* of southern Italy to the rapidly developing north. Italians' per capita income tripled, and the country's social expenditures—financing a newly created welfare state—increased fourteen-fold. Modern Italy rose to a similar economic level as Western Europe and was near both socially and economically to the other founders of the European Economic Community in 1957.

This period of unparalleled achievement ended dramatically in the late 1960s and early 1970s. The *altunno caldo* (hot autumn) of 1969 signaled a frightening change. The occupation of the Fiat factory in Milan and the bombing of the Monument of Vittorio Emanuele II in Rome and the Piazza Fontana in Milan (the latter killing sixteen and wounding ninety) launched the *anni di piombo* (the years of bullets), which saw the killing, wounding, or kidnapping of prominent Italians, including a number of managers of the Fiat Company. Neo-fascist terrorist attack such as the *Golpe Borghese* event and the *Ordine Nuovo* group actions culminated with the March 1978 kidnapping of Prime Minister Aldo Moro by the left-wing *Brigate Rosse*, and his execution 55 days later. The economy slowed down and income levels increased by only a quarter over the next decade. By the end of the 1980s, Italy's entire postwar political system had collapsed and all its leading political parties had disappeared.

A new chapter in Italian politics

The 1990s opened a new chapter in Italian politics. The groundwork for political demagogues was laid. In those years three influential demagogues took over the Italian political arena: Gianfranco Fini, Umberto Bossi, and Silvio Berlusconi. Gianfranco Fini in his youth belonged to the neo-fascist *Movimento Sociale Italiano* and became its leader in 1987. In the 1990s, he reorganized the neo-fascist Movement under the new name of *Alleanza Nazionale*, incorporating the most conservative elements of the disbanded Christian Democratic Party. *Alleanza Nazionale*, although it never turned its back on its neo-fascist origins renounced a number of Mussolini's policies, such as the anti-Jewish legislation adopted at the end of the 1930s, and the more radical legislation passed after 1943. Alessandra Mussolini, the dictator's granddaughter, left the party precisely because it had moved from neo-fascism to ordinary right-wing politics, with close relations with the Catholic Church, with strict law and order, anti-immigration policies, and with an appeal to patriotism, family values and a form of statism. It has strong support in the south. While it won 28 and 25 per cent of the vote in the southern regions of Apulia and Lazio, it received only 6 and 8 percent in the northern Lombardy and Piedmont. *Alleanza* was not an overly centralized organization; several factions existed within the party, including D-Destra, loyal to the neo-fascist past.

Umberto Bossi established *Lega Nord per l'Indipendenza della Padania* party (North League for the Independence of Padania) in 1991. He successfully united several small local parties that had already existed in the north in the 1980s: the *Liga Veneta*, *Lega Lombardia* and others. As the party's name indicates, it was a regional and regionalist party, which advocated the secession of "Padania," a name that was used for the country's richest region in the Po River valley. Bossi advocated getting rid of the "lazy" and backward south and ending the dominance of *Roma ladrona* (Rome, the big thief), that parasitic exploiter of the North. When he dropped the slogan of independence,

he continued to advocate federalization, especially the financial federalization of Italy. His party won roughly 9 percent of the votes and
emerged as the fourth largest party of the country. However, Fini and
Bossi ended up being only the "supporting actors" of the leading demagogue of the age, Berlusconi.

Billionaire Silvio Berlusconi enters the field

Silvio Berlusconi was a successful entrepreneur: first as a real estate de-
veloper who amassed his wealth by building Milano-2, a large modern
suburb of Milan, and then as a media mogul who dominated the country's airwaves with three television channels, owned one of Italy's leading dailies, *Il Giornale*, and was part owner of its largest publisher, *Mondadori*, controlling 40 percent of the country's magazine market. Perhaps
even more important, he was also the owner of FC Milan, one of Italy's best football teams. Football is not merely a sport in Italy, it is a religion that galvanizes much of the population. Berlusconi, who was
knighted in 1977 (Knight of the Order of Merit for Labor) and called *Il
Cavaliere* (the Knight), became the richest man of the country. According to *Forbes* magazine, his wealth was $11 billion in 2006.

In 1993, he suddenly decided to enter politics. Probably he decided
to do so in April of that year in Villa San Martino, his early 18th-cen-
tury mansion in Arcore in the Milanese countryside. This palace with
its 147 rooms (and an added swimming pool), which he bought in 1974,
already symbolized his oversized ambition. This was the most appropri-
ate place to sit down with his close friend and mentor, former Prime
Minister Bettino Craxi, to discuss his plans. Craxi encouraged him to
make the leap. He also informed Gianni Agnelli, the multi-billionaire
owner of Fiat known as the "uncrowned king of Italy," of his intention
to enter politics. In the fall of 1993, he mobilized an army of sales, mar-
keting, and financial executives from his business empire to work on his
political project. "It marked the first time in Western history that a national political party had been designed, engineered, funded and then
launched from inside a major corporation."[1]

At the end of 1993, Berlusconi established the *Forza Italia* party
("Italy Forward!" or "Go Italy," a common inspirational slogan of Ital-

ian soccer teams), and did so without any pre-existing political base—establishing Forza Italia clubs, and even using soccer club networks as bases. At the same time, he began to coordinate with Fini's and Bossi's parties by founding the *Casa delle Libertà* (House of Freedom) coalition. He apprised his clan, his family, and a few closest friends of his plans at a dinner party at his palace in mid-January. A government program was hastily drawn up and, from party headquarters at his Arcore mansion, a well-organized campaign immediately embarked on, saturating the country's television stations with campaign ads. His television and publishing empire launched a totally new kind of political warfare. Paul Ginsborg, in his book on Berlusconi noted that this was "the most ambitious attempt to date to combine media control and political power."[2]

On May 11, 1994, only a few months after he decided to enter politics, Berlusconi won the national elections and became prime minister of Italy. What was the secret behind this unheard of, extraordinary political success? First and foremost was Berlusconi's compelling anti-political demagoguery. He gave speeches, issued statements, granted interviews, wrote articles, and even rebroadcasted an old recording (from February 6, 1994) employing a popular football slogan in a well-calculated manner: "I am taking the field." He decided to enter politics, he told the country, because "I heard that the game was getting dangerous and that it was all being played in the two penalty areas, with the midfield being left desolately empty." This was an altogether novel political style that proved immensely popular, for it conveyed that the candidate was not a politician, but "one of us." Italians loved it.

> I have decided to enter the field with a new movement. . . . It is because I dream . . . of a free society that is made up from men and women who do not live in fear, a society where instead of class envy and class warfare there is generosity and hard work and solidarity. . . . We can no longer accept an Italy that is so politicized, staticised, corrupted, this hyper-regulated Italy. . . . I believe that we must . . . resolve each problem. . . . Italy has need of men . . . that come from the trenches, of life and work, men of hope. . . . We can and we must create . . . a new Italian miracle![3]

The anti-politician businessman

Throughout his campaign, Berlusconi "marketed" himself as an anti-politician and as a proven successful entrepreneur:

> I am a simple man, I don't understand politics with its traps and acrobatics. . . . It is time to end the politics of accusations, of ambushes, traps and indecency. . . . The people want new, capable, and practical men capable of making the state work . . . move from words to deeds.[4]

> I trust in the abilities I've always had: talent, good sense, and the will to do things. . . . In my life I've already accomplished three miracles: as a builder, in sports, as a media owner. . . . Now, together, we must build the new Italian miracle.[5]

> There is no one in Italy who . . . can make this claim with more credibility . . . than the man standing before you now![6]

Berlusconi's populist demagoguery worked because he was an extremely successful businessman who was widely known to the public, and because he hit the nail on the head with his rhetoric by addressing a universal longing for a non-politician who can actively solve problems and recreate the Italian miracle. Italians were well-aware that he was a self-made-man who came from a lower middle-class family, and that he started out with no money singing on cruse-ships and selling vacuum cleaners before amassing his huge fortune. Now he offered his services to the entire nation to duplicate his success for Italy as a whole. Italians sincerely believed what he told them, that he was sacrificing himself for the good of the country. They reasoned that he had no need for political power because he had already attained it through his wealth. They were horribly mistaken.

Anti-communist mission or tax evasion?

Besides a desire for self-sacrifice in service of the nation, Berlusconi suggested—even after the end of his political career—that what motivated him was a determination to prevent communists from taking over Italy. As he remembered it, in July 1993 he met with Giuliano Urbani, a professor of political science, and asked him about the results of national polls he had conducted. "The numbers showed," Berlusconi later mentioned, "that the renamed Communist Party could win almost 40 percent of the votes . . . to control 74 percent of the seats of the Parliament. . . . That was the moment when I decided. Those polling numbers triggered my decision."[7] Others contend more convincingly that his real intention was to avoid prosecution, the prospect of which terrified him throughout the 1990s. Those years were the time of a kind of political revolution in Italy. The collapse of the entire postwar political system had culminated with the *Tangentopoli* (Bribesville) scandal. The Milan Magistrate had embarked on the *Mani Pulite* (Clean Hands) operation to sweep the country of its widespread, unremitting corruption in February 1992. In the end, its inquiries implicated virtually the entire former political elite, including half the members of Parliament, some 5,000 political figures, and a number of leading industrialists. More than 400 city councils had to be disbanded. Quite a few people, including Gabriele de Cagliari, President of the *Ente Nazionale Idrocarburi* (ENI), a major oil and gas multinational company, committed suicide in prison. Bettino Craxi, the head of the Socialist Party and prime minister between 1983 and 1987, was accused of corruption, but escaped just in time and lived out his remaining years in a villa in Tunisia. His party, however, ceased to exist. Political corruption had simply destroyed Italy's First Republic.

In addition, Giulio Andreotti, Italy's prime minister on several occasions in the 1970s and 1989–1992, and minister of interior, defense and foreign affairs in various governments, without question the leading politician of the country, was indicted and sentenced to 24 years in prison in 1993 for mafia connections and the murder of a journalist in Palermo. He was ultimately acquitted by the Court of Appeals and the Supreme Court, but his case was the final blow signaling the demise of Italy's political establishment.

Berlusconi was closely connected with several of those politicians. Craxi and Andreotti made great service for Berlusconi by the Telecommunication Law that helped the Berlusconi Empire. He was a suspect for the Milan Magistrate with good reason, as I will return to it. "Without the reforming zeal of Francesco Saverio Borrelli, the distinguished Magistrate who was to become the Chief Prosecutor of Milan," Ginsborg opinioned, "Silvio Berlusconi would never have been Italy's Prime

Minister. By the beginning of the 1990s, Berlusconi had every reason to be content with his lot."[8]

This view is strongly supported by a few friends and co-leaders of his business empire who belonged to the inner group of Berlusconi. Indro Montanelli, the editor of Berlusconi's journal, *Il Giornale*, revealed that during the 1994 election campaign Berlusconi confided to him: "If I don't enter politics I'll end up in jail and fall into debt." Fedele Confalonieri, head of Berlusconi's Mediaset Group and one of his most faithful lieutenants, bluntly confirmed: "If Berlusconi hadn't entered politics . . . today we'd be sitting under a bridge or in prison accused of mafia offences."[9] Indeed, Berlusconi was ultimately able to postpone and significantly mitigate Confalonieri's prosecution. Regardless of what motivated him, Berlusconi thoroughly enjoyed testing himself on the world political stage. As wealthy as he was, he still liked but was no longer excited in making more money. He yearned for something new and more exciting: to engage the leaders of the world's powers and to be one of them. As he would later recall, "How wonderful it was to sit as the host of a dinner with the most powerful leaders on the planet, with George W. Bush, having a nice conversation with Vladimir Putin to my right."[10] Indeed, within European politics he worked closely with prominent politicians and became friends with two of them: George W. Bush and Vladimir Putin. This meant a lot to him. Years later, he proudly led a journalist to a guestroom in his mansion and gushed: "Here stayed Vladimir Putin."[11] Luigi Cancrini, an eminent Italian psychologist, suggested that Berlusconi is "a personality with unlimited ego-centricity. Up until the point he was a businessman, things were OK. The problems started with his acquisition of political power. And when a normal narcissism is strongly stoked by and combined with too much power, the result is pathology—a genuine personality disturbance. He has an image of himself that is very grandiose . . . dangerously grandiose. . . . This is how people lose contact with reality."[12] This excellent analysis of Berlusconi is certainly valid in various other cases of populist leaders as well.

In other words, he "took the field" when he felt the urge to do so, and he did it at precisely the moment he could plausibly offer an alternative solution to Italy's disastrous political collapse of the early 1990s— a solution that only a demagogue could envision. It was indeed a time of crisis in which Italians despaired of politics as usual. Why?

We need a business genius: rearrangement of the political theater

After the ruinous 1970s, the 1980s and early 1990s witnessed the total col-lapse of Italy's political establishment. For half a century and throughout the Cold War period, Italian politics had been dominated by the Chris-tian Democratic Party and in the later years by Giulio Andreotti person-ally. On the other side of the political spectrum was the main opposition party, the Italian Communist Party, the strongest in Western Europe, with a revered past of partisan resistance to Mussolini, and which had taken part in the immediate postwar government and successfully ran a number of municipal administrations in Italy's "red zone." Admired for its Eurocommunist leanings and its independence from, and criticism of, the Soviet Union, the Italian Communist Party had two million well-or-ganized members and usually won 25–30 percent of the vote.

In 1989–1991, the collapse of communism in Central and Eastern Eu-rope and then in the Soviet Union effectively eliminated communism as an option in Italy. Communism was thoroughly discredited and lost all legitimacy and appeal. Even the extreme left-wing post-Mao Chinese communists turned to capitalism through reforms. The Italian Commu-nist Party lost its bearings and dissolved itself in February 1991. Two new parties came to the fore: the *Partito Democratico della Sinistra,* (PDS) or Party of the Democratic Left, and a small uncompromising *Rifondazione Comunista* or Party of Communist Refoundation. During national elec-tions in 1994, eight mostly small center-left parties (together with the Re-foundation party) formed the Progressive Alliance. The collapse of the two leading parties created a totally new political environment.

The dissolution of the two leading parties would have been enough to assure a completely clean slate in Italian politics. That, however, was not the whole story. The collapse of the entire postwar political system had culminated with the *Tangentopoli* (Bribesville) scandal and the *Mani pulite* (Clean Hands) operation in February 1992. Without these dra-matic changes, Berlusconi, a complete novice in politics, would never have had a chance. But his anti-politics demagoguery, and his promis-es to rid the country of the corrupt and self-serving *partitocrazia,* worked. He established a "movement," not a party. Daniele Zolo called attention to the fact that political parties in Italy would no longer call themselves parties from that time on, but, in a deliberate ploy to distance themselves from the past, became *movements*. This is how the discourse changed regarding the Lega (League), Alleanza (Alliance), Polo (Pole), Casa (House), Rete (Network), Ulivo (Olive Tree).[13]

Berlusconi also vowed to create a new economic miracle and to reduce Italians' tax burden. This would be an extremely popular move everywhere, but was even more so in Italy. Unlike most of the advanced Western countries, Italy possessed an unusually large number of self-employed citizens—small business owners who continually aspired to avoid taxation. They admired Berlusconi and tried to emulate his successes in this domain, and wholeheartedly believed in the promise of his leadership. Moreover, he convinced large numbers that they were in fact right when they cheated the government and declined to pay their taxes, because—as he declared many times—it was not they, but the state with its onerous regulations, that was wrong. He went so far, and this time definitely believed what he said, that "Better Fascism than the bureaucratic tyranny of the judiciary."[14] In a speech in Verona on May 27, 1999, he proclaimed:

> The Treasury which has no faith in the taxpayers, has been set on the assumption that taxpayers, especially self-employed, declare only half of their income. . . . What does the Italian state then do? . . . "I will tax you double because you only declare half". . . . Citizens pay their taxes out of a sense of duty to their fellow citizens.[15]

Many Italians were also convinced that his entrepreneurial skills and business acumen could be applied on the national stage. He offered a complete new start by rejecting the entire political system of the past. Indeed, he won an unbelievable victory in 1994. His program was heavenly music in the ears of self-employed, small business people. In 2001, more than 63 percent of entrepreneurs and professionals and more than 54 percent of shopkeepers, artisans, and self-employed voted for his coalition.

Promises, promises, lies, lies

This remarkable success, however, was short lived. Berlusconi himself was also being investigated for corruption. His brother and business partner, Paolo, had been indicted for bribery and corruption in 1992. Gianni Letta, Berlusconi's chief lobbyist in Rome and vice-president of his Fininvest Group, confessed to bribing a number of political parties in April 1993. Bettino Craxi, the former prime minister and close friend of Berlusconi, also confessed that his Socialist Party, as, indeed, all the other parties, had regularly received money from Italy's biggest corporations such as Fiat, Olivetti, and Berlusconi's *Fininvest*. Prosecutors later found proof of large money transfers from Berlusconi to Craxi's offshore accounts. In 1998, Berlusconi was sentenced to two years and four months in prison for bribing Craxi. Several years later when it seemed that Berlusconi was finally out of politics, he explained in an interview that private sector contributions had become the norm in Italy. "There simply was no other financing of the parties at that time."[16]

In any case, on November 22, 1994, only six months after his electoral victory, the front page of *Corriere della Sera* featured the startling headline: "Berlusconi under Investigation in Milan." He was charged by Antonio Di Pietro of the Milan Magistrate with bribing a tax inspector. The humiliated premier had to resign half a year after he was elected. In 1996, he tried to make a comeback, but he lost the elections primarily because his coalition partners had deserted him. Still, he did not give up and continued on as the leader of the center-right opposition in the Parliament. The legal case against him made him even more popular and seemed to confirm his allegations that the Italian authorities employ excessive and unfair regulations and that a kind of communist conspiracy is at play. In 2000, his publishing empire, *Mondadori*, published his book, *Italy I have in Mind*, which again marketed his 1994 "dream" of renewing Italy and creating a new economic miracle:

> What we want to offer to all Italians is an Italy made by entirely new men. . . . We want to give support and confidence to those who create employment and well-being, we want to accept and beat the great technological and productive challenges faced by Europe and the modern world.[17]

In 2001, he also wrote a 125-page highly illustrated pamphlet, *Una storia italiana*, on his life and accomplishments, and mailed it to more than 12 million families. Before millions of viewers, he appeared on a popular talk-show in May 2001 and signed his *Contratto con gli Italiani* (Contract with the Italians), essentially copying the Republican Party's "Contract with America" in 1994. The five-point program made inordinate promises, all highly appealing to voters: reduction of the tax burden with full tax exemptions for incomes up to € 11,362 per year; tax reductions to 23 percent for incomes up to € 103,291 per year; tax reductions to 33 percent for incomes above € 103,291 per year; abolition of the inheritance tax and the donations tax; implementing the "Plan for the protection of citizens and the prevention of crime," which would result in a sharp reduction of crime from the current 3 million cases annually; raising the minimum pension to at least € 516 per month; halving the current rate of unemployment with the creation of at least 1.5 million workplaces; introducing the *Piano Decennale per le Grandi Opere* (Ten Year Plan for Great Works); and opening sites for at least 40 percent of the investments for construction of roads, highways, subways, railways, water networks, and hydro-geological works to prevent floods. The last paragraph of the Contract promised that Silvio Berlusconi would not resubmit his nomination in the next parliamentary elections should four of the five projects not be achieved in five years' time.[18]

This was presented not as a contract between the people and his party, but a personal contract between Berlusconi and the people. Luca Ostilio Ricolfi, professor at the *Università di Torino*, proved that Berlusconi failed to keep his promises except on one point. Nevertheless, Berlusconi's typical populist demagoguery triumphed and he won more than 43 percent of the votes in 2001. Berlusconi returned to Palazzo Chigi, the prime minister's office in Rome, and ultimately served three terms as the longest reigning politician in postwar Italian history. His promises only grew.

In 2006, during the second televised debate against his opponent, Romano Prodi, Berlusconi turned around a lackluster performance by making a last-minute announcement that an unpopular tax on houses would be abolished if he won the elections. Looking straight into the camera he said: "You have heard it right, we will get rid of this tax."[19] Aside from his bombastic promises, which are characteristic of any demagogue, Berlusconi always went out of his way to blame an enemy—one of the most important weapon of populists—in his case, the Left. During his first political campaign, he tried to frighten the population, especially the middle class, of impending "communist rule" that would destroy the country should he lose the election:

> Those on the left claim to have changed. . . . They say they have be-
> come liberal democrats. But it is not true. . . . They don't believe in the
> free market. They don't believe in private enterprise. They don't believe
> in profit. They don't believe in the individual.[20]

> The threat of the Communists taking over Italy scared lots of business-
> men because we all knew what communist ideology represented.[21]

His warnings of impending "communism" were a flagrant lie in 1994
and throughout the early twenty-first century. Communism posed no
danger at all in Italy after its collapse in Europe in the 1990s. Moreover,
the Italian Communist Party had radically changed its policies and ideology as early as the 1970s. It had long become a West European type
of social democratic party, similar to those in power for years in Britain, Germany, and Scandinavia. Anti-communism had practically disappeared from politics throughout the West, but not in Italy. For Berlusconi, it was crucially important to name the enemy, to paint them in
very dark colors, and to threaten Italians with the peril of a leftist takeover if they did not reelect him.

He articulated these threats again and again in highly agitated
speeches at mass rallies. On May 3, 1997, at the big square in front of
the glorious Gothic cathedral in Milan, Berlusconi, seeking a political
comeback, attacked the center-left government by depicting it as a Soviet-type communist regime:

> Dear Friends. . . . I have been feeling a strong passion, strong convic-
> tion and strong will and could not resist coming to the square . . . to
> bring the concern, the indignation, and the will to react and resist a
> government, a coalition on power that endangers our well-being, our
> democracy, our freedom, our future.

> We are here on this square . . . [to] strongly condemn the left . . . that
> are still impregnated by communism. We are here to accuse the left that
> is building a suffocating and illiberal regime. [Who] occupies every-
> thing . . . the institutions, the bodies of the State and the state compa-
> nies . . . uses the justice system . . . [to] eliminate political adversar-
> ies . . . uses taxes to hit the middle class, [who] destroys the economy,
> risks our firms, our workplaces, our well-being.

During his long speech, beside describing his program for massive
tax reductions, he frightened the audience with the dangers of the com-

munist menace.[22] In his huge, illustrated pamphlet of 2001, beside listing and praising his achievements, he described the Italian political arena as a fight between Good and Evil, between the Blue (his party's and the national football team's color) and the Red (the Left). "There was a terrible fear in the air," he stated, "if the pre- and post-1989 Communists came to power."[23] Giovanni Orsina rightly argues that "Berlusconi's anticommunist position needs to be taken seriously simply because it was the means by which Berlusconi came to be in such close harmony with a considerable section of the electorate."[24]

The role of the media

Berlusconi's attacks on his rivals and his often-empty promises were widely disseminated thanks to an effective use of modern technology. "Whereas most European democracies began to develop features of modern campaigning in the 1960s," Cristian Vaccari noted, "Italian electioneering did not experience a transition from the premodern to the modern era until the early 1980s, when party leaders began using television to bypass party structures and build relationships with voters." Berlusconi's success was closely connected to the "mediatization" of politics employed by his own media empire. The first televised political advertisements appeared in Italy during the general elections of 1983, but only marginally. The real breakthrough took place during the 1994 elections, with the first live televised debate between the two rival coalition leaders was broadcast by the Berlusconi-owned TV channels. In 2001, Berlusconi launched an unprecedented mass electronic advertisement campaign to return to power.[25] Moreover, he successfully personalized politics and offered himself as the guarantor of Italy's success. The entire political culture and activity he embodied was deeply rooted in Italian customs, the traditional patron-client connection, giving gifts, and demanding loyalty.

Good Italians, bad regulations

Berlusconi's successful demagoguery has some important features. One was his convincing argument that Italy and the Italians are fine just as they are, and that it is only the state and its faulty policies and regulations that need to be changed. People loved to hear that.

In a speech in Rome on February 6, 1994, he suggested that Italy is an advanced country only

> because the millions and millions of Italians are continuing to do their duty every day. . . . [This success] we owe to the hard work of our teachers and farmers, to the skill of our entrepreneurs, especially of the managers of small and medium size businesses . . . the genius and talent of our craftsmen, our traders and all of the risk-taking self-employed. . . . Our Mezzogiorno is the only real development tank for the whole of Italy. . . . The Mezzogiorno is on the move. . . . Our duty is to free up these spontaneous forces. . . . We have to change the rules.[26]

Italians loved hearing that it was only the political institutions, the political elite, and the government regulations that were wrong and in need of change. Berlusconi compellingly argued this by employing the Reaganite-Thatcherite line that was so popular in the 1980s. Throughout the twentieth century, he maintained, "state intrusion" became more and more pronounced:

> It is an administrative system which still suffocates us, while the reality . . . is much closer to the Anglo-Saxon model. . . . Forza Italia is about the fight against state oppression, which has gone on for the entire twentieth century.[27]

Berlusconi vowed to make the requisite changes. He promised to bring to the fore

> the same morality in politics that there is in the market. . . . We are the standard bearers of a morality we learned in the market and what is absent in politics what we would like to introduce.[28]

This was music to the ears for many Italians, who were convinced that sound business management practices would change the country's politics for the better.

The Jesus Christ of politics with vulgar language

Another feature of Berlusconi's demagoguery was that he never hesitated to praise himself. His narcissism and egotism compelled him to make statements such as: "I am a man of honor, a truthful person, a gentleman of absolute morality"; "I am the Jesus Christ of politics. I sacrifice myself for everyone"; "Only Napoleon did more than I have done. But I am definitely taller"; "Churchill liberated us from the Nazis, Silvio Berlusconi is liberating us from communists." He presented the NATO summit meeting that took place in Italy in May of 2002 as a historic event for Italy in which he played a central role by meditating between the United States and Russia, making a "titanic effort . . . [that changed the] course of the history of the world . . . [and] put an end to the Cold War."[29] This was a statement typical for someone who forever asked "Who does it better?" and never hesitated to answer "Me of course! I am always *Numero Uno*." He never stopped praising himself and has a "total love for himself."[30]

Another typical feature was Berlusconi's use of popular, at times even vulgar, expressions: once he talked with one of his clients about "the extraordinary qualities of Circassian women's vaginas and," as he stated, "we built up a friendship based on this common 'cultural' basis."[31] Another time, at an open meeting he said, "We could not field a big enough force to void this risk [of rape]. We would need so many soldiers because our women are so beautiful"; "People will vote for Daniela Santanche because she is a beautiful babe"; "I have Italian citizens in too good consideration to think that are so many voting assholes (*coglioni*) around that could vote against their own interests. I apologize for the rude but effective language." At a mass meeting in Udine in 2003 he praised his passing of the Cirami Law, which allowed defendants to protest against judges. He explained: "perhaps one of us has stolen the fiancée of the presiding judge. Such things happen to us, because we're well known to be *tombeur des femmes*. . . . To steel the fiancée of a friend is not the sort of thing we do, but of a magistrate, well that's fine."[32]

At another mass meeting he stated: "When [Italian women are] asked if they would like to have sex with me, 30 percent of women said 'Yes,' while the other 70 percent replied, 'What, again?'"; "It is better to like beautiful girls than to be gay." The 5-foot, 5-inch-tall Berlusconi loved to speak about sex, and his audience loved to hear about it too. During the 2006 elections campaign, as a commentator remarked, he made "probably the most memorable campaign promises ever made by any politician in the history of modern democracy, [when he promised] to abstain from sex in the two-and-a-half months leading up to the election."[33] "For the millions with little interest in, or even an aversion to, politics (or at least politicians)," another expert explained, "Berlusconi's attitude—and stardom—gets their vote. . . . Berlusconi's womanizing and ostentatious wealth gives many middle-aged male Italians a vicarious thrill."[34] Berlusconi, Paul Ginsborg added, was "a leader, who will be chosen because everyone can recognize something of themselves in him, can identify themselves and that which they would want to be."[35]

All this made him hugely popular among ordinary Italians. As one cultural commentator noted: "He loves his children, talks about his mother, likes football, knows how to make money, loves new homes, hates rules, tells jokes, says bad words, adores women." The author also added: "Much of his clowning and lowbrow jokes, which raise eyebrows abroad, chimes with the provincial outlook of his Italian supporters. Many Italians see themselves in Berlusconi."[36]

Finally, as another characteristic of the unique feature of Berlusconi's demagoguery, he never hesitated to deny in the evening what he said in the morning. After the 9/11 terror attack in the United States, he declared: "We must be aware of the superiority of our civilization . . . in contrast with Islamic countries. . . . The West will continue to conquer peoples, even if it means a confrontation with another civilization, Islam, firmly entrenched where it was 1,400 years ago." When his statement was criticized, he flatly retorted: "They have tried to hang me on an isolated word, taken out of context. . . . I did not say anything against the Islamic civilization. . . . It's the work of some people in the Italian leftist press."[37]

Tax evasion and admiration

Many Italians also envied and admired him because he was able to so masterfully avoid paying his fair share of taxes, had survived several bribery scandals, and had paid off various tax officials and law-enforcement officers. He was accused of money-laundering, of associating with the Mafia through his close associates, of tax evasion, and of bribing politicians, judges, and the finance ministry's police. Although he made no fewer than 500 court appearances, endured 106 trials over a twenty-year period, and spent €200 million on legal fees, he remained the consummate survivor. Berlusconi always denied every allegation and blamed everything on a left-wing, communist conspiracy to stage a coup against him.

As prime minister for several years, and contrary to elementary political standards, Berlusconi violated the principle of avoiding any conflicts of interest—he never gave up his multitude of businesses. He formally stepped down from the directorships of his Fininvest Group when he entered politics, but he remained the controlling shareholder. His family continued to run his businesses, and his adult children sat on the plethora of boards in his corporate empire. Until the very end of his political career as prime minister, he skillfully avoided well-deserved prosecution and always remained at the top. This was largely due to his actions in power: he was able to change the law to get himself out of trouble. In the summer of 1994, his government announced the adoption of the Salvaladri ("save a thief") Law "to prevent the judiciary issuing arrest warrants for most crimes relating to political corruption and fraud." A number of criminals already in custody were consequently released. These included ex-ministers, finance police, and political party officials who held millions in hidden accounts abroad. "Overnight, a total of 2,764 suspects walked." Berlusconi later confided to close friends, "We had to pass that decree. The magistrates were after me and my friends. . . . I have to stop them before they become the bosses of Italy." In the summer of 2003, based on the initiative of his government, his majority in Parliament granted legal immunity for persons who held the highest political offices, including the premiership. A law, in other words, tailored for Berlusconi. One of the last pieces of legislation drafted by his second government in December 2005 was Law 251, nicknamed the Save-Previti Law, which drastically shortened the statute of limitations for bribery cases and radically limited the prosecution of criminals. What's more, Italy vetoed a proposal of the European Union Commission for issuing European arrest warrants for those suspected of financial crimes.[38]

The fall: corruption hits back

Nevertheless, in the end Berlusconi failed and was prosecuted. In 1994, a member of the Financial Police reported a bribery attempt by Berlusconi's Fininvest. The case was taken up by Antonio Di Pietro of the popular Milano Magistrate. It is important to note at that point that Berlusconi, due to his usual methods, tried to pay off Di Pietro by offering him the post of Minister of Interior in his government. Di Pietro went to Rome, but rejected the post. By 2001, Berlusconi already had ten court cases. In 2013 he was finally convicted of tax fraud and expelled from the Italian Senate. Another conviction permanently ended his political career in 2015. Let me end his story by quoting two articles from the British weekly the *Economist*—what Berlusconi always dubbed "The Ecommunist," because anyone who criticized him, he insisted, was part of a communist conspiracy against him.

"As often happens in Italy," the *Economist* remarked, "a daunting punishment has been whittled down to a mild reproof. Mr. Berlusconi's four-year sentence was cut to one year because of an amnesty law . . . in 2006. He could not be jailed thanks to another law passed by one of his governments that bans the imprisonment of most [people] over 70."[39] "But it is now clear," another article in the *Economist* concluded,

> that neither the dodgy sex nor the dubious business history should be the main reason for Italians looking back on Mr. Berlusconi as a disastrous, even malign, failure. Worst by far has been a third defect: his total disregard for the economic condition of his country. Perhaps because of the distraction of his legal tangles, he has failed in almost nine years as prime minister to remedy or even really to acknowledge Italy's grave economic weaknesses. As a result, he will leave behind him a country in dire straits. . . . When Europe's economies shrink, Italy's shrinks more; when they grow, it grows less . . . only Zimbabwe and Haiti had lower GDP growth than Italy in the decade to 2010. In fact GDP per head in Italy actually fell . . . the public debt is still 120% of GDP, the rich world's third-biggest. The Berlusconi era will haunt Italy for years to come.[40]

This assessment is shared by other analysts, who conclude that "the Berlusconi government did next to nothing to revitalize the Italian economy."[41]

Thankfully, Berlusconi's populist demagoguery, unlike in many other cases in history, did not lead to war or to the death of tens of thousands of people, nor did it lead to the physical destruction of the country. But his ambition for power had seriously grave consequences on the Italian economy and on the financial standing of the Italian people. As *The Economist* ruefully noted in 2006, the second Berlusconi government was an "abject failure. . . .The Berlusconi government has also undone much of the improvement to the public finances made by its predecessor; the budget deficit and the public debt, the world's third biggest, are both rising once more."[42]

The witty, entertaining, buffoon-type Berlusconi, who in 2003 was nicknamed "Burlesquoni," was not a typical populist demagogue. He was liked by many, enough to elect him three times, despite the fact that during his premiership debts were accumulated and reached a danger zone, the required reforms were not introduced, and the country declined into stagnation. He brought real harm to his country through his demagoguery. He was not the only one to do so at the turn of the millennium in Europe.

Berlusconi gave an interview to two British journalists for the *Spectator* in 2003. At this famous interview Berlusconi said that Mussolini was a benign dictator who did not kill his opponents, but sent them "on holiday to islands such as [the prison island] Ventotene." One of the British journalists was Boris Johnson, who became a quite similar demagogue buffoon a decade later, and played a central role in Brexit, Britain's exit from the European Union.

In 2018, already in his 80s, Berlusconi tried again to regain power, but failed. His party has only received 14 percent of the votes. Unfortunately this lower turnout was due to even more dangerous populist parties with more attractive promises who gained ground in the election. The *Movimento 5 Stelle*, or Five Star movement, established in 2009, developed the most modern of populist programs with combined right- and left-wing programs, and won 32 percent of the votes in the same election. In second place, with 17 percent of the votes, was Berlusconi's old ally, the Lega Nord under the leadership of Matteo Salvini. That party dropped "Nord" (North) from its name and posed as a national, all-Italian party. Although the Lega was in coalition with Berlusconi in the elections, Salvini left Berlusconi and turned to the Five Star Movement and formed a new, more dangerous Eurosceptic nationalist-populist government of Italy in June 2018.

Endnotes

1 Alan Friedman, *My Way: Berlusconi in His Own Words* (London: Biteback Publishing, 2015), 97. Berlusconi attracted a tremendous attention from scholars and writers. Several books were published about him. Mentioning just a few: Alexander Stille, *The Sack of Rome: Media + money + celebrity = power = Silvio Berlusconi* (New York: Penguin Books, 2007); Michael E. Shin and John A. Agnew, *Berlusconi's Italy: Mapping Contemporary Italian Politics* (Philadelphia: Temple University Press, 2008); Alan Friedman, *Berlusconi: The epic story of the billionaire who took over Italy* (New York: Hachette Books, 2015); Michael Day, *Being Berlusconi: The rise and fall from Cosa Nostra to Bunga Bunga* (New York: Palgrave Macmillan, 2015). These and some others will be quoted in the text.

2 Paul Ginsborg, *Silvio Berlusconi: Television, Power and Patrimony* (London: Verso, 2004), 10.

3 Ibid., 104; Donatella Campus, *Antipolitics in Power: Populist Language as a Tool for Government* (Cresskill, NJ: Hampton Press, 2010), 96–97; Geoff Andrews, *Not a Normal Country: Italy after Berlusconi* (London: Pluto Press, 2005), 26–27.

4 *La Stampa*, January 24, 1994; *Corriere della Sera*, February 6, 1994; *Corriere della Sera*, November 25, 1995, all quoted in Campus, *Antipolitics in Power*, 96–97.

5 Ibid, 98. Quotations from *Il Messaggero*, April 3, 1994; *Corriere della Sera*, March 31, 1994.

6 Silvio Berlusconi, *L'Italia che ho in mente: I discursi di Silvio Berlusconi* (Milan: Mondadori, 2000), 23.

7 Friedman, *My Way*, 96.

8 Ginsborg, *Silvio Berlusconi*, 57.

9 Day, *Being Berlusconi*, 46.

10 Friedman, *My Way*, 122.

11 Ibid., 3.

12 Quoted in Day, *Being Berlusconi*, 104.

13 Daniele Zolo, "From 'historic compromise' to 'telecratic compromise': notes for a history of political communication between the First and Second Republic," *Media, Culture and Society* 21, no. 6 (1999): 727–41; Shin and Agnew, *Berlusconi's Italy*, 21.

14 Ginsborg, *Silvio Berlusconi*, 176.

15 Berlusconi, *L'Italia che ho in mente*, 223.

16 Friedman, *My Way*, 91.

17 Campus, *Antipolitics in Power*, 96.

18 See: Luca Ostilio Ricolfi, *Dossier Italia: Ache punto è il "Contratto con gli Italiani"* (Bologna: Il Mulino, 2005).

19 Cristian Vaccari, "The features, impact and legacy of Berlusconi's campaigning techniques, language and style," *Modern Italy* 20, no. 1 (2015): 27, http://dx.doi.org/10.1080/13532944.2014.985583.

20 Friedman, *My Way*, 103.

21 Ibid., 93.

22 Silvio Berlusconi, *Discorsi per la democrazia* (Milan: Mondadori, 2001), 265–73. Speech in Milan on May 3, 1977.

23 Ginsborg, *Silvio Berlusconi*, 95.

24 Giovanni Orsina, *Berlusconism and Italy: A Historical Interpretation* (New York: Palgrave Macmillan, 2014), 76.

25 Vaccari, "The features, impact and legacy," 27.

26 Berlusconi, *L'Italia che ho in mente*, 24–25; Berlusconi, *Discorsi per la democrazia*, 279.

27 Berlusconi, *L'Italia che ho in mente*, 102.

28 Ibid., 116.

29 Ginsborg, *Silvio Berlusconi*, 148.

30 Giorgio Bocca, *Piccolo Cesare* (Milan: Feltrinelli Editore, 2002), 11.

31 Ginsborg, *Silvio Berlusconi*, 125–26.

32 Ibid., 125. Original interview is from *La Republica*, May 12, 2003.

33 Shin and Agnew, *Berlusconi's Italy*, 111.

34 Day, *Being Berlusconi*, 99.

35 Ginsborg, *Silvio Berlusconi*, 112.

36 Day, *Being Berlusconi*, 99.

37 A large collection of Berlusconi's similar statements was published in Day, *Being Berlusconi*; see also "In quotes: Italy's Silvio Berlusconi in his own words," *BBC News*, August 2, 2013, http://www.bbc.com/news/world-europe-15642201.

38 Regarding Berlusconi's legislation to save those indicted for financial crimes, see Day, *Being Berlusconi*, 59, 60, 86, 94.

39 "Silvio Berlusconi, social worker," *Economist*, April 19, 2014.

40 "The man who screwed an entire country," *Economist*, June 9, 2011.

41 Shin and Agnew, *Berlusconi's Italy*, 124.

42 "Basta Berlusconi," *Economist*, April 6, 2006.

CHAPTER 9

Three nationalist demagogues in Yugoslavia and a devastating civil war

The absurd political drama of the collapse of Yugoslavia

This is a unique story, one that is uniquely dramatic and tragic. Three different men at the same time in the same country, Yugoslavia in the late 1980s and early 1990s, arose on the political scene. They had completely different personalities. One of them, Slobodan Milošević, was a product of a disturbed childhood, a devoted communist who was a man of few words, but who became a ruthless nationalist "defender" of the Serbs. The second, Franjo Tuđman, started out as a communist partisan, rose to the rank of Major General, and ended up an ardent anti-communist Croatian nationalist. The third, Alija Izetbegović, a life-long anti-communist and religious Muslim, embarked on a mission to Islamize his people and lead them toward independent nationhood in Bosnia-Herzegovina. The first was an Orthodox Serb, the second a Catholic Croat, the third a Muslim Bosnian. The stage was set at the end of the 1980s for the emergence of nationalist demagogues. Paraphrasing the title of Italian playwright Luigi Pirandello's absurdist play *Six Characters in Search of an Author*, these were three characters in search of a role in what became an absurd and tragic political drama. These men all emerged in politics in the midst of an unprecedented socio-economic and national crisis, a ripe environment for populist demagogues, and found themselves on different sides of the political trenches in Yugoslavia confronting one another head on.

Slobodan Milošević and his background

His first name, Slobodan, means freedom or liberty (*sloboda*) in Serbo-Croatian. His family originated from Montenegro, where his grandfather served as an officer of the Royal Montenegrin Army. Montenegro had been considered a symbol of freedom, for the small mountainous country was the only spot in the Balkans not occupied by the Ottoman Turks. His parents moved to Požarevac, Serbia, in 1941, the year of Slobodan's birth. If one word could characterize his family background, it would have to be *tragic*. He was born in the single worst year of Yugoslav history, the year that Nazi Germany attacked and occupied the country. His parents divorced soon after his birth. His uncle Milislav, a partisan hero, shot himself when Tito broke with Stalin in 1948. His father committed suicide in 1962. His mother hanged herself in her living room in 1972.[1] Slobodan joined the Communist Party at the age of 18 and married his high school sweetheart, Mira Marković, in 1965.

Career based on clientelism

Milošević excelled in his studies both in high school and at Law School (at Belgrade University), but was a taciturn, often depressed young man. His professional career followed the typical Balkan trajectory of kinship and clientelism, as he benefited from his close connections with his friend Ivan Stambolić, the nephew of Petar Stambolić, one of the most senior leaders in Tito's Yugoslavia. With such a tie to an important political higher-up Ivan Stambolić's career accelerated rapidly: he was appointed director general of the state-owned Technogas Company at around the age of thirty, and later director of the Belgrade Chamber of Commerce in 1970. His career culminated in the 1980s with his appointment as secretary of the Central Committee of the Serbian Communist Party and finally as prime minister of Serbia. As he rose from one position to another, he always made sure that Slobodan succeeded him: he had Slobodan take his place at the helm of the Technogas Company in 1970, appointed him to head the country's largest state bank, the Beogradska Banka (Beobanka), in 1975, and placed him in the Executive

Committee of the Serbian Communist Party in 1982. Slobodan soon became the Party chief of Belgrade and in 1986 rose to become the leader of the Serbian League of Communists. Up till this point his career rather routinely exemplified that of a typical apparatchik. Over the next decade and a half, he would gradually emerge as the beloved leader and savior of the Serbs, a dangerous demagogue who climbed to the highest heights only to crash and burn in a calamitous fall.

Crisis of Yugoslavia and the Kosovo question

This final chapter of his story was also connected to Stambolić. In early 1987, the conflict between Albanians and Serbs in the Kosovo province of Yugoslavia reached new heights. This was partly a phenomenon seen throughout communist Central and Eastern Europe, where depleted regimes languished in a debilitating economic crisis beginning in the mid-1970s. The rapid growth and impressive industrialization of their earlier years, which had propelled the legitimation of these regimes, had now all but vanished, replaced by stagnation, decline, debt, and high inflation. Resistance to the regimes sprung up and increasingly intensified. All the regimes were destabilized and, in the space of a few weeks, collapsed in 1989.

Yugoslavia, too, shared this degenerating dynamic, but it had greater problems to contend with: it was a multi-national country precariously comprised of competing, traditionally and mutually hostile ethnicities and nationalities, which now turned against each other and sought independence. The Yugoslav ideal was thrown by the wayside. To understand why requires a short explanation. Yugoslavia was artificially created after World War I. True, the idea of south Slavic unification (the "Illyric" concept) had already existed in the early nineteenth century, when revolts against the half-millennial Ottoman rule began. A politically motivated linguistic reform, the consolidation of a Serbo-Croat (or "Illyrian") literary language, signaled its rise. The Croat Ljudevit Gaj and the Serb Vuk Karadžić were its main propagators. But the Serbs' official goal prior to World War I was not a united "Yugoslavia," but a Greater Serbia that would unite all Serbs, including the 40 percent of them who lived in neighboring countries.[2]

Nevertheless, the international situation in the post–World War I period led to the creation of Yugoslavia, or, as it was then called, the Kingdom of Serbs, Croats, and Slovenes. This was largely the result of French geo-political strategy. The victor in the war and the most powerful country on the European continent, France resolved to create a chain of allied countries behind its arch-enemy Germany and Germany's "natural" ally Austria-Hungary. France's new allies, three relatively small multi-national states that had never existed before, formed the so-called Little Entente. They were western-Slav Czechoslovakia, southern-Slav Yugoslavia, and Greater Romania that was now three times larger with a large minority population.

Yugoslavia was not a homogeneous country. Its regions diverged historically, economically, and culturally. Slovenia had been part of Austria and was highly developed compared to the Balkans. Croatia's kingdom belonged to a dynasty of monarchs reigning in the Hungarian Kingdom for some seven centuries, and Croatia had been an autonomous region of Hungary throughout the modern period. Kosovo was a part of Serbia but had an Albanian majority. Bosnia-Herzegovina had a mixed population, 40 percent of whom were Muslim, and was incorporated into Austria-Hungary after 1880.

The delicate situation of Kosovo—a part of Serbia, indeed, the cradle of Serbia, as it was often called—was especially challenging. Just north of the Albanian border, the region gradually developed an Albanian majority. The ethnic composition of Kosovo was in permanent flux. Kosovar Serbs have continually left the region since 1689, when 37,000 Serbian families settled in Austria. Soon after, nearly 100,000 Serbs, led by Patriarch Arsenije III, trekked across the Balkans, followed by a third wave in 1737 pushed out by the Ottomans. The vacated residences of Serbs were taken over by a steady influx of Albanians. Ethnic animosities between Orthodox Serbs and Muslim Albanians have long festered. When the Serbs took Kosovo from the Ottoman Empire, they expelled 800,000 Albanians from the province and killed 10,000; another 400,000 to 600,000 Albanians fled to the mountains. The Albanians' hatred of Serbs was already evident to the British writer, Edith Durham, who visited the region in the early twentieth century. Indeed, during World War I, Albanians took advantage of the Serbs' losses against Austria to wreak vengeance on their Serbian neighbors. Still, Kosovo's population remained evenly divided between Serbs and Albanians in the 1930s. A large part of the Albanian Kosovar community supported Nazi Germany's occupation during World War II. Kosovar Albanians formed the SS Skanderbeg division and slaughtered or expelled several hundred thousand Serbs.

Tensions between Serbs and Albanians only intensified in the post-World War II period—fueled by Kosovo's economic backwardness and low living standards. In the 1970s and 1980s, Kosovo's standard of living was sorely behind Europe's and equal to Pakistan's. Its economic backwardness increasingly worsened after World War II: Kosovo's GDP was 48 percent the Yugoslav average in 1954, 33 percent in 1975, and a mere 27 percent in 1980. In 1988, the unemployment rate was only 2.5 percent in Slovenia and 8.5 percent in Croatia, but 58 percent in Kosovo.[3]

A new political crisis in Kosovo gradually emerged during the 1980s. Yugoslav troops and police crushed a protest demonstration of Albanian Kosovars in 1981. Three years later, Atanasije Jevtić, the Orthodox Archimandrite of Kosovo, publicly accused Albanians of raping women, including young girls and the elderly. Serbs began voicing complaints of discrimination by the Albanian Kosovar authority. In 1986, the extreme Serb nationalist, Vuk Drašković, wailed against the "organized terror . . . the most brutal and most primitive outpouring of hatred and fascism" of Kosovar Albanians against the Serbian community. A 1987 petition signed by 60,000 Serbs decried that "genocide" was being waged against them. Increasing numbers of Serbian Kosovars fled the region and resettled in Serbia. At the same time, Serb policemen turned on ethnic Albanians. In 1983, nearly 42 percent of political prisoners in Yugoslavia were Kosovar Albanians.

Milošević and the Kosovo crisis

It was in this contentious period that Ivan Stambolić sent his friend and confidant, then Serbian communist party leader Slobodan Milošević, to Kosovo with a mission to "calm things down." At that time the two friends both subscribed to the Titoist, anti-nationalist political platform promoting friendship and coexistence among the country's nationalities. Milošević on several occasions denounced Serb nationalism. His words have often been quoted: "Serbian nationalism today," he declared, "is . . . a serpent deep in the bosom of the Serbian people. . . . Serbian nationalists would do the greatest harm to the Serbian people today."[4] The situation in Kosovo would only improve, he added, if Serbs, Montenegrins, Albanians, and all other Kosovars reinforce their ranks and strengthen brotherhood and unity. At the time, he seemed to be the best person to promote ethnic solidarity within the region.

And yet, something very different happened on his trip to Kosovo—something that would change him and his life forever. He arrived with a prepared speech that he never delivered. A crowd of Serbs congregated in front of his window, bitterly complaining about the Albanian authorities. He spontaneously addressed the crowd:

> You must stay here. Your land is here. Here are your houses, your fields and gardens, your memories. You are not going to leave them, are you, because life is hard and because you are subjected to injustice and humiliation? It was never in the spirit of the Serbs and the Montenegrin peoples to succumb before obstacles, to quit when one has to fight. . . . Yugoslavia and Serbia will not give up Kosovo![5]

Instead of promoting peaceful coexistence and cooperation, he spoke of the Serbs' duty to keep Kosovo Serbian. When the crowd reproached Albanian policemen for beating Serbs, Milošević angrily shouted: "No one will ever dare beat you again." This sentence was repeated again and again throughout the country. This was something new, something that was totally at odds with official Titoist "political correctness." In other words, Milošević had legitimized the Serbs' ethnic grievances against the Albanian majority, which immediately made him the Serbs' trusted leader.

Why did Milošević do this? He certainly realized that communism had to be replaced by nationalism, and that this was the only way for a communist leader to survive. His calculation succeeded. His popularity skyrocketed, and he became intoxicated with fame. "Milošević," two historians noted, "had his first taste of the demonic pleasure of power and fame."[6]

Defending the Serbs

This new stage of Milošević's career thus began in Kosovo, the region of legendary importance for the Serbs, the key element of their national mythos. He seized the opportunity and made a number of speeches employing similar rhetoric. At a Kosovo brotherhood and solidarity rally in November 1988, he addressed his Belgrade audience with much the same demagoguery, noting the Serbs' suffering, the plethora of foreign and domestic enemies, and the need for a heroic Serb struggle:

> The long absence of solidarity with the boundless suffering of the Serbs and Montenegrins in Kosovo constitutes an incurable wound . . . to the heart of all of Serbia. But this is no time for sorrow, it is a time for struggle. . . . We shall win despite the fact that Serbia's enemies outside are plotting against it, along with those inside the country . . . [but] we enter every battle with the aim of winning it.[7]

In another speech, he alarmingly proclaimed:

> There remain a small number of fanatics who still dream . . . of allowing Kosovo to separate from Yugoslavia. . . . I will ensure that these dreams never come true . . . those who hope it will are not only fighting in vain but also exposing themselves to tragic consequences.[8]

But Milošević did not limit himself to making nationalist speeches to Serbian audiences. In an environment of escalating ethnic conflict between 1988 and 1990, when nationalism prevailed throughout Yugoslavia, he resolved to destroy all rival nationalisms. At the end of 1988, he dismissed the Albanian communist chief of Kosovo, Azem Vllasi, who was actually strongly pro-Yugoslav, and ordered his arrest for "counterrevolutionary endangerment of the social order." Kosovo's autonomy was wiped off the books: "the authority of the state in all its forms and at both local and provincial levels was overthrown and handed over to Serbia."[9] Similar steps were made in formerly autonomous provinces within Serbia, such as Vojvodina with its significant Hungarian minority.

Deep economic crisis and nationalist demagoguery

In 1988 and 1989, Yugoslavia—like other communist countries of Central and Eastern Europe—suffered the worst economic crisis in decades. In the second half of the 1980s, its previously rapid economic growth ground to a halt and was replaced with virtual stagnation, with its GDP increasing by only 0.5 percent per year. Living standards dropped by 25 percent, and hyper-inflation paralyzed the economy. Inflation and economic decline were common features of the collapsing communist countries. Poland had a 251 percent inflation rate. Hungary, the best positioned country, had an 18 percent increase in prices in 1989. But Yugoslavia suffered the most. Its inflation rate was 15 percent per year in the 1970s, 40 percent in 1981–83, and 200 percent in 1985–87—followed by uncontrollable hyper-inflation, with 1,300 percent price increases in 1989.[10] A large part of the population fell into severe poverty, especially those living in less developed regions. Not surprisingly, Yugoslavs took to the streets. A series of mass demonstrations and rallies took place in 1988 and 1989—an "anti-bureaucratic revolution" blaming local and federal officials for the public's plight and assailing them for bureaucratic incompetence and theft.[11] Many government officials were consequently dismissed. The number of strikes throughout the country demonstrates the extent of the turmoil: there were 174 strikes with 11,000 strikers in 1982, 696 strikes with 60,000 strikers in 1985, 1,685 strikes with 288,000 strikers in 1987, and 1,851 strikes with 386,000 strikers in 1988. The "ruling working class" was at the forefront of the protests. In October 1988, workers held a mass demonstration at the Federal Assembly building in Belgrade, shouting: "We want wages!" "We want bread!" And quite significantly: "We want Sloba!" Milošević appeared before the cheering crowd and assured them that he backed their demands. Echoing the crowd's reproaches, he denounced the so-called bureaucrats and pointedly linked socio-economic issues with the national one. He spoke of economic reforms that would turn the country around, but also promised to fight counter-revolution in Kosovo. He ended with a populist bromide: "And now, everyone back to work."[12]

On another occasion, when oil was discovered in east Serbia and the first well went into operation, he promised in a televised speech that "Modern Serbia will provide the equivalent of $10,000 income for each one of our citizens."[13] At that time the per capita income in Yugoslavia was less than $6,000, and only $4,000 in Serbia. Milošević frivolously promised to double and triple that number and reach at least half the American level—a feat that would take generations. This withdrawn and taciturn man had clearly perfected the craft of populist demagoguery.

The coronation of Serbia's new leader took place on its most sacred national holiday, St. Vitus Day, on June 28, 1989—the 600th anniversary of the Battle of Kosovo. On that day the Serbs suffered at Kosovo Polje their most devastating defeat by the Ottoman Turks, which ended their political independence for half a millennium. Ironically, the Serbs commemorated this grievous event as their principal national holiday, one that celebrated the moral steadfastness and heroic sacrifices of the Serb nation. In 1989, a time of escalating national conflict in the country, and resurgent Serb nationalism, the Battle of Kosovo Polje attained special symbolic importance.

Serb nationalism had already begun flourishing during the economic crisis of the mid-1980s. A milestone of its rise was the publication of an angry Memorandum of the Serbian Academy of Science and Arts in *Vecernje Novosti* on September 24, 1986. It pays to quote it because of its huge impact on Milošević. The authors of the Memorandum lamented the explicit discrimination against Serbs throughout the entire history of Yugoslavia and cried out for action:

> The Serbian nation . . . did not obtain the right to its own state. Unlike national minorities, portions of the Serbian people, who live in other republics in large numbers, do not have the right to use their own language and alphabet, to organize politically and culturally. . . . The unstoppable persecution of Serbs in Kosovo in a drastic manner shows that those principles that protect the autonomy of a minority (Albanians) are not applied when it comes to a minority within a minority (Serbs . . . in Kosovo). . . . [Yugoslav governments maintained that Serb economic development] would pose a danger to the other nations of Yugoslavia. And so all possibilities are grasped to place increasing obstacles in the way of their economic development and political consolidation. . . . The expulsion of the Serbian nation from Kosovo bears spectacular witness to its historic defeat. . . . The physical, political, legal and cultural genocide perpetrated against the Serbian population of Kosovo and Metohija is the greatest defeat suffered by Serbia. . . . Over two successive generations, the Serbian nation has been exposed to . . . physical extermination, to forced assimilation, to religious conversion, to cultural genocide. . . . [We] must find a modern social and national program.[14]

The President of the Academy (later President of Yugoslavia in the early 1990s), Dobrica Ćosić, promoted the concept of "Greater Serbia."

He introduced a radical nationalist ideology that Milošević later adopted. The American Ambassador, Warren Zimmerman, who held strongly anti-Milošević views, blamed Ćosić for creating "the intellectual foundation, the political framework, the ideology for a totally atrocious savage behavior [of Milošević]."[15]

In addition, the Serbian Orthodox Church was also a principal proponent of Serb national interests. It viewed the solution of Yugoslavia's national question to be the fostering of Serbian national continuity, the celebration of the Serbs' national ethos, and the cult of their national and religious grandeur. The Church demanded the cultivation of the Serbs' national history, literature, and traditional customs. "In that way," one observer noted, "an ideology was formed which deepened the crisis and opened new fronts."[16]

In this atmosphere, Milošević went to Kosovo Polje and addressed the nation. A humongous crowd gathered in attendance, some reports estimating one or even two million Serbs. The staging of the event was itself the embodiment of demagogy: Milošević's arrival was terrifyingly similar to one a half-a-century earlier: Adolf Hitler's landing by plane at the *Reichsparteitag* in Nuremberg, filmed for posterity by Leni Riefenstahl. Milošević made a similarly theatrical entrance: "At noon a black dot appeared in the sunny sky. It was a helicopter slowly preparing to land amid the frenzied mass. . . . Sloba-Sloboda emerged from a cloud of dust, climbed the 18-metre podium and gave a speech."[17] He was surrounded by Orthodox bishops and created the impression that he "presided at his own coronation, replacing communism with nationalism."[18] In his speech to the crowd, he boldly declared:

> The lack of unity and betrayal in Kosovo . . . continue to follow the Serbian people like an evil fate through the whole of its history. . . . When a socialist Yugoslavia was set up . . . the Serbian leadership . . . [made] concessions . . . at the expense of their people [that] could not be accepted historically. . . . Their national and historical being has been liberational throughout the whole of history. . . . They liberated themselves and when they could they also helped others to liberate themselves . . . the Serbs have not used the advantage of being great for their own benefit. . . . This situation lasted for decades . . . and here we are now at the field of Kosovo to say that this is no longer the case. . . . Six centuries later, now, we are being again engaged in bat-

tles and are facing battles. . . . Regardless of what kind of battles they
are, they cannot be won without resolve, bravery, and sacrifice, without the noble qualities that were present here in the field of Kosovo. . . . Six centuries ago, Serbia heroically defended itself in the field
of Kosovo, but it also defended Europe . . . the European culture, religion, and European society. . . . Let the memory of Kosovo heroism
live forever![19]

The main themes of his demagogic pronouncements from previous
years were now repeated: the Serbs' martyrdom and destiny of suffering, the Serbs' resolve to liberate themselves, and the need to fight for
Serbia once again. At the same time, however, Milošević's address retained elements of "Yugoslavism," reflecting his general policy at that
time. There was still a need, he declared, to preserve and defend Yugoslavia's unity. "Equal and harmonious relations among Yugoslav peoples," he added pointedly, "are a necessary condition for the existence of
Yugoslavia." He even declared that the fact that Serbia "has never had
only Serbs living in it," something that is even more true today, is "not
a disadvantage for Serbia." On the contrary, "it is to its advantage."

Nevertheless, his speech effectively echoed the nationalist ideology
of the Academy's Memorandum and the Orthodox Church. He presented Serbia as a victim and warned of unavoidable new battles that required heroic resolve. This new line was strongly at odds with traditional Titoism and the policy of his mentor, Ivan Stambolić.

Extreme nationalism and collapse of Yugoslavia

In point of fact, a conflict with his old friend had already begun in 1987.
In September of that year, Milošević launched an open attack against
Stambolić and his circle in the Central Committee. He called for a special Central Committee meeting that culminated with Stambolić's dis-
missal at the end of the year. Their dispute ended in an ugly and brutal way. In 2000, Ivan Stambolić mysteriously disappeared; later his
corpse was discovered in a remote mountainous area. It then became
public that a Special Operation Unit had in fact killed him, and several members of the unit were indicted for the crime. Rumors abounded
that his former friend and protégé was behind the killing.

Some extreme nationalist Serbians (whom he occasionally denounced), began including Milošević in the extreme nationalist camp. For his part, Milošević was now pushing the Serbs down the road of violent nationalism, which proved to be a bloody and murderous affair. In January 1990, the federatively organized Yugoslav Communist Party, the League of Communists of Yugoslavia, held its 14th Congress. There a conflict immediately erupted: the Slovene delegation walked out of the session and the League was formally disbanded. This was virtually the end of Yugoslavia. Most of the former republican components of the Yugoslav League of Communists now became openly nationalist parties. This was definitely the case in Slovenia, Serbia, and Macedonia. The conventional wisdom was that Yugoslavia was held together by three forces: Tito, the Communist Party, and the Yugoslav Army. Now two of the three had disappeared. The demise of the third, and Yugoslavia itself, would soon follow.

In 1989–90, after nearly a half a century, multiparty elections changed the entire political landscape of Central and Eastern Europe. Their primary focus was democratization and market transformation. Similar elections were held in Yugoslavia as well, but there the preoccupation was national independence of the various republics. Nationalist parties were established in all of those republics alongside their respective Communist Parties, which also jumped on the nationalist bandwagon and blamed Serbian centralization and oppression for the economic crisis. The standard call was for national independence, initially in a confederation of independent south Slavic countries. The most prominent of the new nationalist parties was Franjo Tuđman's Croatian Democratic Union (*Hrvatska Demokratska Zajednica* or HDZ), which was established in 1990 and promptly won 42 percent of the vote in free elections that year. In Serbia, Milošević's Communist Party was revamped as the Serbian Socialist Party (*Socijalistička Partija Srbije*, SPS). Several other new parties, among them the more extreme nationalist Serbian Radical Party, also emerged, but the leading nationalist party was under Milošević's command. In Bosnia three ethnic-religious parties competed with one other: the Muslim Party of Democratic Action (*Stranka Demokratske Akcije* or SDA) of Alija Izetbegovic won 34 percent of the vote, the Serb Party 30 percent, and the Croat Party 18 percent—more or less matching the ethnic ratio within Bosnia-Herzegovina. In Macedonia, the Internal

Macedonian Revolutionary Organization (*Vatreshna Makedonska-Revolucionerna Organizaciya* or VMRO), which originally had been established at the end of the nineteenth century and had been infamously active as a terrorist organization during the interwar period, was reorganized. Winning 37 seats in the Macedonian Parliament, it formed a coalition with the Macedonian Communists (with 31 seats). In Kosovo, Albanians boycotted the first free elections in Serbia and formed an ad hoc government of their own with Ibrahim Rugova serving as shadow president.

Following the Croat and Slovene elections, Milošević refused to consider the independence of the various republics or even the idea of confederation. He had the Serb-led Yugoslav army order the republics' Territorial Defense Forces (formed against a possible Soviet attack in previous decades) to hand over all arms in their possession. The new governments refused to do so and instead began importing more weapons. In a clear escalation, the former Yugoslav republics, now led by their nationalist parties, repudiated the Yugoslav (in reality the Serbian) attempt to preserve a unified multi-national state and declared independence. A referendum was held in Slovenia in December 1990, leading to an overwhelming vote for independence. Croatia held a similar referendum in May 1991, with the same outcome. Both republics declared independence on June 25, 1991. An independence referendum took place in Bosnia-Herzegovina somewhat later in March 1992. The Bosnian Serbs boycotted the referendum, but 99.7 percent of those participating voted for independence. On March 3, the independence of the Republic of Bosnia-Herzegovina was also declared. When the Croats and Bosnians declared independence, the Krajina's Serbs' enclave within Croatia and the Bosnian Serbs also organized plebiscites and declared their own republics, separating from Croatia and Bosnia.

The issue of Serb minorities in Croatia and Bosnia-Herzegovina now became a central part of the conflict. The existence of relatively large Serbian ethnic minorities outside Serbia had long historical roots. Tens and hundreds of thousands of ethnic Serbs escaped from Ottoman occupation during the fifteenth and sixteenth centuries and went north, where they settled in the Habsburg Empire as free warrior-peasants in the border areas. In the Serbian language, this area was called "Krajina," meaning frontier. (This situation was somewhat similar to that of the free Cossack-peasant soldiers in the border areas of the Russian Empire.) As a result of these migrations, roughly 40 percent of modern-day Serbs lived outside Serbia in neighboring regions, now called Croatia and Bosnia-Herzegovina. These Serbs wanted national liberation as much as the Croats and Bosniaks did, and for them that meant joining Serbia.

There was another important element in this chaotic nationalist upheaval. Out of either confusion or bias, the great powers, the United States and the European Economic Community (the soon-to-be European Union), made serious political mistakes. The Bush administration believed—clearly on the advice of the American Ambassador in Yugoslavia, Warren Zimmerman—that after the collapse of communism in Europe Yugoslavia was no longer important and not worth helping.[20] Significantly, George Kennan, the leading Cold War expert in the US and ambassador to Yugoslavia between 1961 and 1963, disagreed. He told Zimmerman: "They [the US government] are wrong. I think events in Yugoslavia are going to turn violent and . . . especially [for] the United States [it will be] one of their foreign policy problems in the next few years."[21]

Western confusion was clearly evident when Secretary of State James Baker visited Belgrade and opposed the secession of Slovenia and Croatia, favoring a confederation instead. On the other hand, the European Parliament passed a resolution on March 13, 1991, declaring "that the constituent republics and autonomous provinces of Yugoslavia must have the right freely to determine their own future in a peaceful and democratic manner and on the basis of recognized international and national borders."[22] Germany rushed to recognize Croat independence in December 1991—a major step in asserting an independent German foreign policy that traditionally turned eastward. Italy and Denmark also supported independence, while France, Britain, and the Netherlands opposed. The European Economic Community recognized independent Croatia on January 15, 1992.

Serbian "self-defense," the civil war, and a new war in Kosovo

In these tense years, Milošević passionately promoted—as he called it—Serbian self-defense. At the Serbian Assembly on May 30, 1991, he characterized the former Yugoslav republics as enemies and issued a call for arms:

Outside factors are already openly giving support to forces of disintegration in Yugoslavia. . . . The state and political crisis in Yugoslavia, which has for a long time involved intra-national conflicts, has acquired the form of an armed showdown with elements of a civil-war.

In an interview on August 7, 1991, he accused the Slovenes and Croats of starting the conflict:

Everything in Yugoslavia started when nationalists in Croatia and Slovenia came to power, and the simple result of that was the decision on secession. Everything else followed. . . . [The Serbs] have always acted in self-defense and nothing else. [The interviewer, Arnot Van Linden, remarked:] They [the Croats and Slovenians] say, however, that everything began in 1987 when you became President of Serbia on the basis of a nationalist policy.[23]

In such an acrimonious environment, nationalist tensions invariably evolved into all-out war—just as Milošević had predicted at Kosovo Polje in 1989. It was he who had actually started the war with his provocative speeches and particularly his decision to send the Serbian-led Yugoslav army to attack Slovenia. True, he soon accepted international mediation and halted the fighting with a dismissive "Let Slovenia go." But the actual war, with all its horrors, had not yet started; that would be between Serbia and Croatia. The whole issue of Croat independence and the Serb minority in east Croatia brought back traumatic memories of the wartime massacres of Serbs by the fascist Ustaše armed forces in "independent" Croatia. (Discussed below in connection with Croat nationalist upheaval.) A full-scale war also broke out both between Serbia (or the Serbs in Bosnia) and Muslim Bosnia and between Croatia and Muslim Bosnia.

Initially Milošević strove to keep Yugoslavia together, but it soon became clear that that was impossible. He then pivoted to the idea of Greater Serbia, his oft-stated promises of defending and uniting the Serbs residing in Croatia and Bosnia. Within those Serbian enclaves, he operated mostly through local Serb paramilitary units, even though he would occasionally bump heads with these extremist, often murderous, gangs.

One of the war's most grotesque episodes was the invitation that Milošević extended to one of his arch enemies, Croatia's extreme nationalist leader Franjo Tuđman, to meet at Karadjordjevo (Tito's hunting lodge) on Mach 25, 1991.

The topic was Bosnia. In a strange way, the two men were bound together; they were like Siamese twins who had one heart. And that heart
was Bosnia. . . . Where they differed was on the matter of territory. Both
wanted the whole of Bosnia . . . they decided to reach an agreement at
the expense of the Bosnian Muslims. The two men shared the view that
the Muslims were not a distinct nation. Tuđman actually contended that
the Bosniak Muslims are Croats, whereas Milošević insisted that they
were Serbs. . . . The understanding they reached at Karadjordjevo was
that the Bosnian republic should disappear from the map. . . . Indeed,
the two men soon held another secret meeting on the Serb-Croatian
border . . . [to] discuss details of the Bosnian division. . . . [Their] en-
voys met secretly more than thirty times to discuss maps and population movements (what later became known as ethnic cleansing).[24]

Whatever the causes, the Yugoslav Civil War would end in tragedy.
Most of the killing was carried out by Serb paramilitary units. These included Vojislav Šešelj's men, the "seseljevci" Chetniks or the "White Ea-
gels," and especially Željko Raznatović's crew, nicknamed Arkan'smen, the
"arkanovci" or "Tigers." A United Nations report determined in 1994 that
no fewer than 83 different paramilitary organizations had operated in Bosnia "and were responsible for some of the worst atrocities of the war."[25]

When Serbia lost the war in 1994–95, Milošević rediscovered his former self and played a positive role in Dayton in 1995, when the United
States forced the three leaders to sit down and reach an agreement on
Bosnia. He was the most realistic and talented of the three and provided crucial assistance to US Ambassador Richard Holbrook and Secretary of State Warren Christopher. His role was widely recognized—a role
that was pivotal when Izetbegović refused to sign the final agreement because he wanted more. Milošević was even prepared to make concessions
on Sarajevo that would be very unpopular with Serbs to reach an agreement. As the author of an important book on the Yugoslav tragedy concluded, Milošević "served as an invaluable partner to Holbrooke in over-
coming stumbling blocks, . . . such as the question of who would
exercise control over Sarajevo."[26] Thorwald Stoltenberg, the United Nations negotiator in Bosnia in 1995, concurred that "President Slobodan
Milosevic had played a key role in the peace process in Yugoslavia."[27]

Quite unfortunately, however, this tragic scenario was repeated a few
years later, when war broke out in Kosovo at the end of the 1990s. Ruth-

less Serb militias killed, raped, and uprooted Kosovar Albanians, and the equally brutal Albanian Kosovo Liberation Army, the KLA (*Ushtria Çlirimtare e Kosovës*), killed and expelled Serbs from their homes. In 1997, the Kosovo Liberation Army had launched a campaign which, for the most part, "meant warfare in the shadows, ambush, assassination, murder, and torture, leaving in its wake a trail of destroyed towns, burned villages, and wrecked families." By 1998, these guerilla actions "had reached significant proportions and elicited brutal Serb countermeasures."[28] Moreover, the KLA sought to escalate the war by spreading it to Macedonia in order to "liberate" the Albanians there as well.

The savage war in Kosovo was the occasion when the United States and the NATO finally intervened militarily in the Yugoslav conflict. In March 1999, both began a devastating bombing campaign on Serbia. Milošević's response to the bombing was the ethnic cleansing of Kosovar Albanians. Hundreds of thousands of Albanians were uprooted from their villages and expelled to neighboring countries. Milošević stubbornly posed as a Serb martyr, duplicating Prince Lazar's performance at Kosovo Polje six centuries earlier to fight till death and not surrender or compromise. He recalcitrantly rebuffed Richard Holbrooke's last minute offer for an agreement. "He was fatalism itself . . . and he chose this path despite warnings that it would mean the physical destruction of Serbia,"[29] and to him personally: the International War Crimes Tribunal in The Hague charged him of crimes against humanity on May 27. On June 3, he capitulated and withdrew from Kosovo, which, per UN Security Council Resolution 1244 of 10 June 1999, became an international protectorate. A steadfast Milošević addressed the nation that evening and told his Serb compatriots that they have ultimately survived and defended the country.[30]

He was mistaken. Despite Russian opposition, the Western powers and the international community settled the Kosovo war nearly a decade later by recognizing Kosovo's independence from Serbia. The *New York Times* reported on February 18, 2008:

> The province of Kosovo declared independence from Serbia on Sunday, sending tens of thousands of ethnic Albanians streaming through the streets to celebrate what they hoped was the end of a long and bloody struggle for national self-determination. Kosovo's bid to be recognized

as Europe's newest country—after a civil war that killed 10,000 people a decade ago and then years of limbo under United Nations rule—was the latest episode in the dismemberment of the former Yugoslavia, 17 years after its dissolution began.[31]

There was little logic to the West's actions. A decade earlier, in 1995, the United States had forced an agreement on the combatants in Dayton to end the Bosnian war. At that time, both the Serb and Croat communities in Bosnia-Herzegovina had voted for independence from Muslim Bosnia and sought to join their respective Serb and Croat states. But their demands were rejected, and a multi-ethnic independent Bosnian state was created. In 2008, however, the Alban ethnicity in Kosovo won the West's recognition of independence from Serbia, incorporating a Serbian minority within an independent Kosovo. This time the West decided against a multi-ethnic solution. Regretfully, the Western powers were not in their best form throughout the Yugoslav civil war.

Less than a decade later, independent Kosovo became a hot-bed of Islamic fundamentalism. To quote the *New York Times* again (from May 22, 2016):

> Since then [the American-led intervention] . . . Saudi money and influence have transformed this once-tolerant Muslim society at the hem of Europe into a font of Islamic extremism and a pipeline for jihadists . . . [Hundreds] of Kosovars . . . have gone abroad to join the Islamic State, the highest number per capita in Europe. . . . It is a stunning turnabout for a . . . people that not long ago was among the most pro-American Muslim societies in the world.[32]

The war criminal

Slobodan Milošević undoubtedly went too far by employing nationalist demagoguery to mobilize the Serbs and then launch a devastating war. The International Criminal Tribunal in The Hague set up by the United Nations (Resolution 827), indicted Milošević in 1999 with "genocide, crimes against humanity, grave breaches of the Geneva Conventions and violations of the Laws or Customs of War." The prosecutor charged him with criminal responsibility for war crimes, which "he planned, instigated, ordered, committed, or in whose planning, preparation, or exe-

cution he otherwise aided and abetted. . . . 'Committed' in this indictment refers to participation in a joint criminal enterprise as a
co-perpetrator . . . [between] 1 August 1991 and continued until at least
31 December 1995."[33]

Milošević was voted out of office in national elections in 2000. His
successor as president of Yugoslavia, Vojislav Koštunica, had him arrested and handed over to the International Tribunal in The Hague. He died
in prison of a heart attack in 2006. He defended himself quite successfully at his trial, and it is not at all clear what the trial's outcome might
have been had he lived. Especially, since Serbia's deputy prime minister
Šešelj,[34] who was an even more extreme Serb nationalist who had urged
the members of his paramilitary Chetnik gang "to use 'rusty spoons' to
gouge out their enemies' eyes," was acquitted in The Hague in 2016.

The International Tribunal indicted more than 160 people for war
crimes in Yugoslavia. Neither Tuđman, who died in 1999, nor Izetbegović,
who died in 2003, were indicted. Although their actions will be discussed below, it's worth quoting Michael Barratt Brown on the subject:

> The majority of world opinion has accepted the Croatian nationalist
> propaganda line . . . to the effect that it was a result of Serbian nation-
> alism stoked by a demonic character named Slobodan Milosevic. . . .
> There were a lot of other nationalists about in other republics, even more
> extreme than Milosevic, looking for the opportunity to transfer power
> to themselves if Yugoslavia broke up.[35]

Milošević, and to an extent Serbia were demonized by the international community and a great part of the scholarly literature as the principal culprits responsible for the war, the atrocities, and the killings.
Not without reason. Although responsibility was shared by Tuđman and
Izetbegovič, the primary initiator for the war, atrocities, and mass killing was Milošević.

Franjo Tuđman—from communist to rightwing nationalist

This extreme nationalist Croat leader, who was president of the country during the entire civil war, was also responsible for the immense
tragedy in those years, second only to Milošvić. "Carl Bildt, the United

Nations envoy, suggested that Tudjman was equally deserving of indictment."[36] Some accounts of the Yugoslav civil war rightly maintain that "Tudjman was in a sense a perfect match for Milosevic."[37]

Born in 1922, Tuđman was nineteen years older than Milošević. A year after the latter's birth, Tuđman, then 19, joined the 10th Zagreb Corp of Tito's communist partisan army, along with his father Stjepian, a tavern owner. His family background was somewhat similar to Milošević's. His mother died when he was 7 years old; his father remarried, but he and his second wife were found dead at home in April 1946, in what was believed to be a murder suicide.

The beginning of Tuđman's career was determined by his partisan background. After the war, he graduated at the military academy at the age of 30. Already a colonel at that time, he rose to the rank of major general in 1959. At just shy of 40, he was the youngest major general in the Yugoslav Army. But then his life suddenly changed. In 1961, he decided to leave the army to pursue an interest in Croat nationalism, and he began an academic study reinterpreting Croatian history from a nationalist point of view. He became a professor at Zagreb University. His doctoral dissertation on "The Causes of the Crisis of the Yugoslav Monarchy from Unification in 1918 until Its Breakdown in 1941" was rejected by Zagreb University in 1965, but then accepted by the University of Zadar. It was later discovered that four-fifths of his dissertation had been lifted from the work of another historian. He was expelled from the university for plagiarism and retired at the age of 45 in 1967.

Croat nationalism and "independent" fascist state

Tuđman became preoccupied with Croat nationalism, and he manifested increasing anti-Serb, anti-Yugoslav attitudes. These ideas had a long history in Croatia. One cannot understand his mind-set without understanding its historical roots. Croat-Serb conflicts had accompanied all of Yugoslavia's history. After a few years of brief enthusiasm for southern-Slav unity at the end of World War I, intense conflicts between Croats and Serbs resurfaced again in the mid-1920s. The founder and leader of the Croatian People's Peasant Party, Stjepan Radić, renounced the idea of a united Yugoslavia and declared it dead already in 1927: "This state has buried its own idea. . . . Nothing is left of the Slavic and Yugoslav idea."[38] He was assassinated the following year during a parliamentary session. Only the dissolution of all political parties and the introduction of a Royal Dictatorship in 1929 saved the unity of Yugoslavia—albeit temporarily.

The Croatian independence movement, however, was not buried with Radić. An even more radical, this time right-wing secessionist party, the Croatian Party of Rights (*Hrvatska Stranka Prava*, or HSP), emerged during the 1920s. A Zagreb lawyer, Ante Pavelić, became its leader, but was forced to flee to Mussolini's Italy when the Royal Dictatorship was introduced. There, he formed a Croatian terrorist organization, the Ustaše. Its most successful action was the assassination of Yugoslavia's King Alexander in Marseille during his state visit to France in 1934.

After years of tension and atrocities, the opportunity the Croat nationalists were waiting for came in 1941, when Hitler attacked Yugoslavia. Pavelić immediately ordered Croat soldiers in the Yugoslav army to "Use your weapons against the Serbian soldiers and officers. . . . We are fighting shoulder to shoulder with our German and Italian allies."[39] A puppet Independent State of Croatia (*Nezavisna Drzava Hrvatska*, NDH), incorporating all of Bosnia-Herzegovina, was declared under the tutelage of Hitler and Mussolini. Working side by side with Nazi troops, the fascist Croat state launched a brutal war against the Serbs and the Yugoslav partisan army. Massacres began in the Serbian village of Gudovac in Bosnia-Herzegovina in April and turned into a genuine genocide with the killing of tens of thousands of Serbs, Jews, and Gypsies. The Croats' infamous Jasenovac concentration camp was on par with Nazi extermination camps.

The Serb partisan army avenged the Croat atrocities by the end of the war. One of the most infamous incidents was dubbed the Bleiburg affair, named after the Austrian border town where tens of thousands Ustaše soldiers were killed by Tito's forces. The Ustaše army had wanted to surrender to the British, and not to Tito's partisan army. The British, however, handed the Croat soldiers to the Serb-led Yugoslav army, which promptly massacred them.

Tito's new constitution—towards national revival

Yugoslavia was reunited at the end of World War II without really healing the deep wounds, thanks to the efforts of an exceptional leader, Josip Broz Tito. This larger than life partisan hero, admired internationally for his brave and successful resistance against the century's most powerful dictators, Hitler and Stalin, held the country together with an iron hand and a firm resolve to create and maintain peaceful ethnic coexistence. The communist state suppressed nationalism and imprisoned nationalist activists—among them two of the main actors of this story—and it tried to develop a Yugoslav nation and national consciousness.

Before his death, Tito tried to create institutional protections of that unity. He changed the country's constitution to stabilize it after his death. The 1974 Constitution had allotted equal status to each republic and introduced a semi-confederal system: the Bosnian Muslims and Kosovar Albanians were given de facto autonomy; the Albanian language was given the same recognition as Serbo-Croatian; and an Albanian university was opened in Pristina. Collective leadership was also introduced to take the place of the Yugoslav Presidency, comprising one representative of each of the eight Yugoslav republics and autonomous provinces, elected by their parliaments for a five-year period. These prescient actions by Tito not only failed but proved counterproductive. The new constitution, Susan Woodward observed, "whilst trying to halt atavistic nationalism, actually fueled them by situating political power at the level of the national groups, promoting the further ethnic stratification of Yugoslav politics."[40]

In addition to the age-old ethnic strife, another factor intensified nationalist tensions in the country. Economically speaking, Yugoslavia was not a single, homogenous country. As a Slovene historian noted,

> Yugoslavia was at the level of Turkey in terms of per capita gross domestic product at purchasing power parity in 1985. Kosovo, the less-developed part of Yugoslavia, was at the level of Pakistan. The most developed part, Slovenia, was compared with Spain and New Zealand. Vojvodina and Croatia approached Greece and Portugal. Bosnia-Herzegovina and Macedonia were compared with Thailand and Mexico, and Serbia with Turkey.[41]

The economic gap or more precisely, the economic abyss in the country was simply unbridgeable. This applied as well to the various regions' unemployment rates. In 1988, unemployment was only 2.5 percent in Slovenia and 8.5 percent in Croatia, but it topped 25 percent in Bosnia-Herzegovina and Montenegro and 58 percent in Kosovo.[42]

For this reason, Susan Woodward concluded that

> The conflict is not a result of historical animosities and it is not a return to the pre-communist past; it is the result of the politics of transforming a socialist society to a market economy and democracy. A critical element of this failure was economic decline. . . . More than a decade of austerity and declining living standards corroded the social fabric [of Yugoslavia].[43]

But this conclusion is incorrect. One certainly cannot ignore the fact that economic conditions exacerbated old conflicts and ethnic tensions among the various groups in the country. One also cannot ignore the fact that, less than half a century earlier, those nationalities, organized in independent states, literary cut each other's throats in unspeakable carnage. It is therefore easy to understand how mass dissatisfaction and desperation in Yugoslavia can almost naturally be transformed into bloody nationalist conflict once again. Indeed, one may use the term "naturally" in a country where the wealthiest republics (Slovenia and Croatia) had living standards two-to-four times higher than those in the poor provinces, and where Yugoslav national consciousness barely existed—except for about five percent of the population, some of whom were in mixed marriages. The wealthier Slovenia and Croatia, trapped in a quasi-confederation not of their choosing, wanted to rid themselves of the less developed parts of Yugoslavia. One should not forget that the primary slogan throughout Central and Eastern Europe in 1989 and 1990 was "Back to Europe!"—an earnest desire to join the European Union. For the Slovenes and the Croats, such a dream appeared more attainable without Serbia and the even more backward regions of Yugoslavia. But even if all this were natural, it was not inevitable. Nationalist demagogues began to appear on the political scene and were very much responsible for the events that followed.

Tuđman the far-right nationalist leader

Franjo Tuđman became more and more involved in nationalist ideas in the 1960s. This was a time of major turmoil in Yugoslavia. With its economic reforms beginning in 1965, the country began to move more and more away—both economically and politically—from the Soviet model. The government enacted severs market reforms, promoted worker self-management, and passed constitutional amendments in 1967, 1968, and 1971 that strengthened the autonomy of its constituent republics. These reforms invariably weakened the power of the central government, which in itself enabled traditional Croat nationalism to thrive. This culminated in the *Croatian Spring* movement,[44] which denounced Serb centralism and demanded more autonomy, insisted on a greater share of tourism revenue, and—an important symbolic change—called for the abolition of the Serbo-Croat language. This last demand, issued by the Declaration of the Name and Position of the Croatian Literary Language in 1967, was publicly backed by Tuđman. It was repeated a second time in 1971, when *Matica Hrvatska*, a traditional Croat cultural institution, openly rejected the existence of Serbo-Croatian and demanded the recognition of two separate Croat and Serb languages. In November 1971, at the height of the Croat national movement, 30,000 students of the University of Zagreb demonstrated in support of these national demands.

These were very tense years in Yugoslavia generally. The Soviet Bloc had militarily suppressed the "Prague Spring" in Czechoslovakia in 1968, and the Brezhnev Doctrine vowing to "defend socialism" in other socialist countries renewed the fear of a possible Soviet invasion. Tito enacted the Law on Total National Defense to establish republican defense forces.

All of this strongly influenced Franjo Tuđman, who joined the Croatian Spring movement. Tito was determined to suppress Croat nationalism: he accused the Croat party leaders of supporting nationalism and removed the popular Miko Tripelo and Savka Dabčević-Kučar from their posts. Tuđman was also arrested in the purge and sentenced to two years in prison for subversive activities. However, he was released nine months later. Tuđman's imprisonment pushed him further into the nationalist camp. Throughout the 1970s and 1980s, he continued to reinterpret Croat history along nationalist lines. He published a 1980 study arguing that Bosnia-Herzegovina was "by historical right and geographical logic an integral part of Croatia."[45] He began building up connections with the Croatian diaspora. In 1977, he travelled to Sweden to meet with prominent émigrés. He was imprisoned for three years for statements he made on Swedish television, but, once again, was released just 11 months later. In 1987, he traveled to Canada to link up with nationalist and often former Ustaše fascist émigré organizations there.

He was finally able to make his ideas a reality at the end of the 1980s. Tuđman founded the Croatian Democratic Union party in 1989 and won the national elections in 1990. He moved ahead with an independence referendum in May and declared Croatia's independence in June 1991, which was recognized by Germany at the end of the year. Throughout the election campaign he regularly used "inflammatory nationalist remarks [and] suggested that Bosnia was naturally in the Croatian sphere of interest."[46] His statements reminded Serbs living in Croatia of the Ustaše's rhetoric about protecting the "Arian blood and honor" of the Croatian nation; at one point he indeed proudly proclaimed that "Thank God my wife is not a Jew or a Serb."[47] The connections he built with the nationalist and even fascist émigré organizations immediately consolidated his political position. He "openly courted the Ustashe exile organizations. He invited Ustashe émigrés to Croatia and issued visas upon their arrival at the airport."[48] As Tuđman himself described it, this was "a turning point in my life." "The key to Tudjman's success," concluded one historian, "was an alliance with the militant nationalist émigrés who had been associated with the Ustashe, who fled to North and South America and Australia after World War II." Indeed, the old Ustaše slogans such as *"Mi Hrvati ne pijemo vina/nego krv Srba iz Knina"* (We Croats don't drink wine, rather we drink the blood of Serbs from Knin) or *"Srbe na vrbe"* (Hang Serbs from willow trees) appeared all over Croatia.[49]

Tuđman believed he represented the legacy of independent World War II Croatia, regardless of its fascist and murderous nature. He pushed for rehabilitating the wartime Ustaše state, and he adopted its symbols, including the checker-board flag. He also initiated a nationalist language reform to replace Serbo-Croat and foreign (including English sports) words with "genuine" or invented Croat ones. Most of all, he planned to reestablish the borders of the former Ustaša state. Ian Traynor writes,

[At] one crisp morning in January 1991, six months before the wars began and less than a year after he became president, he received me in the locker room at his tennis court on the outskirts of Zagreb. Tudjman had just won a doubles match. The mood was one of backslapping bonhomie with mid-morning champagne by the crate. . . . Tudjman revealed his ideal vision for Yugoslavia. The country, he laughed, would be reorganised along the lines last tried in 1939, when the Serbs and Croats reached a deal to turn Yugoslavia into a Greater Croatia and a Greater Serbia. That, of course, meant wiping Bosnia off the map.[50]

War criminal—without indictment

Tuđman's nationalist regime immediately advocated the idea of Greater Croatia, which meant incorporating Bosnia-Herzegovina into Croatia, as had the wartime Ustaša state. The American Ambassador Warren Zimmerman recalled a conversation with Tuđman in which the latter insisted that the Bosnian Muslims were planning a Greater Bosnia that would spread to Turkey and Libya, that their leader, Alija Izetbegovic, was a fundamentalist front-man for Turkey, and that the Bosnians would eradicate both Catholics and Orthodox alike. He also informed the ambassador that he and Milošević were planning to divide Bosnia among themselves. He "modestly" conceded: "Let Milošević take the larger part. . . . We can do with less than fifty percent."[51]

Franjo Tuđman was absolutely convinced of his eternal place in Croatia's history books. He was sure that he was always right and was always inclined to "bark orders, grunt disapproval, and interrupt whoever was speaking. He would later do himself no favours by repeating the rudeness with various US secretaries of state."[52] He was adamant that every word he uttered was important and resolved to preserve all his private conversations and telephone correspondences on tape. (Some called him the Croat Nixon.) After his death, Stipe Mesić's Social Democratic Party took office and handed the tapes over to The Hague. On June 18, 2000, when the existence of the tapes became public, *The Telegraph* reported under the title "Tudjman tapes reveal plans to divide Bosnia and hide war crimes" that the "recordings lay bare the scale of Zagreb's co-ordination of Croatia extremists in Bosnia and Tudjman personal complicity in war crimes, theft and corruption." The records also showed that he covered the manslaughter in the Bosnian Ahmici village in April 1993 when 100 Muslims were killed by Croats. Although in 1994, after an investigation, he named five men as responsible, he also "ordered that they be given new names and identities and allowed to leave Croatia." At a meeting, he warned his associates about the possibility of an indictment by The Hague Tribunal: "It is clear our generals and all of you who are sitting here now with me could end up there."[53] It did not happen.

Tuđman's speeches were typically demagogic. A good example of his style was his "State of the Nation" speech to the Joint Session of the Croat Parliament when he addressed on December 22, 1994, the alarming demographic decline, the lack of reproduction, and the decrease of the population:

> [Demographic decline is] the most severe and the most baleful consequence of the rule over the Croatian people by the artificial Communist system and anti-Croatian Yugoslav state. It is such that the Croatian people would be faced with extinction if we did not take decisive steps. The natural population of Croatia has been decreasing for 45 years (since 1950) and [birth rate] is now lower than the death rate.

Duplicating similar programs of Mussolini and Hitler, Tuđman announced the preparation and implementation of a demographic revival program.

> A mother of four (and more) children should be given the average salary of her rank so that she could devote herself to bringing up her children and be existentially secure. Families with more children should enjoy housing priority. Single persons should pay higher taxes. The award of shares to families with more children and newborn children should also be considered.[54]

Tuđman's pedigree as a dangerous demagogue was fully on display during his victory speech after the Serbs' defeat in Krajina. In the first stages of the war, the Serbian paramilitary forces were brutal and effective against the Croats and were able to occupy a Serb-inhabited region in Croatia. But the Croats were able to reverse this in 1994–95 and reoccupy Krajina. At the end of their "Operation Storm" in 1995, the Croat paramilitary "Merčep's Gang" (known as the "Croatian Knights") chased out some 250,000 Serbs from the region and slaughtered the few thousand who remained behind. On this occasion, Tuđman delivered a jubilant victory speech on August 30, 1995:

> And from today, this is Croatian Knin. And there can be no return to the past, to the times when they the Serbs were spreading cancer in the heart of Croatia, cancer which was destroying the Croatian national being . . . to be the master in its own house. . . . Our nation will celebrate its freedom and build its Croatia for which, since King Zvonimir [in the] 11th century, too many Croatian people died and too many of our sons suffered in the dungeons of Venice, Vienna, Budapest, and Belgrade. . . . Croatian future can be secured.[55]

Franjo Tuđman's Croatia fought the Yugoslav civil war in the same brutal manner as did the Serbs. His striking national demagoguery and his embrace of the wartime fascist Croat state legitimized the country's war crimes and inspired the most barbaric behavior in his troops. He attempted to occupy all of Bosnia-Herzegovina, expelled Croatia's Serb minority and ethnically cleansed Krajina. His country was nevertheless supported by the Western allies and he was never indicted by The Hague Tribunal for war crimes. He conveniently died at the end of 1999, just in time to avoid indictment. Reporting his death on December 11, 1999, the BBC correctly noted that "Unlike Serbia's President Slobodan Milosevic, Mr. Tudjman managed to promote his equally rampant nationalism without attracting widespread condemnation."[56] As the *Guardian*'s obituary rightly observed, "Tudjman was a nationalist zealot, obsessed with his place in history. His nationalist drive brought him to purge the language of foreign elements and Yugoslavisms to rename the currency, streets . . . and to preside over a creeping rehabilitation of the quisling Ustashe regime."[57]

Alija Izetbegović and his background

The third politician who also shared some responsibility for the Yugoslav tragedy was the Bosnian Muslim Alija Izetbegović. His background and personality diverged from his Serb and Croat counterparts, but he was also guilty of the most egregious demagoguery. Unlike Milošević and Tuđman, he had never been a communist, and in fact had always been an ardent anti-communist. He never had any position in the Yugoslav state and had never played any role in politics, had spent several years in Tito's prisons, and overall had a much milder persona than Milošević or Tuđman. Nevertheless, as the *Guardian* observed in 2003, "in the political, military, and diplomatic games of the Balkans, he was no angel either. . . . In opting for ethnic politics, Izetbegovic was as guilty as the Serbian and Croatian fanatics who hated him so viscerally."[58]

Alija Izetbegović was born to a Bosnian Muslim family in 1925. Part of the south Slavic population had converted to Islam during the nearly five hundred-year Ottoman Turkish occupation of the Balkans, especially members of the landowning class who could only keep their estates as Muslims. His family background was indeed aristocratic, though they had lost their land long ago. His father worked as an accountant.

A large number of Bosnian Muslims did not like living in either an Orthodox or a secular Yugoslav state. During World War II, after Hitler had established a fascist Croat state and incorporated Bosnia-Herzegovina as part of that state, Bosnian Muslims sided with the Croatian fascists and fought alongside the Ustaše and the Germans in their genocidal struggle against the Serbs and Serb-dominated Titoist partisans. Bosnian Muslims had even established the first non-German Hadzhar Waffen SS Mountain Division, whose symbol was a Nazi swastika with a hand holding a Turkish dagger, the hadzhar. A group of Bosnian Muslims even wrote to Adolf Hitler in November 1942 asking him to annex Bosnia-Herzegovina to the Reich. The 17 year-old Alija had supported the Muslim SS division, for which he was sentenced to three years in prison after the war.

Islamska Deklaracija and his program of a world-wide federal Islam Caliphate

As a devoted Muslim, Izetbegović was a co-founder of the *Mladi Muslimani* (Young Muslims) organization at the age of 22 and published *Islamska Deklaracija* (Islamic Declaration) in 1970. In a 1990 reprint, the 127-page Declaration unveils a complex, imprudent program that seeks to channel "ideals and plans into organized action." It was a bold and demagogic treatise that insisted

There can be no peace or coexistence between the Islamic faith and non-Islamic societies and political institutions. . . . Our objective is the Islamization of Muslims. . . . Our motto is to have faith and fight. . . . A world of 700 million [Muslim] people with enormous natural resources . . . their colossal cultural and political traditions . . . cannot long remain in a state of vassalage. . . . We announce . . . that Muslims are determined to take the fate of the Islam world into their own hands and arrange that world according to their own vision. . . . It is a natural function of the Islamic order to gather all Muslims and Muslim communities throughout the world into one. Under present conditions this desire means a struggle for creating a great Islamic federation from Morocco to Indonesia, from tropical Africa to Central Asia. . . . In the struggle for Islamic order all methods are permitted . . . except crime. . . . We are not announcing an age of peace and security. [59]

Izetbegović was a passionate political agitator in the early 1990s, who urged Bosnian Muslims to attain their ultimate goal of national independence in the face of their internal and external enemies. He grounded his independence program with a somewhat modernized Islam. He criticized the traditionalists, the "Hajjs and Sheikhs . . . [who want to] drag Islam into the past," but he went after the Westernizers even more:

So-called progressives, Westernizers, modernists . . . are the exemplification of real misfortune throughout the Muslim world. . . . The modernizers raised a front against all that the [Islam] idea represents. . . . Schooled in Europe, from which they return with a deep sense of their own inferiority towards the wealthy West . . . [they] destroy local ideas, customs and convictions, while introducing alien ones. [60]

He also denounced the "alien education" that leads to an "admiration for the might and wealth of the foreigner" and to the development of a "vassal mentality." A lack of Islamic education, he asserted, is "paralyzing the minds and will." He had nothing good to say about Kemal Atatürk, for, he insisted, his westernizing measures in Turkey had destroyed a mighty empire and made it backward. His criticism of Atatürk's secularization was an indirect attack on Bosnian Muslims, who in their vast majority had become secularized in Tito's Yugoslavia. Izetbegović noted ruefully that the Bosnian people want both Islamic activism with a westernized intelligentsia, but, he insisted, the former cannot be attained with the latter. Izetbegović therefore fervently called for the creation of a "new intelligentsia, which thinks and feels Islam. This intelligentsia would then fly the flag of the Islamic order."[61] He argued for the "Islamization" of the Bosnians:

> [What we need is] a period of internal purging and the practical acceptance of certain fundamental moral principles. All power in the world starts out as moral firmness. Every defeat begins as moral failure. All that is desired to be accomplished must first be accomplished in the souls of men.[62]

Izetbegović also laid out his religious-political program in the introduction of his book, *Islam Between East and West*, published in the United States in 1984:

> Islam is not only a religion or way of life, but primarily the principle of the organization of the Universe. Islam existed before man and it is . . . a principle by which man was created. . . . [Islam is a] unity of faith and politics. . . . Every true Islamic movement is also a political movement. . . . Muhammed was a warrior.[63]

His aggressive rhetoric mapping out a grandiose vision of a federalized Islamic Caliphate the world over, represented the worst political demagoguery in crisis-ridden Yugoslavia. His was one of the very first fundamentalist Islamist programs, a precursor of what was to come in the Middle East decades later, propagated on European soil.

During his long prison term in the 1980s, Izetbegović wrote numbered notes and comments on his readings. These notes were later published in a book, and they tell us a great deal about his views. On note number 3,096, he comments on Draža Marković's published diary with the quip: "One comes to the old question if Yugoslavia is the state of the Yugoslav people, or is a state of Slovenians, Macedonians, Montenegrins, as well as a state of Albanians, Italians, Bulgarians, Hungarians, Slovaks, etc. Where are the Muslims here!" In another note he affirms his oft-expressed belief of Islamic superiority by declaring "while nationality is based on a natural relation link, Islam is a relation based on spirit, law and morality." Islam, he repeats several times, is superior to other religions and to materialistic communism.[64]

Towards independent Bosnia and the civil war

In 1983, Izetbegović was sentenced to 18 years in prison for writing *Islam Between East and West*, but was pardoned in 1988 after serving only five years. He emerged from prison in the midst of Yugoslavia's implosion and immediately threw himself into the political fray. He founded the Muslim Party of Democratic Action in Bosnia in 1989. "Muslims have had no political leaders," he argued, "we need a big party, then we need political power."[65] The party tactically refrained from openly propagating its ultimate goal of a Muslim state but instead feigned support for multiculturalism. As one analyst noted:

> The crucial element in his [Izetbegović's] strategy was to make the idea of "multiculturalism" his rallying cry. The multicultural platform was a brilliant tactical move that endowed the Muslims with a higher claim to public virtue. It also set Izetbegović apart, in Western eyes, from his Serb and Croat opponents, the two predatory neighbors. . . . While preaching multiculturalism, Izetbegović embraced Islamism as his ideology.[66]

Large numbers of Bosnian Muslims were secular and did not support Islamization. "Early on, some Bosnian Muslim intellectuals issued public warnings: Izetbegović, they said, was against a modern, multicultural Bosnian state; he was exploiting religion for political purposes; and his 'hidden agenda' included the partition of Bosnia and the creation of a purely Muslim state in Europe." Two secular Bosnian Muslims, Musadik Borogovać and Sven Rustempasić, observed that "Izetbegović is not interested in becoming part of Bosnia's history, but a part of the history of Islam—the man who established the Muslim state on European soil."[67]

This was true. Izetbegović immediately began the battle for an independent Muslim Bosnia-Herzegovina. Following the precedents in Serbia and Croatia, he too organized a referendum and then declared independence. Armed conflict was easily foreseeable and was not something he sought to avoid. He never articulated his vision of a vast Muslim world power, but he acted accordingly. He travelled to Pakistan, Saudi Arabia, and Turkey in 1991 seeking support, and won Iran's assistance to build up his army. He also flew to the United States seeking political backing. Saudi Arabia played an instrumental role in convincing President Bush to recognize the Bosnian Muslim state, as did Egypt and Syria. On April 6, 1992, the US recognized independent Bosnia.

As we've seen, the Serbs and the Croats sought to divide Bosnia-Herzegovina among themselves during the Yugoslav civil war. For his part, Izetbegović tried to keep the entire province together in a Muslim state—even though only 44 percent of the Bosnian population were Muslim. A third were Serbs and the rest were Croat. He dismissed Milošević as the "Serb Stalin" and Tuđman as "the Croat Hitler" and rebuffed both. Choosing either of them, he suggested, would be "like choosing between leukemia and a brain tumor." He opted to fight instead.

His Islamist demagoguery contributed to the genocidal and devastating war that broke out in Bosnia. His actions and propaganda also had a destructive impact on the country. A Bosnian armed force, called the "Patriotic League," was set up under the command of the militant imam Hasan Čengić. Assistance began pouring in from Muslim nations. An illegal arms pipeline helped supply the Bosnian soldiers, and Jihadist fighters came from around the Arab world. Osama Bin Laden visited Bosnia and met with Izetbegović in 1993 and 1994, and was even issued a Bosnian passport.[68]

As was the case in the civil war generally, the Serbians enjoyed great success in the first stage of the Bosnian war. Ratko Mladić, the military commander of the Bosnian Serbs, declared independence and took control of 70 percent of Bosnia-Herzegovina. One of the war's most infamous massacres took place in Srebrenica and turned the entire Western world against the Serbs. But war crimes were committed on both sides. Muslim forces slaughtered Serbs in Bratunac on January 16, 1992, and the vengeance they meted out for Srebrenica was severe. As the British media reported, after the Serbs had fled Srebrenica in May 1992, the Muslim commander Naser Orić burned 192 villages and killed 1,300 villagers over a three-year period, including the Christmas massacre of 46 Serb worshipers in Karvica.[69] The French United Nations Commander in Bosnia, General Philippe Morillon, told French Parliamentary representatives investigating the Srebrenica massacre: "I am not afraid to say that it is Sarajevo that deliberately provoked the dramatic events. It was the Presidency, it was Izetbegovic."[70]

Atrocities by Serb and Croat paramilitary forces certainly made up the bulk of the war's killings, but the responsibility for the bloodshed was clearly shared by all. A large number of Bosnians had no desire for war, as was evident by the 50,000 Bosnians' demonstrating in Sarajevo in July 1991. They rejected Izetbegović's hard line, pronouncing to the Bosnian Parliament on February 27, 1991: "I would sacrifice peace for a sovereign Bosnia-Herzegovina, but for the peace in Bosnia-Herzegovina I would not sacrifice sovereignty."[71] His Islamist-national demagoguery and his mobilization of Middle Eastern Muslim states as his suppliers and supporters also played a role in the Yugoslav tragedy.

The international community tried to impose peace with an ethnic division of Bosnia. In January 1993, the Vance-Owen Plan proposed forming 10 ethnic cantons: 3 Serb, 3 Croat, and 4 Muslim. The Owen-Stoltenberg Plan in May 1993 preferred three ethnic states, while the Contact Group Plan 2 endorsed a Muslim-Croat federation and a Serb state in March 1994. To avoid further bloodshed, United Nations peace keepers were stationed in Bosnia. The end solution, however, came with a Muslim-Croat military agreement that led to the defeat of the Bosnian Serb military. At last, the United States forced the Dayton Agreement on all parties in 1995, which offered 51 percent of Bosnian territory to a Muslim-Croat Federation and 49 percent to a Bosnian Serb Republic. Having blithely acceded to the dissolution of multi-ethnic Yugoslavia, the West created a tripartite multi-ethnic "small-Yugoslavia" in Bosnia-Herzegovina. Izetbegović initially refused to sign the agreement and tried to obtain more concessions, but in the end was forced to accept it.

Izetbegović died at age 77 of a heart attack in the fall of 2003. Although his obituary in the *Guardian* described him as a decent, mild-manner man "who alone among the rival leaders retained a moral stature," the article nevertheless concluded that "he too, ended up a nationalist leader."[72] His Islamist "national" demagoguery played a role in the Bosnian bloodbath—no fewer than 65,000 were killed—and in the Yugoslav tragedy as a whole.

* * *

Nothing quite like it had happened in Europe during the second half of the twentieth century. Three demagogues called for the "defense of their nations," insisted on independence and fought to defend their peoples on enemy territories and/or to rid their countries of rival ethnicities. The human catastrophe that unraveled was unfathomable. Some 120,000–150,000 Muslims, Croats, and Serbs were killed, and roughly a million were expelled from or fled their homelands. Sexual violence was regularly employed to humiliate and punish rival populations. Expulsions and ethnic cleansing were routinely carried out on all sides. This carnage distinguished itself as Europe's bloodiest conflict during the second half of the twentieth century.

Endnotes

1 A similar tragedy befell the family of his wife, Mirjana (Mira) Marković. They were more than a couple. They met in school, attended university together and became inseparable. They were each other's best friends and political advisors. Mira's mother, Vera Marković-Miletić, was a communist partisan, worked in the underground in Belgrade and became the secretary of the Belgrade communist organization. She was the partner of Moma Marković, a renowned partisan hero. The story of what happened to Vera remains a mystery. In March 1943, she was arrested by the Gestapo and broke under torture. Soon the entire Belgrade resistance was eliminated. No one knows whether she was killed or escaped. Moma Marković condemned her as traitor. Mira (later she used this name, which was her mother's underground name) was raised in Požarevac by her grandparents. Her mother had disappeared and her father abandoned her immediately after the war.

2 This concept goes back to 1844, when Ilija Garasanin, one of the first statesmen of the independent Serb state in the making, outlined Serbian territorial aims on the Balkans.

3 Zdravko Petak, "The Political Economy Background of Yugoslav Dissolution: Between Economic Nationalism and Europeanization," paper presented at the Conflict Resolution and Self-Governance in Africa (and Other Regions) Mini-Conference, May 3–5, 2003, Workshop in Political Theory and Policy Analysis, Indiana University, Bloomington, Indiana, http://citeseerx.ist.psu.edu/viewdoc/download?doi=10.1.1.563.1504&rep=rep1&type=pdf.

4 See Diana Johnstone, *Fools' Crusade: Yugoslavia, NATO, and Western Delusions* (New York: Monthly Review Press, 2002), 19. Lenard J. Cohen took this quotation as the title of his book on Milošević, see *Serpent in the Bosom: The Rise and Fall of Slobodan Milošević* (Boulder, CO: Westview Press, 2001).

5 Quoted in Dusko Doder and Louise Branson, *Milosevic: Portrait of a Tyrant* (New York: The Free Press, 1999), 39.

6 Doder and Branson, *Milosevic*, 3, 43–45.

7 "Slobodan Milosevic at Kosovo Brotherhood and Solidarity Rally in Belgrade," November 21, 1988, http://www.slobodan-milosevic.org/documents/sm112188.htm.

8 Quoted by Vidosav Stevanović, *Milosevic: The People's Tyrant* (London: I.B.Tauris, 2004), 39.

9 Alex J. Bellamy, *Massacres and Morality: Mass Atrocities in an Age of Civilian Immunity* (Oxford: Oxford University Press, 2012), 9.

10 European Bank for Reconstruction and Development, *Transition Report, 2001* (London: EBRD, 2001), 61.

11 Nebojša Vladisavljević, *Serbia's Antibureaucratic Revolution: Milošević, the Fall of Communism and Nationalist Mobilization* (Houndsmills: Palgrave Macmillan, 2008).

12 Ibid., 156.

13 Stevanović, *Milosevic: The People's Tyrant*, 34.

14 For the Memorandum, see "Serbian Academy of Arts and Sciences (SANU) Memorandum, 1986," http://chnm.gmu.edu/1989/items/show/674.

15 Doder and Branson, *Milosevic*, 40.

16 Radmila Radić, "Srpska pravoslavna crkva u poratnim I ratnim godinama 1980–1985," *Republika* 7 (August 31, 1995): 24, quoted in Cohen, *Serpent in the Bosom*, 154.

17 Stevanović, *Milosevic: The People's Tyrant*, 44.

18 Doder and Branson, *Milosevic*, 4.

19 St. Vitus Day National Address at Kosovo Field, June 28, 1989, http://www.slobodan-milosevic. org/spch-kosovo1989.htm.

20 Michael Barratt Brown, *From Tito to Milosevic: Yugoslavia, the Lost Country* (London: The Merlin Press, 2005), 137.

21 Doder and Branson, *Milosevic*, 105.

22 Susan L. Woodward, *Balkan Tragedy, Chaos and Dissolution after the Cold War* (Washington D.C.: The Brookings Institution, 1995), 157, 161.

23 "Serbian President Interviewed Denies Involvement in Croatian Conflict," text of August 7, 1991, interview with Sky Television, http://www.slobodan-milosevic.org/news/milosevic080791.htm.

24 Doder and Branson, *Milosevic*, 88–89.

25 Ibid., 117.

26 Cohen, *Serpent in the Bosom*, 159.

27 Brown, *From Tito to Milosevic*, 10.

28 Doder and Branson, *Milosevic*, 7.

29 Ibid., 8.

30 Ibid., 9.

31 Dan Bilefsky, "Kosovo Declares Its Independence from Serbia," *New York Times*, February 18, 2008.

32 Carlotta Gall, "Making Kosovo Fertile Ground for ISIS," *New York Times*, May 21, 2016.

33 See the webpage of the International Tribunal, the text of the Indictment of Milošević, and the Amended Incitement at https://www.icty.org/x/cases/slobodan_milosevic/ind/en/mil-ai040421-e.htm.

34 For his indictment, see the website of the *United Nations, The International Criminal Tribunal for the former Yugoslavia*, at www.icty.org/case/seselj/4.

35 Brown, *From Tito to Milosevic*, 121, 136. Another author went so far as to state: "The rise of Milošević personally as leader had little to do with a nationalist programme, contrary to the assertion of scholars of Yugoslavia." Vladisavljević, *Serbia's Antibureaucratic Revolution*, 75.

36 David Owen, *Balkan Odyssey* (London: Indigo, 1996), 365.

37 Doder and Branson, *Milosevic*, 1999, 81.

38 Mark Biondich, *Stjepan Radić, the Croat Peasant Party and the Politics of Mass Mobilization, 1904–1928* (Toronto: University of Toronto Press, 2000), 207.

39 Howard Ball, *Genocide: A Reference Handbook* (Santa Barbara, CA: ABC-CLIO, 2011), 124.

40 Ibid., 160–61.

41 Neven Borak, "Economic Background to National Conflicts in Yugoslavia," in *Economic Change and the National Question in Twentieth-Century Europe*, ed. Alice Teichova, Herbert Matis, and Jaroslav Pátek (Cambridge: Cambridge University Press, 2000), 312–13. Indeed, the total GDP was 5,988.8 billion dinar in Bosnia-Herzegovina with a population of 4.4 million; thus 1,361 dinar per capita. Compare that to 7,614.3 billion dinar in Slovenia with 1.9 million inhabitants; thus more than 4,000 dinar per capita.

42 Petak, "The Political Economy Background of Yugoslav Dissolution."

43 Woodward, *Balkan Tragedy*, 15.

44 Ante Batović, "The Balkans in Turmoil—Croatian Spring and the Yugoslav position Between the Cold War Blocs 1965–1971," *LSE Ideas*, LSE Cold War Studies Programme, 2009.

45 Brown, *From Tito to Milosevic*, 141.

46 Cohen, *Serpent in the Bosom*, 153.

47 Doder and Branson, *Milosevic*, 82.

48 Ibid.

49 Ibid.

50 Ian Traynor, "Franjo Tudjman," *Guardian*, December 13, 1999.

51 Doder and Branson, *Milosevic*, 89.

52 Traynor, "Franjo Tudjman."

53 Philip Sherwell and Alina Petric, "Tudjman Tapes Reveal Plans to Divide Bosnia and Hide War Crimes," *Telegraph*, June 18, 2000.

54 Franjo Tudjman, "The Necessity of Croatia's Demographic Revival," see at http://chnm.gmu. edu/history/faculty/kelly/blogs/h300f07/tudjman-speech/index.html.

55 For the full text of the speech, see "Croatian President Franjo Tudjman's Speech on 'Freedom Train' Journey," at emperors-clothes.com/docs/tudj.htm, posted on March 17, 2006.

56 "Franjo Tudjman: Father of Croatia," *BBC News*, December 11, 1999, news.bbc.co.uk/2/hi/europes/294990.stm.
57 Traynor, "Franjo Tudjman."
58 Ian Traynor, "Alija Izetbegovic," *Guardian*, October 20, 2003.
59 Alija Izetbegović, *Islamskaja Deklaracija* (Sarajevo: BOSNA, 1990); see also Alija Izetbegović, *Islamic Declaration: A Programme for the Islamization of Muslims and the Muslim Peoples* (Sarajevo: SR Bosnia, 1990); excerpts available online at www.hraicjk.org/islamic_declaration.html.
60 Izetbegovic, *Islamic Declaration*, 10–11.
61 Ibid., 20–21, 25.
62 Ibid., 49–50.
63 Alija Izetbegović, *Islam Between East and West* (Indianapolis: American Trust Publication, 1984), iv, 146, 155, 156, 179.
64 Alija Izetbegović, *Izetbegović of Bosnia and Herzegovina: Notes from Prison, 1983–1988* (Westport: Praeger, 2002), 91, 189.
65 Doder and Branson, *Milosevic*, 92.
66 Ibid., 91–92.
67 Ibid., 92.
68 See *London Times*, March 5, 2002; Davin Binder, "Alija Izetbegovic, Muslim Who Led Bosnia, Dies at 78," *New York Times*, October 20, 2003.
69 *Daily Telegraph*, 08, 01, 1993.
70 Brown, *From Tito to Milosevic*, 148.
71 Doder and Branson, *Milosevic*, 91.
72 Traynor, "Alija Izetbegovic."

CHAPTER 10

Two British Brexit fighters:
Boris Johnson and Nigel Farage

Boris Johnson and Britain's relation with the European Union

Britain's relationship with continental Europe and with European integration has always been ambiguous and complex. In the post–World War II period, Winston Churchill, the leading British politician in modern times, defined his country's policy toward Europe. He was the first influential statesman who, as early as in 1946, called for the creation of the United States of Europe, based on French and German reconciliation. A cold-war warrior, he wanted to create a strong Western alliance against the Soviet Union. Nevertheless, he clearly expected that Britain would support such integration from the *outside*. He and other leading British politicians, Tories and Laborites alike, repeated again and again during the postwar period that Britain's first consideration is the Commonwealth, their English-speaking "kinship," and also their "special relations" with the United States. He and his successors at 10 Downing Street strongly resisted Presidents Truman and Eisenhower's attempts to pressure Britain into leading or at least taking part in European integration. As the Americans were seriously hammering out a Western alliance system, they had little patience for British foot-dragging, which in the end proved to be a futile exercise. Moreover, when the European Economic Community was established in 1957, Britain formed a rival organization, the European Free Trade Association (EFTA), of seven member countries.

The "independence" of the island country was an *idée fixe* for Britain's political elite, based on the myth of (in reality rapidly evaporating)

Britain's status as a world power. This myth even survived the collapse of its gargantuan 450 million-strong colonial empire, which began after the war and was an accomplished fact by 1960. The Commonwealth emerged from its remnants. The memory of Britain's world leadership, when the British pound reigned as the world's currency and Britain as the world's first industrialized nation, still dominated the country's thinking in the postwar period. The recent victory in World War II, when Britain prevailed against all odds, kept this sentiment alive.

True, the debacle of the Suez campaign in 1956, the decline of its "gunboat diplomacy" after two hundred years of success, and the collapse of its colonial empire clearly pointed to a grim new reality. At the same time, an integrating Europe became much more prosperous. Britain was suddenly a small country with a partly obsolete economy. During the 1960s, this situation strongly undermined Britain's self-image as a great world power. Consequently, Britain applied for membership in the European Economic Community (EEC) during that decade. After two rejections because of Charles de Gaulle's veto, Britain finally joined in 1973.

Nevertheless, even as an EEC member over the next half a century, Britain always kept one foot out the door. It held a referendum on whether to leave or stay only two years after joining. Several Tory and Labor governments fought all attempts at further integration and any move towards supranationalization. Britain opted not to join the common currency and opposed the Schengen Agreement for a borderless Europe. Margaret Thatcher waged an undeclared war against Brussels and the European "super-state" in the 1980s and successfully cut British payments to the Community. Thirty years later, David Cameron waged a campaign to "reform" the European Union by reducing it to a mere free trade zone. The only EU institution that London enthusiastically embraced was the Single Market, because Britain never intended to become part of anything other than a free trade zone, which was considered to be an immense playground for the "City," the center of its powerful banking sector. All in all, Britain has always remained an "inside-outsider" in the European Union.[1]

The 2008 financial crisis hit Europe hard and soon evolved into a severe debt crisis for several EU member countries that nearly destroyed the common currency and made Britain's political elite became more and more euro-sceptic. As the crisis continued well into the mid-2010s, an enormous migration crisis challenged the entire integration process and strengthened anti-EU sentiment significantly. Part of the British political elite pushed for leaving the EU. A great part of newspaper articles and most of the tabloid press vehemently attacked "Brussels" and European integration. A tsunami of populist, nationalist, and xenophobic voices rose to the fore clamoring to leave the European Union and halt immigration. A third of the governing Tory Party's representatives demanded an exit from the EU. Prime Minister David Cameron, trying to quell the divisions within his party, made a perilously risky maneuver: he announced that the government would hold a referendum on EU membership.

Tapping into the widespread anti-integrationist views, the prevailing "island country and great power" sentiment in the UK, and banking on Britain's enduring ambivalence about its EU membership, right-wing populists launched a massive campaign to leave the Union. The conditions could not have been better for the Brexit demagogues. Several emerged from the pack as Brexit's primary leaders: one of them, Boris Johnson, a Tory politician and the popular Mayor of London, became a central figure.

The Eurosceptic Boris Johnson enters politics

Alexander Boris de Pfeffel Johnson was born in 1964 in an ethnically mixed family background, raised in an upper middle class family and was the product of the same elite schools that had produced the country's upper class overlords for generations: the famous Eton boarding school and Oxford University. At the latter, he fraternized with the future conservative leaders David Cameron, William Hague, Michael Gove, and Jeremy Hunt. He started off his career as a journalist and was stationed in Brussels. Johnson knew that city well, for his father had worked for the European Commission beginning in 1973 and was thus one of the "Brussels bureaucrats" whom his son would later so sarcastically lambaste. As a child Boris studied at the European School in Brussels and became fluent in French.

It seems that the driving force of Johnson's life was to be different. He developed his uniquely "eccentric British persona" while at Eton.

Psychologically speaking, this was more than understandable. Boris Johnson could have been called Boris Kemal had his grandfather not changed his name. His great-grandfather, Ali Kemal, was a Muslim Turkish journalist and politician. Boris himself described him,

> As interior minister in the government of the last [Ottoman] sultan, [he] signed the arrest warrant for Ataturk, now acknowledged to be the father of modern Turkey. . . . A short while later, my great-grandfather . . . was beaten to death and stuck in a tree [by the revolutionary crowd]. That is why my paternal grandfather, who was born Osman Ali, arrived in this country in search . . . [of] asylum.[2]

In truth, Johnson liked to write about his family background, partly because he loves to write, partly because the story is somewhat exotic, and partly because he is bent on proving that he is not an immigrant-hating xenophobe. The following quotation is quite characteristic for his attitude:

> You can't call me a racist, no sir, not when my own family is the product of more than one country; not when the Johnsons have enough nationalities in our immediate inheritance to make up a UN peacekeeping force. . . . In desperation [I] played my ace. . . . I am the grandson of an asylum seeker. . . . I am the first member of a thousand generations of Johnsons (or Johnsonoglus, or whatever our Turkish name was) to sit in the House.[3]

Indeed, in addition to his Turkish origins, Boris Johnson also has some French and Jewish background on his mother's side, and thus had a quite unique Muslim, Jewish, and Christian ancestry. As he succinctly put it, I am "a one-man melting-pot." With an unconventional hairstyle and an endless array of eccentric outbursts, Johnson always aspired to be witty and interesting (mostly successfully), and in the process would quite often insult others, including world political leaders. His desire to be clever and original is part of his charm. In 2008, he memorably compared Hillary Clinton to the infamous Nurse Ratched in *One Flew Over the Cuckoo's Nest:* "She's got dyed blonde hair and pouty lips, and a steely blue stare, like a sadistic nurse in a mental hospital." He also had some ugly words for President Obama when the latter advised Britain to remain in the EU: the "part-Kenyan President," he suggested, was guided by an "ancestral dislike of the British Empire." He described the leader of the Scottish National Party, Nicola Sturgeon, as "a fox in a henhouse, a jewel thief, King Herod, and voracious weevils."[4] He once asserted that Africa would have been better off had it continued to be governed by the former colonial powers. As Mayor of London, he commuted to work each day by bicycle.

At the beginning of his career as a reporter from Brussels, he never intended to be realistic and balanced. He had nothing positive to say about the EU, which he always described with the most biting sarcasm. He arrived in Brussels in the spring of 1989, only a half a year after Prime Minister Margaret Thatcher had delivered her famous Bruges speech attacking the "utopian, abstract intellectual concept" of integrating the member states into "a single, bureaucratic European super-state." Boris Johnson wholeheartedly propagated this idea while in Brussels. As he later put it: "The longer I stayed in Brussels—and I served five happy years—the more obvious it was that Europe would never work."[5] He pointedly added that "it has been the object of 500 years of British diplomacy to ensure that continental Europe is not united against our interests."[6]

Johnson was a convinced euro-sceptic who attacked every possible step towards further integration beyond the common market. In reality, the 1980s, especially the second half of them, were the most promising years for the development of European integration, led as they were by the "Troika" of President Mitterrand, Chancellor Kohl, and the President of the European Commission, Jacques Delors. Johnson perennially attacked Delors, who, he flippantly suggested, "presides over 16 fellow senior bureaucrats and about 13,000 junior functionaries. To call him President Delors . . . is a misnomer, a silly equivocation. . . . And the exact status of Delors, homo foederalis has become ever more mysterious."[7] On another occasion he dismissively "reported" that the "European Community foreign ministers were stunned yesterday to learn of a plan by Jacques Delors to transform the Brussels Commission into a 'European government,' with himself . . . becoming a fully-fledged, elected 'President of the European Community' with executive power."[8] He was also quick to ridicule Delors's "extreme Clouseau-ish accent when attempting English."[9] In an 1992 article entitled "Delors Plan to Rule Europe," Johnson alleged that, following the signing of the Maastricht Treaty in February of that year, Delors planned to propose greater centralized power in Brussels. Johnson would later proudly claim that his article had led to the Danish "No" vote on Maastricht.

> They photocopied it [his article] a thousandfold. They marched the streets of Copenhagen with my story fixed to their banners. And on June 2, a spectacularly sunny day, they joyously rejected the treaty and derailed the project.[10]

He conveniently "forgot" that the Danes in fact ratified the treaty a year later after another referendum in 1993. Praising himself—indirectly, if need be—is an intrinsic part of his personality. To quote one of his typical boasts:

> I rang the Foreign Desk [of his journal] during the first Gulf War and begged to be sent out [to Iraq]. . . . "Hur hur," said the Foreign Desk. "Nah, Boris, we reckon you're too valuable where you are."[11]

During his Brussels years, Johnson consistently opposed European integration: "The reason I became a sceptic about integration was that it continually involved a Procrustean squeezing or chopping of national interests."[12] The original considerations that led to integration, he suggested, no longer apply: "There will be no war between France and Germany, and the Soviet threat is a busted flush. That leaves no urgent necessity to create a tightly unified Little Europe, except in the hearts of those who are so anti-American that they would abandon national independence . . . [to] creating a rival superstate."[13] Then he added: "Why is Europe so feeble? . . . The answer is that Europe is not a natural political unit."[14]

Johnson regularly joked about the EU's regulations and dismissed them as nonsensical bureaucratic maneuvers. In reality, it is not enough to eliminate tariffs and borders if one wants to create a common market. The common market's products must be standardized throughout if they are to be sold in other member countries. Cars, for instance, must be subject to identical emission standards if they are to be sold throughout the common market. These are elementary facts. Britain earned billions because it was able to exploit these standardized markets. Ignoring this basic reality, Johnson tried to caricature EU standardization by cherry-picking a few extreme examples. On this, too, he emphasized the huge importance of his articles on Thatcher on these issues:

> After five months' study the EEC Commission has decided snails should be categorized as fish, not meat.[15]

Then he added:

> Brussels bureaucrats have shown their legendary attention to detail. . . . All 12 member states have agreed that an unstretched condom should be 16 centimeter long. However, the EC has dismissed Italian plans for a maximum condom width of 54 millimeters. . . . Spokesman of the Commission's standards division, said: This is a very serious business.[16]

For years, Boris Johnson depicted European integration as serving foreign (meaning not British) interests and acting against Britain:

> The European Community . . . is ruled by France. . . . [They] are dressing up French national interests as the European dream. . . . It was widely remarked that [the new] French government contains Martine Aubry, daughter of M. Delors. . . . But did you know that Pascal Lamy, M. Delors' chef de cabinet has just been offered the same job in the French government? . . . Delors and Lamy now have a dense network of *gauleiters* . . . [Using the Nazi term.] There is no British counter network. . . .[17]
>
> But whatever you think of the French, they deserve admiration for one huge geo-political coup. They have created the European currency.[18]

He often drops not-so-subtle hints suggesting France and the EU have identical interests. One way he does so is to describe an EU Commissioner as a French bureaucrat: "There is the Brussels commission, with its strange pipe-puffing Frenchmen . . . who decide the price which they may export . . . and what premium they receive for a ewe."[19] Johnson continually insists that the Commission is unabashedly anti-British and decries its "semi-annual humiliation of the British Government."[20] In an article entitled "Revelation on the road from Hastings to Maastricht," he goes so far as to compare the Battle of Hastings in 1066 with the EU's suspension of national veto rights and adoption of a qualified majority vote. This comparison was meant to provoke, as Britain had lost the Battle of Hastings and was consequently invaded by the Normans:

[The Battle of Hastings], in the words of the historian John Gilling-ham, "a catastrophe for the English". . . . As William of Malmesbury wrote in 1125, "England today is the home of foreigners and the domain of aliens." The memory of the conquest is one of those many things that put us in two minds, about whether to rejoice in our links with the con-tinent, or whether to be dismayed.[21]

Qualified majority voting, Johnson maintains, is the simplest way to vote against the British government—an argument often made by the Brexiters. The *Guardian*, however, has shown just how exaggerat-ed this is: "A swathe of EU policies is now decided by these weighted-majority votes, such as environment, agriculture and transport. More sensitive policies, including tax, defence and foreign policy, have to be agreed by unanimity." The British daily carefully described the actual situation:

Under QMV, a law passes if it is backed by 16 out of 28 countries that make up at least 65 percent of the EU population. The UK has 13 per-cent of the EU population, so gets a 13 percent vote share. Research by the London School of Economics found that the UK was on the win-ning side 87 percent of the time between 2009 and 2015. So the British government does have to accept some EU decisions it didn't vote for. One of the most high-profile losses in recent years was when the chancellor, George Osborne, was outvoted on an EU law to restrict bankers' bonus-es. In this case, more than three quarters of the British public, includ-ing 68 percent of Conservative voters, supported the EU proposal.[22]

In other words, the picture Boris Johnson paints is so one-sided it is virtually a lie. Writes Martin Fletcher in the *New York Times*: "For decades, British newspapers have offered their readers an endless stream of biased, misleading and downright fallacious stories about Brussels. And the journalist who helped set the tone—long before he became the mayor of London or the face of the pro-Brexit campaign—was Boris Johnson."[23] The *Guardian*'s John Palmer, one of Johnson's former col-leagues, concurs: "As a journalist he is thoroughly irresponsible, mak-ing up stories." *Liberation*'s, Jean Quatremer, who is also well-acquaint-ed with Johnson, adds that Johnson's motto is: "Never let the facts interfere with a good story."[24] Boris Johnson has built an entire career on rejecting European integration and mocking the European Union.

His demagoguery was based on bombastic statements about regaining Britain's lost world status—good music for British ears. On this topic, he has made several false, or at the very least, mistaken pronouncements. A more ungenerous interpretation is that he deliberately lies. Permit me to fact check (in brackets) his published remarks in this quotation:

> What is the Remain camp offering? Nothing . . . but the steady and miserable erosion of parliamentary democracy in this country. If we vote Remain, we stay locked in the back of the car, driven by someone with an imperfect command of English [a masked xenophobic remark], and going a direction we don't want to go. . . . If Britain votes to Remain in the EU, then we continue to be subject to an increasingly anti-democratic system that is now responsible for 60 per cent of the laws. . . . We no longer control our destiny. . . . We will remain prisoners of a trade regime that will not allow this country—the fifth biggest economy on earth—to negotiate with America or China or India . . . because that privilege is reserved exclusively for the hierarchs of the European Commission [which represents all the member countries and thus has a much stronger position in trade deals than any single European country], of whose vast staff only 3.6 per cent come from this country [again a clear anti-foreigner reference]. If we stay, we will find our global influence and weight not enhanced, but diminished—as the EU ruthlessly cuckoos us aside . . . from the IMF and the UN and the WTO [in reality, Britain is one of the five members of the UN Security Council].

Johnson then proceeded to glorify Britain's regained independence that, he promises, will lead to Britain's resurgent global status:

> We can take back control of our borders. . . . [Britain had opted out of the Schengen Agreement, and thus has control over its borders] We can do global trade deals that . . . could generate another 300,000 jobs. Above all we could take back control of our powers to pass laws and set tax rates [the EU has no uniform tax rates, as each country sets its own rates] in the interest of the UK economy. We can reorient the UK economy to the whole world, rather than confining ourselves to an EU that now amounts to only 15 per cent of global GDP. [Britain earmarked 56 percent of its trade to the EU, while and only 12 percent to its Commonwealth; the EU produces 24 percent of the world GDP, more than the US's 22 percent or China's 13 percent or Japan's 6 percent.][25]

On another occasion, Johnson depicted the EU as an anachronistic failure:

> Whatever the noble ambitions on which it was founded, the EU is an anachronism. It is increasingly anti-democratic [actually it is increasingly democratic, for the directly elected Parliament shares decision making with the representatives of the member countries]; its supranational system is being imitated nowhere else on earth; and its economic policies are causing misery in many parts of the EU. It is sclerotic, opaque, elitist . . . [run] by a centralised bureaucracy. . . . It is an attempt to build a United States of Europe.[26]

An independent fact checking institution in Britain immediately corrected these statements about the European Commission's supposed rule over Europe and, by quoting the "Remain" camp's statement, declared: "The European Commission doesn't make laws. It only makes proposals, which are then debated, amended and passed (or rejected) by elected national governments and directly-elected MEPs [Members of the European Parliament]."[27] The idea of a United States of Europe was actually introduced by Churchill after the war, and was not on the EU's agenda. Overall, the EU's bureaucracy is actually much smaller than Britain's.

As one can see, Johnson's arguments are full of "mistakes" or misleading lies. However, his most egregious lie was one that was key to winning 52 percent of the vote, especially among elderly voters. To quote Boris Johnson: "Think of what we can achieve if we vote Leave. We can take back control of huge sums of money—£10.6 billion net per year—and spend it on our priorities. . . . We could do with having that cash back."[28] In an open letter to the Prime Minister, Johnson and Michael Gove stated:

> We already know the official bill for our membership is due to rise to £20.65 billion per year by 2020–2021. . . . A vote to stay is a vote to keep sending more and more money to a dysfunctional bureaucracy. . . . [Together with other expenditures to the EU our] payouts could be as high as £43 billion by 2021, a huge sum of money that would be better spent on schools and hospitals.[29]

Britain will continuously be part of the Single Market (?)

Another fundamental falsehood that Boris Johnson disseminated was that the Single Market would remain open to Britain even without EU membership. In other words, there was nothing to lose, but everything to win:

> Does [anyone] worry about tariffs, if we left? Of course not. The Germans would not dream of it: we Brits buy 820,000 German cars every year, worth about 20 billion euros. In fact we buy one fifth of Germany's entire car output. . . . Tariffs would mean the Germans would be cutting their own throats.[30]

After Brexit he self-confidently declared:

> It is overwhelmingly in the economic interests of the other EU countries to do a free-trade deal, with zero tariffs and quotas, while we extricate ourselves from the EU law-making system. . . .[31]

> The "single market" is in reality a political project that is turning inexorably into a single government of Europe. There is no need to be part of this expensive legislative machine in order to export goods or services into the EU.[32]

Before and after the referendum, Johnson persistently lied about Britain's continuing ability to engage in free trade and take part in the EU's Single Market. Or was this perhaps not lies, but rather simply ignorance of the basic facts? After Brexit, as Foreign Secretary in Theresa May's cabinet, he declared that Britain, out of the EU, would continue to enjoy all the advantages of the Single Market without having to adhere to EU regulations or accept migrants from EU member countries.

German Finance Minister Wolfgang Schäuble and his French counterpart Michel Sapin were asked about Johnson's remarks at a news conference. . . . The two ministers shot glances at each other before the German host responded:

> We just looked at each other because we're used to respecting foreign ministers a lot. If we need to do more, we will gladly send her majesty's foreign minister a copy of the Lisbon Treaty. Then he can read that there is a certain link between the single market and the four core principles in Europe. . . . So if clarification is necessary we can pay a visit and explain this to him in good English.

Sapin, in a French twist added: "There are four freedoms and they cannot be separated. So if we want to make good European paté then there are four freedoms that together make up the paté in question."[33]

At the end of November 2016, a leaked note on the government's Brexit strategy revealed that this was still defined by the idea to "have your cake and eat it," something that "critics described as delusional." Indeed, Johnson, the then "foreign secretary and leading pro-Brexit campaigner once notoriously claimed that Britain could leave behind everything it did not like about the European Union . . . but keep everything it did like (such as the unencumbered trade with European countries)." Or, as Johnson himself put it in his usual cheerful and witty manner, "My policy on cake is pro having it and pro eating it."[34]

Probably a lack of basic knowledge on the subject and a sense of misguided optimism led Johnson to be so sanguine about continued British access to the Single Market. Whatever the case, he should have known that the free trade agreement could not possibly have opened the continental financial market for Britain's banking industry, because such services are not covered in the agreement. More importantly, as Charles Grant of the Centre for European Reform reported after discussing the matter in several EU countries, the European Union is firmly united on pursuing a hard line on Brexit. France and several other countries have long decided on a firm response because they have a political interest to weaken their own Eurosceptic opposition (Marine Le Pen and others). Further, they consider the so-called "four freedoms" as indivisible, as they always have before. Grant predicts that Britain will face an extremely difficult transition period, in stark contrast to Johnson's quixotic forecasts. It will have to join the World Trade Organization and then, within two years of leaving the EU, negotiate bilateral free trade agreements with 53 separate countries. All in all, it was simply not true that Britain has nothing to lose but everything to gain.[35] As *The Economist* correctly noted,

> Brexiteers say that, once outside, Britain would eventually negotiate low or no tariffs on its trade with the EU. Yet, even if it did, tariffs are less than half the problem. Without harmonised regulations [that Johnson has earlier mocked so viciously] British firms will discover that their products do not meet European requirements, and vice versa. And it is unlikely that a trade deal between Britain and the EU would cover ser-

vices, including the financial sorts that are among Britain's biggest exports. A study by the Treasury . . . estimated that the hit to GDP within two years of Brexit would be nearly twice as large if Britain left the single market than if it remained a member.[36]

A complete lack of knowledge of basic issues was even more apparent regarding a number of important but largely ignored details. At the moment, there are several EU institutions in Britain. A total of 45 European Union agencies, including the European Banking Authority and the European Medicines Agency, are located in Britain and have some 40,000 employees. EU member countries have long competed with one another to house such institutions, as there are loads of advantages for host countries. The Medicine Agency, for example, has 890 employees, an annual budget of $300 million, and a 25-year lease on a building in London, and it regularly holds meetings and conferences that require hotel accommodations for at least 350 people on any given day. These agencies will now have to leave Britain, which will be costly indeed for the local economy.[37] No one appears to have taken this into consideration.

Fueling hate and calling for the exclusion of foreigners

The Brexit campaign stirred up hatred and xenophobia against foreigners—Poles, Romanians, other East Europeans, and non-Europeans alike. As Boris Johnson and Michael Gove declared in an open letter:

> The Eurozone's economic crisis is fueling the rise in migration. Millions of people in southern Europe, particularly young people, are giving up hope of their countries escaping recession. Unsurprisingly, migrants from those countries are disproportionately coming to Britain. . . . If we stay, we are tying ourselves to a broken Eurozone economy while simultaneously accepting unlimited migration of people. . . . The only way to restore democratic control of immigration policy is to vote to leave on 23 June.[38]

Although he identified immigration as an important reason for leaving the EU, Boris Johnson was certainly not a racist. On several occasions he emphasized that he had genuine compassion for asylum seekers, but he has also spoken of his "natural" racist instinct. Mentioning his mixed ethnic background, he made assurances that

> I have a predisposition to be sympathetic to those who have come to this country, in fear of their lives or not, with the intention of making a new start.[39]

> Am I a racist? I jolly well shouldn't be. Look at my life. . . . [My] kiddies . . . are the produce, within the space of four generations, of India, Turkey, France, Germany, Russia, international Jewry, Wales and England. [However,] I have prejudged [certain ethnic groups] about the greater likelihood of being mugged by young black males than by any other group. And if that is racial prejudice, then I am guilty. And so are you baby . . . racism is "natural."[40]

Johnson does not subscribe to the views of the right-wing British politician Enoch Powell, who predicted in his "Rivers of Blood" speech in 1968 that an ethnic civil war would break out in Britain if immigration from the Commonwealth continued. On the contrary, Johnson asserted: "As a prophet, Powell was crushingly wrong. Where is the foaming river of blood? . . . I don't see a race war; I see innumerable examples of colour-blind cooperation."[41] He also questioned any racial distinction: "[Are there] any legitimate grounds for worry about the changing racial mix of Britain? I don't think there are."[42]

However, he condemned multiculturalism. The problem, Johnson explained, was that they were not demanding and abetting all immigrants' assimilation, but rather acceding to their cultural isolation:

> No one had the guts to talk about Britishness, or whether it was a good thing to insist . . . on the basic loyalty of immigrants to the country of immigration. . . . It is a cultural calamity . . . and we must begin now with what I call . . . the re-Britannification of Britain.[43]

After the Brexit vote, Johnson defensively insisted—in sharp contrast to the facts—that the referendum had nothing to do with immigration, and immigrants—except for extremists—would continue to be welcomed in Britain: "There is no risk whatever to the status of the EU nationals now resident and welcome in the UK, and indeed immigration will continue—but in a way that is controlled, thereby neutralising the extremists."[44]

Leftist anti-corporate populism?

The conservative and elitist Boris Johnson, like other populists, did not hesitate to employ leftist rhetoric in order to present Brexit as a populist project against big corporations:

> It is we who want to give power back to people. It is we who want to stand up against the corporatist and elitist system that will never admit its mistakes. . . .[45]

> Although some very large banks and multinational companies profit from the EU system, the situation is very different for small and medium sized businesses, the backbone of the economy. . . . The European Court will continue to prioritise the rights of big companies . . . EU membership helps some people and some businesses but they are disproportionately those with power and money.[46]

In the midst of a bitter political debate, Johnson decided to oppose two thirds of his party and its prime minister and take the helm of the "Leave" campaign. Demagoguery worked, the countryside, the less educated and less informed, and the older generations voted to leave. David Cameron's gambling failed and he resigned. Many politicians rushed to exploit the situation and elevate on the waves of Brexit. One of them, Theresa May, who voted for remaining in the EU, but became the successor of Cameron, jumped to the other camp. Moreover, she even argued for "hard Brexit," leaving even the Single European Market and reestablishing Britain as a "global power." Boris Johnson also recognized the opportunity. He became foreign secretary in the May government. After Theresa May's attempt to hold an early election to strengthen her position proved to be a miscalculation—one that lost her a majority in Parliament and significantly weakened her position as prime minister and leader of the Tory Party—Boris Johnson felt that his time had arrived. In October 2017, at the Tory Party conference in Manchester, he played the central role. He positioned himself as leader of the hard-Brexit faction and his attention-grabbing tactic has seemingly worked:

> Shaggy-headed, bombastic and full of bravado and sunny optimism as he brushed aside the clouds hanging over Britain's fraught withdrawal from the European Union, Foreign Secretary Boris Johnson was exactly

where he wanted to be . . . —at the center of attention. . . . Mr. Johnson's jovial, bumbling persona belies a ferocious ambition, and, after weeks of cabinet leaking, backstabbing . . . , a battle to succeed Mrs. May is emerging from the shadow.[47]

Brexit definitely helped his carrier. Boris Johnson indeed became prime minister of the UK and led the country into leaving the EU. What will be its outcome for Britain—is another question.

Nigel Farage

Nigel Farage, one of the leading Brexit demagogues and anti-EU crusaders, unlike Boris Johnson, is not an educated man. He was not part of the British Eton-Oxford educated political elite. Following in his father's and grandfather's footsteps, Farage became a metal merchant in the City, Britain's banking center. He established his own trading company, Farage Futures, in 1993, but he closed his business after a decade in order to pursue politics full-time. His political career got off the ground very slowly: he ran for the British Parliament several times unsuccessfully. He began his political career as a Tory, but left the party when the John Major government voted for the Maastricht Treaty. In 2006, he became the leader of an alternative populist, anti-EU, and anti-immigration party, the *UK Independence Party*. As representative of that party, he became a member of the European Parliament as early as 1999. He used his position there to deliver provocative speeches against the EU and organize noisy demonstrations during its proceedings. After the Lisbon Treaty, he was behind the scandalous catcalling that erupted during the speech of the Portuguese prime minister, which, he later mused, he enjoyed tremendously: "there was so much heckling and barracking from the floor—I was the ring-leader of all of that. It was a bit like being at school."[48] He proudly noted: "Between 2004 and 2006, I became well known as the most controversial member of the European Parliament."[49]

Farage, like several other nationalist demagogues, had a mixed ethnic background. His French Huguenot ancestors had immigrated to Britain, and one of his great-grandfathers had been born to German parents who migrated to London in the 19th century. Farage's wife herself was a German immigrant, and his children are half-Germans. It is a psychological common place that neophyte citizens are often the most extreme nationalists. Who else could have been then a more ideal nationalist, anti-immigration, and pro-independence leader in Britain than Farage?

Nigel Farage displayed a fair amount of political acumen when the Brexit referendum neared. This period seemed to be tailor-made for him. Like most populist demagogues in politics, he benefited mightily from anti-establishment sentiment and attacked the elite:

> In their cowardice, our politicians, in league with their mutually dependent banks, have sustained their position only by spending our children's money. . . . The people had started to acknowledge what the fight was really about . . . and had recognised, I think, that we, fallible and sometimes amateur as we were, were not part of the self-serving, self-perpetuating cabal of professional politicians who scorned them.[50]

He even referred to his party as the people's army against the establishment. During a televised debate with the head of the Liberal Democratic Party, "I looked straight into the camera and urged viewers to join our 'People's Army' and help us bring down the political establishment."[51] A born demagogue with an aggressive character and unlimited "chutzpah," Farage rose from the pack during the rancorous Brexit debates that so divided the British public. Lacking the wit and flair of Boris Johnson, he compensated through public displays of compassion for his followers, with whom he would regularly share drinks at local pubs, and with a knack for posing as a simple man living among the people for whom he was ready to sacrifice everything:

> It all started with anger and frustration at politicians' lies. . . . He who rides a tiger cannot dismount. Am I glad that I took up tiger-riding? . . . Had I stayed on in the City, I suspect I would now be looking forward to prosperous retirement. Instead, I have an aged Volvo. I have just remortgaged my home and will be lucky to retire to a dinky villa in Worthing. I have sorely neglected my family. . . . I have worked seven days a week for fifteen years.[52]

Farage has waxed rhapsodic about how much he works for the people—a self-sacrificing man who sleeps only a few hours a night. In typical demagogic fashion, he describes present reality in apocalyptic terms in dire need of urgent remedies:

> Religion has all but gone. The extended family has gone. The nuclear family . . . is all but gone. . . . Hereditary cultures and dialects swept away by imports. . . . And now even nations and cultures are things of which, we are told, we should be ashamed. . . . Social mobility has rarely been less . . . success is defined not by achievement . . . but by material possessions Aspiration and originality are not encouraged in education . . . education is at the lowest level in modern history—no, in all history. . . . The privileged . . . live in gated communities. . . . And then there is immigration . . . 80 percent of all new jobs in Britain are going to migrant workers. . . . We are in an unholy mess.[53]

Farage regularly portrayed Britain as a Third World country and the EU as a totalitarian super-state similar to Nazi Germany and Stalinist Russia. He shamelessly used baseless lies in a way that is rare for even the most extreme anti-EU demagogues: "Thanks to [the EU Treaty of] Lisbon, we are entering a second protectorate in which neighbor spies upon neighbor."[54] Europe-wide standardization, a favorite subject for Brexiters, as Farage argued:

> After 1986 the City became more and more regulated . . . talent, intuition, flair and fun were all but outlawed. . . . Every aspect of human life in Britain was becoming the subject of homogenising intervention. Not just my market—the financial—was being prowled by unimaginative jobsworths intent upon standardization, but the very street market where I bought my morning apple, the pubs where I ordered a pint. . . . [They are] pointless regulations . . . [a] one-size-fits-all colonialism—entirely contrary to the British tradition.[55]

Of course, "pointless regulations" make the European single market a real unified market, very advantageous for the British economy. Farage hopefully does not think that "colonialism . . . was entirely contrary to the British tradition." But this demagogic attitude toward standardization was successful, like in the case of Boris Johnson, as a pointless bureaucratic endeavor. Truth was not a priority when trying to convince the British public to oppose the EU. And convince them he did.

Farage, like several other demagogues, is fond of insulting others, often in unusually rude and vulgar language. At the session of the Euro-

pean Parliament, after the speech of the European Council's newly elected President, the former prime minister of Belgium Herman van
Rompuy, Farage delivered an unprecedented harangue:

> I don't want to be rude but, really, you have the charisma of a damp rag
> and the appearance of a low-grade bank clerk and the question I want
> to ask is: Who are you? Nobody in Europe had ever heard of you. . . .
> Your intention is to be the quiet assassin of European democracy and
> of European nation states. . . . Perhaps that's because you come from
> Belgium which, after all, is pretty much a non-country.[56]

Farage was so proud of his attack that he reminisced about it in both
his books. He also recalled a similar incident, when he gave a speech to
the EU Parliament:

> In the speech, I said to Baroness Ashton that I was grateful that she was
> the EU's High Representative of the Union for Foreign Affairs and Se-
> curity Policy . . . because if we had someone in that job who was com-
> petent and decisive we might actually be quite dangerous. Goodness
> knows what would happen if we had someone in the job who had a clue
> what they were doing.[57]

Using coarse and hostile language is his routine. He commonly refers to EU officials as "Brussels's Beria" (equating them to Stalin's worst
henchman and secret police chief). He suggests that professors of European universities who received prestigious Monnet Chairs were "paid to
teach the party line." (To identify the EU with the Soviet system.) He
derisively describes EU officials as "self-proclaimed and self-perpetuat-
ing mediocracy whose only excellence appears to lie in the prodigious
ability to remember acronyms." Cynically employing left-wing slogans,
as populists often do, he decries the "unholy alliance of bankers and professional politicians now passing the vast cost of their imperialist dream
onto the people of Europe." For Farage, Europe's politicians and EU's officials are nothing but "power-crazed idiots spouting gibberish."[58]

Since 2013, however, Farage has become one of Britain's most renowned and successful politicians: he came in second in the *Daily Telegraph*'s poll of the Top 100 most influential right-wingers in October
2013, and was named "Briton of the Year" by *The Times* in 2014. Rod
Liddle penned an article in *Spectator* in July 2016 entitled "In Praise of

Nigel Farage," which described him as "the most important British politician of the last decade and the most successful." Indeed, Farage understood that he had a clear chance to bring UKIP into the British political mainstream as a third party of equal standing. As part of this
effort he simply equated all the main parliamentary parties—from Tory
conservatives to social democrats—as completely identical. Thus establishing that a new, different sort of opposition party was needed in the
political arena. For instance, in 2006 he asserted:

> We've got three social democratic parties in Britain—Labour, Lib Dem
> and Conservative are virtually indistinguishable from each other on
> nearly all the main issues . . . [and] you can't put a cigarette paper be-
> tween them and that is why there are nine million people who don't
> vote now in general elections that did back in 1992.[59]

Farage envisioned a special role for himself and his party, and he relished playing that role: "Farage almost relishes playing the stage villain,
the bounder or rotter, and he sails through it all with the accusations
running off him like rain off his waterproof Barbour coat."[60] As another journalist described him:

> Nigel Farage delights in the game of politics and in his role as an in-
> surgent, a man of the people, a new kind of unlikely hero of the work-
> ing class, as some of his supporters would have it. It's cold and dry and
> the lunchtime crowd bustles and swirls around us. People keep ap-
> proaching to shake his hand—"Keep it up, Nigel"; "You're doing a great
> job, Nigel"; "Stick it to them, Nige"—and he receives them with inter-
> est and warmth. I ask if he ever grows weary of the attention. "Never.
> It's huge fun," he says, laughing loudly.[61]

Farage, indeed, attracted thousands of people and established his base.

Brexit demagoguery

What were the main arguments that Brexit proponents made to successfully convince more than half of Britain's voting public? Exit poll
statistics suggest that the most susceptible to Brexit demagoguery were
rural people, the less-educated, and the elderly. What were the core is-

sues of Brexit's demagoguery? Regaining independence, reestablishing democracy, and rising to global prominence. One of the Brexit proponents' primary issues was "regaining" British independence and sovereignty. Britain, Farage insisted, must rid itself once and for all of the EU, with its endless laws and regulations and its overpaid "Brussels bureaucrats." Once Britain leaves, he maintained, it would be able to reestablish its "lost democracy" and self-governance. This was fundamental for Farage, as reflected by the following statements:

> We've got to get back control of our country. We're in deep denial about how we've given away control of almost everything. When you get back control of your country you get proper democracy. You get back proper debate.[62]

> They call it integration, but what it was in practice was Whitehall giving away . . . our inherited rights and freedoms to a bunch of unelected, unaccountable technocrats in Brussels. . . . We had given up our sovereign rights for anything.[63]

> Brussels would increasingly seek to control more of our industry, regulate it more and, as a result, drive it away. Brussels hates . . . the City and . . . it began bombarding Britain's financial services industry with a blizzard of compliance and red tape.[64]

It's ironic that the very bankers and industrialists whom Farage portrayed himself as protecting had such totally different views about the EU. Prior to the Brexit referendum, the City's leading financial institutions and the representative bodies of British industrialists were all against leaving the EU and financially supported the "remain" campaign. After the referendum, some of them moved their headquarters to Ireland to remain in the EU.

As the costly and inefficient "Brussels bureaucracy" was one of the core issues in the Brexit debate, and a favorite argument of Farage, it pays to quote Nick Clegg, the leader of the Liberal Democratic Party, in response to Farage on April 2, 2014: "The total size of the European bureaucracy is about exactly the same size as the number of people employed by Derbyshire County Council. Some super-state!" Indeed, there were roughly 36,000 public sector employees in Derbyshire County Council in 2013, and it is still somewhat shocking that the European Commission has only 33,000 employees.[65]

Farage described the "Brussels bureaucracy" and the deputies of the EU Parliament (although he was one of them) as corrupt and parasitic. He regularly depicts them as pampered bureaucrats who "insist on exercising their right to being picked up in a chauffeur-driven Mercedes, ferried around and having the car door opened for them. . . . Who do they think they are?"[66] Farage's populist demagoguery presented EU membership as a terribly bad business for Britain. To "prove" that he, similarly to Boris Johnson, flatly lied about the cost of membership Britain paid. In a televised debate with Nick Clegg, he asked the viewing audience:

> Would you join a club that charges £55 million a day as a membership fee? . . . And would you sign up to a club that would open your borders to 485 million people who can live in your country, bring their families and do as they wish?[67]

This was probably the "Leave" campaign's most compelling argument, for it repeatedly claimed that money saved by leaving the EU would be invested in the ailing healthcare system. This was a highly popular statement. The only "problem" with this promise was that it was entirely made up. What are the real facts? Britain, indeed, officially pays £350 million per week to the EU. However, Margaret Thatcher had long ago fought for and successfully received a reduction of Britain's fee to £259 million/week—a fact that Farage and other Brexiters had conveniently "forgotten." They similarly forgot to deduct the EU's payments to Britain in the framework of the Common Agricultural Policy and the so-called Cohesion Policy, which support agriculture and relatively backward, "rust belt" regions in member countries (areas with less than 75 percent of the EU's average GDP). Adding these EU payments, Britain's weekly net contribution to the EU drops to £126 million. In addition, the EU foots the bill for international aid (a £1 billion value that would otherwise have come from Britain's own budget), and research grants (£1.4 billion per year) for British scholars and universities—all of which one can further deduct from Britain's contribution to the EU's budget. Between 2007 and 2013, British scientists received $3.7 billion from various EU programs. The European Union finances 40 percent of British cancer research, 62 percent of nanotechnology research, and 67 percent evolutionary biology research. British scholarship, research, and higher education are all highly dependent on the EU. Britain's universities attracted 30,000 scientists and researchers, no less than 20 percent of their teaching and research staff, from other EU member countries.[68] And the European Single Market generates an annual £6.5 billion additional income for the British economy.

After Brexit, Britain will have to support its own farmers, subsidize its own regions, finance its own research, and pay for its own international aid programs out of its own national budget. It will have to revamp its foreign trade and—depending on the agreement it reaches with the EU—pay tariffs on its exports to the EU. Investing £350 million a week in the health-system—as all of the Brexiters "promised" after having left the EU, was totally out of the question. The British daily *The Telegraph* has made the real facts public, showing that Brexiters deliberately misled the public through outright lies on this issue. After the referendum, the "Remain" camp demanded an admission of the falsehoods and an apology from the demagogues: "They cannot walk away from it now, disown it or pretend it never happened. They must either admit it was a lie and apologise to their voters, or justify it and explain when it is coming." Anna Soubry, a Tory leader of Open Britain, the successor to the Remain campaign, added: "They should all hang their heads in shame. There were many people, particularly in less wealthy areas, who were convinced by Leave's claim that if we left the EU we would be able to pour millions more into the NHS [the National Health Service]. The danger now is these people will become even more disillusioned with all politicians because this lot misled them."[69]

Indeed, after the referendum, Nigel Farage readily admitted that the promise to invest Britain's weekly EU fee in the health service was a "mistake."[70] The *Guardian* bitterly noted after the Brexit vote, Farage and other Brexiters "prospered by treating public life as a game," by grabbing media attention with dramatic overblown statements, and debating vitally important issues with an utter disregard of the truth.[71] Farage's Brexit propaganda was also invariably infused with extreme anti-foreigner and anti-immigration sentiment. It was the cause of increasing hatred and even violence against foreigners, such as the murder of a Polish worker and a Czech citizen by an angry mob a few weeks prior to the referendum, and the murder of a pro-European Labor parliamentarian.

Immigrants, Farage insisted, caused the failure of the National Health Service because they were such a huge financial burden. Instead of spending vast sums of money on immigrants with HIV, "what we need to do is put the National Health Service there for British people and families who in many cases have paid into this system for decades."[72] Here we are treated with a double dose of demagoguery. Not only is NHS money being squandered on undeserving immigrants in the place of legitimate taxpayers, but those very immigrants are importing dangerous diseases (more frequent among homosexuals) to Britain. Farage also painted frightful portraits of immigrants placing unbearable burdens on housing, schools, and hospitals: "Local authorities have no idea how many extra primary school places we will need, and GP surgeries have no idea how many new patients will be trying to register."[73] Farage posed as the defender of workers whose wages are declining because of immigrants:

> British workers have been hit hard by the effect of cheap labour, that the influx of migrants eager to do the same job for less.[74]

> The mass of cheap labour on our shores undercuts local wages for British workers. In some sectors—such as construction and local household services—the minimum wage has effectively become the maximum wage.[75]

Farage also forgets to mention that there are not enough British workers to fill the jobs available in these sectors. He was also quick to denounce Muslims for "coming here to take us over." In 2015, he warned of the existence of a "fifth column" of Islamic extremists in the United Kingdom. Farage also affirmed that the "basic principle" of the well-known right-wing politician, Enoch Powell's famous racist "Rivers of Blood" speech in 1968, was in fact correct.[76] Powell had fervently declared that Britain was "literally mad" to allow high levels of immigration from the Commonwealth and that will lead to civil war and bloodshed. But Farage nuanced Powell's ranting by asserting that the question is "not about color," as Powell had said, "but it is about identity, and it is about community."[77] He also replaced Commonwealth immigrants with East Europeans, declaring in 2014 that he would be "concerned" if a group of Romanian men moved next door to him.[78] When a journalist later asked Farage what exactly it is about people from Eastern Europe that so unsettles him, he replied:

Look, I got into terrible trouble by pointing out that 92 per cent of ATM crime in London is [committed] by one nationality. . . . I did once say I caught a train and nobody spoke English around me, and this again was treated with horror in London.[79]

Here Farage employs another populist stereotype: immigrants are the ones committing crimes. Like Boris Johnson, he expressed perennial unease about the dangers they posed. A week before the referendum, Farage's UKIP distributed a poster of a huge crowd of immigrants, with Farage standing in the forefront. The *Guardian* commented:

If you are thinking of voting to leave the EU, if you want Britain to take back control, if you believe the Brussels oligarchs are throttling our democracy, and, yes, if you think immigration has to be regulated and that can best be done if we have proper national borders again, look at this poster, for it is very informative. A crowd is flowing towards us. Face after face, an apparently unending human tide. . . . They are not just strangers but they are, perhaps, alien. For this poster makes plain what is commonly fudged in all the heated talk about free movement within the EU. The long snaking line seems to deliberately quote the queue of unemployed people in the famous *Labour Isn't Working* poster in 1979.[80]

The resemblance to that old Labour poster was quite intentional: both professed the typically populist line that immigration causes unemployment.

The Brexit propaganda on foreign workers was an utter fabrication. The conservative *Economist* noted:

The supply of workers and students from the EU has helped Britain grow faster than any other member state in recent years. To avoid suffocating industry, ministers have already indicated that they may let in financial-services employees, as well as seasonal agricultural workers. There are sure to be more exceptions as bottlenecks emerge.[81]

While conceding that he is a big believer in meritocracy and neo-liberal competition, Farage also employed far-left populist rhetoric in order to recruit working-class voters:

I see replicated in what happened to British society over the last twenty-five years—a shocking widening of the class system, where the rich have got a lot richer and the poor are robbed of opportunity to attain their best. . . . Two-thirds of children in the state education system were not achieving their potential.[82]

Nigel Farage flatly rejects the idea of being either left-wing or right-wing. As is the case throughout modern Europe, populist demagogues use an amalgam of right-wing and left-wing ideas to win as much support as possible. As Farage declared: "There is no left and right any more. Left and right is irrelevant."[83]

Farage, with other Brexit demagogues, were extremely successful. They were able to influence the less educated and the elderly living in the countryside, altogether 52 percent of voters voted to leave the EU. Interesting and noteworthy is the fact that a majority of young people, urbanites, and the educated wanted to remain in the EU. 75 percent of the vote in Cambridge and 60 percent in London voted to stay. A majority of those under 35 did so as well. An overwhelming majority of the population of Northern Ireland, Scotland, and Gibraltar voted to stay as well. British big business and its banking industry also financed the Remain campaign. Nearly half the British public (48 percent) did not fall for the Brexit demagoguery. However, they will most certainly have to pay for it. The "United" Kingdom post-referendum can hardly be called "united" at all.

The Theresa May Tory government, preparing for the Brexit talks with the EU, has used quite strong language: "Brexit means Brexit." Nevertheless, Britain may ultimately embrace a half-way solution. *The Economist* does not exclude the possibility that Britain will end up a temporary member of the European Economic Area, as is Norway. If it does, Britain should agree to pay the membership fee and accede to the migration quotas as well, for this is the only way it can continue to reap the benefits of the EU's single market. After three long years of uncertainty, the general elections on December 12, 2019, ended the performance of the Brexit tragicomedy with an impotent government and parliament.

As one of the leading British newspapers, the *Guardian* summed up the next day in its editorial, Johnson's Tory party was the undisputed winner with 365 seats, up 48 seats from the previous parliament, securing an 80-seat majority. The Conservatives had not achieved such a success in 32 years. The biggest loser of the election was Jeremy Corbin's Labour Party, which lost half of their blue-collar voters and altogether secured only half of the Parliamentary seats they won in 2001. It was the worse election result for the party since 1935. Johnson's election slogan, "Get Brexit done," was effective and resulted in 56 percent of the seats in the Parliament backing Brexit. There was no question that Britain would be leaving the European Union in January 2020.

However, behind the numbers of the election results, the outcome of the troubled Brexit process is much more ambivalent. Although Johnson won 56 percent of the seats, he had only 44 percent of the votes. Altogether, only 47 percent of the voters supported parties that wanted to leave the EU, while 51 percent voted for parties that advocated a second referendum on the issue. Britain remains a sharply divided country, and increasingly so with the possibility of the end of the United Kingdom. The Scottish National Party, a vocal advocate for Scottish independence and for remaining in the EU, became much stronger, while both the conservative and labor parties lost about half of their seats in Scotland. This exceptional success, as the party's leader stated, sent a "very clear message" to England and a "strong endorsement" for a new referendum on independence. Northern Ireland, for the first time, also elected more Irish nationalists than unionists and the drive to join the Irish Republic became stronger than ever. The price for leaving the EU might be very high.[84]

Brexit will be done, but the agreement with the EU and the reaction of the British business world remains uncertain. The Brexit enthusiasts' dreams of regaining Britain's nineteenth century global power in the changing world order of the twenty-first century will certainly remain a dream.

Endnotes

1 See Ivan T. Berend, *The Contemporary Crisis of the European Union* (London: Routledge, 2017).

2 Boris Johnson, *Have I Got News For You* (London: Harper Perennial, 2006), 129; see also "BBC: Who Do You Think You Are? Boris Johnson—How we did it," *BBC One*, http://www.bbc.co.uk/whodoyouthinkyouare/new-stories/boris-johnson/how-we-did-it_2.shtml, accessed on July 22, 2019.

3 Boris Johnson, *Friends, Voters, Countrymen: Jotting on the Stump* (London: Harper Collins, 2001), 185, 189, 239.

4 David A. Graham, "A Short History of Boris Johnson Insulting Foreign Leaders," *Atlantic*, July 13, 2016, https://www.theatlantic.com/international/archive/2016/07/boris-johnsons-foreign-strained-relations/491237/.

5 Johnson, *Have I Got News For You*, 5.

6 Johnson, *Friends, Voters, Countrymen*, 39.

7 Boris Johnson, *Lend Me Your Ears* (London: Harper Collins Publisher, 2003), 49–50.

8 Ibid., 55.

9 Ibid., 52.

10 Johnson, *Have I Got News For You*, 6.

11 Ibid., 8.

12 Ibid., 7.

13 Ibid., 203–4.

14 Ibid., 8.

15 Johnson, *Lend Me Your Ears*, 29.

16 Ibid., 37–38.

17 Ibid., 43–45.

18 Ibid., 263.

19 Johnson, *Friends, Voters, Countrymen*, 144.

20 Ibid., 48.

21 Ibid., 178–81.

22 Jennifer Rankin, "Is the EU undemocratic?," *Guardian*, June 13, 2016.

23 Martin Fletcher, "Who Is to Blame for Brexit's Appeal? British Newspapers," *New York Times*, June 21, 2016.

24 Josh Lowe, "Boris Johnson's Best Brussels Dispatches," *Newsweek*, February 22, 2016.

25 Boris Johnson, "Please Vote Leave on Thursday, because we'll never get this chance again," *Telegraph*, 19 June 2016.

26 Boris Johnson, "When it comes to the single market, you don't have to be in it to win it," *Telegraph*, June 12, 2016.

27 https://fullfact.org/europe/eu-facts-behind-claims-brussels-bureaucrats/, accessed April 25, 2016.

28 Johnson, "Please Vote Leave on Thursday."

29 Boris Johnson and Michael Gove, "Getting the facts clear on the economic risks of remaining in the EU—Vote Leave's letter to David Cameron," *Telegraph*, June 5, 2016.

30 Johnson, "When it comes to the single market."

31 Boris Johnson, "Tory candidates need a plan for Brexit—here's mine in 5 points," *Telegraph*, July 3, 2016.

32 Johnson, "When it comes to the single market."

33 "France and Germany brush off Johnson's EU 'baloney' jibe," *Guardian*, September 23, 2016.

34 Katrin Bennhold, "What Is U.K.'s 'Brexit' Plan? Glimpse of a Notepad Stirs Up Intrigue," *New York Times*, November 29, 2016.

35 Charles Grant, "Why the 27 are taking a hard line on Brexit," *Centre for European Reform*, October 3, 2016, https://www.cer.eu/insights/why-27-are-taking-hard-line-brexit.

36 "The Road to Brexit," *Economist*, October 8, 2016.

37 Stephen Castle, "EU agency in limbo as hidden 'Brexit' costs mount," *New York Times*, December 26, 2016.

38 Johnson and Gove, "Getting the facts clear on the economic risks of remaining in the EU."

39 Johnson, *Have I Got News For You*, 9, 12.

40 Johnson, *Lend Me Your Ears*, 209–10.

41 Johnson, *Have I Got News For You*, 127.

42 Johnson, *Lend Me Your Ears*, 211, 218.

43 Johnson, *Have I Got News For You*, 139.

44 Johnson, "Tory candidates need a plan for Brexit."

45 Johnson, "Please Vote Leave on Thursday."

46 Johnson and Gove, "Getting the facts clear on the economic risks of remaining in the EU."

47 Stephen Castle, "British Foreign minister is center of attention at a party conference," *New York Times*, October 4, 2017.

48 Nigel Farage, *The Purple Revolution: The Year that Changed Everything* (London: Biteback Publishing, 2015), 141.

49 Ibid., 142.

50 Nigel Farage, *Flying Free* (London: Biteback Publishing, 2011), 304.

51 Farage, *The Purple Revolution*, 14

52 Farage, *Flying Free*, 279.

53 Ibid., 282, 285–86, 288, 293.

54 Ibid., 227.

55 Ibid., 56–58.

56 Ibid, 238, 240; see also "Ukip's Nigel Farage tells Van Rompuy: You have the charisma of a damp rag," *Guardian*, February 25, 2010.

57 Farage, *The Purple Revolution*, 164.

58 Farage, *Flying Free*, 222, 226, 227, 274, 280.

59 "UKIP 'voice of British majority,'" *BBC News*, October 7, 2006, accessed on December 19, 2013.

60 "Nigel Farage and his U.K. Independence Party Want Out of Europe," *New York Times Magazine*, May 14, 2014.

61 Jason Cowley, "Nigel Farage: 'I'm not on the right or left. I'm a radical,'" *New Statesman*, November 12, 2014, www.newstatesman.com/politics/2014/11/nigel-farage-i-m-not-right-or-left-i-m-radical.

62 Ibid.

63 Farage, *The Purple Revolution*, 124.

64 Ibid., 126.

65 Owen Spottiswoode, "EU debate: does Brussels employ fewer bureaucrats than Derbyshire?," Full Fact, July 4, 2016, https://fullfact.org/europe/eu-debate-does-brussels-employ-fewer-bureaucrats-derbyshire/.

66 Farage, *The Purple Revolution*, 131.

67 Ibid., 7–8.

68 "Britain's Scientists Fear a 'Brexit' Brain Drain," *New York Times*, October 18, 2016.

69 Toby Helm, "Brexit camp abandons £350m-a-week NHS funding pledge," *Guardian*, September 11, 2016.

70 Helen Lewis, "How the Brexit campaign lied to us—and got away with it," *New Statesman*, June 30, 2016.

71 Nick Cohen, "There are liars and then there's Boris Johnson and Michael Gove," *Guardian*, June 25, 2016.

72 Rowena Mason, "Nigel Farage's HIV claim criticised by leaders' debate rivals," *Guardian*, April 3, 2015, https://www.theguardian.com/politics/2015/apr/03/nigel-farage-hiv-claim-criticised.

73 Farage, *The Purple Revolution*, 13–14.

74 Ibid., 18.

75 Ibid., 294.

76 Georgia Graham, "Nigel Farage: 'the basic principle' of Enoch Powell's River of Blood speech is right," *Telegraph*, November 19, 2014.

77 Cowley, "Nigel Farage: 'I'm not on the right or left. I'm a radical'."

78 Interview by LBC Radio Station's host James O'Brien with Nigel Farage, May 16, 2016. When O'Brien pressed him on the difference between having Romanian men as neighbors and a family with German children (Farage's wife and children are German), Farage replied: "You know what the difference is." https://www.lbc.co.uk/radio/presenters/james-obrien/watch-nigel-farage-v-james-obrien-live-from-1130-9/.

79 Cowley, "Nigel Farage: 'I'm not on the right or left.'"

80 Jonathan Jones, "Farage's poster is the visual equivalent of Enoch Powell's 'rivers of blood' speech," *Guardian*, June 16, 2016.

81 "The Road to Brexit," *Economist*, October 8, 2016.

82 Farage, *The Purple Revolution*, 50.

83 Cowley, "Nigel Farage: 'I'm not on the right or left.'"

84 "The Guardian view on the 2019 election result: a new political landscape," *Guardian*, December 13, 2019.

CHAPTER 11

A "freedom fighter" against the EU: the Dutch Geert Wilders

The rise of the eccentric personality of Geert Wilders as a moderate politician

Geert Wilders was born in 1963 in the southern part of the Netherlands to a Catholic family from the Dutch East Indies. He was a difficult, rebellious boy without any particular interests. He sported a leather jacket, had long brown hair, and was enamored with anarchist groups. In those years he even left his parents' faith. "[I]declared myself an atheist in the fervor of my youth. As I have grown older and wiser, my atheist radicalism has mellowed into agnosticism. . . . Moreover, I realize now how important religion is for the vibrancy and the very survival of a culture."

Wilders also acknowledged that "I was a rebellious, difficult kid, especially between the ages of ten and eighteen; I must have driven my parents crazy."[1] Some analysts suggest that he suffered from post-colonial trauma and "identity estrangement," not uncommon among returnees from former colonies. His attempt to rid himself of the "shame of his origin" may explain his curious habit of bleaching his hair.[2] His eccentric and flamboyant platinum blond hair had earned him the nickname of "Captain Peroxide" and the distinction of being "the most famous bleach-blond since Marilyn Monroe." His narcissistic character is probably a better explanation for his unusual appearance. He was always bent on being different and, like most demagogues, was forever seeking the limelight. Colleagues and co-workers describe his insatiable hunger for media coverage. As a former personal assistant recalled, Wilders kept a precise record of how many times and in what instances his name was mentioned in the media and on the internet, and expected a detailed report presented to him every morning on the topic. According to a former colleague, "if no media were going to turn up to an event, then he wouldn't go either." Once he planned to go to Gouda to talk to people about a Moroccan attack there (one of his favorite topics), but changed his mind when he learned that the media would not be attending.[3]

Wilders had no interest in studying or finishing high school, and instead decided to leave the Netherlands and discover the world. "I wanted to go to Australia; the country appealed to me." Lacking money, he instead landed in Israel, where he immediately "felt at home. . . . I was happy and relaxed. . . . I have since returned to Israel over fifty times, at least once a year, sometimes even three times."[4] He today considers Israel as his second homeland. He also traveled to Syria and the Arab world and developed, as he later related, a certain aversion to Islam. His antipathy intensified when he moved to Utrecht's Kanaleneiland district in 1985. As he would later describe it, the area was a little Casablanca or Istanbul full of Turkish shops and women wearing headscarves. Non-Muslims were regularly attacked and pressured to leave. He provided a detailed description of one attack against him: "They had probably been following me for a while. . . . When they caught up with me, they sprayed some sort of gas in my face, causing intense pain and blinding me. I fell on the pavement as they beat me, grabbed my wallet, and ran off."[5]

Indeed, the 1980s and 1990s were a period of massive immigration to the Netherlands from the former Dutch colonies and other parts of Asia and Africa. Only 200,000 non-Western immigrants resided in the country in 1970 (only 1.5 percent of the population). That number would increase to 1.6 million (9.7 percent of the population) by 2000. Lacking requisite skills and language fluency, these immigrants suffered unemployment rates three times higher than that of the Dutch people as a whole, and many ended up on welfare rolls.

Wilders took a course on health insurance in Amsterdam and got a law certificate at the Dutch Open University, whereupon he began working at the government organ that supervised the country's social security system. This position provided him personal experience on the problems the Dutch welfare state encountered with immigrant communities. He could soon pinpoint the major faults and abuses in the system. Both employers and employees took advantage of the Disability Insurance Act either to avoid working or to dismiss workers. Designating a worker disabled became inordinately easy. "The public interest," Wilders declared, "was sacrificed to the interest of certain groups."[6]

These early experiences pushed Wilders toward politics, and he joined the *Volkspartij voor Vrijheid en Democratie*, VVD (People's Party for Freedom and Democracy), in 1988. Lacking a formal higher education and devoid of political experience, he was made a social security adviser of the Party's Parliamentary group at the age of 27. He worked as a speechwriter and later as a parliamentary assistant to party leader Frits Bolkestein from 1990 to 1998. These years were Wilders's apprenticeship years. His mentor Bolkestein was one of the first anti-immigration and anti-Muslim Dutch politicians, and one who commanded a sharp confrontational style. Wilders was a quick learner and rapidly rose up the ranks of the VVD. He was elected member of the Utrecht City Council in 1997 and Parliament in 1998.

Throughout the 1990s, Wilders held basically moderate views. He was a supporter of the European Union, backed the introduction of the common currency, and was all for the EU's eastward enlargement and even its negotiations with Turkey on membership. He worked on a bill stipulating equal opportunities for foreigners on the labor market. He essentially emulated Ronald Reagan's and Margaret Thatcher's neo-liberal line. As late as 2012, he declared: "My favorite American president is Ronald Reagan," and pointedly added (exhibiting an ignorance of real history and repeated cheap propaganda slogans): "the man who saved the West from the Soviet threat and helped liberate Eastern Europe and Russia from communism. Reagan understood the evil nature of totalitarianism . . . [and remains] a source of inspiration for many freedom loving people."[7]

Wilders exhibited moderation that time when he criticized the populist anti-Islam politician Pim Fortuyn, who called for a "Cold War on Islam." In September 2001, Wilders proclaimed:

A Cold War against Islam is objectionable, for he [Pim Fortuyn] is generalizing about Muslims when he says this. I have said from the start: there is nothing wrong with Islam; it is a religion that deserves respect.

Most Muslims around the world and in the Netherlands as well, are good citizens. The problem lies with a handful of Muslim extremists.[8]

True, in 1999, during his first year in the Parliament, he presented a report on the danger of Muslim extremism and of weapons of mass destruction in the Middle East. At that time he asserted:

[E]xtremism in those countries is threatening the stability of Europe and the Netherlands. It is set to become the greatest problem of the coming decade, as immigration will bring extremism to the Netherlands. It is happening already, though no one seems to talk about it.[9]

In 2002, he became the spokesman for the VVD, and in that capacity became quite well known as an opponent of Islamic extremism.

Turn towards extremist demagoguery

Wilders soon surpassed his master. In 2004, he left the VVD because he rejected the party's positive stance towards Turkey's accession to the European Union. He established his own party two years later, the *Groep Wilders* (Wilders Group), later called *Partij voor de Vrijheid*, PVV (Party for Freedom). From that time on, he held sway as a crusader against the "Islamization of the Netherlands." He revised his earlier comments and now affirmed that Islam is not a religion but an ideology, and he compared the Quran to Hitler's *Mein Kampf.* In his political manifesto, *Klare Wijn* ("Clear Wine") in March 2006, he laid out a program for introducing an extreme anti-immigrant regime. Among other things, he demanded that the Dutch constitution be amended by eliminating the "guarantee of equality under the law" and stipulating the cultural dominance of Judeo-Christian traditions. He also demanded a 5-year moratorium of additional immigration of non-Westerners, a similar moratorium of establishing new mosques and Islamic schools, and a ban on preaching in languages other than Dutch. He called for shutting down radical mosques and expelling radical Muslims, for imposing administrative detention on terrorist suspects, for sentencing street terrorists to boot camps, and for stripping immigrant offenders of their citizenship and deporting them. In his one-page party program for 2017, titled "The Netherlands [should/will be] ours again," he proclaimed:

> Millions of Dutchmen are fed up with the Islamization of our country. Fed up with mass-immigration, asylum, terror, violence and insecurity. Instead of financing the whole world, and people that we don't want here, we will spend our money on regular Dutchman. . . . The Netherlands will be sovereign again. So we must leave the European Union.[10]

What caused this dramatic turn in Geert Wilders's views and politics? It gradually came about between 2001 and 2004. The first shock was the 9/11 Islamist attacks in the United States in 2001. This was followed by two highly publicized murders in the Netherlands. In May 2002, Pim Fortuyn was murdered. This professor of sociology became a highly celebrated populist politician who espoused Samuel Huntington's prophesy about a clash of civilizations, rebelled against the Dutch elite, called for restricting further emigration, and insisted on the mandatory assimilation of immigrant minorities to Dutch society. In the elections held after his death, his party won 1.5 million votes (17 percent of the vote) and became the country's second largest party. (The Fortuyn List's election victory actually led to the loss of Wilders's Parliamentary seat. He was not reelected on his party's list.)

In November 2004, Theo van Gogh, the outspoken anti-Muslim filmmaker, was also murdered by a Dutch-Moroccan Muslim fundamentalist, Mohammed Bouyeri. This was in retaliation for his film *Submission*, which had premiered in August of that year, and dealt with the oppression of women in Muslim society. The two murders over a one-and-a-half year period shocked the traditionally tolerant Netherlands. These three events not only radicalized Geert Wilders, but also pointed him down a path upon which he could realize his ever-growing political ambitions. A political vacuum was clearly created in the country after Pim Fortuyn's assassination, and Wilders quickly jumped to fill it. Turning to extreme anti-Islamism was not a difficult move, as he knew much about it from his readings. The highly popular Italian journalist, Oriana Fallaci, had published two books, *The Rage and the Pride* (2001) and *The Force of Reason* (2004), precisely during the period when Wilders became the real Wilders. He borrowed Fallaci's idea of the Islamic colonization of a decadent Europe. In Wilders's favorite book, Fallaci drearily described Europe as a continent that had sold itself as a prostitute to the sultans, caliphs, viziers, and mercenaries of a new Ottoman Empire. Fallaci coined the term "Eurabia" as well, and provided the details for Wilders's new program.

Wilders also began cooperating with the co-creator of Theo van Gogh's film, Ayaan Hirsi Ali, a Somali refugee and the darling of Dutch left-wing intellectuals. Hirsi Ali renounced her Islamic faith, advocated Muslims' assimilation into Dutch society, and denounced the Prophet Muhammad as a "pervert and a tyrant." Wilders was fascinated with Hirsi Ali and co-wrote a number of articles with her. In the *NRC Handelsblad*, they called for a "liberal Jihad" and the stripping of elemental rights from those attacking the foundation of Dutch society. They equated Islam with National Socialism and harshly criticized the tolerant political attitudes of the West. Wilders's views and rhetoric evolved from criticizing Islamic extremism to rejecting Islam altogether in the most extreme manner. As he put it a few years later:

> The Quran calls for Muslims to kill non-Muslims, to terrorize non-Muslims and to fulfil their duty to wage war: violent jihad . . . a duty for every Muslim. . . . Mohammed was a warlord, a mass murderer, a pedophile, and had several marriages—at the same time. Islamic tradition tells us how he fought in battles, how he had his enemies murdered and even had prisoners of war executed. . . . Let no one fool you about Islam being a religion . . . in its essence Islam is a political ideology. . . . If you want to compare Islam to anything, compare it to communism or national-socialism, these are all totalitarian ideologies.[11]

Death threats and growing popularity

Wilders predictably provoked Islamic extremists, and they predictably began issuing death threats: "Wilders you are a dead man. . . . We are going to cut your head off."[12] They tried to kill both him and Hirsi Ali in November 2004. The two attackers from the so-called *Hofstadgroep* were captured in The Hague. After this attempt and a number of other threats, Wilders was considered the most threatened person in the Netherlands and had to be put under permanent security protection for more than a decade. He is always surrounded by six plainclothes police officers, meets only those who have been searched and cleared, and resides in a heavily guarded state safe-house with bullet-proof windows. He is driven around in armored police vehicles and always wears a bulletproof vest. At certain times he was able to meet his Hungarian born wife, Krisztina, only once a week.

Writes Winston Ross of *Newsweek* in 2015:

> Death threats regularly arrive at his office. . . . When I ask him how he's doing, he raises his eyebrows and answers: "Surviving." It's an understandable response for a guy who has spent the better part of a decade wearing a bulletproof vest and being shuttled between safe houses to avoid assassination. "I'm not in prison," he says. "But I'm not free, either. You don't have to pity me, but I haven't had personal freedom now for 10 years."[13]

"But for Wilders," the journalist correctly noted, "it only added to his appeal. Since the attack, his Freedom Party has surged in national polls. It was already the most popular party in Holland, but if the 2016 parliamentary elections were held today, he'd pick up 31 seats out of 150, more than double his current figure."[14] Indeed, Wilders's Freedom Party has gradually increased in strength. In 2006, in the first elections it ran in, it won only 6 percent of the vote and was awarded 9 seats out of 150. By 2010, the PVV had risen from 9 to 24 seats, winning 15.5 percent of the vote and becoming the third largest party. It then won 17 percent of the vote in the EU parliamentary elections in May 2014. Since 2010, Wilders's political position has been quite strong. In that year Wilders took part in negotiations and signed a "support agreement" leading to the formation of Prime Minister's Mark Rutte's minority cabinet. He withdrew his support of the government in the spring of 2012 on the pretext of disagreeing on budgetary issues, as he now felt strong enough to seek power on his own. Both the death threats and his increasing popularity gradually established him as a leader of a near mainstream party and further radicalized his political stances.

The anti-Islam, anti-Eurabia crusader

Wilders emerged as the country's most outspoken and radical anti-Islam crusader. In a speech to Parliament, he declared:

Islam is the Trojan Horse in Europe. If we do not stop Islamification now, Eurabia and Netherabia will just be a matter of time. One century ago, there were approximately 50 Muslims in the Netherlands. Today, there are about 1 million Muslims in this country. . . . We are heading for the end of European and Dutch civilization as we know it. . . . I can report that [Dutch people] have had enough of burkas, headscarves, the ritual slaughter of animals, so-called honor revenge, blaring minarets, female circumcision, hymen restoration operations, abuse of homosexuals . . . Sharia exams . . . and the enormous over-representation of Muslims in the area of crime, including Moroccan street terrorists.[15]

Geert Wilders showed himself to be a master instigator when he described the situation in his country and Europe as a whole as a tragically lethal crisis. His rhetoric proved compelling for many since he used real facts and genuine circumstances but in an extremely over-dramatized and exaggerated way: "Street terrorism is on the rise throughout the Netherlands. These are no longer isolated incidents. This is an Islamic intifada."[16] When Wilders exaggerates the extent of crime among Moroccan immigrants, and his opponents respond that what he says is not true for all Moroccans, Wilders's followers can comfortably ignore the counter-arguments by insisting that "Wilders identifies the problems, while his opponents seek to downplay them and even defend Islam. . . . The more you magnify the dangers, the less the counter-arguments matter."[17] Hans de Bruijn calls our attention to Wilders's *totum pro parte* rhetorical tactic, that is using the whole to refer to the part, all for emotional effect. It is this emotional connotation that gives strength to the rhetoric.

We are losing the Netherlands . . . to Moroccan thugs who go through life cursing, spitting and beating up innocent people; thugs who terrorize our streets and playgrounds; who stick up a finger at funeral processions. . . . They are happy to accept our social benefits, our houses and our doctors, but not our norms and values.

Although Wilders is always criticized, "as long as the moral outrage is strong enough this may work in his favour. . . . Exaggeration seems to be understandable for many people."[18] Thus, Wilders has gone on to declare that moderate Islam does not exist, that Muslims are settlers occupying Europe, and that they will be the majority relatively soon. It pays to quote at length one of his speeches in 2008:

> All throughout Europe a new reality is rising: entire Muslim neighborhoods where very few indigenous people reside or are even seen. . . . It's the world of head scarves, where women walk around in figureless tents, with baby strollers and a group of children. Their husbands, or slaveholders if you prefer, walk three steps ahead. . . . These are Muslim ghettos controlled by religious fanatics . . . and they are mushrooming in every city across Europe. These are the building-blocks for territorial control . . . of Europe. . . . Many European cities are already one-quarter Muslim: just take Amsterdam, Marseille and Malmo in Sweden. In many cities the majority of the under-18 population is Muslim. Paris is now surrounded by a ring of Muslim neighborhoods. . . . In England sharia courts are now officially part of the British legal system. . . . Jews are fleeing France in record numbers. . . . A total of fifty-four million Muslims now live in Europe . . . a staggering 25 percent of the population in Europe will be Muslim just 12 years from now . . . [and] a Muslim majority by the end of this century. . . . I call the perpetrators "settlers". . . . They do not come to integrate into our societies, they come to integrate our society into their Dar-al-Islam.[19]

In the same speech, given in the United Sates, Wilders delivered an apocalyptic portrayal of the threat of Europe's imminent Islamization:

> I come to America with a mission. All is not well in the old world. There is a tremendous danger. . . . We might be in the final stages of the Islamization of Europe. The danger I see looming is the scenario of America as the last man standing.[20]

Several years later, talking again to American audience, he further warned of the dangers of Islamic immigration:

> Almost all terrorists seem to be Muslims today. . . . Islam and freedom, Islam and liberty are incompatible.[21]

To establish his bona fides as a prophet against Islamization, he published a book in English in 2012—the title of which aptly expresses his none-too-subtle narcissism: *Marked for Death: Islam's War Against the West and Me*. Striving to write the iconic anti-Islamization handbook, Wilders provides an amateurish "historical analysis" of the entire history of Islam. In his reading, the history of Islam is nothing but a history of attacks against non-Muslims in order to kill or to subordinate them, with the goal of conquering and Islamizing the entire world. Islam means poverty and slavery; Islam is nothing less than totalitarianism, on par with Nazism and communism. Its portrayal of Islam is analogous to a history of Christianity that mentions nothing but the Inquisition, torture, burnings at the stake, religious conflict, forced Christianization, and the waging of colonial wars under the guise of a Christian "civilizing mission."

Wilders also routinely launches vitriolic attacks against Muhammad and depicts him as a bloodthirsty warlord and perverted pedophile: "Muhammad may be sacred in Islam, but we in the West are entitled to critically research his life and legacy. . . . Let [the Muslims] suffer the truth."[22] Appealing to deeply rooted Cold War and anti-communist sentiment, Wilders draws a rather convoluted historical parallel:

> Defeated Nazi Germany was subject to de-Nazification, [but there was] no de-Marxification after the fall of communism. . . . Islam is the communism of today—the worldwide menace that threatens the West and all our rights and freedom. But our failure to come clean with communism has prevented us from standing up to Islam.[23]

Wilders also regularly relates stories of Muslims' crimes in various West European countries, and repeatedly links them to the Koran and with Islam generally:

> Viewing the world as Islam sees it, we come to understand why some Muslims consider it only natural to extract money out of the infidels, whether by robbing and raiding them or by making them pay jizya, the welfare payment they receive in the West.[24]

In *The Agenda of Hope and Optimism*, his political platform published during the 2010 election campaign, Wilders denies any possibility of Muslim assimilation. If they appear to be assimilated, it is only mimicry, due to the Muslim concept of *taqiyya*, the masking of one's real intentions and appropriating those of the enemy, or of *hudna*, the deceptive truce necessary in Holy War against the infidel until Islam attains the strength to prevail.[25] To support his arguments, Wilders likes to quote then Turkish Prime Minister Recep Tayyip Erdoğan, who declared in 2008 that "assimilation is a crime against humanity." He also likes to quote a 1974 speech of the former Algerian president Houari Boumediene: "One day, millions of men will leave the Southern Hemisphere to go to the Northern Hemisphere, and they will not go there as friends. Because they will go there to conquer it. And they will conquer it with their sons. The wombs of our women will give us victory."[26]

Wilders predictably draws overgeneralized and hyperbolic conclusions regarding the "crux of Islam": "an ideology of global war . . . terrorism, atrocities, betrayal, deception, deceit, assassination and hostage-taking are all *halal* (permitted) because Muhammed himself set the 'good' example."[27] Accordingly, Muslims have attempted to occupy Europe: first in 732, when their force was stopped at Poitiers, then in 1683, when they were defeated in Vienna. Now they are trying again, according to Wilders, but in a different way: by sending immigrants instead of armies. In an interview in 2015, Wilders declared that "My focus has always been on Islam. . . . That's what I wake up in the morning and what I take to bed at night; it's what I think about every second."[28]

In a manner of populists, Wilders equated Muslim Moroccans with criminals:

> Just look at these past weeks: Moroccan fortune-seekers stealing and robbing in Groningen, abusing our asylum system, and Moroccan youths terrorizing entire neighborhoods in Maassluis, Ede and Almere. I can give tens of thousands of other examples. . . . We are Dutch and this is our country . . . people with Moroccan nationality are overrepresented in the Netherlands in crime, benefit dependency and terror. . . . [W]e want . . . expelling criminals with Moroccan nationality after denaturalizing them of their Dutch nationality . . . 43% of the Dutch people, around 7 million people, agree with me.[29]

Wilders does not attack all migrants and minorities, for instance, those who arrived during the interwar period or during the 1950s and 1960s—mostly Hungarians, Czechs, and Poles who have assimilated into Dutch society. He is also quite tolerant toward the Chinese and the Vietnamese. But along with his favorite targets, Moroccans, Wilders has called for the exclusion from the Dutch labor market of all recent East European immigrants who came to the Netherlands after their countries had joined the European Union. His party created a website in 2011 to register complaints against East Europeans. This issue comprises an important part of Wilders's anti-EU stance against the EU's principle of the free movement of people and the right to work in other countries.

Developing a complex populist program

Wilders soon recognized that anti-Islam and anti-immigration proclamations are not enough to attract voters and attain power. It was obvious that he had to include a "Law and Order" component in his political platform. He unveiled the details of his new program during the 2010 election campaign. One proviso calls for the forced internment of all drug addicts in government labor camps, where they will be "rehabilitated." His platform decries that "large parts of the Netherlands are very unsafe. Where crime used to be limited to isolated incidents, we are now seeing whole neighborhoods being taken over. Street terrorists are in control."[30] The culprits, the platform specifies, are immigrants.

Driven by unmitigated ambition, he haphazardly borrowed various elements from other populist parties to assemble his program. One of its most important elements is an unwavering denunciation of the Dutch political elite. This has become part and parcel of every speech he makes. In 2005, when he announced that he intended to run in the 2007 elections, Wilders published his "Declaration of Independence" from the "self-satisfied political elite who lost their way long ago and are at the point of saying farewell to age-old Dutch roots in exchange for multiculturalism, culture relativism and a European super state."[31] When he was tried for "hate speech,"[32] a criminal act in several European countries including the Netherlands, he used the opportunity to proclaim:

> Speaking about one of the biggest problems of our country—the problem with Moroccans—is now punishable according to the elite. And hence we are slowly but surely losing our freedom of speech. Even asking a question is no longer allowed. Even though millions of people agree. . . . If you say something about Moroccans, you are now a racist. . . . Only meant to shut you and me up. . . . The Netherlands is running the risk of becoming a dictatorship. It looks like Turkey. . . . The opposition is silenced.[33]

In typical populist fashion, Wilders labeled the elite as a bunch of cowardly liars: "What is the use of political cowards who no longer dare to speak the truth? Who are silent about the problems in our country? Putting one's head in the sand is cowardice."[34] He also maintained that Europe's elite had betrayed the West and had forged an alliance with Islam after the oil crisis of 1973:

> When the Arab countries used oil as a weapon to punish European nations that had allied with Israel, European Union leaders began building an alliance with the Islamic world to ensure Europe's oil supply. . . . The multicultural elite suppressed dissent by denouncing as racists.[35]

In his book, he tried to put his anti-elitism in a general, all-European context: "Every day Europeans have been victimized by a cynical, condescending cultural elite that loathe their own people's supposed illiberalism, intolerance. . . . These ruling cosmopolitans do not see European culture as a tradition worth defending."[36] The culmination of Wilders's anti-elitism is a demand for direct democracy. His election platform of 2010 plainly states: "Only radical democratization can break the dominance of the left-wing elite." Accordingly, he called for the Netherlands to be governed by binding referenda, which would apply to the elections of mayors and the prime minister: "Let the people have their say—collectively, they know more than the left-wing clique."[37] At the same time, his party has also advocated a number of liberal policies. Wilders supports the right to abortion, euthanasia, and equal rights for homosexuals. He has also suggested putting animal rights into the constitution. These views, however, are entirely common for populists who often combine right-wing and left-wing policies and seek to gain support from previously right- and left-leaning parts of society.

The representative of the "Henks and Ingrids"

In stark contrast to the political and cultural elite, which, he assures us, betrays the populace on an everyday basis, Wilders, in a typical way, presents himself as an integral part of the "ordinary people," the Hanks and Ingrids, as he began calling them in 2010. At his trial in 2016, he described himself and his voters thus:

They are ordinary people, ordinary Dutch. The people I am so proud
of. They have elected me to speak on their behalf. I am their spokesman. I am their representative. I say what they think. I speak on their
behalf. . . . When you judge me, you are not just passing judgment on
a single man, but on millions of men and women in the Netherlands
. . . you will convict half of the Netherlands.[38]

Assembling his populist program, Wilders has borrowed from kindred
parties in Europe and America. As one of his closest collaborators put it:
"Wilders gains his knowledge from reading reports; he is a practical man,
not an intellectual. . . . The conservative canon, including authors like
Thomas Hobbes, Edmund Burke and Leo Strauss, was virtually unknown
to him."[39] Another close collaborator reveals that he has limited interests
in general. Wilders is exceedingly one-dimensional; his single interest in
life is politics.[40] On one of his trips to the United States where he con-
ferred with an advisor of President Ronald Reagan, he got the idea of advocating for a tax cut. "In the Netherlands, we don't have a party dedicat-
ed to lowering taxes. That opens up possibilities," Wilders verbalized his
thoughts in front of a Dutch journalist.[41] Consequently, his Party of Freedom includes a provision for cutting €16 billion in taxes. He has also
picked up a number of other policies from the US, such as demanding
smaller government, reducing regulation, cutting social security, and arguing that the welfare state erodes people's work ethic. In his "Declaration of Independence" in 2005, he suggested that "an extensive and detailed system of benefits, subsidies and services has made many citizens
dependent on a government."[42] Wilders would partially reverse himself a
year later. While continuing to rail against big government and pushing
for deregulation and a tax cut, he now described himself as the true follower of Willem Drees, the Dutch prime minister of the 1950s and the
"father of the Dutch welfare state." He promised to preserve the welfare
state and insisted that he was the best representative of Drees's legacy.

Against the European Union

Similarly to other populist parties in Europe, Wilders is opposed to the
European Union. This has become a core element of his anti-establishment rhetoric. In an Op-ed piece in the *New York Times* in November

2015, Wilders asserted: "The importation of a huge number of immigrants [would] be the biggest mistake in their country's postwar history. Millions now want to come to Western Europe. . . . Other European countries should not be the victims of Ms. Merkel's policies. . . . There is a perfectly good alternative to the European Union—it is called the European Free Trade Association, founded in 1960. . . . Leaving the European Union would . . . be beneficial for the Netherlands.[43] Wilders situates his party as part of the anti-European Union rebellion:

> A worldwide movement is emerging that puts an end to the politically correct doctrines of the elites and the media that are subordinate to them. That has been proven by Brexit. That has been proven by the US elections. That is about to be proven in Austria and Italy. That will be proven next year in France, Germany, and the Netherlands . . . everywhere in the West we are witnessing the same phenomenon. The voice of freedom cannot be imprisoned.[44]

In June 2016, Wilders, enthusiast for Donald J. Trump's election as president of the US, travelled to America and spoke at the Republican convention that nominated Trump as its presidential candidate. There he declared that the EU project is "collapsing" due to "a decades-long policy of open borders and cultural relativism."[45] After the election in November 2016, he celebrated Donald Trump's victory as a turning point for Europe. On Twitter he enthusiastically connected Trump's upset with his assumed victory next year: "A historic victory! A revolution! We too will give our country back to the Dutch! . . . Trump's winning proved to me that people are fed up with politically correct politicians."[46] As part of his extreme anti-establishment campaign, Wilders has also called for abolishing the United Nations. This was his response to the United Nations' High Commissioner for Human Rights Zeid Ra'ad al-Hussein's speech in The Hague in September 2016, which condemned Wilders for employing "lies and half-truths, manipulations and peddling of fear." Wilders's demagoguery, Zaid suggested, reminded him of the Balkans war in the 1990s, where he had served as a peacekeeper and learned that the cruelty he witnessed "flowed from this same factory of deceit, bigotry and ethnic nationalism. . . . We must pull back from this trajectory . . . the atmosphere will become thick with hate [which could] descend rapidly into colossal violence." Angrily reacting to Zeid's speech, Wilders in a text message to AFP dismissed the Jordanian prince as "an utter fool. . . . [This is] another good reason to get rid of the UN."[47]

Geert Wilders travelled to Cleveland to build an alliance with Donald Trump in 2016. Alliance-building became a new feature of his policy in general. He changed his attitude towards fellow European populists as well. Previously he had not aligned himself with right-wing European populists and had denounced the French Jean-Marie Le Pen and the Austrian Jörg Haider, at times calling them fascists. Now he reconsidered and began to cooperate with Marine Le Pen to form an anti-EU faction in the European Parliament. He also wanted to include the Austrian Freedom Party, the Italian Northern League, and the Belgian Flemish Interest into this alliance, which was to serve as the resistance against Islamization since

> Islam is threatening the survival of all free peoples. Dutchmen, Americans, Canadians, Australians, Indians, Germans, Brits, Russians, Irishmen, Frenchmen, Italians, Danes, Swiss, Israelis and others should unite against our common adversary.[48]

Wilders's alliance-building with European populists is linked to his larger nationalist agenda. As have other European populists, he has naturally combined his anti-immigrant and anti-EU policy with nationalism. "The people of the free world," he suggested, "can defend their liberties only if they can rally around a flag with which they identify."[49] However, he has called for not only "regaining" national sovereignty, but also for uniting all Flemish people, including those in the northern part of Belgium. In 2008, Wilders co-authored an article in the *NRC Handelsblad* proposing a Flemish-Dutch Union. He began referring to Northern and "Southern" Netherlands (the latter meaning Flemish Belgium), which share a common history: "We are about to find out that we will also have a shared future. The Netherlands must embrace the Flemish Lion and say, welcome home, we have never forgotten you." He has considered calling for a referendum on unification, exploiting the conflicts between the southern Walloon and northern Flemish parts of Belgium.[50]

The end game?

In traditionally tolerant and liberal Holland, Geert Wilders's populist demagoguery has appeared to have succeeded. His eccentric personality, his overly dramatic depiction of the country's problems, and his tactical employment of exaggerated half-truths have indeed made an impact on a part of the Dutch populace. The repeated assassination attempts against him and the need for him to live in hiding under guard for more than a decade, have served to provide him a propaganda coup and garner him increasing legitimization. His demagoguery has resonated with those experiencing uncertainty in their lives or fear for the future. The dangers posed to him personally seemed to verify his claims of Islam's threat to the country. His trial did more good for his reputation in the Netherlands than did any proposal his party has made to address the country's problems.

In October 2016, *The Economist* correctly observed that

> a court in The Hague did the PVV's campaign prospects a favour. It allowed the country's public prosecutors to go ahead with trying Mr. Wilders for incitement to hatred based on a speech he delivered in 2014 calling for "fewer Moroccans" in the country. The trial . . . , if past precedent is any guide . . . will lead to a boost in the PVV's popularity.[51]

This "prophecy" has already been proven true by the polls conducted after the trial in November. According to polls of Maurice de Hond, the Netherlands' most prominent pollster, the PVV would become the largest party in parliament if elections were held today: Wilders party would get 33 seats in the 150-seat lower chamber.[52] The fractured political structure of the country almost always requires at least a three-party coalition, with the head of the largest coalition party winning the premiership. The March 15, 2017, elections in the Netherlands were anticipated with great interest and trepidation across Europe. Would the populist trend of Brexit and the election of Donald Trump triumph in the Netherlands as well?

The Dutch populace was mobilized to a great degree, with more than 80 percent of eligible voters casting ballots, and, contrary to the forecasts, defeated the rising demagogue. Wilders won only 20 seats, hardly more than 13 percent, and Mark Rutte's governing Peoples Party finished in first place with 33 seats, or 22 percent. Even the Christian Democrats and Liberal Progressive parties were virtually tied with Wilders (each winning 12.7 percent), and the left-leaning Green Party, with its thirty-year old half Moroccan leader, Jesse Klaver, increased its seats from 4 to 14, thus more than 9 percent. To build a majority government (76 seats) there needed to be a four-party coalition. All four parties support the European Union and reject Wilders's xenophobic populism.

This election indicated that the advance of populism, at least in some countries, has temporarily stopped in Western Europe. Wilders miscalculated the "Trump effect." In contrast to his hope and belief, the similarly narcissistic, bombastic American demagogue did not pave his way to power in the Netherlands but just the opposite, probably pushing the Dutch electorate away from populism.[53]

Endnotes

1 Geert Wilders, *Marked for Death: Islam's War against the West and Me* (New York: Regnery Publishing, 2012), 31.

2 Lizzy van Leeuwen, "Wreker van zijn Indische grootouders: De politieke roots van Geert Wilders," *Groene Amsterdammer*, September 2, 2009, quoted by Koen Vossen, *The Power of Populism: Geert Wilders and the Party for Freedom in the Netherlands* (London: Routledge, 2017), 2. I used this book and some of its quotations in the entire chapter.

3 "Koen Vossen's interview with former MP Louis Bontes," quoted in Vossen, *The Power of Populism*, 93.

4 Wilders, *Marked for Death*, 73–74.

5 Ibid., 139.

6 Geert Wilders, *Kies voor Vrijheid: Een eerlijk antwoord* (Groep Wilders: 2005), 26, quoted by Vossen, *The Power of Populism*, 5.

7 Wilders, *Marked for Death*, 130.

8 "Wie is Wilders en wil hij wel regeren?", video webpage NRC, https://www.nrc.nl/nieuws/2017/03/08/wie-is-wilders-enwil-hij-wel-regeren-7137192-a1549304, quoted in Laurens-Jan Danen, "The need for information: The EU and countering populism," manuscript.

9 Quoted by Vossen, *The Power of Populism*, 10.

10 Partij voor de Vrijheid concept party program "Nederland weer van ons": http://www.pvv.nl/images/Conceptverkiezingsprogrammma.pdf, quoted by Danen, "The need for information," 46.

11 "Speech Geert Wilders in New York, 25 September 2008," https://www.pvv.nl/index.php/component/content/article.html?id=1310:geert-wilders-spreekt-bij-het-hudson-institute-te-new-york.

12 Wilders, *Marked for Death*, 8.

13 Winston Ross, "Geert Wilders: The 'Prophet' Who Hates Muhammad," *Newsweek*, January 19, 2015.

14 Ibid.

15 "Mr Wilders's contribution to the parliamentary debate on Islamic activism," PVV website, September 6, 2007, https://pvv.nl/index.php/7-nieuws/nieuws/464-mr-wilderss-contribution-to-the-parliamentary-debate-on-islamic-activism.html.

16 Wilders's statement in the Parliament on September 17, 2008, quoted by Hans de Bruijn, *Geert Wilders Speaks Out: The Rhetorical Frames of a European Populist* (The Hague: Eleven International Publishing, 2011), 27.

17 Ibid., 29, 31.

18 Ibid., 38.

19 "Speech Geert Wilders in New York, 25 September 2008," https://www.pvv.nl/index.php/compo-nent/content/article.html?id=1310:geert-wilders-spreekt-bij-het-hudson-institute-te-new-york.

20 Ibid.

21 "Press Conference: Geert Wilders Warns America against Islamic Immigration," Limits to Growth, May 1, 2015, https://www.limitstogrowth.org/articles/2015/05/01/press-conference-geert-wilders-warns-america-against-islamic-immigration/.

22 Wilders, *Marked for Death*, 124.

23 Ibid., 131–32.

24 Ibid., 153.

25 *De Agenda van Hoop en Optimisme*, Wilders election program in 2010, quoted by Vossen, *The Power of Populism*, 32.

26 Wilders, *Marked for Death*, 162.

27 Ibid., 78, 87.

28 P. Jansen, "Geert Wilders: Mijn focus is altijd op Islam gericht," *De Telegraaf*, February 28, 2015, quoted by Vossen, *The Power of Populism*, 58.

29 Geert Wilders, "Final Statement of Geert Wilders at his Trial," November 23, 2016, *Gatestone Institute*, https://www. gatestoneinstitute.org/9404/wilders-trial-closing-statement.

30 "Justitie en Politie met Ambitie: Plan PVV voor een effectieve aanpak van de criminaliteit," quoted by Vossen, *The Power of Populism*, 48.

31 "Geert Wilders returns from US and writes Dutch 'Declaration of Independence' from the EU—calls for closing of Islamic schools," *Militant Islam Monitor*, March 14, 2005, http://www.militantislammonitor.org/article/id/500.

32 The proceedings were the result of a speech Wilders gave in a cafe in The Hague in 2014. He asked a room full of supporters if they wanted to see "more or fewer" Moroccans in the Netherlands. The audience enthusiastically answered with "fewer, fewer." Wilders replied: "OK, we'll take care of that." "'I will never be silenced,' Wilders tells court on final day of 'fewer Moroccans' trial," *DutchNews.Nl*, November 23, 2016.

33 Baron Bodissey, "Geert Wilders: No Cowardly Prosecutor Will Get Me on My Knees!," *Gates of Vienna News Feed*, November 18, 2016, https://gatesofvienna.net/2016/11/geert-wilders-no-cow-ardly-prosecutor-will-get-me-on-my-knees/.

34 Ibid.

35 Wilders, *Marked for Death*, 177, 208.

36 Ibid., 180.

37 Quoted by Vossen, *The Power of Populism*, 39.

38 Wilders, "Final Statement of Geert Wilders at His Trial."

39 "Statement by Bart Jan Spruyt," quoted by Vossen, *The Power of Populism*, 21.

40 Koen Vossen's interview with Johan Driessen, in Vossen, *The Power of Populism*, 92.

41 M. Chavamnnes, "Wilders snuift in de Verenigde Staten conservatieve thema's op," *NRC Handelsblad*, January 15, 2005, quoted by Vossen, *The Power of Populism*, 21.

42 Quoted in Vossen, *The Power of Populism*, 47.

43 Geert Wilders, "Let My People Vote," *New York Times*, November 20, 2015.

44 Wilders, "Final Statement of Geert Wilders at His Trial."

45 Nick Gutteridge, "The EU is collapsing due to open borders, Dutch MP tells Trump support-ers," *Express*, July 20, 2016, https://www.express.co.uk/news/politics/691327/European-Union-Dutch-MP-Geert-Wilders-Donald-Trump-supporters-Republican-Convention.

46 Rob Virtue, "'Trump win is latest in west's patriotic spring,' Dutch anti-migrant politician rejoices," *Express*, November 9, 2016, https://www.express.co.uk/news/world/730468/Geert-Wilders-US-election-Donald-Trump-Freedom-Party.

47 "'Demagogues and cheats': UN rights chief condemns Trump and Wilders," *Guardian*, September 20, 2016.

48 Wilders, *Marked for Death*, 216.

49 Ibid., 215.

50 G. Wilders and M. Bosma, "Nederland en Vlaanderen horen bij elkaar," *NRC Handelsblad*, July 31, 2008, quoted by Vossen, *The Power of Populism*, 44.

51 "Dutch far-right leader Geert Wilders will face trial for hate speech," *Economist*, October 15, 2016.

52 Michael van der Galien, "Geert Wilders on Track to Become Next Prime Minister of the Netherlands," *PJ Media*, November 27, 2016, https://pjmedia.com/trending/2016/11/27/geert-wilders-on-track-to-become-the-netherlands-next-prime-minister/.

53 "The World Waits and Wonders about Donald Trump," *New York Times*, November 12, 2016.

CHAPTER 12

Three demagogues exploit the difficult transformation: Viktor Orbán in Hungary and the Kaczyński brothers in Poland

The eighteenth-century Polish proverb, *"Polak, Węgier, dwa bratanki"* (Pole and Hungarian cousins shall be), reflects the historically close relations between the two nations. Indeed, in East-Central Europe, where neighboring peoples have traditionally been enemies—where Czechs look down on Slovaks, Hungarians revile Romanians, and Croats spurn Serbs, where each nation considers its eastern border as the end of Europe and thus disdains its eastern neighbors as non-Europeans—Poles and Hungarians have traditionally been friends.

How do we account for this anomaly? Both countries have fundamentally similar pasts. Both were medieval great powers but later lost independence and were incorporated into neighboring countries.[1] Both fought for independence from time to time. Both suffered national humiliation, lost territories through forced partition, have been frequently occupied, and embraced extreme nationalism during the nineteenth and twentieth centuries. Given their commonalities, Poles and Hungarians have historically sympathized with one another. Poles had even elected Hungarian kings in earlier centuries, and had participated in the Hungarian struggle for independence in 1848. For its part, Hungary, although Hitler's staunch ally, allowed Polish soldiers to escape to Hungary and on to the West to avoid German prisoner of war camps during World War II. Both countries were occupied by the Soviet army and were part of the Soviet Bloc after World War II, and both—alone in the region—staged revolts against Soviet occupation in 1956. The Hungarian revolution actually began as a demonstration of solidarity with Poland's struggle at the statue of József Bem, a Polish general who was one of the military leaders of the Hungarian 1848 revolution. Communism had first collapsed in these two countries in 1989.

These similarities persisted during the difficult transition from authoritarian communism to democratic capitalism. The primary slogan in both countries in 1989 was "Back to Europe!"—although they had never really belonged to the European core, but only to its periphery. Neither country had any kind of genuine democratic system during modern times. Authoritarian regimes predominated. After 1989 they began to follow a new path, suffering terrible decline in the first years, but then making solid progress around the turn of millennium. The transformation from communism to capitalism caused major social shock in both countries. After a long era when everything was strictly regulated with little personal choice, people suddenly had to adapt to the new laws and regulations of a free market society, and adopt new behavioral patterns and life strategies. An egalitarian social system was replaced by one of striking income inequality. Seemingly overnight, new oligarchy of multi-millionaires emerged with close ties to power, while large numbers of citizens fell into poverty. The transition was therefore extremely difficult, engendering not only a new set of winners, but also a multitude of losers.

Both Hungary and Poland became permeated with Western corporations, and both of their banking systems came to be dominated by leading Western banks. Their modern new industries became subsidiaries of Western multinational companies, and those working in them earned twice as much as workers in domestic companies. Both countries sought to join the European Union and NATO as quickly as possible, and they were indeed quickly accepted. Both received massive financial assistance from the EU and benefited from NATO's military protection, though they garnered little influence within those Western-dominated organizations. Both ultimately became prey to a rapid resurgence of right-wing nationalism in the twenty-first century Europe in its quite extreme form.

The situation was similar in other transitioning countries that also became the playground of populists and political demagogues. Slovakia has a long history of populist demagoguery from the early stage of transformation under Vladimír Mečiar in the 1990s up to the Robert Fico's leadership during the 2010s. The Czech Republic is facing a populist breakthrough by the electoral victory of the billionaire—the country's second richest populist, Eurosceptic demagogue—Andrej Babiš in the fall of 2017. Slovenia followed in June 2018 when the country elected a populist party to government.

Conditions were exceedingly ripe in most of the transition countries in Central Europe for right-wing nationalist and populist demagogues. Two countries of the region are already dominated by well-established right-wing, anti-EU demagogues who triumphed in elections in the early twenty-first century. The identical twins Lech and Jarosław Kaczyński rose to power in Poland, and Viktor Orbán, their political "twin brother," took control of Hungary. They skillfully undermined democratic institutions in order to cement their authoritarian rule, what Orbán described as "illiberal democracy."

"Over the past several years," George Friedman noted,

> Hungary and Poland have been heavily criticized within the European Union. Both have been scolded, but neither have had sanctions imposed against them. . . . Since 2010, the government of Hungarian Prime Minister Viktor Orbán has been criticized for . . . impeding on press freedoms and independence of the judiciary, as well as undermining checks and balances and the rule of law. In Poland, after coming to power in October 2015, the new government of the Law and Justice party has introduced laws that . . . limit the independence of the media. Moreover, the government triggered a constitutional crisis when it took steps that undermined the ability of the Constitutional Tribunal to function.[2]

Viktor Orbán

Viktor Orbán was born to an impoverished rural family in Hungary in 1963. His parents, however, made the most of the advantages allotted by the state socialist Kádár government. His father, Győző Orbán, joined the communist party in 1966, attended evening college courses free of charge, and earned an engineering degree. The family rose to a solid middle-class status. Viktor was sent to the Eötvös Loránd University in Budapest and graduated from its law school in 1987.

This was the time when Hungary initiated a unique transformation process. By the following year, the Kádár regime, which had emerged after the 1956 revolution, would be a thing of the past with the retirement of the communist leader. Reform communists took over the party and government and implemented radical reform. New opposition party formations were allowed. The "1956 counter-revolution"—taboo up till then—was reevaluated as a genuine people's uprising and a struggle for independence against Stalinism and Russian occupation.[3] A genuine privatization of the economy and banking system commenced, and the country saw the introduction of real market prices and the opening of the first subsidiaries of Western multinational companies on Hungarian soil. The reforms culminated in February 1989, when the Central Committee of the Hungarian Communist Party resolved to hold free multi-party elections in the spring of 1990. By the time those elections took place, communism had collapsed in Poland and the region's first anti-communist Solidarity government was formed and even welcomed by Mikhail Gorbachev's transforming Soviet Union.

The newly graduated Viktor Orbán began working at a Management Training Institute, but became a professional politician in 1989. He is a born leader who loves power. In high school he served as the head of the school's Communist Youth Organization. As he later explained, he was a naïve and devoted supporter of communism. In March 1988, he established the *Fiatal Demokraták Szövetsége*, Fidesz (Alliance of Young Democrats) party with 36 of his friends and schoolmates. By the end of the year, there were 21 political parties in existence in the country, and their number would rise to 60 the following year, when the regime collapsed entirely.

Orbán became a devoted (and certainly also a "naïve") liberal democrat. The communist regime had virtually dissolved and left the country waiting in anticipation for the first free elections in more than forty years. A few months before the election, Imre Nagy, the executed communist leader of the 1956 revolution, was reburied. Orbán was one of the speakers at the catafalque before a crowd of 250,000 on Heroes' Square in Budapest on June 16, 1989. He delivered a spirited and passionate anti-communist speech that earned him considerable renown across the country. In an aggressive and threatening tone, he demanded free elections (which had already been decided on and announced some time earlier) and the withdrawal of the Soviet troops from Hungary. Fidesz won 5.4 percent in the first free elections in March 1990, and he became vice-chairman of the Liberal International.

In 1993, Fidesz's collective leadership disbanded and Orbán took over as the party's unquestioned leader. In September of that year, Orbán met with the prominent Austrian journalist Paul Lendvai in Vienna.[4] As Lendvai would later report, Orbán at that time made a strong impression as a consistent liberal democrat who strongly criticized the right-wing nationalist policies of the first post-communist government of József Antall. In the next elections in 1994, Fidesz barely exceeded the 5 percent threshold and became a minor parliamentary party. The results suggested to Orbán that Fidesz had little chance of winning elections if it remained one of many liberal democratic parties. He also recognized that there was a vacuum on the other side of the political spectrum. The power-loving Orbán did not hesitate to transform his party into a right-wing nationalist organization in April 1995. His party proceeded to leave the Liberal International and join the Europe-wide "family" of European Peoples Parties in 2000. At about the same time, the atheist, anti-clerical Orbán, who chose not to be married in a church, suddenly became religious and endorsed the political ascendancy of the church in Hungary. He and his wife were again married in a church eleven years after their civil marriage. When he lost the elections in 2002, he told his party associates, "Let's pray!"

Orbán's strategy worked spectacularly: his party won 42 percent of the vote in the 1998 election, and he formed a coalition government under his premiership. His first government took steps towards authoritarian rule and declared that "the Parliament works without opposition." However, a number of scandals, corruption cases, forced resignations of close collaborators, and the implosion of his governing coalition led to Fidesz's defeat in the 2002 elections. The Socialist Party took over the government, and won reelection in May 2006. After that victory, the socialist prime minister Ferenc Gyurcsány delivered a secret speech to the Socialist Party's parliamentary caucus in a resort at Balatonöszöd. Seeking to mobilize the party to address a number of enduring economic problems in the country, Gyurcsány spoke openly about the party's crucial mistakes over the previous years and the lies they told to cover up their failed economic policies. He used crude and vulgar language to shock his colleagues. A recording of the speech was leaked and broadcast on the radio in September 2006.[5]

An unprecedented scandal erupted. Orbán masterfully exploited the public's outrage and called for daily demonstrations demanding the government's resignation. An unruly mob, including fascist skinheads and members of the openly anti-Semitic far-right Jobbik Party (formed from *Jobboldali Ifjúsági Közösség*), was mobilized—launching a three-and-a-half-year period that Paul Lendvai described as a "Cold Civil War." "It was clear," the Austrian correspondent Ernst Gelegs reported, "that Orbán made an alliance with Jobbik Party at that time outside the Parliament."[6] An endless array of riots ensued, including attacks on the state television headquarters and the occupation of the main square in front of Parliament (with crowds sleeping in pitched tents and cooking in open air kitchens). Clashes with the police resulted in injuries of 326 civilians and 399 policemen, some of them seriously. The Socialist Party simply could not cope with the scandal. Orbán's second electoral victory in 2010 was therefore predictable, and it turned out to be a landslide, with 57.2 percent of the votes. The neo-fascist Jobbik Party won an additional 17 percent of the vote, reflecting the astounding shift of three-quarters of the population to the political right. Viktor Orbán's performance as a successful populist demagogue began that year.

His demagoguery was partly based on the traditionally strong nationalism of much of Hungary's population. The key political agenda of the extreme nationalist Horthy regime of the interwar period was the revision of post–World War I Trianon Treaty, which left Hungary with only a third of its prewar territory and made 3 million Hungarians minority citizens of Romania, Yugoslavia, and Czechoslovakia. Horthy's Hungary allied itself with Mussolini and joined Hitler's war to regain its lost territories. Most Hungarians were intoxicated by extreme right-wing nationalism—hence the success of the Hungarian "Arrow-cross" or Nazi Party. In 1939, the Hungarian Nazi Party emerged as the country's largest party when it won 40 percent of the vote in the first secret-ballot elections in Horthy's Hungary. Under communism, nationalism was suppressed for four decades and Trianon was rarely mentioned. This did nothing to eradicate the entrenched nationalism of a significant part of the population, a nationalism that was expressed in even stronger tones when people were free to do so after 1989.

Orbán's demagoguery was partly based on this traditionally strong nationalism, which provided him a huge throng of supporters. He began speaking of a nation of 15 million Hungarians (rather than the 10 million living in Hungary), including even the children and grandchildren of the one-and half million Hungarians who left the country before World War I. He designated the anniversary of the Trianon Treaty the "Day of National Unity." At a mass rally in July 2014, he accused all previous liberal governments with neglecting national interests and declared himself the savior and unifier of the Hungarian nation:

> Liberal democracy was not capable of openly declaring, or even obliging, governments with constitutional power to declare that they should serve national interests. Moreover, it even questioned the existence of national interests. It did not oblige subsequent governments to recognize that Hungarian diaspora around the world belongs to our nation and to try and make this sense of belonging stronger with their work.[7]

In his "State of the Nation" speech in 2014, he mused that "We are also familiar with the hoary old joke that Hungary is the only country in the world which has borders with itself—in fact all the way round, in every direction."[8] This "joke" reminded Hungarians living as minorities in the surrounding countries (Slovakia in the north, Romania in the east, Serbia and Croatia in the south, and Austria in the west) that they in fact belong to Hungary. "Accepting the restrictions of EU membership, Fidesz wants to change the meaning of Hungary's borders, rather than the borders themselves. It has tried to do this by giving all 'ethnic Hungarians' citizenship of Hungary, though preferring them to remain in the ancient lands of pre-Trianon Hungary."[9] In 2017, Orbán congratulated himself as the spiritual unifier of Hungarians living beyond the country's borders.[10]

Searching for historical roots, Orbán quite predictably linked his regime to the extreme nationalist, authoritarian Horthy era. He denied Hungary's responsibility in the Holocaust, in which half of the country's Jewish citizens perished, and attributed their deaths solely to the German occupation of Hungary in March 1944. Hungary and the Horthy regime, he insisted, bore no responsibility for the country's murderous past. He went so far as to praise the "outstanding diplomatic and military accomplishments" of the Horthy regime—a regime that was deeply hostile to the West and closely allied to Mussolini and Hitler. Horthy's decision to join Hitler's war resulted in the country's total defeat and led to the death of nearly one million Hungarian citizens. But Orbán has defiantly rewritten the history of the Horthy period:

> Because this is the time when we may finally build . . . a national Christian era. . . . We could also define our current situation in comparison with the Horthy era. . . . We can . . . say that, despite our losses, the dismembering of our country and the Great Depression, we [i.e. Hungary during the Horthy regime] managed to stand up, and . . . we started flourishing and achieved outstanding diplomatic, military and economic results. Our gross national product per capita exceeded that of Spain, Ireland, Finland and Portugal—not to mention Poland, Yugoslavia and Romania.[11]

In a classically demagogic way, Orbán cherry picks historical facts that serve his agenda and rejects others that do not. In the same speech he also declared:

> The 1918–19 revolution can be found in [historical accounts] devoted to Bolshevik anti-Hungarian subversion launched in the service of foreign interests and foreign ambitions. . . . The tradition of 1919, too, is still with us—though fortunately its pulse is just a faint flicker. . . . After its leaves and branches have withered, its roots will also dry up in the Hungarian motherland's soil, which is hostile to internationalism.[12]

While referring to the "1918–19 revolution," he forgot to mention that it actually comprised two revolutions: a democratic one in 1918 under the leadership of President Count Mihály Károlyi, and a communist one in 1919 led by Béla Kun. The statue of Mihály Károlyi, which stood next to the parliament building, had already been conveniently removed.

Declining West and the "Eastern Wind"

Orbán bitterly criticized the "decline of the liberal West." He denounced the "decadent and 'money-based' West" and embraced a "work-based society . . . of a non-liberal nature."[13] Misinterpreting liberalism, he stated that "the strength of American 'soft power' is deteriorating, because liberal values today incorporate corruption, sex, and violence and these liberal values discredit the US and American modernization. . . . Western Europe was so preoccupied with solving the situation of immigrants that it forgot about the white working class."[14]

By rejecting "decadent" Western liberal democracy, Orbán pointed Hungary in a new direction. After his election victory in 2010, he called for reorienting the country toward the East. He unveiled a new approach to economic policy and summarily discarded Western liberalism. "We are sailing under a Western flag," he lamented at a September 5, 2010, meeting, "though an Eastern wind is blowing in the world economy."[15] What was the meaning of his reference to an "Eastern Wind"? He made it clear soon enough:

> [There is a] race to figure out a way of organizing communities, a state that is most capable of making a nation competitive. This is why . . . a trending topic in thinking is understanding systems that are not Western, not liberal, not liberal democracies, maybe not even democracies, and yet making nations successful. Today, the stars of international analyses are Singapore, China, India, Turkey, Russia. And I believe that our political community rightly anticipated this challenge. . . . We are searching for, and we are doing our best to find, ways of parting with Western European dogmas, making ourselves independent from them.[16]

In the same speech, Viktor Orbán continued to predict the West's economic decline and outlined his "new" principle of state organization based on work. He predicted that

> probably societies founded upon the principle of the liberal way to organize a state will not be able to sustain their world-competitiveness in the following years, and more likely they will suffer a setback. . . . [W]e can consider three ways to organize a state that we so far knew, as a starting point: the nation state, the liberal state, and then the welfare state, and the question is, what is coming up next? The Hungarian answer is that the era of a workfare state . . . that in character it is not of a liberal nature. . . . [W]e have to abandon liberal methods and principles of organizing a society.[17]

This reasoning is quite convoluted. He presents the nation state, the liberal state, and the welfare state as if they were species of the same taxonomic genus. He forgets that welfare states had in fact been introduced by liberal nation states. Even more confounding is the idea of the so-called "workfare state" as a new state formation. What is perfectly clear, however, is that Orbán rejects both liberal democratic principles and the "declining" West, and that he idealizes the anti-democratic one-party rule of Putin's Russia, Erdoğan's Turkey, and Communist China. Orbán expressed his clear preference for strong power: "If you ask what we expect from Turkey, we say that our number one priority is stability." He was also quick to praise Donald J. Trump after his election "as a gift" portending the demise of the "liberal elite" in the West and the onset of dramatic political change around the world.[18]

Authoritarianism and re-nationalization

This "new" ideology served to legitimize the new policies of the Orbán government: the introduction of a regime that approaches state-dirigist authoritarianism. He regularly employs classic populist demagoguery to pose as the protector of the "little people" against the banks, and as the defender of the nation against foreign dictates. He denounces Western individualism, propagates "Christian values," and tops it off with a "lefty" agenda:

> [W]hat happened is that . . . the stronger neighbor told you where your car entrance is. It was always the stronger party, the bank that dictated how much interest you pay on your mortgage, changing it as they liked over time. . . . [T]hat was the continuous life experience of vulnerable, weak families that had smaller economic protection than others during the last twenty years.[19]

In the name of protecting the people's interests, Orbán re-nationalized a number of important assets that had been privatized after the collapse of communism. This included more than 200 companies in the banking, energy, manufacturing, and other industries during the first half of the 2010s. These steps have significantly increased the government's power and control over the economy, while providing highly paid positions for cronies and supporters.[20]

In another speech, Orbán expounded on his concept of three levels of interests: individual, community, and national.

Liberal democracy . . . did not protect public wealth. . . . [I]n Hungary liberal democracy was incapable of protecting public property that is essential in sustaining a nation. . . . Then, the liberal Hungarian state did not protect the country from indebtedness. . . . [W]hat is happening today in Hungary can be interpreted as an attempt of the respective political leadership to harmonize the relationship between the interests and achievement of individuals—that needs to be acknowledged—with interests and achievements of the community, and the nation. Meaning, that the Hungarian nation is not a simple sum of individuals, . . . the new state that we are building is an illiberal state, a non-liberal state. It does not deny foundational values of liberalism, . . . but it does not make this ideology a central element of state organization, but applies a specific, national, particular approach in its stead.[21]

Who is responsible for representing the supreme interests of the state and nation? In authoritarian states, it is the charismatic supreme leader—in the past the *Duce*, the *Führer*, the *Conducător*, the *Nemzetvezető*,[22] and in today's Hungary, the current prime minister. As Jan-Werner Müller first described it, the Orbán regime has effectively become a "Führer democracy." Indeed, Viktor Orbán has (certainly) unknowingly reinvented Mussolini's dictum:

If the nineteenth century was the century of the individual . . . [the twentieth century] is the collective century and therefore the century of the State . . . all the political, economic, and spiritual forces . . . circulate within the State. . . . The Fascist concept . . . accepts the individual only in so far as his interests coincide with those of the State.[23]

Without knowing it, he has also duplicated the ideology of the Romanian fascist Corneliu Zelea Codreanu, who, like Orbán, spoke of three levels of interests: the individual, the national community, and the future interests of the nation. The three levels represented a hierarchy, with the lower level subordinated to the higher, the individual to the community, and both to the future interests of the nation.[24]

In order to raise his status as the charismatic Leader, Orbán is moving his office to the former royal quarter, lurking above the city at the top of the Buda hills.

Towards authoritarian rule[25]

When, in the autumn of 2010, the Constitutional Court struck down a statute that would have been implemented retroactively, Fidesz immediately retaliated by amending the constitution and constraining the Constitutional Court's powers. Thus, the Constitutional Court was transformed overnight from a controlling body—a real check on legislative power—to a feeble overseer of the application of the law. Previously, the president of the Constitutional Court had been chosen by the judges themselves; now, under the new rules, he/she was to be appointed by parliament, where Orbán had a majority. In addition, the number of judges was increased from eleven to fifteen, and the court was promptly packed with Orbán's cronies—right-wing personalities close to Fidesz. The Constitutional Court was thus politically checked and could no longer overrule the decisions of the Parliament and government.

The Orbán government proceeded to pass laws that gave it the power to immediately dismiss public employees without cause. This led to the purge of the entire government apparatus and its replacement with loyal cronies. Dismissing and hiring officials on loyalty alone was the primary means of centralizing the government's power without institutional change. This was the lesson Orbán learned when he sought to subordinate the independent National Bank to his government in 2011 and was met with immediate EU opposition. At that time he had to renounce the legal changes he made to the Bank, but he was able to subordinate it nonetheless by appointing his close friend as its new president. In 2010, another former Fidesz representative became president of the Media Authority, and another was made the head of the newly-created National Judicial Office. The Financial Supervisory Authority and the Budgetary Council came under political control as well. The new president of the National Cultural Fund was also a Fidesz politician, who simultaneously served as president of the Parliamentary Cultural Committee, and was thus the overseer of his own position. A loyal government official took charge of the Ombudsman Office, virtually eliminating the institution's independence. Most of these appointments were made for nine to twelve-year stints, thereby preventing future governments from making changes.

Orbán did not stop at the subordination of the Constitutional Court. With a special law, he cut the retirement age for judges from 70 to 62 years, thus enabling him to uproot the justice system with the appointment of his cronies. For the first time in Hungarian history, a small group of close friends hold all the leading positions of the government: he and his closest friends hold the offices of prime minister, president of the state, president of the Parliament, and the president of the National Bank. Those who have made the mistake of opposing some of Orbán's decisions have been labeled traitors and dropped from the leadership.

Beside occupying institutions by appointing close associates and loyal followers, an additional method—discussed and analyzed by Kim Lane Scheppele of Princeton University—is the use of the parliamentary majority to change laws and even the constitution. Orbán enacted a new constitution, but then amended it five times to serve the party's immediate interests. He also changed the electoral law to make his party almost unbeatable.[26] After a new election victory in 2018 which brought Fidesz again an absolute majority in the Parliament, laws were enacted to ban demonstrations if they "disturb people in the neighborhood." A new law requires government permission for "two or more people" to discuss public issues in public places. The regime attacks elementary democratic principles and practices. The shift toward an authoritarian system is increasingly apparent, and the regime has at last been indicted by the Sargentini Report and the acceptance of the report by the European Parliament.[27]

Enjoying the advantages but decrying the "colonization" of the EU

As part of defending Hungary's national interest, Viktor Orbán's permanent "fight for national independence" was also directed against the European Union. He is a fervent adversary of the rules and values of the EU. Along with several other countries of Central and Eastern Europe, Hungary was eager to join the European Union immediately after the fall of communism in 1989. Eight of them were accepted as members in 2004, after they had completed their democratic transformation and had successfully installed a market economy. Hungary benefited from EU membership in various ways.

As part of an integrated continent, Hungary enjoyed the advantages of an immense European market and a multitude of Western investments. The latter totaled over $37 billion for the entire region during the membership candidacy period prior to 2004. Western corporations purchased technologically obsolete factories and transformed them into modern, competitive powerhouses. They established practically the entire modern banking system of the country, as well as a number of new high-tech and medium high-tech industries in the electronics, electric industry, and automobile sectors. These served as the country's new export sectors and generated rapid economic growth.

EU membership assured that Hungary's banks would continue to be financed during the Great Recession after 2008 and during the 2010s. Since 87 percent of all banking assets were in the hands of Western banking institutions in the region, financing would be endangered if those banks had stopped crediting their customers, as most indeed did across the continent. To avoid such an outcome, the EU convened a meeting with the IMF, the World Bank, the European Bank for Reconstruction and Development and some 40 major private banks in Vienna in March 2009, and together resolved to keep crediting the new EU member countries of Eastern Europe. This so-called Vienna Initiative saved the region, including Hungary. As a result, these countries did not have to bail out their banks, as Ireland and Spain did—a calamity that led to great indebtedness in those countries and required an EU bail out. In other words, the EU saved Hungary and the region from financial collapse.

EU membership also provided an impressive aid package to Hungary, partly to its non-competitive agricultural sector, and partly to the entire country as a "backward region" of the EU (defined as having a per capita GDP that was less than 75 percent of the EU's average). Hungary received a significant amount of EU assistance even before it became a member in 2004. The so-called pre-accession aid for the ten candidate countries, as well as assistance during the first years of membership, amounted to €2.7 billion. As prime minister, Viktor Orbán signed a new budget agreement with the EU (for the years 2014–2020) that itself provided €36 billion ($40 billion) to Hungary—a country with an annual GDP of $125 billion.

In addition, only in the 2010s some 600,000 Hungarians have recently taken advantage of the opportunities provided by the EU's Schengen agreement and have gone to work in Western EU countries. These workers send significant amounts of money home to their families. Altogether, aid from the EU and money sent home by Hungarian guest workers comprised 4.5 percent of the GDP in 2014–15 and more than 3 percent in the long run.[28] One could safely say that, without the European Union, Hungary's economy would have stagnated.

Nevertheless, Orbán is fond of praising Hungary's economic success as his own achievement. In speech after speech, he forever congratulates himself for his courage and vision in lifting Hungary to the top of Europe. He insists that his spectacular success is in sharp contrast to the previous governments' dismal failures:

> It is hard to explain why we Hungarians became so pathetically incompetent. While the others were rising [around 2004], we found ourselves mired in growing sovereign debt, crippling foreign currency mortgage loans, high budget deficits, rampant inflation, a balance of payments deficit, and rising unemployment. This was eventually followed by financial ruin, a dog-collar and leash held by the IMF, and debt slavery. . . . [W]ithin three years the civic-Christian government had led the country out of this hopeless, ruinous situation with a . . . new national policy. . . . Within five years we have reduced personal income tax from 35% to 15%. . . . We have reduced household utility bills by 25%, and within five years the minimum wage in Hungary has increased by 50%.[29]

Two years later, in January 2015, he delivered another speech celebrating his triumphs as "a reflection on five years of governance." He again castigated the previous governments as total failures, citing statistics on the impact of the post-2008 international recession on Hungary: "Consider life in Hungary until recently: Economic growth in negative territory. Government debt at over 85% of GDP. Inflation over 6% a year. The budget deficit close to 7%. Unemployment rate heading 12%."[30]

Orbán described his record as one of unparalleled achievement. In an article in January 2017, he blithely compared "his" success to what occurred in the previous half-century: "We restored health to the Hungarian economy in record time to make up for the inertia of the last fifty years."[31] In another speech he gushed: "I have been able to run off a list of fifteen unprecedented achievements that have occurred in Hungary over the last five years—fifteen towering columns that prove that this nation [meaning him] has courage and vision."[32]

Some of these achievements can unquestionably be attributed to his government. As have other populist regimes, Orbán's has indeed passed popular legislation—including a significant tax reduction by introducing a flat tax (for individuals and corporations) that rose the population's income, particularly the wealthy elite. Other genuine achievements were a drastic decrease of monthly utility bills, a reduction of mortgages, and a significant increase of the minimum wage. In early 2017, he had a personally signed letter mailed to every retired person in the country commemorating the economy's great success with an attached check of $34 to each recipient. These measures did indeed help many people. Most of the government's successes, however, are closely connected to the new international economic recovery after the 2008 economic crisis, to the European Union's huge assistance and the various advantages that the EU provides, including free market access and the investments from Western EU countries. Without these, Hungary's GDP and living standard would be at least 15 percent lower than before the 2008 crisis. But, while exploiting these opportunities, Orbán has always refused to credit the EU and instead applauds himself.

In reality, the country's economic successes were not nearly as triumphant as the government claimed. With all the lavish assistance it has received, Hungary can claim a per capita GDP of only $12,755 in 2015, which is roughly twenty per cent lower than its pre-Orbán high point of $15,600 in 2008.[33] The World Economic Forum's Global Competitiveness Report of 2014–2015, which compares the economies of 144 economies, clearly paints a negative picture of Hungary. The report has dropped it from 29th place in 2001 to 60th place, behind most of the Central and East European countries, as well as Brazil and Panama.[34]

In late 2016, the European Central Bank (ECB) completed a comparative analysis of the wealth of the euro-zone countries, including Poland and Hungary. As Hungary's leading economic magazine (*Heti Világgazdaság*) revealed in the shocking title of its report of the ECB's findings, "The average Slovak [is] twice as rich as the average Hungarian." This was especially unpleasant news for Hungarian nationalists because Slovakia had been the poorer northern region of Hungary before World War I. It was also devastating that the country was in second-to-last place (19 out of 20), with only Lithuania in worse shape. Moreover, the average GDP of the twenty euro-zone countries (€104,000) was four times higher than Hungary's (€26,000). Not only the wealthiest Belgium (€217,000) and Austria (€85,900), but even Poland (€57,100) and Slovakia (€50,300), were doing much better. This was alarming news, given that Poland and Slovakia had been behind Hungary throughout most of the transformation period.[35]

Orbán can never find a positive word to say about the EU, which has aided Hungary a great deal. At mass rallies, such as a speech on March 15, 2012, he vehemently shouted: "Hungarians won't live according to the commands of foreign powers!" "We will not be the colony [of the EU]!" Four years later his rhetoric became even more duplicitous and melodramatic:

> Today Europe is as fragile, weak, and sickly as a flower being eaten away by a hidden worm. Today, one hundred and sixty-eight years after the great freedom fights of its peoples [in 1848], Europe—our common home—is not free. . . . In Europe today it is forbidden to speak the truth. . . . It is forbidden to say that Brussels is stealthily devouring ever more slices of our national sovereignty. . . . The peoples of Europe may have finally understood that their future is at stake. . . . We cannot allow Brussels to place itself above the law. . . . [W]e must put steel in our spines, and we must clearly answer . . . with a voice so loud so that it can be heard far and wide . . . "Shall we be slaves or men set free—That is the question, answer me!"[36]

In the spring of 2017, Orbán signed and mailed a personal letter to every Hungarian citizen with the title: "We have to stop Brussels!" "I am writing to you because we are before major decisions again. Brussels prepared several plans that are endangering our national sovereignty and the security of our country." Attached to this letter a questionnaire with six questions offered the choice of alternative answers. The choices were extremely manipulatively phrased to gain a kind of supportive referendum for the government.[37] When the Kaczyński regime was established and began to implement similar polices in Poland, Orbán enthusiastically "defended" Poland against "Brussels," and announced a joint Polish-Hungarian struggle against the EU:

> As always throughout our shared thousand-year history, now, too, we are standing by you in the battle you are fighting for your country's free-

dom and independence. We are with you, and we send this message to Brussels: more respect to the Polish people, more respect to Poland! . . . We Hungarians and Poles know how to [fight for independence].[38]

This is demagoguery at its most exorbitant! Europe is in chains and the European Union is the prison of its many peoples. Hungary, together with the Poles and others, must wage a new battle for independence. Orbán also lied to his audience when he suggested that assistance from the EU is not assistance at all: "Hungary is *entitled to* [these EU funds], *these resources do not come as a gift*—as I said we are entitled to them."[39] "Hungary opened its doors to Western companies. Everyone profited from this: Western companies repatriated as much money from Hungary as the European Union sent here. We are quits, and we have nothing to call each other to account for."[40] The sum Hungary gets form the EU is thus just a form of Western "repayment." This was classic populist anti-Western, anti-corporatist, and even communist arguments intermingled with right-wing demagoguery.

The opposition as traitors

The attacks on liberalism and the European Union were always combined with an assault on domestic opponents, who were condemned as traitors in the service of foreign interests.

> If we look at civil organizations in Hungary, the ones in the public eye—debates concerning the Norwegian Fund have brought this to the surface—then what I will see is that we have to deal with paid political activists here. And these political activists are, moreover, political activists paid by foreigners. . . . If we would like to reorganize our nation state instead of the liberal state, then we should make it clear that these are not civilians coming against us, opposing us, but political activists attempting to promote foreign interests.[41]

As a columnist of the *Guardian* rightly noted: "Nationalism is combined with authoritarianism, with the government increasingly cracking down on media and NGOs considered 'disloyal' to the nation (i.e. to Orbán and Fidesz), and with strong populism, which presents Orbán as the authentic voice of the Hungarian people who are fighting off a (EU-sponsored) leftwing conspiracy."[42]

Similarly, in his quest to destroy every liberal stronghold, Orbán attacked the Hungarian-born American billionaire philanthropist, George Soros's Open Society Fund and also attempted to close the Central European University (CEU), established by Soros in 1991. He rushed through Parliament legislation targeting Central European University, which led to tens of thousands of protesters marching in the streets of Budapest and widespread international criticism. The Commission of the European Union, most of the world's top universities, and even the US government harshly opposed Orbán's actions and publicly clamored against them. After Trump's victory, one of the closest lieutenants of Orbán, Szilárd Németh, Vice Chairman of Fidesz, blundered out "These organizations must be . . . swept out, and now, *the international conditions are right for this with the election of a new* [US] *president.*"[43]

The Orbán government's hysterical anti-Soros campaign only followed in the footsteps of Orbán's idol, Vladimir Putin, who had already destroyed various non-governmental (NGO) organizations that supported liberal values and defended human rights in Russia, signing the first laws against them in 2012. Putin, building his autocratic regime, openly and consistently destroyed his opponents—politicians, journalists, or rich oligarchs alike—who turned against him. They were shot in the streets, imprisoned, or pushed out from the country. He also closed all of the Soros-financed NGOs working in Russia in 2015–16. The official Russian statement regarding this already explicitly mentioned the "anti-government activity" of George Soros. An important sentence of this statement strongly recommended following the Russian measures in other Central European countries: "This list [of NGO organizations] will be interesting for the East European and Balkan countries as well; banning the fake civil organizations under Western control and the groups that collaborate with them is highly recommended for the East European countries as well."[44]

Orbán followed Putin by curbing checks and balances, changed the legal and even constitutional system, and led to the introduction of a quasi-authoritarian regime. *Foreign Affairs* accurately observed: "Like Moscow, the governments of these countries [of Eastern Europe] are careful to maintain their democratic façade by holding regular elections.

But their leaders have tried to systematically dismantle institutional checks and balances, making real turnover in power increasingly difficult."[45]

Exploiting the migration crisis

Viktor Orbán's demagoguery culminated during the 2015 migration crisis, when a momentous wave of more than a million Middle Eastern, African, and Asian migrants "invaded" Europe. A seemingly endless number of Syrian, African, and Afghan refugees and economic migrants traversed the Balkans and Hungary on their way to Germany. Although Germany itself had accepted a million migrants, the EU resolved to send less than 1,300 of them to Hungary. The European Union was caught unawares and had made critical mistakes of accepting the migrant invasion as a *fait accompli* without controlling it. Orbán refused to accept any refugees and masterfully exploited the crisis.

His popularity in Hungary was at its lowest point at that time, leading to speculation of his possible electoral defeat. But at precisely that moment, he stepped up as the defender of Christian Europe and even of Hungarian Jewry. First, he created a chaotic crisis in Budapest where he assembled tens of thousands of migrants in front of a railway station but prevented them from leaving the city. The Hungarians' brutal treatment of the migrants sparked international outrage. Then, he decided to build a massive barbed wire fence along Hungary's southern border with Serbia and Croatia. He was the first to do that, and was soon followed by others. He was also the first to openly oppose the EU and Angela Merkel's migration policy, but was soon seconded by others. He hammered out an Eastern bloc of the so-called four Visegrád countries of Eastern Europe that rejected the EU's quota of a few thousands refugees. In the eyes of large numbers of people, he emerged as a savior of Hungary and a strong advocate of protecting Europe from the migrant hordes. His anti-immigration and anti-EU demagoguery now reached its highest point:

> It is forbidden to say that today we are not witnessing the arrival of refugees, but a Europe being threatened by mass migration. It is forbidden to say that tens of millions are ready to set out in our direction. It

is forbidden to say that immigration brings crime and terrorism to our countries. It is forbidden to say that the masses of people coming from different civilizations pose a threat to our way of life, our culture, our customs, and our Christian traditions. . . . We shall not allow [the EU] to force upon us the bitter fruit of its cosmopolitan immigration policy. We shall not import to Hungary crime, terrorism, homophobia, and synagogue-burning anti-Semitism.[46]

In the same speech Orbán added: "We know how these things go. First we allow them to tell us whom we must take in, then they force us to serve foreigners in our country. In the end we find ourselves being told to pack up and leave our own land."[47] His speeches decry the acceptance of 1,300 Muslim refugees (!) as posing a perilous danger for Hungary: "our national culture—which is slowly finding its feet once again—is also in danger. What is more, not only does this danger threaten the things which we have, but also the things which we may have in the future. . . . We shall teach Brussels, the people smugglers and the migrants that Hungary is a sovereign country. . . . [G]angs shall not hunt our wives and daughters."[48]

With his rhetoric vowing to defend the borders and to protect Hungarians, including the Jewry from Muslim terrorism, Orbán has also tried to alter Hungary's long-enduring reputation for anti-Semitism and anti-Roma prejudice. His close associates behind the "House of Terror" museum have forever equated communism and communist terror with Jews in general. The last episode of the Holocaust, the murder of half of Hungary's Jews a few months before the war's end, has been persistently interpreted by Orbán's camp as a German crime alone, even though it could never have happened without the collaboration of Hungarians. Orbán also exploited deeply rooted anti-Semitism in Hungary with his anti-Soros campaign. Accusing Soros of having a plan for the Islamization of Hungary and Europe offered the possibility of both an anti-capitalist, anti-American, and hidden anti-Semitic campaign without saying the word "Jew." Regardless, everybody in the country understood the message. The demagoguery, indeed, worked. Orbán's approval rate jumped from 30 to 80 percent. He emerged as the uncontested winner of the new elections in 2014.

Like most other Central and Eastern European populist demagogues, Viktor Orbán has built, as some called it, a "mafia" state behind a façade of popular nationalist, xenophobic, and anti-EU demagoguery. Following Vladimir Putin's example, Orbán has established a patron-client relationship with the business elite. While he "destroys the relative autonomy of the oligarchs . . . [he] aims to integrate them into [his] own chain of command. . . . It is the political regime that milks the economic actors . . . by way of contracts and privileges ensured to its subjugated oligarchs." They have enriched themselves to a great degree and support the government in various ways. Those who turn against the "patron" are subject to harsh retribution.[49] Orbán has also found allies in Kaczyński's Poland and became the unofficial leader of the neighboring Visegrád-four countries. In November 2016, after Donald Trump's victory in the US elections, Orbán celebrated the event as a triumph for democracy. He was in fact the first and only European head of government to endorse Trump before the election. Nationalist-populist demagoguery abroad effectively strengthens his position at home. His rule is seemingly cemented in Hungary for the foreseeable future.

The identical Polish twins, Lech and Jarosław Kaczyński

Lech and Jarosław Kaczyński were born in 1949—Jarosław 45 minutes earlier than his twin brother. Their father, Rajmund, was a member of the underground *Armia Krajowa* (Home Army) and had fought in the Warsaw uprising. The identical twins had a close personal bond. In 1962, they earned a modicum of fame as child actors in the movie of *The Two Who Stole the Moon*. Both graduated from Law School. Their peers found it difficult to distinguish one from the other, even though they were actually quite different. Lech was married and was more the extrovert; Jarosław was not interested in women and lived with his mother until her death. He was a perennial loner who never traveled, spoke no foreign languages, and whose primary form of entertainment was watching television at home, sometimes until three o'clock in the morning, surrounded by his two cats. In many ways he lived firmly in the past: he did not use a computer and opened his first bank account only in 2009. When his mother became ill, he traveled to Częstochowa, the holiest shrine in the country, and vowed to stay away from alcohol if she recovered.

From opposition to power

The brothers shared the same political views and were not interested in money. Their only interest was power. They were also virulently anti-communist. They joined the Solidarity Movement in the 1980s. Lech was already a member of the underground Workers Defense Committee (KOR), and later became an adviser to Lech Wałęsa. He was imprisoned in 1981 when the communist government imposed martial law.[50] He took part in the Roundtable discussions that led to the agreement between Solidarity and the government and to Solidarity's electoral victory. Jarosław became the editor of Solidarity's weekly newspaper, and later a member of Parliament. Lech became a senator and vice-Chairman of Solidarity's Trade Union, then Minister of Justice and Attorney General of the Solidarity government.

The Solidarity movement, however, soon imploded, and the twin brothers established their own right-wing, nationalist-conservative party, *Prawo i Sprawiedliwość*, PiS (Law and Justice). Within a year, Lech would be elected Mayor of Warsaw. The brothers quickly established a populist platform and began indulging in demagogic rhetoric. Lech's first public speech as mayor attacked crime and corruption, and he combined a policy of modernization with traditionalism. He berated the public prosecutor's offices and pushed them to adopt stronger positions. He attacked judges who passed light sentences, and pushed for applying the death penalty in more cases. One of their well-working arguments was accusing the previous governments of high corruption. "The ensuing debate on corruption," noted an observer, "made a once neglected topic into the most contentious issue in domestic politics, and led society to adopt a more uncompromising definition of what should be understood under corruption. As a result, the impression strengthened that the land really was ridden with corruption."[51]

In 2005, the twins' party won the election and formed a government in coalition with a left-populist and a conservative party. Lech was elected president, while Jarosław ran the party and government from behind the scenes. When the coalition disbanded, Jarosław became Prime Minister in 2006. It pays to quote Kate Connolly, who characterized the brothers in the *Guardian* this way:

They speak together on the phone at least 10 times a day. They complete each other's sentences. Both are silver-haired, rotund and 5ft 5in tall. . . . They are two men who appear to operate as one, and their central mission since coming to power . . . has been to restore Polish pride. . . . Vehemently homophobic and nationalist, the Roman Catholic twins have certainly engendered a new climate of fear in Poland in their short time in control, largely as a result of their paranoia about a "grey network" of former communists they believe to be at work in every corner of national life.[52]

Naming the enemies

The brothers tried to exacerbate and exploit discontent in the country, which was clearly reflected in public opinion polls: large numbers expressed distrust of the authorities, of non-Poles, and of every neighboring country. Their populist demagoguery focused on the corrupt elite and promised to create a new one. They tried to remove former communists and corrupt Solidarity leaders. They saw conspiracy and betrayal around every corner. As Jarosław ominously declared: "In Poland, there is the bad tradition of national treason. This takes place in the genes of some people who are the worst sort of Poles. And right now this worst sort is incredibly active."[53] In their battle against internal enemies, the brothers pushed through the *lustracja* (vetting) law, which encouraged the examination of communist police records with the intent to expose prominent Poles as past informers—bringing about a wholesale purge of the old elite. They also unearthed communist party documents that tainted the reputation of the legendary Solidarity leader Lech Wałęsa, suggesting that he was a paid agent of the secret police. The brothers also attacked intellectuals and politicians who, in their estimation, were "fed from the hands of the Germans." Their ardent anti-communist rhetoric was combined with anti-Russian and anti-German bombast. As a member of parliament, Jarosław launched an infuriated attack against traitors in August 2004:

> In Poland, there was and . . . still is a genuine front for the defense of German interests. . . . This front . . . consists of informants of the German secret services. . . . This is a very big group of people who live from German money and act as if they were independent scholars and journalists.[54]

Poland: the Jesus Christ of nations – Katyn and the Russian enemy

The Kaczyński brothers have followed the traditional path of Polish nationalism. As a consequence of their unfortunate history, Poles characteristically suffer from a surfeit of self-pity. Poles have periodically waged heroic battles that were usually lost causes in the face of invincible enemies. They engaged in several confrontations with the expanding Ottoman Empire, and waged three hopeless revolts against Tsarist Russia in the late eighteenth and nineteenth centuries. The Polish cavalry— legend has it—fought German tanks in 1939. The Polish Home Army carried out fruitless attacks against Russian troops at the end of World War II. Poles never hesitated to fight against formidable enemies even when they had no chance of winning.

Traditional Polish nationalists have always considered themselves to be innocent victims of external and internal enemies. They were always convinced that they were right, and that all their adversaries, especially their arch enemies—the Russians to the east and the Germans to the west—were wrong. The most celebrated Polish national poet, Adam Mickiewicz, put it in 1832: "We defended the West and are the crucified, the Jesus Christ of nations, who will rise again or be resurrected and redeem the human race . . . the [Polish] nation shall arise and free all of the peoples of Europe from slavery."[55] This sense of victimization has always been strong among Poles, and the Kaczyński brothers apply their rhetoric accordingly. This is the background of their foreign policy. As an analyst rightly noted: "A thick streak of historical revanchism runs through the party's foreign policy: Kaczyński never misses a chance to dredge up past crimes committed against Poland and harbors a special distrust for Germany and Russia, the country's neighbors and historic foes."[56]

As President of Poland, Lech Kacziński traveled to Russia on a Polish military airplane to commemorate Stalin's massacre of Polish officers in Katyn in 1941. He planned to hold a separate ceremony there with the victims' families on April 10, 2010. The plane's pilot disregarded Smolensk's air controller's warning of bad weather and crashed while landing, killing all 96 notables aboard, including the President, his wife, and a large number of Poland's political and military leaders. His brother never believed that it was an accident, but was convinced that a secret Russian conspiracy had been behind the crash. In the next election campaign, he promised a thorough investigation to uncover that conspiracy. He insisted in an interview that "We will continue all of our efforts, from trying to uncover the truth about the Smolensk tragedy to defending democracy . . . and to combating the de-Christianization [of Poland]."[57]

Lech Kaczyński, who died in the crash, never delivered his prepared speech in which he repeated nationalist stereotypes on various enemies, denounced communism and Russia, and even brought up the 1939 Nazi-Soviet pact against Poland:

> Over 21,000 Polish prisoners were in April 1940 taken from the NKVD's camps and prisons and murdered. . . . The alliance of the Third Reich, the Ribbentrop-Molotov pact and the aggression against Poland of 17 September 1939 culminated in the shocking Katyn crime. These citizens of the II Polish republic, people who formed the basis of our statehood, unconquered in the service of their fatherland, were murdered. . . . The families of the victims and thousands of other inhabitants of Poland [were] deported [and] murdered.[58]

His pathological hatred of Russia was expressed even more clearly in an earlier speech in August 2008, when he rushed to Tbilisi to express solidarity with Georgia in its conflict with Russia. At a mass rally there, he declared:

> We are here to take up the fight. For the first time in years our eastern neighbors show their true face that we have known for hundreds of years. . . . They think other nations should be subordinated to them. We say no! That country is Russia . . . which had brought disaster upon all of Europe.[59]

Facing the past?

Facing the past, especially the history of Polish anti-Semitism, has been a delicate issue for the Kaczyńskis. Jarosław used the occasion of the 75th anniversary of the Nazis' infamous destruction of the Great Bialystok Synagogue (on June 27, 1941)—a major event of the Holocaust—to impart blame solely on Germany. Polish complicity in the destruction of Polish Jewry has long been documented by historians. But speaking at the site of the Great Synagogue, Jarosław made no mention of Polish anti-Semitism or the Poles' contribution to the Holocaust:

> On 27 June 1941, the German army occupying Bialystok carried out a monstrous crime. It murdered around 2,500 Jews—around 1,000 of them were burned alive in the synagogue. This was the beginning of the Holocaust . . . this monstrous, inconceivable, genocidal crime. We also need to remember . . . to appropriately address responsibility and blame. It was the German state and German nation that supported the leadership of Adolf Hitler. The blame is clear-cut and we need to talk about it to remember . . . in which culture the greatest threats to Europe . . . exist.[60]

Somewhat later his Parliament enacted a law that criminalized speaking about Polish responsibility.

Copying the "Orbán" model – building an authoritarian regime

Orbán and Kaczyński share similar ideologies and seek to build national "reconstruction" on that basis. Both are populist politicians; both reject Western democratic values and liberalism; and both denounce "the dictates of Brussels" and oppose the EU. Since Orbán's rise to power, Hungary has served as a model for Kaczyński, who seeks to "build a Budapest in Warsaw."[61] Indeed, he has closely followed in Orbán's footsteps. First, he neutralized the Constitutional Court. To achieve this, his regime appointed five new judges to the court, all party loyalists, and changed the Court's decision-making procedures by requiring a two-thirds majority for all rulings instead of a simple majority. The government also stripped the court of the power to prioritize cases, and forced it to decide cases in the order of their arrival. As a British journalist noted, these changes rendered the Court "toothless." The Constitutional Court ruled that the changes were in fact illegal, but in vain. The court's ruling was not even published. When human rights groups decried these efforts as an "assault" on democracy, Kaczyński responded by labelling the critics "enemies of Poland."[62] At the end of 2016, when the term of the Court's President, Andrzej Rzepliński, expired, he stated that the Kaczyński regime is "systematically weakening the checks and balances provided by the courts, the press and other institutions, and is leading the country 'on the road to autocracy.'"[63]

Pursuing that agenda, the government has also sought to control all Non-Government Organizations (NGO) in the country and bar liberals, including foreign donors like George Soros, from exerting any influence. A new media law was also enacted that gives the government complete control of state television and radio stations. The government purged 130 liberal journalists and replaced them with its loyal followers. It ignored EU objections and appointed Jacek Kurski, who once described himself as Kaczyński's "bull terrier," as the new head of public television. Taking effect immediately, the media law empowers the treasury minister to hire and fire broadcasting directors of public television and radio networks. The government also banned journalists of the private media from broadcasting from Parliament; the right to do so would now be the state media's alone. Party representatives spoke about the "re-Polonizing" of the country's press, and complained that Polish outlets had too many foreign shareholders. According to Kaczyński, the reason for Western criticism of the new media law is that much of Poland's media is "in German hands."[64]

In an interview with the German *Bild Magazine*, Foreign Minister Witold Waszczykowski, justified the elimination of independent media and affirmed that the government was "curing" the country's "illnesses" that had been caused by previous left-wing regimes: "illnesses . . . [such] a new mixture of cultures and races, a world made up of cyclists and vegetarians, who only use renewable energy and who battle all signs of religion. . . . What moves most Poles [is] tradition, historical awareness, love of country, faith in God, and normal family life between woman and men."[65] Before the end of his party's first year in government, Kaczyński sought to crown his Christian conservative agenda by imposing a total ban on abortion although the existing law from 1993 was itself the strictest in Europe. It allowed abortion only in cases of rape and incest, the life or health of the mother or severe fetal deformities. Unborn babies with Down syndrome and other disabilities had been allowed to be legally aborted. In 2015, there were only a thousand or so known abortions in the country of nearly 40 million. But that was not enough. The new law would criminalize any kind of abortion, except when the mother's life is endangered. Performing abortions became subject to up to five-year imprisonment.[66] Hundreds of thousands of women, dressed in black, demonstrated throughout the country against the new law that, at first reading, was overwhelmingly supported in Parliament. Thanks to the mass resistance, Kaczyński decided to withdraw the new abortion bill.

This incident taught the regime that it had to go even further and restrict the right to demonstrate against the government. Kaczyński called this and similar restrictions a "cultural counterrevolution against all those liberals. This is a time of reaction."[67] In early December 2016, the Law and Justice Party's parliamentary majority passed a law stipulating that gatherings of any size had to reserve demonstration sites for a period of three years. Government and Church organizations were granted priority to use any site for public gatherings. Even the already debilitated Supreme Court ruled that the law was unconstitutional, "the right to freedom of peaceful assembly is universally granted." Commenting on the new law, the legendary Solidarity leader Lech Wałęsa bemoaned that "this is the worst government Poland has ever had. They are populists and demagogues. Even Communists were better."[68]

Opposing the EU and Germany, but accepting aid

The Kaczyński brothers' demagogic attacks on their neighbors went hand in hand with a fervent euro-skepticism and an angry rejection of "European Union's dictates." During the immigration crisis, the Kaczyński regime, stressing the Catholic character of Poland, joined Viktor Orbán in refusing to accept the EU's decision on distributing refugees—a decision that would have dispatched a total 7,000 migrants to Poland, a country of nearly 40 million inhabitants. Decrying the collapse of European civilization in a speech to Parliament on September 16, 2015, Jarosław Kaczyński painted a false and overly dramatized picture of Europe, mendaciously asserting that Muslim Sharia Law had already been implemented in roughly fifteen regions in Sweden, and claiming that migrants had used churches as toilets in Italy.[69]

Attacks on the European Union first began when the EU sharply criticized the government's subversion of the Constitutional Court.[70] In response to the criticism, Poland's hard-line justice minister—echoing the prime minister—hit back with an acerbic letter comparing EU scrutiny to the Nazi occupation during World War II. Kaczyński did not hesitate to reject the EU's requirement to return to democratic norms:

> No pressure, no threats, no words . . . *particularly by Germans*, will make us turn back from this path. . . . We won the election but have no right to create laws, to remodel Poland, to make decisions instead of a handful of people bought by foreigners and internal forces that don't serve Polish interests.[71]

Jarosław Kaczyński is an authoritarian ruler who alone decides on just about everything. As Timothy Garton Ash accurately observed: "For the political blitzkrieg of the past two months suggests that the strategy of the Law and Justice party . . . and specifically of its one true leader, Jarosław Kaczyński, is to do the dirty work of transforming the political system rapidly, even brutally. . . . He has the parliamentary majority to do this."[72] Indeed, the spokesman of the Polish President has declared precisely what Kaczyński demanded: "Our country is now run by politicians accountable to Polish voters, not to German, British or French left-wing intellectuals."[73] His other puppet, the Minister of Defense Antoni Macierewicz, conveyed Kaczyński's clear message to a group of American senators, who had also warned Poland about destroying democratic norms: "People who were only building their country in the 18th century are telling us what democracy is—a nation that already had structures of representative democracy in the 13th and 14th centuries?"[74]

In addition to demanding the West's continued defense of Poland against Russia, the country is the largest beneficiary of European Union assistance among the 28 EU member states. Poland has received one-and-half times more aid from the EU than did the sixteen countries receiving Marshall Plan assistance over a four-year period after World War II. In the current seven-year financial period, Poland, a country with a GDP of $518 billion in 2013, will receive $318 billion of EU assistance between 2008 and 2020. Poland today is receiving $26.5 billion per year up through 2020. This lavish assistance provides an additional 5–7 percent to the county's GDP.[75] The Poles have also been the biggest winners of the EU's Schengen Agreement allowing the free movement of people within the EU. Some two million Poles are working in other EU countries, and they regularly send money home to their families. Nevertheless, Kaczyński, echoing Orbán, insists that the EU money is not a gift, but an entitlement.

Promises, promises...

The other *leit motif* of the brothers' demagoguery is a typical populist agenda to protect the "little people." Jarosław described his program prior to the 2015 election, asserting that everything had declined in Poland during the previous quarter of a century, and that he and his party will increase wages, lower the retirement age, adopt more egalitarian policies, and stimulate economic growth to raise the country to Western standards. Most of all, they will lift Poland up, and create a country that would make Poles proud to be Polish. One could not promise more:

> The road ahead is clear. . . . We want to improve Poland . . . [to] eliminate the divisions between us and our western neighbors. . . . The first step is to establish a government, strong in its foundation. . . . Our country is the instrument in our hands. This instrument must serve our entire nation. It must not be used for the advantage of the privileged, lobby groups or schemes, which unfortunately happens today. . . . The promises already made, such as 500 PLN per child, such as bringing the retirement age back down to what it used to be, increasing the tax-free income threshold. . . . We the Polish people, do not earn enough. . . . Equality does not exist in today's Poland.[76]

The Kaczyński brothers' nationalist-populist demagoguery is the spitting image of Viktor Orbán's rhetoric: take everything you can get—Western defense, investment, and economic assistance and opportunities—and at the same time pose as the savior of Poland's independence against the malevolent foreigners, neighbors, the European Union, and domestic traitors. Preaching democracy to Europe, they undermine democracy at home and strengthen their authoritarian power. Kaczyński found his most loyal followers in the Polish countryside. A rural electoral wave swept the party into power. In the village of Kulesze Kościelne, for instance, 83 precent of the church-going population voted for Kaczyński's party, but only a third of Warsaw's population did so.

Endnotes

1 Poland was partitioned by Russia, Prussia, and the Habsburg Empire in the late eighteenth century (and later a second time). Two thirds of the country became part of the Russian Empire. Hungary became part of the Habsburg Empire in the early sixteenth century and then—with autonomy—of the Austro-Hungarian Empire from 1867.

2 Georg Friedman, "Hungary, Poland and illiberal democracy," *Euractiv*, March 22, 2016, https://www.euractiv.com/section/global-europe/opinion/hungary-poland-and-illiberal-democracy/.

3 Ivan T. Berend, "Történelmi utunk: A munkabizottság állasfoglalása a jelen helyzet kialakulásának történeti okairól" [The Historical Road of Hungary: Report of the Working Committee on the Historical Causes of the Crisis Situation], *Társadalmi Szemle*, Special Issue (1989): 1–80.

4 Paul Lendvai, *Orbáns Ungarn* (Vienna: Verlag Kremyr & Scheriaut, 2016). I will use this excellent work in the following analysis, as I do with an earlier book of József Debreczeni, *Orbán Viktor* (Budapest: Osiris Kiadó, 2002).

5 According to certain information, a party rival of Prime Minister Gyurcsány had stolen the tapes and made them public in a quest to replace Gyurcsány.

6 Ernst Gelegs and Roland Androwitz, *Schöne Grüße aus dem Orbán-Land: Die Rechte Revolution in Ungarn* (Vienna: Styria Verlag, 2013), quoted by Lendvai, *Orbáns Ungarn*.

7 [Viktor Orbán], "Full text of Viktor Orbán's speech at Băile Tuşnad (Tusnádfürdő) of 26 July 2014," translation by Csaba Tóth, *Budapest Beacon*, July 19, 2014, https://budapestbeacon.com/full-text-of-viktor-orbans-speech-at-baile-tusnad-tusnadfurdo-of-26-july-2014/.

8 [Viktor Orbán], "Prime Minister Viktor Orbán's State of the Nation Address," February 28, 2016, *Cabinet Office of the Prime Minister*, http://www.miniszterelnok.hu/prime-minister-viktor-orbans-state-of-the-nation-address/.

9 Cus Mudde, "The Hungary PM made a 'rivers of blood' speech . . . and no one cares," *Guardian*, July 30, 2015.

10 Viktor Orbán, "Hungary and the Crisis of Europe," *Hungarian Review* 8, no. 1 (January 24, 2017).

11 [Orbán], "Prime Minister Viktor Orbán's State of the Nation Address," February 28, 2016.

12 "Speech by Prime Minister Viktor Orbán on 15 March," March 15, 2016, *Cabinet Office of the Prime Minister*, http://www.miniszterelnok.hu/speech-by-prime-minister-viktor-orban-on-15-march/.

13 Edy Kaster, "EU urged to monitor Hungary as Orbán hits at 'liberal democracy,'" *Financial Times*, July 30, 2014.

14 [Orbán], "Full text of Viktor Orbán's speech at Băile Tuşnad."

15 "Eastern Opening," *The Orange Files: Notes on Illiberal Democracy in Hungary*, last updated on May 21, 2018, https://theorangefiles.hu/eastern-opening/.

16 [Orbán], "Full text of Viktor Orbán's speech at Băile Tuşnad."

17 Ibid.

18 Orbán, "Hungary and the Crisis of Europe," 8.

19 [Orbán], "Full text of Viktor Orbán's speech at Băile Tuşnad."

20 See Péter Mihályi, "A privatizált vagyon visszaállamosítása Magyarországon, 2010–2014," Discussion Papers, MT-DP-2015/7, MTA Közgazdasági és Regionális Tudományos Kutató Központ, Közgazdaság Tudományi Intézet, Budapest, 2015,

21 [Orbán], "Full text of Viktor Orbán's speech at Băile Tuşnad."

22 *Conducător* in Romanian and *Nemzetvezető* in Hungarian means Führer.

23 Benito Mussolini, *Fascism: Doctrine and Institutions* (Rome: Ardira Publisher, 1935), 10–11, 26–31.

24 See Chapter 3 in this volume.

25 This sub-chapter was based to the summary of András Bozóky and Kinga Györffy, "The Crisis of Democracy in Hungary," *Heinrich-Böll-Stiftung*, May 21, 2012, https://www.boell.de/de/node/276334.

26 See several studies by Kim Lane Scheppele of Princeton University: "On constitutionalism and the rule of law in Hungary," *Budapest Beacon*, December 11, 2014, http://budapestbeacon.com/public-policy/scheppele-on-democracy-constitutionalism-and-rule-of-law-in-hungary/, accessed on December 11, 2014; "Hungary, an Election in Question," *New York Times*, published within Paul Krugman's blog *The Conscience of a Liberal*, February 28, 2014, https://krugman.blogs.nytimes.com/2014/02/28/hungary-an-election-in-question-part-1/; "Writing the Rules to Win—The Basic Structure," http://krugman.blogs.nytimes.com/2014/02/28/hungary-an-election-in-question-part-2/.

27 European Parliament resolution of 12 September 2018 on a proposal calling on the Council to determine, pursuant to Article 7(1) of the Treaty on European Union, the existence of a clear risk of a serious breach by Hungary of the values on which the Union is founded (2017/2131(INL)), http://www.europarl.europa.eu/doceo/document/TA-8-2018-0340_EN.html?redirect.

28 László Csaba, "A magyar paradoxon—töprengés hosszú távú dilemmákról," *Educatio* 26, no. 4 (Winter 2016).

29 [Orbán], "Prime Minister Viktor Orbán's State of the Nation Address," February 28, 2016.

30 Viktor Orbán, "Notes Towards a Definition of Civic Conservatism: Reflections on Five Years of Governance," *Hungarian Review* 6, no. 4 (July 2015), 29.

31 Orbán, "Hungary and the Crisis of Europe," 10.

32 Orbán, "Notes Towards a Definition of Civic Conservatism," 31.

33 *The World in 2017* (London: The Economist, November 2016), 101.

34 Klaus Schwab, ed., *The Global Competitiveness Report 2014–2015* (Geneva: World Economic Forum, 2014), 13. Accessible at http://www3.weforum.org/docs/WEF_GlobalCompetitivenessReport_2014-15.pdf.

35 "Az átlag szlovák kétszer olyan gazdag, mint az átlag magyar," *Heti Világgazdaság*, December 27, 2016, https://hvg.hu/gazdasag/20161227_vagyon_europa_gazdagok. The number of average wealth includes the value of ownership of homes and this is far the greatest part of the wealth figures.

36 [Orbán], "Speech by Prime Minister Viktor Orbán on 15 March," March 15, 2016. The quotation in the last sentence is of the mid-nineteenth century Hungarian poet, Sándor Petőfi's 1948 poem that started the Hungarian revolution of that year.

37 "Állítsuk meg Brüsszelt! Nemzeti Konzultáció," circular letter sent to every citizen in 2017.

38 [Orbán], "Speech by Prime Minister Viktor Orbán on 15 March," March 15, 2016.

39 [Orbán], "Full text of Viktor Orbán's speech at Băile Tuşnad."

40 [Orbán], "Prime Minister Viktor Orbán's State of the Nation Address," February 28, 2016.

41 [Orbán], "Full text of Viktor Orbán's speech at Băile Tuşnad."

42 Mudde, "The Hungary PM made a 'rivers of blood' speech."

43 Rick Lyman, "Eastern Europe's populists emboldened in limiting foreign groups," *New York Times*, March 2, 2017. Emphasis added.

44 László Valki, "A felsőoktatási törvény módosítása," in *Jogtörténeti Parerga II: Ünnepi tanulmányok Mezey Barna 65. születésnapja tiszteletére*, ed. Gergely Gosztonyi and Mihály Révész T. (Budapest: Eötvös Kiadó, 2018), 271–82. Quoted from "Nemkívánatossá nyilvánítják Soros György alkalmazottait," *Hidfo.ru*, May 24, 2015, http://www.hidfo.ru/2015/05/nemkivanatossa-nyilvanitjak-soros-gyorgy-alkalmazottait/.

45 Jan-Werner Müller, "Eastern Europe goes South: Disappearing democracy in the EU's newest members," *Foreign Affairs*, March/April 2014, 15.

46 [Orbán], "Speech by Prime Minister Viktor Orbán on 15 March," March 15, 2016.

47 Ibid.

48 [Orbán], "Prime Minister Viktor Orbán's State of the Nation Address," February 28, 2016.

49 See Bálint Magyar, *Post-Communist Mafia State: The Case of Hungary* (Budapest: CEU Press, 2016), 76–79.

50 Jarosław was not imprisoned because the police had thought his name (with the same date of birth) was only a misprint.

51 Klaus Bachman, "Reason's cunning, Poland, populism, and involuntary modernization," *Eurozine*, Web Special, 7, https://www.zeitschrift-osteuropa.de/site/assets/files/4066/2007-08-10-bachmann1-en.pdf.

52 Kate Connolly, "Divide and Control," *Guardian*, October 17, 2007.

53 Derek Monroe, "No law, no justice and no civic values: Why Poland's constitutional crisis can only get worse," *RT*, January 4, 2016, https://www.rt.com/op-ed/327882-poland-political-crisis-eu/.

54 Minutes of the 82nd session of the 4th Sejm, August 25, 2004. Quoted by Bachman, "Reason's cunning, Poland, populism," 8–9.

55 Adam Mickiewicz, *Books of the Polish Nation and Pilgrimage* (London: James Ridgway, [1833] 1986), 202.

56 Henry Foy, "Poland's New Majoritarians," *The American Interest* 12, no. 1 (June 2016), https://www.the-american-interest.com/2016/06/07/polands-new-majoritarians/.

57 Pawel Sobczak and Justyna Pawlak, "Divisive Kaczynski shuns limelight in Polish election," *Reuters*, October 23, 2015, https://www.reuters.com/article/us-poland-election-kaczynski/divisive-kaczynski-shuns-limelight-in-polish-election-idUSKCN0SH20N20151023.

58 "Full text of Lech Kaczynski's letter to Katyn families," published by Andrew Rettman, *Euobserver*, April 15, 2010, https://euobserver.com/opinion/29868.

59 "Kaczynski in Tbilisi: 'We are here to take up the fight,'" posted on August 13, 2008, www.freerepublic.com/focus/news/2061279/posts.

60 "Jaroslaw Kaczynski gives a speech in front of the monument of the Great Synagogue in Bialystok," *Poland.pl*, July 12, 2016, https://poland.pl/politics/home/jaroslaw-kaczynski-gives-speech-front-monument-great-synagogue-b/.

61 Olga Cichowlas, "Poland's Right-Wing Government Scares Europe by Going After the Media," *VICE News*, January 9, 2016, https://www.vice.com/en_us/article/43mqp9/polands-right-wing-government-scares-europe-by-going-after-the-media.

62 Foy, "Poland's New Majoritarians."

63 "Poland's Tragic Turns," *New York Times*, December 22, 2016.

64 Cichowlas, "Poland's Right-Wing Government Scares Europe."

65 Quoted in Foy, "Poland's New Majoritarians."

66 Micaiah Bilger, "Poland Initially Approves New Law Banning All Abortions and Protecting Unborn Children," *LifeNews.com*, September 23, 2016, https://www.lifenews.com/2016/09/23/poland-poised-to-approve-new-law-banning-all-abortions-and-protecting-unborn-children/; Don Murray, "Poland's proposed ban on abortion part of broader push to turn back history," *CBC News*, October 4, 2016, www.cbc.ca/news/world/poland-abortion-law-1.3789335.

67 "Poles protest new law on public gatherings," *New York Times*, December 14, 2016.

68 Ibid.

69 Jarosław Kaczyński's speech in the parliament on September 16, 2015, seehttps://www.youtube.com/watch?v=6NlRstWinSU.

70 The European Commission formally censured the Polish government for subverting the rule of law by changing the makeup and procedures of the country's Constitutional Court. The government has also tightened control over state media to ensure that it relays the nationalist and conservative ideology of the Law and Justice Party. More than 150 state television employees, including prominent news anchors and reporters, have been fired or forced out.

71 Vince Chadwick, "Jarosław Kaczyński enters Polish judges row," *Politico Europe*, December 14, 2015, https://www.politico.eu/article/jaroslaw-kaczynski-enters-polish-judges-row/.

72 Timothy Garton Ash, "The pillars of Poland's democracy are being destroyed," *Guardian*, January 7, 2016.

73 "Is Poland a failing democracy?" *Politico*, January 13, 2016, https://www.politico.eu/article/poland-democracy-failing-pis-law-and-justice-media-rule-of-law/.

74 Jan Cienski, Joseph J. Schatz, and Benjamin Oreskes, "Polish-American romance sours," *Politico Europe*, March 15, 2016, https://www.politico.eu/article/nato-poland-obama-kaczynski-russia-putin-venice/.

75 *New York Times*, October 5, 2014.

76 Jarosław Kaczyński 2015 parliamentary elections speech, *Poland Current Events*, October 24, 2015, http://www.currenteventspoland.com/news/Jaroslaw-Kaczynski-speech-on-2015-parliamentary-elections.html.

Conclusion

The last hundred years—the worst of times

Charles Dickens's first sentence in his *A Tale of Two Cities* famously stated about the past: "It was the best of times, it was the worst of times."[1] The historian, looking back to the century of European history between World War I and the Great Recession of 2008 can also repeat this statement. Yes, it was the worst of times with two singularly destructive world wars, an unprecedented Great Depression in the 1930s and the Great Recession that exploded in 2007–8 and determined the 2010s. That was the century of the dramatic rise of Fascism, Nazism, Communism, and their equally dramatic fall, all culminating in a neo-liberal, globalized, democratic free-market capitalist system across Europe. Even positive changes had significant negative repercussions on many societies. As with all major social and political change, the transformation of Central and Eastern Europe from impoverished, shortage-ridden, closed communist societies to thriving market democracies required equally dramatic changes in social behavior and resulted in widespread uncertainty and social distress in the 1990s and 2000s.[2] As a result, authoritarian-leaning crony capitalism, in some cases "mafia state" type regimes have come to the fore in certain Central and Eastern European countries.

The last hundred years—the best of times

However, this was also a period when Europe internalized the bitter lessons of its calamitous wars and turned toward cooperation among former enemies and integration of its economy. In the process, it achieved great economic prosperity, played an important role in a new communication and technological revolution, comparable only to the First Industrial Revolution, raised living standards to unheard of levels, established a new model of the capitalist welfare state and, with unity and integration, reclaimed the continent's global dominance and competitive edge. In unprecedented fashion, the affluent countries in the integrating Continent—while also serving their own interests—helped the less developed countries at the periphery to catch up. This was the time that Europe attained its greatest historical achievement: the founding of the European Union.

Radical changes with winners and losers

World War I radically changed the map of Europe. Huge empires exploded, several new independent countries were created, and several others were mutilated. The pre-war "first globalization"³ was replaced by economic nationalism, tariff wars, and hostility among neighboring countries. The peace was a winner's peace that created tremendous political chaos and quick preparations for revenge. The world's greatest depression uprooted millions of people. Europe gradually slid into a new and even more devastating war that decimated the continent.

The last hundred years was a period that saw several other dramatic changes as well. For a century and a half ago, Europe had been a continent of emigration with some 50–60 million Europeans leaving their homelands for better shores. In the second half of the twentieth century, however, Europe became a continent of immigration, one that reached perilous and unprecedented dimensions in the 2010s. This new reality terrified a large part of the Europe's populace, as the proportion of immigrants from the Near East, Asia, and Africa rose to more than 10 percent of the total population and comprised 13–15 percent of the labor force in several countries.

This metamorphosis went hand in hand with other major changes. From the last third of the twentieth century, a new age of neo-liberal globalization held sway, with Europe playing a major role. Europe began to regain its competitive edge and international stature through *regionalization*, by hammering out a strong and modernized economy, and by creating a thoroughly integrated European market with a harmonized legal system, regulatory regime, common standards, and institutionalized pan-European banks and corporations. An integrated market assured the free flow of factors of production—goods, capital, and labor—throughout a borderless EU. Although regionalization was in some ways a part of—or at least contemporary with—globalization, it was also very much a *defense* against it.[4] As a result of the creation of the Single Market, Europe's multinational corporations pulled much of their business from the global market. The Dutch-British Unilever, one of the first multinational companies in the world, sold more than 70 of its factories and subsidiaries outside Europe and turned toward the European market. Germany drastically decreased its investments outside Europe, from 40 to 17 percent, and channeled them into other European countries. This new development was also connected with a change in the international division of labor. After Britain's Industrial Revolution and until roughly the 1960s, a division of labor had existed between advanced industrialized and less developed non-industrialized countries of Europe and beyond. The former sold industrial goods to the latter and in turn purchased raw materials and agricultural products. During the last half century, advanced countries developed a new kind of division of labor among themselves, both on national and industrial sectorial levels.

Europe itself, while employing much less labor in agriculture than before and in several other regions, became an agricultural exporter. Modern high-tech industries used markedly less raw materials. This change strongly influenced the direction of investment that was also directed toward other advanced countries.

Europeanization created a free flow of goods and capital from the prosperous core to the less advanced peripheries, and created a flow of migration, first from the poor Mediterranean countries and then later from the impoverished eastern European periphery, toward the Western core countries. A borderless Europe, one in which former boundaries can be crossed with ease, brought dramatic changes that came as a shock to many and rattled the continent. For a great number of people, such changes are not easy to digest, for great changes always produce winners and losers. Most of the losers often could not understand the real and rather complex causes of their predicament. Was it the result of the globalized free trade system, the free flow of goods and factors of production such as capital and labor? (For left-wing dissenters, but later for right-wing populist opponents, this explains everything.[5]) Or was it the increasing imports from newly industrializing Asian countries, with their cheap labor forces, that caused the loss of so many European jobs? Were the problems caused by the free flow of labor, the growing number of immigrants coming from less developed, poorer regions and willing to work for lower wages? Or were they the consequence of the ongoing technical revolution that dramatically transformed the communication and energy system, automated various industries, and radically reduced the number of people employed in industry, causing de-industrialization and service revolution?

Fertile soil for demagogues' half-truth explanations and the spreading of hatred

Increasing numbers of people readily embraced the over-simplified "explanations" that a new wave of anti-establishment politicians, mostly populist demagogues, provided. They believed their half-truths and deliberate lies that promised easy and immediate solutions. Listening to the demagogues, they felt that they suddenly understood the true causes of their misery and could finally identify their true enemies: those countries exporting artificially cheap products, those free trade policies of the political elite, those ethnic and religious minorities, those incessantly invading immigrants, those filthy rich fat cats rolling in money, or those perceived as the menacing other. They enthusiastically followed their new saviors, especially the less educated living in declining "rust-belt" regions and the countryside, who believed the demagogues were speaking their language and were their true representatives.[6] The refreshing straight talk of these rabid rabble-rousers, and their welcome renunciation of "political correctness," convinced large numbers of people to follow populist demagogues who were not members of the established elite such as the Hungarian Béla Kun or the Romanian Corneliu Zelea Codreanu, or even demagogues who were members of the professional political elite, such as Geert Wilders in the Netherlands, or demagogue billionaires from the business elite, like Italy's Silvio Berlusconi.

All of this was perhaps predictable given the dramatic last hundred years in Europe, which provided fertile soil for various kinds of left-wing and right-wing populist demagoguery, and occasionally a combination of both. Populist demagogues played a surprisingly large role in European politics in the twentieth- and early twenty-first centuries. They often made their way to power, especially after World War I and during the Great Depression,[7] and had a toxic impact on society even when they didn't.

For several decades after World War II, a period that saw relative peace and prosperity, the rise of welfare capitalism, declining income disparities, and immense and enduring optimism, Europeans had little time for demagogues, and they kept marginalized provocateurs like Jean-Marie Le Pen or Jörg Haider at a safe distance. But populist demagogues would return with a vengeance at around the turn of the millennium, and they would again prevail in the political scenes of several European countries.

Demagogues quickly attracted whole segments of European society—capturing in several countries 15 to 30 percent, but in some even more than 60 percent of the population. They appealed to all those terrified of the rapid and radical changes in their countries, to those unnerved by the vast uncertainties and the unknown dangers of the times, and to those alarmed by their stagnating or deteriorating living standard. The losers of the fundamental transformations taking place across Europe, those rendered redundant while wealth conspicuously abounded at the very top, directed their wrath at the political establishment. This anger and discontent—a recurrent phenomenon in Europe over the last hundred years—was shrewdly channeled by populist demagogues and directed against a whole list of nefarious "enemies:" capitalists, neighboring countries, Jews, immigrants, the "dictators of Brussels," or the concept of neoliberal globalization or European integration.

The vast numbers who felt ignored and forsaken invariably turned to anti-establishment, nationalist, and often xenophobic populist demagogues. Corneliu Zelea Codreanu of Romania and Gyula Gömbös of Hungary supplied easy, ready-made answers to the plight of hordes of landless, starving, and uneducated Romanian and Hungarian peasants, or the mass of unskilled workers suffering in poverty in both countries during the interwar period. According to them it was the Jewish bankers, land-renters, shopkeepers and money-lenders, and the hostile machination of the neighboring countries that was the cause of their poverty. Few were inclined, therefore, to resist the most horrendous retaliation against those accused parties.

Similarly, workers bogged down by stagnating wages or who were stripped of their positions found it easy to believe that their jobs had been stolen by foreign countries that had flooded their country's markets with their products. These workers believed that the elite had betrayed them by failing to defend the domestic market, or to protect the country's industries and their jobs. They were reassured to hear that the solutions to unemployment like the introduction of tariffs and other restrictions would be easy. Once they "grasped" that the corrupt establishment politicians had "sold" them out or had totally forgotten them, they were only too ready to believe the empty promises of populist demagogues.

Changing political landscape

The political landscape of Europe dramatically changed. The traditional parties lost their members and supporters, and new parties and political movements rose to the fore. The lower layers of society in rural and industrial regions that had hither to backed left-wing socialist parties now clamored behind right-wing, often xenophobic, and at times fascist movements. This political change seemed at first glance to be counterintuitive, but in fact it wasn't. These people were pursuing the same anti-establishment and anti-elite agenda, but they were applying it in a different direction. In the interwar period a part of the Left's constituency was captured by the extreme Right. These same people returned to the Left after the war, but the collapse of communism delegitimized the communist parties and rendered leftist politics bankrupt. Large numbers again turned to the Right and railed against new enemies.

The nationalism card

Whenever populist demagogues gained power, they usually implemented populist policies, hence, the embrace of so-called economic nationalism across Europe during the interwar period. Self-sufficiency became the program and tariff-wars the practice. But economic isolationism soon proved counter-productive, and Europe (at least its western part) returned to free trade, adhered to an international division of labor, and gradually eliminated its borders in half a century after World War II. This was a time when the idea of the nation state had lost its appeal. The smaller countries of Europe had come to realize that their sovereignty was more fiction than reality during the war-torn centuries prior to the European Union.

Scholarship ultimately clarified that nations had been "created" some two and a half centuries ago by homogenizing various ethnic and linguistic groups, who were imbued by the state to embrace a national identity and a sense of belonging to the national community. Whole populations were indoctrinated by the schools, the media, and by political propaganda to willingly sacrifice their lives and, if need be, kill others for the nation. Nineteenth-century nationalist regimes, the various wars engaging Europe, and especially the two world wars in the twentieth century profoundly embedded nationalist sentiment and stirred up nationalist hatred of others. Nationalism prevailed in Europe even though its countries were hardly cohesive, but rather divided into ethnic, religious, and social groups often pursuing conflicting interests. In other words, the nation is only an "imagined community," as Benedict Anderson so convincingly argued.[8] The Austrian philosopher Rudolf Bauer built upon Anderson's thesis when he referred to the nation as an "Imagi-Nation" and an "Indoctri-Nation."[9]

If national identity can be created, some scholars wonder, then why can't a European identity be created as well? If India can become (or at least be considered) a nation with its innumerable languages, religions and social divides, then certainly Europe, John Pinder suggests, can do so as well.[10] In other words, national sovereignty is hardly something eternal and sacrosanct.

Nevertheless, a new populist attack was launched at around the turn of the millennium against the international system and against the comprehensive Europeanization of the continent. Defending the nation state and upholding national sovereignty were placed firmly on the agenda once again. (It is interesting to note that some of the main advocates of nationalism in several countries came from surprisingly diverse ethnic-national backgrounds as the children or grandchildren of immigrants, like, for instance, the Hungarian Gömbös, the Romanian Codreanu, and the English Johnson and Farage.)

At the beginning of the twenty-first century, populist demagoguery attributed all of Europe's problems, including its shrinking security, to mass immigration and the "growing Islamization" of the continent. They called for punishing the elite for supporting multiculturalist policies that were behind both phenomena. Indignant demands for defending national borders and preserving national identity followed. Having subjugated the continent in the interwar period, but swept under the rug after World War II, nationalism was back with full force in Europe. However, a new type of rhetoric emerged, what Rogers Brubaker described as "civilizationism."[11] Populist demagogues warned that traditional Christian European civilization was in fact endangered, for immigrants and the blindness and impotence of the European Union were undermining it and were subverting the basis of European and national identity. They called for defending Christian-European values, which was interpreted by most North-Western European populist demagogues in a secular, and not a religious, way. For them, Christian-European values were cultural phenomena that, among other things, promote liberal values such as the freedom of speech, philo-Semitism, women's equality, and gay rights. Nationalist xenophobia and Islamophobia were thus transformed into the defense of secular Christian values, and reinterpreted using a unique mix of right-wing and left-wing ideologies. Anti-Semitism was dropped even from right-wing populist programs. Marine Le Pen, who went along with her father Jean-Marie's openly anti-Semitic policies for decades, and who continued to surround herself with close friends and associates who are overt Nazi-sympathizers and anti-Semites,[12] quite suddenly dropped anti-Semitism and readily expelled her father from the Front National and changed the name of the party to make it *comme il faut* to govern France. The Hungarian neo-fascist Jobbik Party also dropped its openly anti-Semitic program and rhetoric. Anti-Semitism is still virulent but often covert and rarely openly advocated by demagogues on the continent. It is not accidental that various populist politicians reject the old divisions of Left and Right and identify themselves as neither.

In Central and Eastern Europe, however, all interpretations of Christian-European values do not incorporate liberal ideals, but are restricted to a rigorous defense of the "Christian nation" against foreign influences of any kind, including foreign loans and investments and the spread of Western liberalism by foreign agents, non-governmental organizations (NGOs), and the European Union.[13] Here the system that is applauded is "illiberal democracy," because the demagogues of the region reject liberal values and freedom, but retain a façade of democracy through multi-party elections and other ostensibly liberal institutions. Opposition parties and journals remain legal but are suppressed, and opposition leaders are not imprisoned or killed, although sometime this has happened as well.

Toxic populist demagoguery attacking liberal rule or in power

As history has demonstrated, populist demagogues seek to attain a great deal of power, if possible even authoritarian rule. This was the norm during the interwar period and in some areas even after World War II. Hitler rose to power through free elections and then introduced a totalitarian dictatorship. Followers of Mussolini, Hitler, or Stalin built dictatorial states throughout Europe.

Demagogues in power have been extremely dangerous. They have been able to stir up intense hatred and mobilize huge crowds against specified "enemies," be they minorities, other ethnicities, or neighboring countries, and they have often been behind horrendous atrocities and crimes against humanity. The number of victims of these demagogues over the last hundred years is in the tens of millions.

Demagogues were extremely influential in several countries even without attaining power. As some of the cases in this volume clearly documented, Gyula Gömbös in Hungary and Corneliu Zelea Codreanu in Romania played huge roles in establishing dictatorial and murderous anti-Semitic regimes in their countries while remaining in the opposition and without rising to power themselves. They were very much responsible for creating a large base of supporters for anti-Jewish legislation and the murder of half the Jewish population of their countries.

In most Central and Eastern European countries, the regime changes of the 1990s and their joining the EU in the early 2000s were the most positive changes in their entire history. In some cases, however, demagogues exploited the trials and tribulations of the transition and pushed their followers into civil war. In Romania, a successful and briefly popular communist demagogue, Nicolae Ceaușescu, created a uniquely catastrophic situation that provoked a civil uprising that killed several hundreds of people. Similar civil conflicts were seen in several former Soviet republics a few years later. Armed conflicts and civil wars among different ethnic groups or fighting with Russia took place in Georgia, Moldova, Ukraine, and elsewhere. The most dramatic fallout was seen in the former Yugoslavia, as highly effective Serbian, Croatian, and Bosnian demagogues (Slobodan Milosevič, Franjo Tuđman, and Alija Izetbegovič) pushed their peoples toward civil war.

Populist demagogues do not always commit crimes against humanity or transform their countries into clear-cut dictatorships. Italy's Silvio Berlusconi hardly did so while in power, though he has been elected three times. Jörg Haider never attained real power in Austria, though his party did take part in a coalition government for a short period. Haider also never committed any crimes, which is also true of the Brexit demagogues, Nigel Farage and Boris Johnson.

Still, all of them caused serious economic or political damages in their countries. Berlusconi's self-promoting regime, with its enormous tax cuts and its rampant tax evasion, dramatically increased Italy's indebtedness to near intolerable levels, and was the cause for the long-term stagnation of the Italian economy. Haider's demagoguery—equating Nazi crimes with acts of retribution after the war and painting Nazi SS soldiers as patriots serving the homeland and defenders of Europe from a Soviet invasion—was part of the factor behind the Austrians' enduring silence about their Nazi past. The Haider effect helped postpone the nation's soul searching of the past that was so essential for educating younger generations and strengthening democracy.

The most successful anti-EU demagogues swayed slightly more than half of Britain's electorate to vote "yes" on leaving the EU in 2016 through lies and propaganda. Their influence grew further when Prime Minister Theresa May joined their ranks and repeatedly proclaimed that "Brexit means Brexit," while ominously suggesting a "hard landing" with Britain's exit from Europe's Single Market. Britain may indeed pay a high economic price for following the demagogues, who may challenge the United Kingdom since both Scotland and Northern Ireland have voted to remain in the EU.

In the 2010s, demagogues challenging establishment parties and governments in the Netherlands, Italy, France, Britain, and Germany have had a detrimental effect on domestic politics, as they have pushed traditional conservative and centrist parties more to the extreme Right. In their drive to be competitive, Nicolas Sarkozy and François Fillon in France, and Mark Rutte in the Netherlands, have appropriated large parts of the extremist programs of Marine Le Pen and Geert Wilders.

After both the defeat of fascism and the collapse of communism, populist demagogues were incapable of installing openly authoritarian, dictatorial regimes in Europe. The international situation around the turn of the millennium and the existence of the European Union were strong impediments to self-appointed dictators. Still, autocratic demagogues in power have been able to erode democracy in more tactful and indirect ways. In some countries they undermined the rule of law, wore down institutional checks and balances, neutralized supreme courts, and, with sufficient majorities, repealed laws and even constitutions— all in the quest of suppressing opposition, restricting non-governmental organizations, and silencing the media.

After Donald J. Trump's victory in 2016, and following Putin's Russia's example, a coordinated attack has been launched in various Central European countries against George Soros's Open Society Fund and the Central European University in Hungary in a bid to rid the region of institutions that embody liberal democracy. A newspaper in Bulgaria denounced Soros as a "liberal terrorist," and one in Serbia highlighted Soros's Jewishness by linking him to the Rothschilds. Szilárd Németh, Vice Chairman of Viktor Orbán's Fidesz party, openly called for the elimination of all NGOs: "These organizations . . . must be swept out, and now . . . the international conditions are right for this with the election of a new [American] president."[14] These attacks meanwhile gave the opportunity to use a hidden, coded anti-Semitism to gain votes.

Another weapon in the demagogues' arsenal is their flexibility: right-wing demagogues like Nigel Farage do not hesitate to use left-wing rhetoric and policies to court voters. While in power, they have occasionally increased the minimum wage, lowered the age of retirement, and reduced utility bills and home mortgages—Hungary's Viktor Orbán and Poland's Jarosław Kaczyński have been masters in doing the same. Such popular measures naturally consolidate their hold on power. Behind the scenes they have been busily building crony capitalism, mafia states, enriching themselves and their oligarch allies, and creating formidable political dynasties—as is all too apparent in the transforming countries of Central and Eastern Europe. The demagogues have made it extremely difficult to challenge their rule. They fully intend to stay in power for the long haul. This is happening in early twenty-first century Hungary and Poland, whose rulers openly embrace "illiberal democracy," which is code for anti-democratic dictatorship and placation to their right-wing and xenophobic followers. Exploiting the long-nurtured nationalism and xenophobia of a part of their populace is also something Orbán and Kaczyński have mastered. They stand at the forefront of anti-immigration endeavors and are quite tolerant of anti-Jewish or anti-Roma sentiment, though they have not launched violent campaigns against the minorities in their countries. These demagogues are instead focused on stabilizing their power, as well as building anti-European Union alliances with their counterparts in other countries (such as the so-called four Visegrád countries in Central Europe or Geert Wilders and Marine Le Pen's attempt to build an anti-EU coalition) and strengthening right-wing nationalism across Europe. They pose a significant danger to Europe's democratic order and are the central subverters of European solidarity.

As a rule, populist demagogues are not easy to dislodge from power. It took the total military defeat of Hitler, Mussolini, and their Vichy-French, Hungarian, Romanian, Croatian, Bulgarian, and Slovak allies to finally put an end to the pernicious rule of Europe's interwar demagogue fascist dictators. The following normalization—which included retribution, often with collective punishment[15]—was an exceedingly partial and often painful process and in several cases took many years to complete or even failed.

The Yugoslav civil war in the 1990s paralleled the situation in Europe after World War II, in that it took the intervention of the great powers to finally end the military conflict, legalize the creation of several independent states in the place of the former Yugoslavia, and re-move nationalist demagogues from power. Western intervention and the positive influence of the European Union only gradually stabilized the peace and assured the political normalization and democratization in the Balkans. None of this could have happened without ridding the re-gion of its nationalist demagogues, which is a *sine qua non* for the re-turn of stability and prosperity in the area.

In peaceful times, demagogues cannot be removed from power by mil-itary force, but it cannot be emphasized enough the extent of the danger that they pose. Within the European Union, their vicious attacks on in-tra-European cooperation and their nationalist, "illiberal," authoritarian-leaning regimes are pernicious influences that may undermine Europe-an integration. Several of these demagogues want their countries to leave the eurozone or follow the British out of the EU. In principle, the Eu-ropean Union has the legal right to stabilize member countries, defend their democracies, and act against these demagogues. All candidate members of the EU had to meet rigorously defined prerequisites for membership (the so-called *acquis communautaire*), which included hav-ing a "functioning democratic system." If a member country violated these requirements, the EU could suspend its voting rights and halt fi-nancial aid. However, the European Union does not regularly resort to such measures. The EU provides billions of euros of assistance to Poland and Hungary, more than what the Marshall Plan allotted to 16 countries over a four-year period after the war. Billions more go to Poland and Hungary thanks to the EU's cohesion and agricultural policies.[16] This is the case even though the governments of both countries regularly vio-late elemental democratic requirements of membership. The Union spe-cifically requires a campaign against corruption before accepting any new member, but it looks the other way when it comes to the rampant cor-ruption in Greece, Italy, Bulgaria, Romania, Hungary, and other mem-ber countries. The European Union's intervention on regulatory and fi-nancial matters could make a difference in countering demagogues and "illiberal" quasi-authoritarian rulers in its member countries. It is in-cumbent that the EU uses the weapons at its disposal—or even creates new ones, because the existing ones are not enough to handle the rebel-lion—to stabilize the system of cooperation in the European Union. Not doing so may undermine integration altogether.

Attacks on the European Union

Populist nationalists in the early twenty-first century have effectively attacked the "dictatorial bureaucrats of Brussels" and decried their lost sovereignty. They again call for embracing nationalism with slogans like Berlusconi's "Italy First" and Haider's "Austria First." They seek to "regain" Christian national identity and rid themselves of Muslim immigrants. They have successfully influenced up to at least one-quarter of the population in Austria, France, and the Netherlands, and were able to mobilize more than half of Britain's and three quarters of Italy's electorate. They have won majorities in parliaments of several Central and Eastern European countries, such as Hungary and Poland. Millions are susceptible to their rabble-rousing attacks on "dictatorial," "colonizing," and "self-promoting" EU bureaucrats who don't have to answer to elected bodies. Rather than addressing the EU's genuine shortcomings with necessary reforms, more and more people look to simple solutions like ending the common currency or leaving the European Union and "regaining independence." During the crisis years of the 2010s, large numbers in quite a few countries have lost confidence in the integration process and believe that the EU is harmful to their countries.

The populist demagogues have also been adept at exploiting a number of the EU's missteps, such as its long delays at solving the euro- and debt-crises and, most of all, its initial mistaken response to the migration crisis, when it allowed more than a million migrants to enter Europe in a chaotic manner without proper controls. At the same time, they mercilessly attack the EU for "dictating heartless austerity measures against poor peripheral countries" like Greece.[17] An austerity policy was unavoidable after the 2008 financial-economic crisis, which exposed the reckless spending and endemic tax evasion in some peripheral countries inside the EU. In 2011, Greece ranked as the 80th most corrupt country, out of 185 countries around the world, a level of corruption far beyond what is typical in Europe. As the deputy-head of Greece's tax collecting bureau suggested, if tax collection worked "there would be no debt problem."[18]

Both individuals and, in certain cases, governments of formerly poor peripheral, now *nouveau-riche*, countries, abounding in cheap EU credit, spent far beyond their means and attained a much higher level of home ownership (about 80 percent) than has Switzerland, Germany (with hardly more than 50 percent), and the United States (67 percent). Greece spent four times more for armament in relative terms (6–7 percent of GDP) than did Germany (less than 2 percent). Their banks and state coffers fell into bankruptcy and had to be bailed out three times.

Austerity measures demanding a reduction of spending and a rise in state revenues had a kind of "educational" mandate to require a reasonable fiscal policy from the eurozone member countries. Actually this was a bitter pill that worked remarkably well in Ireland, Spain, and Portugal. The accusation that the austerity policy was ruthless exploitation is not only one-sided, it is contrary to the facts.

Populist demagogues rightly blame the EU for slowly responding to serious challenges. Yet their criticism is not meant to improve the EU, but to destroy it. With their incessant attacks, demagogues jeopardize the most promising development in post–World War II Europe. True, recent demagogues have waged relatively few wars and caused little bloodshed compared to those of the mid-twentieth century, but nevertheless, their role in reviving nationalism is deleterious to the extreme, and in the long run may lead to unpredictable and dangerous consequences.

Defending the European Union against the nationalist-populist attacks of demagogues is the most important task of its member countries. The EU has established a peaceful continent and reestablished Europe's position in the world. It enjoyed exceptional economic growth and rapidly rising living standards prior to the 2008 crisis, and it did so within the framework of an integrated Europe. Several countries and regions achieved remarkable transformations from economic backwardness to growth and advancement and from political dictatorships to popular democracies, once they were incorporated into the European Union: Ireland beginning in the 1970s; Greece, Spain, and Portugal in the 1980s; and the Central and East European former communist countries in the 2000s. These kinds of dramatic historical changes are often pregnant with intense conflict. The European Union, with its plentiful political and economic assistance, led to a much smoother transformation of the former peripheral countries of Europe. In some cases their impressive progress and ability to catch up with the most advanced countries of Western Europe was nothing less than extraordinary. Nevertheless, populist demagogues still viciously attack the European Union.

Populist demagoguery has deep roots in Europe. Path dependence, the survival of old behavioral patterns, entrenched ideology, and cultural norms persist under the surface of official political institutions, and social conditioning in familial and small communal settings keeps the past alive in contemporary Europe. With the 2016 election of an unpredictable demagogue, Donald J. Trump, as president of the United States, America's role as the post–World War II benign hegemon determining world politics and ensuring European stability is certainly over. An inward looking US ("America First!") may change the international political environment and boost nationalism and populist demagoguery throughout the world. A new American policy—one that no longer seeks to keep an over-ambitious Vladimir Putin under control—creates immediate dangers for some of Russia's neighbors, especially in the Baltics.

The demagogues in Europe, from Geert Wilders and Marine Le Pen, to Nigel Farage and Viktor Orbán, exuberantly celebrated the election of Donald Trump. They believed that the American election signaled that their time had truly arrived. As the *New York Times* rightly stated,

> In the immediate wake of the election, the chorus of excited reactions from Europe's far right, which has made common cause with Mr. Trump's anti-globalization, anti-immigration and anti-establishment messages, reflected a sense that its cause had been given a huge boost. Marine Le Pen had seen in Mr. Trump's election a "great movement across the world" to open the status quo. In the Netherlands, Geert Wilders . . . declared the election "historic." In Britain, Nigel Farage . . . declared that he could not be happier.[19]

This enthusiasm, however, was premature. A significant portion of Europe's population was frightened by the start of the Trump era in the United States, with its chaos, its lies, and its betrayal of the electorate. Two months after Trump's election, a large majority of Dutch voters took heed of the dangers and deserted Geert Wilders. The same *New York Times* noted with satisfaction that "for the Dutch, both the British vote to leave the European Union and Donald J. Trump's election in the United States broke political dikes, leaving the Dutch ill at ease with the conflict and uncertainty that has ensued." The article also quoted a local observer who stated that "in Europe we all see the developments in the United States, and that's not where we want to go." These developments, concluded another observer, "helped shift the mood in the Netherlands."[20]

At the same time, Europe seemed even more endangered. Additional integration, including of the financial systems, and a strengthening of Europe's defense and energy independence were now more important than ever. Populist demagogues are preventing the European Union from addressing the new challenges and introducing reforms that will stabilize and strengthen the Union. Their victory in Italy in the early spring of 2018 signals a new danger for common actions.

The endangered EU and the chances of its reinvigoration

All in all, populist demagogues are unquestionably dangerous for their own countries and for Europe as a whole. All availing political forces must therefore be mustered in the fight against them, for they should not be allowed to acquire any additional power. This battle must not, however, be limited to political campaigns and elections. It requires long-term measures and additional social and political change. To limit the demagogues' influence, countries must cultivate effective social institutions, revitalize the welfare system in states where it has practically collapsed, decrease the income disparities and assist the losers of the ongoing socio-economic transformations in society. Governments must mitigate the social shocks, reverse the economic malaise, and assist the vulnerable members of society. The European Union must address and remedy its significant shortcomings in order to stabilize the integration process.

Does Europe have any chance of doing so? Or will a domino effect of mounting victories of nationalist-populist demagogues uproot the entire landscape? One of the most striking circumstances of the recent period is just how easily demagogues can spread their lies and influence large numbers in their societies. An unrestricted social media has effectively magnified this danger and has significantly enhanced the demagogues' ability to disseminate lies. Scientifically based polls and statistical analyses have indicated that in the modern period the less educated are the most vulnerable to demagoguery, fabrications, and quixotic promises are the most prone to support demagogues. In several countries it has become all too apparent that demagogues particularly attract the less educated, the more elderly, the residents of the countryside, and the "forgotten" workers hurt by de-industrialization, job losses, and stagnating wages. This was precisely the dynamic of Britain's referendum to leave the European Union, as it was during Berlusconi's numerous election campaigns and even more so in the case of the newly emerging Italian Lega of Matteo Salvini and the Five Star Movement in early 2018. These elements comprise the strongest base behind Marine Le Pen's and Geert Wilders's and they are the most loyal supporters of Orbán in Hungary and Kaczyński in Poland.

Perhaps one lesson to be gleaned from these facts is the importance of education in the long-term struggle against demagoguery. Strengthening basic education, which should be offered free of charge, and retraining all those whose skills have become obsolete because of technological and structural changes in the economy must be an organic part of the struggle against populist demagoguery. Governments must not ignore this critical lesson. Education and occupational training help protect the vulnerable against both social decay and populist demagoguery.

Democratic governments have a permanent responsibility of preventing demagogues from prevailing by unmasking their over-simplified "solutions" to complex questions and exposing their half-truths and lies with genuine facts. This is, however, not nearly enough. Confronting demagogues also requires sound social and educational policies.

One of history's most renowned philosophers, Georg Wilhelm Friedrich Hegel, once offered a profoundly pessimistic reading of history when he noted: "What experience and history teaches us is that people and governments have never learned anything from history, or acted on principles deduced from it." This has been proved time and time again over the centuries. Still, post–World War II Europe has also showed that the old continent was in fact capable of learning from its dismal history—particularly the two calamitous world wars in the first half of the twentieth century. Europe embarked on a new age after an endless period of recurrent warfare. The historical reconciliation of former enemies and the integration of a divided continent is Europe's glorious answer to its disastrous history. Today, with this integration process in serious danger, Europeans must again demonstrate that they are fully capable of learning from history.

On March 25, 2017, Europe's leaders assembled in Rome to commemorate the 60th anniversary of the foundation of the European Union. As the *New York Times* gloomily observed, there is, however,

> little to celebrate. . . . The main question facing the European Union, 60 years later, is one of reinvigoration. How can it recapture the optimism, restore the solidarity and reassure its core members while delivering economic opportunity to its poorer members and to its youth? That will be not easy. . . . Its troubles are so numerous and structural that they threaten to undo the bloc.[21]

Indeed, in early 2017 the prospects for reinvigoration were hardly promising. Still, one cannot but wonder whether Brexit and the incessant populist assault on the European Union may spark a genuine defense of unity and integration, and lead to serious soul searching about the future of Europe. Perhaps only then will the EU finally make the necessary reforms and renew both itself and the confidence of its many peoples. As a commentary on a 2017 European Parliament debate exploring the future development of the European Union noted:

> If the EU is to boost its capacity to act, restore citizens' trust and make the euro zone economy more resilient to outside shocks, it needs to make full use of the Lisbon Treaty. But to go further, it needs to reform itself more fundamentally.

In the same spirit, a member of the parliament said:

> Citizens expect solutions from Europe, and they are angry because they do not see answers being delivered. This is evident in a time with many challenges, but there are many problems that can only be solved together. The Lisbon Treaty offers plenty of possibilities for making the EU more efficient, accountable and transparent, which have not yet been tapped.

Or to put it another way, using the words of another MP summing up the response the EU should give to the challenge posed by populism:

The European Union doesn't need a populist revolution. It needs peace and to adapt to the necessities of our time. This means coping with democratic challenges, providing citizens with social, fiscal, and ecological protection, defending their right to safety in a degraded international context and delivering on our moral obligations to our neighbors.[22]

These statements, unfortunately, are just as valid today as when they were delivered.

Endnotes

1 "It was the best of times, it was the worst of times, it was the age of wisdom, it was the age of foolishness, it was the epoch of belief, it was the epoch of incredulity. . ." Charles Dickens, *A Tale of Two Cities* (London: Chapman & Hall, 1859).

2 This phenomenon is brilliantly explained by Karl Polanyi, *The Great Transformation: The Political and Economic Origins of Our Time* (Boston: Beacon Press, [1944, 1957] 2001). Polanyi, among others, uses the example of the social shock caused by the British Industrial Revolution.

3 This term was introduced by Kevin H. O'Rourke and Jeffrey G. Williamson, *Globalization and History: The Evolution of a Nineteenth-Century Atlantic Economy* (Cambridge, MA: MIT Press, 2001).

4 See, among others, Robert Gilpin, *The Challenge of Global Capitalism: The World Economy in the 21st Century* (Princeton: Princeton University Press, 2000); Renato Ruggiero, "Regionalism Vs. Globalism? Do the United States and the EU have a special responsibility to advance global trade?," *The Globalist*, June 20, 2003, https://www.theglobalist.com/regionalism-vs-globalism/; Grahame Thompson, "Globalisation versus regionalism?," *The Journal of North African Studies* 3, no. 2 (1998): 59–74, http://dx.doi.org/10.1080/13629389808718320.

5 See Perry Anderson, "Why the system will still win," *Le Monde Diplomatique*, March 2017.

6 Exit polls after the Brexit vote clearly reflected this phenomenon. The less educated and older people from the countryside voted for leaving the EU, while the more educated, younger, urban population overwhelmingly supported the "remain" camp.

7 It pays to note that the American writer and Nobel laureate, Sinclair Lewis, wrote a book entitled, *It Can't Happen Here* in the 1930s about an imagined populist-authoritarian political turn in the United States.

8 Benedict Anderson, *Imagined Communities: Reflections on the Origin and Spread of Nationalism* (London: Verso, 1983).

9 Rudolf Bauer, "Die nachträgliche Nation: Gedanken zu einer unvollständigen Gegenwart," in *Zukunft denken: Festschrift für Wolfgang Schüssel*, ed. Andreas Kohl, Reinhold Lopatka, and Wilhelm Molterer (Vienna: Oldenbourg, 2005), 21–38, quoted by Ferdinand Kühnel, "The silent disappearance of ethnic minorities from gravestones," in *Central Europe (Re-)visited: A multi-perspective approach to a region*, ed. Marija Wakounig and Ferdinand Kühne (Vienna: LIT Verlag, 2015).

10 John Pinder, "European Community and Nation-State: A Case for a Neofederalism?," in *International Affairs* 62, no. 1 (Winter 1985–1986): 41–54.

11 Rogers Brubaker, "Between Nationalism and Civilizationism: The European Populist Movement in Comparative Perspective," *Journal of Ethnic and Racial Studies* 40, no. 8 (2017): 1191–1226.

12 See Adam Nossiter, "Concern that aides have Nazi leanings clouds Le Pen in France," *New York Times*, April 15, 2017.

13 Ibid.

14 Rick Lyman, "Eastern Europe's populists emboldened in limiting foreign groups," *New York Times*, March 2, 2017.

15 Retaliations for ethnic cleansing and war crimes took place after the war. Moreover, the concept of collective responsibility led to the expulsion of 13 million Germans from Eastern Europe. The brutality of this process was excellently analyzed and dramatically presented in a case study of Czechoslovakia. See Benjamin Frommer, *National Cleansing: Retribution against Nazi*

Collaborators in Postwar Czechoslovakia (Cambridge: Cambridge University Press, 2005). Tens of thousands of Nazi collaborators were also lynched without due process, especially in France and Italy. Retribution was sometimes combined, however, with personal vendettas. Old family enemies could be accused and killed without cause during the immediate postwar years. See István Deák, *Europe on Trial: The Story of Collaboration, Resistance, and Retribution During World War II* (Boulder, CO: Westview Press, 2015).

16 See Ivan T. Berend, *The Contemporary Crisis of the European Union: Prospects for the Future* (London: Routledge, 2017), 95.

17 The austerity policy was equally attacked from both the Right and the Left. On the latter, see Perry Anderson, "Why the system will still win," *Le Monde diplomatique*, March 2017.

18 Adéa Guillot, "Greece struggles to address its tax evasion problem," *Guardian*, February 24, 2015.

19 "The World Waits and Wonders," *New York Times*, November 12, 2016.

20 Alissa J. Rubin, "Trump may have pushed Dutch voters away from populism," *New York Times*, March 17, 2017.

21 Steven Erlanger, "Divided EU turns 60 with little to celebrate," *New York Times*, March 25, 2017.

22 "Parliament sets out its vision for the future of Europe," *European Parliament*, Press Release, February 16, 2017, https://www.europarl.europa.eu/news/en/press-room/20170210IPR61812/parliament-sets-out-its-vision-for-the-future-of-europe.

Bibliography

Abromeit, John. "Transformation of Producerist Populism in Western Europe." In *Transformation of Populism in Europe and the Americas: History of Recent Tendencies*, edited by John Abromeit, Bridget Maria Chesterton, Gary Marotta, and York Norman. London: Bloomsbury, 2016.

Anderson, Perry. "Why the system will still win." *Le Monde Diplomatique*, March 2017. https://mondediplo.com/2017/03/02brexit.

Andrews, Geoff. *Not a Normal Country: Italy after Berlusconi*. London: Pluto Press, 2005.

Bachman, Klaus. "Reason's cunning, Poland, populism, and involuntary modernization." *Eurozine*, Web Special, 7. https://www.zeitschrift-osteuropa.de/site/assets/files/4066/2007-08-10-bachmann1-en.pdf.

Berend, Ivan T. *The Contemporary Crisis of the European Union: Prospects for the Future*. London: Routledge, 2017.

―――. *Decades of Crisis: Central and Eastern Europe before World War II*. Berkeley: University of California Press, 1998.

―――. *An Economic History of Twentieth-Century Europe: Economic Regimes from Laissez-Faire to Globalization*. Cambridge: Cambridge University Press, [2006] 2016.

Berend, Ivan T., and György Ránki. *Economic Development of East-Central Europe in the Nineteenth and Twentieth Centuries*. New York: Columbia University Press, 1974.

―――. *The Hungarian Economy in the Twentieth Century*. Beckenham, Kent: Croom Helm, 1985.

―――. *Magyarország a fasiszta Németország "életterében," 1933–1939*. Budapest: Közgazdasági és Jogi Kiadó, 1960.

Berlusconi, Silvio. *Discorsi per la democrazia*. Milan: Mondadori, 2001.

―――. *L'Italia che ho in mente: I discursi di Silvio Berlusconi*. Milan: Mondadori, 2000.

Betz, Hans-Georg. *Radical Right-Wing Populism in Western Europe*. New York: St. Martin's Press, 1994.

Borsányi, György. *The life of a communist revolutionary, Béla Kun*. Boulder, CO: Social Science Monographs, 1993.

Brown, Michael Barratt. *From Tito to Milosevic: Yugoslavia, the Lost Country*. London: The Merlin Press, 2005.

Brubaker, Rogers. "Between Nationalism and Civilizationism: The European Populist Movement in Comparative Perspective." *Journal of Ethnic and Racial Studies* 40, no. 8 (2017): 1191–1226.

Bruijn, Hans de. *Geert Wilders Speaks Out: The Rhetorical Frames of a European Populist*. The Hague: Eleven International Publishing, 2011.

Campus, Donatella. *Antipolitics in Power: Populist Language as a Tool for Government*. Cresskill, NJ: Hampton Press, 2010.

Carsten, Francis. *Revolution in Central Europe, 1918–1919.* Berkeley: University of California Press, 1972.

Castells, Raymond. *Hitler, Le Pen, Megret: Leur Programme.* Paris: Raymond Castells, 1998.

Ceaușescu, Nicolae. *Romania on the Way of Completing Socialist Construction: Reports, Speeches, Articles July 1965–September 1966.* Vol. 1. Bucharest: Meridiane Publishing House, 1969.

———. *Romania: Achievements and Prospects: Reports, Speeches, Articles, July 1965–February 1969.* Bucharest: Meridiane Publisher, 1969.

Chakotin, Serge. *The Rape of the Masses: The Psychology of Totalitarian Political Propaganda.* New York: Alliance Book, 1940.

Cichowlas, Olga. "Poland's Right-Wing Government Scares Europe by Going After the Media." *VICE News,* January 9, 2016. https://www.vice.com/en_us/article/43mqp9/polands-right-wing-government-scares-europe-by-going-after-the-media.

Codreanu, Corneliu Zelea. *For My Legionaries: The Iron Guard.* Madrid: Editura Libertatea, 1976.

Cohen, Lenard J. *Serpent in the Bosom: The Rise and Fall of Slobodan Milošević.* Boulder, CO: Westview Press, 2001.

Cowley, Jason. "Nigel Farage: 'I'm not on the right or left. I'm a radical.'" *New Statesman,* November 12, 2014. www.newstatesman.com/politics/2014/11/nigel-farage-i-m-not-right-or-left-i-m-radical.

Davies, Peter. *The National Front in France: Ideology, Discourse and Power.* London: Routledge, 1999.

Day, Michael. *Being Berlusconi: The rise and fall from Cosa Nostra to Bunga Bunga.* New York: Palgrave Macmillan, 2015.

De Felice, R. *Mussolini il rivoluzionario.* Torino: Einaudi, 1965.

Debreczeni, József. *Orbán Viktor.* Budapest: Osiris Kiadó, 2002.

Doder, Dusko, and Louise Branson. *Milosevic: Portrait of a Tyrant.* New York: The Free Press, 1999.

Eibicht, Rolf-Josef, ed. *Jörg Haider: Patriot im Zwielicht?* Stuttgart: DS-Verlag, 1997.

Farage, Nigel. *Flying Free.* London: Biteback Publishing, 2011.

———. *The Purple Revolution: The Year that Changed Everything.* London: Biteback Publishing, 2015.

Felton, Keith Spencer. *Warriors' Words: A Consideration of Language and Leadership.* Westport, CT: Praeger, 1995.

Fieschi, Catherine. *Fascism, Populism and the French Fifth Republic.* Manchester: Manchester University Press, 2004.

Foy, Henry. "Poland's New Majoritarians." *The American Interest* 12, no. 1 (June 2016). https://www.the-american-interest.com/2016/06/07/polands-new-majoritarians/.

Friedman, Alan. *Berlusconi: The epic story of the billionaire who took over Italy.* New York: Hachette Books, 2015.

———. *My Way: Berlusconi in His Own Words.* London: Biteback Publishing, 2015.

Ginsborg, Paul. *Silvio Berlusconi: Television, Power and Patrimony.* London: Verso, 2004.

Gömbös, Gyula. *Válogatott politikai beszédek és írások.* Edited by József Vonyó. Budapest: Osiris Kiadó, 2004.

Graumann, Carl F., and Serge Moscovici, eds. *Changing Conceptions of Crowd Mind and Behavior.* New York: Springer Verlag, 1986.

Gyurgyák, János. *A zsidókérdés Magyarországon: Politikai eszmetörténet.* Budapest: Osiris Kiadó, 2001.

Heinen, Armin. *Die Legion "Erzengel Michael" in Rumänien: Soziale Bewegung und politische Organisation.* Munich: Oldenburg, 1986.

Ionescu, Ghita, and Ernest Gellner, eds. *Populism: Its Meaning and National Characteristics.* London: Weidenfeld and Nicolson, 1969.

Iordachi, Constantin. "God's Chosen Warriors: Romantic Palingenesis, Militarism and

Fascism in Modern Romania." In *Comparative Fascist Studies: New Perspectives*, edited by Constantin Iordachi, 316–357. London: Routledge: 2009.

Izetbegović, Alija. *Islam Between East and West*. Indianapolis: American Trust Publication, 1984.

———. *Islamic Declaration: A Programme for the Islamization of Muslims and the Muslim Peoples*. Sarajevo: SR Bosnia, 1990.

———. *Izetbegović of Bosnia and Herzegovina: Notes from Prison, 1983–1988*. Westport: Praeger, 2002.

Johnson, Boris. *Friends, Voters, Countrymen: Jotting on the Stump*. London: Harper Collins, 2001.

———. *Have I Got News For You*. London: Harper Perennial, 2006.

———. *Lend Me Your Ears*. London: Harper Collins Publisher, 2003.

———. "Please Vote Leave on Thursday, because we'll never get this chance again." *Telegraph*, June 19, 2016.

———. "Tory candidates need a plan for Brexit—here's mine in 5 points." *Telegraph*, July 3, 2016.

———. "When it comes to the single market, you don't have to be in it to win it." *Telegraph*, June 12, 2016.

Johnson, Boris, and Michael Gove. "Getting the facts clear on the economic risks of remaining in the EU—Vote Leave's letter to David Cameron." *Telegraph*, June 5, 2016.

Johnstone, Diana. *Fools' Crusade: Yugoslavia, NATO, and Western Delusions*. New York: Monthly Review Press, 2002.

Kazin, Michael. *The Populist Persuasion: An American History*. Ithaca, NY: Cornell University Press, 1995.

Kessel, Stijn van. *Populist Parties in Europe: Agents of Discontent?* Houndsmill: Palgrave Macmillan, 2015.

Kun, Béla. *Válogatott írások és beszédek*. Budapest: Kossuth Kiadó, 1966.

Lakoff, George. *Don't Think of an Elephant!: Know your Values and Frame the Debate*. White river: Chelsea Green Publishing, 2004.

Lattes, Gianfranco Bettin, and Ettore Recchi, eds. *Comparing European Societies: Towards a Sociology of the EU*. Bologna: Monduzzi Editore, 2005.

Le Bon, Gustave. *The Crowd*. Harmondsworth: Penguin [1895], 1977.

———. *The Psychology of Socialism*. New Jersey: Transaction Publishers, 1982.

Le Pen, Jean-Marie. *Les Français d'abord*. Paris: Carrere-Michel Lafon, 1984.

———. *Pour la France*. Paris: Albatross, 1985.

Le Pen, Marine. *Pour que vive la France*. Paris: Grancher, 2012.

Lehman-Horn, Knut. *Die Kärtner FPÖ 1955–1983: Vom Verband der Unabhängigen (VdU) bis zum Aufstieg von Jörg Haider zur Landesparteioberman*. Klagenfurt: Universitätsverlag Carinthia, 1992.

Lendvai, Paul. *Orbáns Ungarn*. Vienna: Verlag Kremyr & Scheriaut, 2016.

Mackay, Charles. *Memoires of Extraordinary Popular Delusions and the Madness of Crowds*. Wells, VT: Page, [1841] 1932.

MacRae, Donald. "Populism as an Ideology." In *Populism: Its Meaning and National Characteristics*, edited by Ghita Ionescu and Ernst Gellner, 154–65. London: Weidenfeld and Nicolson, 1969.

Magyar, Bálint. *Post-Communist Mafia State: The Case of Hungary*. Budapest: CEU Press, 2016.

Mény, Yves, and Yves Surel, eds. *Democracies and the Populist Challenge*. New York: Palgrave Macmillan, 2002.

———. *Par le Peuple, Pour le Peuple: Le Populisme et les Démocraties*. Paris: Fayard, 2000.

Moscovici, Serge. "The Discovery of the Masses." In *Changing Conceptions of Crowd Mind and Behavior*, edited by Carl F. Graumann and Serge Moscovici, 5–25. New York: Springer Verlag, 1986.

Mudde, Cas, ed. *The Populist Radical Right: A Reader*. London: Routledge, 2017.

Mudde, Cas. "The Populist Zeitgeist." *Government and Opposition* 39, no. 4 (2004): 542–63.
———. "The Hungary PM made a 'rivers of blood' speech . . . and no one cares." *Guardian,* July 30, 2015.
Mudde, Cas, and Cristóbal Rovira Kaltwasser. *Populism: A Very Short Introduction.* Oxford: Oxford University Press, 2017.
Mudde, Cas, and Rovira Kaltwasser. "Populism and Political Leadership." In *Oxford Handbooks Online,* edited by R. A. W. Rhodes and Paul 't Hart, doi:10.1093/oxford-hb/9780199653881.013.016.
Mussolini, Benito. *Fascism: Doctrine and Institutions.* Rome: Ardira Publisher, 1935.
Nagy-Talavera, Nicholas M. *The Green Shirts and Others: A History of Fascism in Hungary and Romania.* Stanford: Hoover Institution Press, 1970.
Orbán, Viktor. "Hungary and the Crisis of Europe." *Hungarian Review* 8, no. 1 (January 24, 2017). http://hungarianreview.com/article/20170124_hungary_and_the_crisis_of_europe.
———. "Notes Towards a Definition of Civic Conservatism: Reflections on Five Years of Governance." *Hungarian Review* 6, no. 4 (July 2015). http://hungarianreview.com/article/20150716_notes_towards_a_definition_of_civic_conservatism_reflections_on_five_years_of_governance.
———. "Full text of Viktor Orbán's speech at Băile Tuşnad (Tusnádfürdő) of 26 July 2014." Translation by Csaba Tóth. *Budapest Beacon,* July 19, 2014. https://budapestbeacon.com/full-text-of-viktor-orbans-speech-at-baile-tusnad-tusnadfurdo-of-26-july-2014/.
———. "Prime Minister Viktor Orbán's State of the Nation Address." February 28, 2016. *Cabinet Office of the Prime Minister.* http://www.miniszterelnok.hu/prime-minister-viktor-orbans-state-of-the-nation-address/.
———. "Speech by Prime Minister Viktor Orbán on 15 March." March 15, 2016. *Cabinet Office of the Prime Minister.* http://www.miniszterelnok.hu/speech-by-prime-minister-viktor-orban-on-15-march/.
Orsina, Giovanni. *Berlusconism and Italy: A Historical Interpretation.* New York: Palgrave Macmillan, 2014.
Ottomeyer, Klaus. *Jörg Haider, Mythenbuildung und Erbschaft.* Klagenfurt: Drava Verlag, 2009.
Owen, David. *Balkan Odyssey.* London: Indigo, 1996.
Petak, Zdravko. "The Political Economy Background of Yugoslav Dissolution: Between Economic Nationalism and Europeanization." Paper Presented at the Conflict Resolution and Self-Governance in Africa (and Other Regions) Mini-Conference, May 3–5, 2003, Workshop in Political Theory and Policy Analysis, Indiana University, Bloomington, Indiana. http://citeseerx.ist.psu.edu/viewdoc/download?doi=10.1.1.563.1504&rep=rep1&type=pdf.
Piketty, Thomas. *Capital in the Twenty-First Century.* Cambridge, MA: Harvard University Press, 2014.
Polanyi, Karl. *The Great Transformation: The Political and Economic Origins of Our Time.* Beacon Hills: Beacon Press, [1944] 1957.
Quer, Giovanni Matteo. "Israel-Washing: The Radical Right in Europe, Anti-Semitism, and Israel." In *Central Europe (Re-)visited: A Multi-Perspective Approach to a Region,* edited by Marija Wakounig and Ferdinand Kühnel, 105–122. Vienna: LIT Verlag, 2015.
Rajsfus, Maurice. *En Gros et en Détail: Le Pen au quotidien, 1987–1997.* Paris: Mediterranée, 1998.
Reznek, Lawrie. *Delusions and the Madness of the Masses.* Lanham, MD: Rowman & Littlefield, 2010.
Sakmyster, Thomas. *Hungary's Admiral on Horseback: Miklós Horthy, 1918–1944.* Boulder: East European Monographs, 1994.
Sassoon, Donald. *One Hundred Years of Socialism: The West European Left in the Twentieth Century.* New York: The New Press, 1996.

Seton-Watson, Hugh. *Eastern Europe Between the Wars, 1918–1941.* New York: Harper Torchbooks, 1967.

Shin, Michael E., and John A. Agnew. *Berlusconi's Italy: Mapping Contemporary Italian Politics.* Philadelphia: Temple University Press, 2008.

Simmons, Harvey G. *The French National Front: The Extremist Challenge to Democracy.* Boulder: Westview Press, 1996.

Starhemberg, Ernst Rüdiger. *Between Hitler and Mussolini: Memoires.* New York: Harper and Brothers, 1942.

———. *Die Erinnerungen.* Vienna: Amalthea Verlag, 1991.

———. *Die Reden des Vizekanzlers E.R. Starhemberg.* Vienna: Oesterreichischen Bundespressedienst, 1935.

Stevanović, Vidosav. *Milosevic: The People's Tyrant.* London: I.B.Tauris, 2004.

Sully, Melanie A. *The Haider Phenomenon.* New York: East European Monographs, 1997.

Taggart, Paul. *Populism.* Buckingham, PA: Open University Press, 2000.

Vaccari, Cristian. "The features, impact and legacy of Berlusconi's campaigning techniques, language and style." *Modern Italy* 20, no. 1 (2015): 25–39. http://dx.doi.org/10.1080/13532944.2014.985583.

Vladisavljević, Nebojša. *Serbia's Antibureaucratic Revolution: Milošević, the Fall of Communism and Nationalist Mobilization.* Houndsmills: Palgrave Macmillan, 2008.

Vonyó, József. *Gömbös Gyula és a jobboldali radikalizmus: Tanulmányok.* Pécs: Pannonia Könyvek, 2001.

———, ed. *Gömbös pártja: A Nemzeti Egység Pártja dokumentumai.* Budapest: Dialóg Campus Kiadó, 1998.

Vossen, Koen. *The Power of Populism: Geert Wilders and the Party for Freedom in the Netherlands.* London: Routledge, 2017.

Warren, Kenneth F., ed. *The Encyclopedia of U.S. Campaigns, Elections, and Electoral Behavior.* Thousand Oaks, California: SAGE Publications, Inc., 2008.

Weber, Max. *Economy and Society: An Outline of Interpretive Sociology.* Berkley, CA: University of California Press, [1922] 1978.

———. *Politik als Beruf.* Stuttgart: Reclam Verlag, [1919] 1992.

Weyland, Kurt. "Clarifying a Contested Concept: Populism in the Study of Latin American Politics." *Comparative Politics* 34, no. 1 (2001): 1–22.

Wilders, Geert. "Final Statement of Geert Wilders at His Trial." November 23, 2016. *Gatestone Institute.* https://www. gatestoneinstitute.org/9404/wilders-trial-closing-statement.

———. *Kies voor Vrijheid: Een eerlijk antwoord.* Groep Wilders: 2005.

———. "Let My People Vote." *New York Times,* November 20, 2015.

———. *Marked for Death: Islam's War against the West and Me.* New York: Regnery Publishing, 2012.

Wodak, Ruth. *The Politics of Fear: What Right-wing Populist Discourses Mean.* London: Sage Publications, 2015.

Wodak, Ruth, and Anton Pelinka, eds. *The Haider Phenomenon in Austria.* New Brunswick: Transaction Publisher, 2002.

Woodward, Susan L. *Balkan Tragedy, Chaos and Dissolution after the Cold War.* Washington D.C.: The Brookings Institution, 1995.

Index